# Three Invaders

D1613299

# Three Invaders

## The Deliberate Revision of History & The Secrets and Lies Behind Today's World

### Saleem I. Abdulrauf, M.D.

St. Louis, Missouri
USA

Published by Saleem I. Abdulrauf
St. Louis, Missouri, USA
www.ThreeInvaders.com
info@ThreeInvaders.com

Hardcover ISBN: 978-0-578-70624-5
Paperback ISBN: 978-0-578-70191-2

Library of Congress Control Number: 2020912617

Printed on acid-free paper.

*I saw the blood of my soldiers*

*I saw the blood of my enemies*

*I could not tell the difference*

# Preface

**I have written two books in the field of neurosurgery, and this is** my first book that deals with a different type of challenge. As a neurosurgeon, I have treated patients with complex brain tumors and aneurysms. This has taught me how to systematically and scientifically break down a problem to come up with solutions. In this book, I am employing the same strategy to evaluate long-standing conflicts in order to find novel solutions. I decided to utilize my skills to deal with the vexing challenge of our time, the puzzle that is the "Middle East" and the perceptions about its people, Arabs and Muslims. To truly treat a patient with a brain aneurysm or tumor, I had to know everything about it before going into surgery. Therefore, in the attempt to treat the problem we call the "Middle East," I pose a number of questions that I must answer:

- How did a people with a glorious civilization (the Islamic civilization), the people who built the first-ever university for higher education in the history of the world (University of Al-Karaouine) in the city of Fez, Morocco, in AD 859, under the direction of a woman no less (Fatima al-Fihri), end up in their current unenviable position?
- *Back to the Future*, about time travel set in America's 1950s, is one of the most iconic movies of a generation. Why did Steven Spielberg, in this science fiction movie, choose to make the bad guy an Arab character? In a recent survey, a Pittsburgh-based research firm posed the question "Should Americans, as part of their school curriculum, learn Arabic Numerals?"; 56% of the 3,200 respondents said no, and 15% had no opinion. Perhaps many among the respondents did not know that Arabic numerals are the numbers 0 to 9 which we use every day, reflecting a deep bias. How is this bias connected to the movie *Back to the Future*?

- In the fifteenth century, the German-born Chief Rabbi of Edirne, in an effort to convince Jews to move to the Ottoman Empire in order to escape persecution in Christian Europe, wrote a message circulated to European Jewish communities: "Is it not better for you to live under Muslims than under Christians?" Thousands of Jews were welcomed into the Muslim Ottoman Empire once they were expelled from Spain in 1492. How did we go from the time in which the Muslims were saving Jews from Christian persecution in Europe to the current situation in which the world sees Muslims and Jews as enemies?

- The "Middle East". . . Middle of what? East of what? Where did the name come from? And what does it imply?

- The dominant perception is that Islam is more associated with terrorism than Christianity or Judaism; is that based on facts or is it a created alternative reality, a myth?

- How did the most antagonistic president toward the Islamic faith in US history, Donald Trump, become the closest and most trusted US ally to the leader of Saudi Arabia, the country which claims to be the protectorate of the Islamic faith?

- Spanish Christians call God *Dios*, French Christians call God *Dieu*, Arab Christians call God *Allah*, and Muslims call God *Allah* or *Elah*. In the US, while *Dios* and *Dieu* would be considered the same as *God* in English, many in the media and the public consider the term *Allah* to be a different entity than what they define as *God*. Why is that? Especially since Jesus, the son of Mary, who spoke Aramaic and not English, used the word *Elaha* for God, which is akin to the Arabic *Allah* or *Elah*. Jesus would not have even recognized the English word *God*.

- The term Judeo-Christian is commonly used by politicians and the media when addressing issues of values and morals. There are clear biblical connections between Judaism and Christianity. However, the only two religions in the world that believe that Jesus, the son of Mary, was the Messiah are Christianity and Islam, and these are the only two religions which hold the Virgin Mary as their most important female figure. Judaism regards Jesus as a false prophet and

Christianity a false religion. Judaism and Islam are the only religions to prohibit the eating of pork. The Qur'an calls Jews and Christians "People of the Book," and the only two religions that Islam permits Muslims to marry are Jews and Christians. So, why is the term Judeo-Christian used rather than Judeo-Christian-Islamic?

- Have Christians or Muslims killed more Jews?
- Terrorists planted a bomb in the basement of a church, and in the ensuing explosion, four young girls—11-year-old Denise McNair, and three 14-year-olds, Addie Mae Collins, Carole Robertson, and Cynthia Wesley—were killed. This occurred on September 15, 1963, in the city of Birmingham, Alabama. The four girls who died that day were African American. The terrorists who committed the bombing were White Christian extremists belonging to the KKK, for whom this was the third terrorist bombing in Birmingham in 11 days. Why did the mainstream media never label these men terrorists and the KKK a terrorist organization?
- Besides violence and religious extremism, what deeply connects Islamist terrorists and Christian White nationalist terrorists?
- After every terrorist attack committed by Christian White nationalists, the media and politicians invariably raise the specter of mental illness as a potential cause. Why is mental illness never raised following Islamist-based terror attacks?
- For over a thousand years, Islam's holiest sites, Mecca and Medina, were ruled by descendants of the Prophet Muhammed, during which there were no suicide attacks and no terrorism. Winston Churchill, during the British colonization of the "Middle East" in the early 1920s, came across a Bedouin chieftain, Abdulaziz ibn Saud, from the deep deserts of the Arabian Peninsula. Churchill, in a speech to the House of Commons on June 14, 1921, stated that Abdulaziz and his followers "kill all who do not share their opinions" and "make slaves of their wives and children. Women have been put to death in Wahabi villages for simply appearing in the streets. . . . Austere, intolerant, well-armed, and bloodthirsty . . . very dangerous to the holy cities of Mecca and Medina, and to

the whole institution of the pilgrimage." After that honest account, Churchill financially supported Abdulaziz to topple the rule of the descendants of the Prophet Muhammed. Abdulaziz ibn Saud did so by invading Mecca in 1924 and Medina in 1925. Why would Winston Churchill support this? Why did the takeover of Islam's holy places by the Al-Saud family push the Islamic world toward a more extremist direction?

- As a surgeon and scientist, I believe in the principle of controlled experiments. Jerusalem was invaded more than once by each of the three Abrahamic faiths: Jews, Christians, and Muslims. This provides a unique setting for a controlled observational study! How did each of the three treat the local population of Jerusalem?

- Let me quote a young man who wrote the following on a wall: "Then there came to our places a large army, who killed many men and took me and brought me to the great sea and sold me into the hands of the Christians, who bound me and sent me on board a great ship and we sailed upon the great sea a month and a half . . . I reside in this our country by reason of great necessity. Wicked men took me by violence and sold me to the Christians." This was written in Arabic on the wall of a jail cell in North Carolina by Omar ibn Said, who had been captured in Western Africa in 1807 and sold as a slave in the United States. Is slavery in the US yet another flashpoint in the interaction between Christianity and Islam? Were there forced conversions to Christianity? Why was the Bible used for proselytizing slaves, known as the Slave Bible, so heavily edited? Are there millions of Christian African Americans in the US today who are descendants of proud Muslim families from Western Africa?

- The concentration camps for Muslims in China, the genocide of Muslims in Burma, the targeting of Muslims by Prime Minister Modi in India, the apartheid system for Muslims in the occupied territories of Israel—none of these would be tolerated singularly, let alone in combination, by world powers if the victims were Christians or Jews. Such a question was asked by Edward Luce of the *Financial Times* in January of

2020: "Imagine if China had incarcerated upwards of a million Christians. Or India said it would take all refugees except Christian ones. The west would be in a state of frenzy." So why are these egregious acts tolerated by the world's civilized societies and governments?

- What is in the hearts and minds of a whole generation of young Muslim boys and girls around the world that the fanatic terrorists are tapping into to radicalize them? In July 2019, a group of 22 countries issued a joint statement to the UN high commissioner on human rights rebuking China's detention of over a million Chinese Muslims (known as Uyghurs) in internment camps. Not a single Arab or Muslim country president, dictator, or king joined in signing this statement criticizing China! Quite the contrary, the leaders of Saudi Arabia and Pakistan issued statements supporting China, and Iran held joint naval exercises with China. Why are these Muslim leaders supporting China's torture of its Muslim population? Besides the economic ties, could it be due to the fact that the largest collective abusers of Muslim populations in the world are the presidents, dictators and kings of the Arab and Muslim countries, and if they were to criticize China, the lens could quickly turn on them?

- How can one be deeply anti-Semitic and be an ardent supporter of the state of Israel at the same time? This may sound hypocritical but is a real phenomenon that I term the *duplicitous syndrome* in this book. This syndrome has had a deep implication on the formation of what we call the "Middle East" in the twentieth century.

# Contents

# Three Daggers
# to the Heart

# Chapter 1

# Invaders from the East: Destruction of the City of Knowledge

I vividly remember seeing the movie *Back to the Future* (Universal Pictures) with my friends in Kansas City in the summer of 1985. I was mesmerized by this movie in which the seventeen-year-old Marty McFly (played by Michael J. Fox) travels back to 1955 and meets his then-teenaged parents using a time machine built from a modified DeLorean by his friend Emmett "Doc" Brown. At the edge of our seats, we watched as Marty jumped into the DeLorean to make the thirty-year leap—when, out of the blue, a van full of "Arab terrorists" speeds onscreen, shooting at Marty and Doc!

As is normal among young boys, my friends teased me after the movie, poking fun at my Arabic background given the pejorative representation of Arabs in the movie. I was a "Westernized" boy who did not know much about the history of my ethnic culture, and I was very upset about the portrayal of Arabs in the movie and the taunting by my friends. Once I got home from the movie theater, I called my favorite uncle, whom I regarded as a worldly, intellectual man. He could tell I was hurt, and I remember the words he tried to console me with: "Saleem, you come from a great heritage." That one sentence by my uncle that day started me on a journey that has led me to write this book.

From 1985's *Back to the Future*, whose plot traveled 30 years backward, let's fast forward 30 years to July 2016. At the Republican National Convention in Cleveland, Ohio, Iowa's US Representative Steve King said, "I'd ask you to go back through history and figure out, where are these contributions that have been made by these other categories of people [other than white Western people] that you're talking about, where did any other subgroup of people contribute more to civilization?"

Hollywood has depicted Muslim characters and Islamic civilization in a large number of movies, but these representations don't typically reflect the great civilization my uncle was talking about. The Islamic Empire was once the intellectual center of the world for the sciences and arts—but you won't find that in cinema. Just like *Back to the Future*, which became one of the most culturally beloved movies of all time, *The Exorcist* (1973, Warner Bros. Pictures) has been considered one of the greatest horror films of all time. *The Exorcist* depicts the demonic possession of a 12-year-old girl, played by Linda Blair. Where did the demon come from? Iraq.

Hollywood has depicted Muslim characters and Islamic culture in a large number of movies in a nefarious manner. A key question I intend to answer in this book is "Why does Hollywood intentionally demonize Arabs and Muslims and their culture?"

In *The Exorcist*, Iraq is portrayed as a source of evil, but the true story is much more complicated. The real Baghdad, Iraq, was not a birthplace of demons; it was the source of one of the greatest civilizations of human history.

## Baghdad

Human civilization was established in 14,000 BC in a land that lies between the Tigris and the Euphrates Rivers (current-day Iraq). This is also where the birth of writing took place in 3300 BC. The Caliph al-Mansur in the eighth century decided to construct the city of Baghdad to serve as the capital of the Islamic Empire. This empire, with Baghdad as its capital, would go on to be larger than the Roman Empire at its height.

Al-Mansur came from the Abbasid family, who were descendants of the family of the Prophet Muhammad, and they came into power in the Islamic Empire within about 100 years of the Prophet's death. They were driven by the core Islamic concept of seeking and expanding knowledge. Baghdad became the world's center of learning in the eighth and ninth centuries, a time in which Europe was embroiled with violence and religious extremism. Its school Bayt al-Hikma (House of Wisdom) translated texts from various languages into Arabic; particularly noteworthy was the translation of early Greek texts into the Arabic language. For over 700 years, the international language of science was Arabic.

In this intellectually vibrant culture, Mohammad ibn Musa al-Khwarizmi wrote *Kitab al-Jabr (The Compendious Book on Calculation by Completion and Balancing)*, and to the dismay of high school students for generations to come, created the mathematical field of algebra. Al-Khwarizmi (Fig. 1-1) also invented algorithms, a step-by-step method of performing a set of operations; in fact, the word *algorithm* is based on the Latinized version of his name.

**Figure 1-1:** A stamp issued on September 6, 1983, in the Soviet Union which commemorated Al-Khwarizmi's 1200th birthday. Renowned American author and historian Michael Hamilton Morgan described the impact of Al-Khwarizmi on the modern world: "His numbers and new ways of calculating will enable the building of 100-story towers and mile-long bridges; calculating the point at which a space probe will intersect with the orbits of one of Jupiter's moons; the reactions of nuclear physics; the language and intelligence of software; and the confidentiality of a mobile phone conversation."

Al-Khwarizmi also introduced the "missing link"—the number zero—to mathematical calculations. (Previously, the concept of zero had been first described by the ancient Indian mathematician Pingala and the seventh-century Indian mathematician Brahmagupta, who explored the concept of using zero in calculations.) Al-Khwarizmi's work is why people today use Arabic numerals instead of the cumbersome Roman numerals used in Europe at the time (Fig. 1-2). University of Surrey Professor Jim al-Khalili, a British theoretical physicist, has said that Al-Khwarizmi's work has helped create the modern world; according to him, science today would be impossible without it.

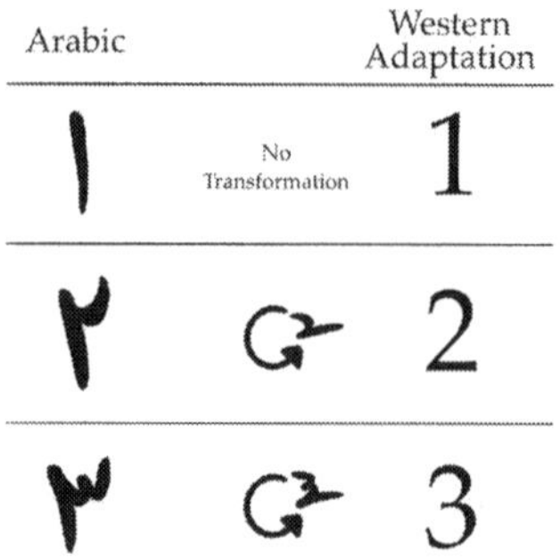

| Arabic | Western Adaptation |
|---|---|
| ١ | No Transformation   1 |
| ٢ | ᏻ   2 |
| ٣ | ᏻ   3 |

**Figure 1-2:** Arabic numerals were adopted to become the Western standard for the numbering system. Please note the counterclockwise rotation of the Arabic numbers that led to the creation of current Western numbers.

In his 2016 book *Wonderland: How Play Made the Modern World*, Steven Johnson described how scholars in Baghdad's "House of Wisdom" invented the concept of computational thinking and programmability. The combined concepts of algorithms and programming became the basis of data processing and computer development. Alan Turing, an English mathematician in the early twentieth century, figured out how a machine could follow an algorithmic instruction to solve a mathematical problem, ultimately giving birth to the computer era.

Scholars in the Islamic Empire also contributed to our scientific understanding of the natural world. The concept of light as we know it today was first described by Ibn al-Haytham; in his monumental textbook *Book of Optics*, he theorized that light was composed of rays and traveled in straight lines. Before him, the understanding of light was rooted in second-century Greek mathematician Ptolemy's theory that the human eye is where light came from. The later development of the camera was based on Al-Haytham's concept. Al-Haytham's impact was much larger than our understanding of light, though. He questioned scientific assumptions until proven by objective testing and suggested that test results have to be reproducible in order to have validity. By declaring this process, he laid the foundation of what we call today the *scientific method*, a foundational concept across all scientific disciplines (Fig. 1-3).

**Figure 1-3:** Johannes Hevelius, the German astronomer who is considered the founder of lunar topography, for the title page of his monumental AD 1647 publication, *Selenographia*, paid tribute to the two men with the biggest impact on science to date, Al-Haytham (left) representing "Reason" and Galileo (right) representing the "Senses."

## The First Doctors

From the early Islamic civilization's culture of science emerged three physicians who became the forefathers of the three main disciplines of Western medicine: internal medicine, surgery, and pediatrics. The five-volume *The Canon of Medicine* by Ibn Sina, known as Avicenna in the West, encompassed all known medical knowledge at the time. First published in AD 1025, it was translated from Arabic to Latin and was typically required reading for medical students in Europe until the eighteenth century (Fig. 1-4).

**Figure 1-4:** Stamp printed by Poland in 1952 shows Avicenna, or Ibn Sina, a thinker of the Islamic Golden Age whose works were required readings for medical students in Europe for several centuries.

Abu al-Qasim al-Zahrawi, known in the West as Abulcasis, wrote a 30-volume encyclopedia of medicine called *Kitab al-Tasrif*, its chapter on surgery became the standard textbook on surgery in Europe for 500 years, all the way up to the late 1800s. As a neurosurgeon I would like to mention that Al-Zahrawi provided the first clinical description of operating on children with hydrocephalus (water on the brain). Along with the nineteenth-century Englishman Joseph Lister, who developed the antiseptic technique, Al-Zahrawi is considered one of the fathers of modern surgery (Fig. 1-5).

Abu Bakr al-Razi, known in the West as Rhazes or Rasis, wrote the first ever book on pediatrics, which was called *The Diseases of Children.* He was the first to characterize and distinguish between smallpox and measles, and the World Health Organization (WHO) credits his essay on infectious disease as "the first scientific treatise on the subject."

**Figure 1-5:** Al-Zahrawi (Abulcasis) blistering a patient in the hospital at Cordoba (current-day Spain). Oil painting by Ernest Board.

As a physician, I was touched to learn that although each of these physicians were sought after by royal courts in Baghdad and Europe, they had tremendous compassion and dedication toward the poor and instilled these values in their students as well (Fig. 1-6).

The Islamic Empire under the visionary Abbasids developed the wider concept of a unified health-care system. Licensing exams to become a doctor were instituted in the tenth century in Baghdad. A new concept, philanthropy, emerged as well; this development led to some of the first organized hospitals in history. These hospitals were built to provide health care to the poor, as they could not afford to pay doctors to come to their homes. For the first time in history, official state funding was directed toward research. The first large-scale state-funded scientific project was the construction of the Baghdad observatory in AD 828.

**Figure 1-6:** Painting by Robert Thom of Al-Razi (Rhazes) attending to a sick child. Depicted here, Rhazes was the first to describe something neurologists and neurosurgeons do in practice every day when examining a patient: check the pupil's reaction to light.

## Sending Kids to Universities

Today, many well-to-do families from around the world send their children to attend universities in the US and Western Europe, but there was a time when families in Europe would send their children to cities in the Muslim Empire for their education. The world's first degree-granting university was founded in the Islamic Empire—and it was founded by a woman. Fatima al-Fihri, born in AD 800 in present-day Morocco, received a formal education at her father's insistence; formal schooling for girls was essentially unheard of in Europe at that time. After Al-Fihri's father died, she went on to establish the first university, the University of al-Karaouine in the city of Fez in AD 859. The university's library is the oldest in the world, containing more than 4,000 manuscripts (Fig. 1-7).

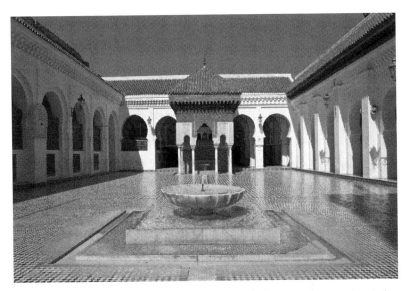

**Figure 1-7:** The first center for higher education (a degree-granting university) in the history of the world, the University of al-Karaouine in the city of Fez (current-day Morocco) was established by a female Muslim intellectual, Fatima al-Fihri in AD 859.

One young man from France whose family sent him away to study was Gerbert of Aurillac. He went abroad to study in the Islamic Empire's cities of Cordoba (present-day Spain) and North Africa. He later introduced the Arabic numerical decimal system to Europe and went on to become Pope Sylvester II from AD 999–1003 (Fig. 1-8). Another young man, Leonardo Fibonacci (Fig. 1-9), lived in Muslim North Africa (current-day Bugia, Algeria), where

he learned Arabic numbers and math; after returning to Europe, he published *Liber Abaci* (*Book of Calculation*) in 1202. Through this highly influential book, Fibonacci introduced Arabic math to Europe at large, and the new numbering system, now a cultural standard, was labeled "Arabic numerals."

**Figure 1-8:** Pope Sylvester II (AD 946–1003), originally known as Gerbert of Aurillac, was a prolific scholar who introduced the Arabic decimal system to Europe. This is his statue in Aurillac, Auvergne, France.

**Figure 1-9:** Leonardo Fibonacci (AD 1170–1240), who studied in Muslim schools as a child, later became the most influential European mathematician of the Middle Ages; he is credited with introducing and converting the world to the "Arabic numerical" system.

## The Chess Game of Kings and Empires

Just as the United States has been a leader on the world stage for the last century, the Abbasid Caliphate in Baghdad commanded international respect in the eighth through the eleventh centuries. When President Donald Trump visited Saudi Arabia in 2017, King Salman and his son Mohammad ibn Salman (MBS) invited leaders from 55 Arab and Muslim countries to Riyadh to showcase the close relationship they had with a US president. Similarly, during the Abbasid Caliphate, the eighth-century English King Offa, one of the most powerful Anglo-Saxon kings, minted gold coins for his kingdom that contained Arabic letters from the Abbasid Caliphate, thus demonstrating to his subjects and the other European leaders his closeness to the Islamic rulers in Baghdad (Fig. 1-10).

**Figure 1-10:** This gold coin (Mancus) of King Offa of England is now housed in the British Museum. It is copied after the Abbasid coin (Dinar). In the center is the word Offa and in the periphery, inscribed in Arabic, is the Muslim profession of the oneness of God ("there is no God but Allah, and Muhammad is the messenger of Allah").

As the superpower of its time, the Abbasid Caliphate in Baghdad was keen on conducting international diplomacy, and its alliance with the Frankish Carolingian dynasty, the most powerful player in Europe, was important to them. In AD 807, the Caliph Harun al-Rashid sent a gift to Charlemagne, the king of France and the Holy Roman Emperor who ruled most of Western and Central Europe at the time. Harun al-Rashid made sure the gift was unique and had never been seen in Europe. He sent Charlemagne a clepsydra, a water clock, described at the time by a member of the Frankish court: (Figs. 1-11, 1-12)

> . . . marvelously contrived by mechanical art, on which the course of the twelve hours was marked by a clepsydra, with the right number of little bronze balls, which would fall into a basin when the hour was complete and make it sound. [This clock] also had the same number of horsemen, and they would, through twelve windows, come forth at the end of the hours.

The gift was intended to show respect as well as technological superiority. That some in the Frankish court thought the device was "possessed" is not surprising. This is very similar to the reported reaction of the Wahhabis of Saudi Arabia during the early-mid-twentieth century when cars, radios, and TVs were first introduced—these were the devil transformed!

**Figure 1-11:** Harun al-Rashid's envoys presenting the water clock to Charlemagne.

**Figure 1-12:** As part of the Abbasid–Carolingian (French) alliance, Harun al-Rashid is depicted here receiving a delegation sent by Charlemagne at his court in Baghdad. Painting by Julius Köckert in 1864.

Why did this intellectual, science-oriented culture flourish in the Islamic Empire? Because the leadership in Baghdad fostered a spirit of openness toward other cultures and religions and freedom of expression was welcomed. More importantly, the leaders made the conscious decision to separate science from extremist religious orthodoxy. Social justice and protection of minority rights were the hallmarks of this era.

Baghdad was home to 28 Jewish synagogues at that time, more than most Western cities today. This was in stark contrast to Europe at the time. While science, math, and medicine were prospering in the Islamic world, Europe was entrenched in religious ideology. The church used its overwhelming power to suppress scientific thought and promote religious extremism, which at the time was strongly linked to anti-Semitism. In fact, in the thirteenth century, Étienne Tempier, the then bishop of Paris, prohibited the Arts Faculty of the University of Paris from teaching the works of Aristotle and the Muslim scholar Ibn Rushd (known in Europe by his Latinized name, Averroes), as their works were considered too progressive for Christendom at the time (Fig. 1-13).

**Figure 1-13:** Statue of the twelfth-century Muslim philosopher Ibn Rushd (Averroes) in Cordoba, Spain. His concepts were considered too progressive and were banned by the Catholic Church, but he was among a number of Muslim scholars who provided foundational seeds for the Renaissance movement in Europe.

The intersection between Islamic and European politics and culture reached beyond the formal diplomatic meetings of their leaders. Allow me to share an anecdote. In the game of chess, a micro-form of political warfare, the term "checkmate" comes from the Arabic "shah mat." Shah is a Persian term for King, and "mat" is the Arabic term for dead. From early centuries of cross-cultural interaction on the international playing board, it's clear that the Islamic Empire was truly a cultural and political world power.

During my research to write this chapter, I found the book by Michael Hamilton Morgan *Lost History: The Enduring Legacy of Muslim Scientists, Thinkers, and Artists* to be one of the most eloquent accounts of the impact of Islamic civilization on the scientific and cultural developments of Europe during the Renaissance and Enlightenment eras.

_Saleem I. Abdulrauf_

## The Economist and the President

When asked about his signature support for supply-side economics at a news conference on October 1, 1981, President Ronald Reagan said supply-side economic principles dated back to the Islamic economist and historian Ibn Khaldun (1332–1406), who is considered one of the greatest philosophers of all time. Reagan's attribution of his twentieth-century policies to this early thinker's pioneering works on economics illustrates the long-lasting impact of Islamic scholarship in Western civilization's economic fabric, the quality that many consider its distinguishing feature (Fig. 1-14).

**Figure 1-14:** Ronald Reagan, the 40th president of the United States, was a strong proponent of supply-side economics, and he credited this principle to the fourteenth-century Islamic economist and historian, Ibn Khaldun. The author Stephen Frederic Dale wrote, "Thucydides invented history, but Ibn Khaldun turned it into a science."

## The Omitted History

Getting back to the question of Representative Steve King: "Where did any other subgroup of people [other than white people] contribute more to civilization?" It is easy to dismiss King's comments as prejudice, but it is important to note that the historical revisionism which led to the omission of many Arab Muslim scientists from textbooks means that King may have never learned about Al-Khwarizmi, Al-Haytham, and Ibn Sina in his high school classes. It is, however, almost certain that he learned about the European scholars Galileo, Newton, and Einstein. The question therefore extends beyond individual politicians such as King: Why do many Americans know about the contributions that European scholars have made to civilization but never learn about scholars and thinkers from the East who contributed to the same civilization?

Historical documents show that from the twelfth to the seventeenth centuries, European scholars and textbooks gave credit to Arab scientists for their monumental contributions to scientific discoveries and thought. However, in the eighteenth century, those names were systematically removed, and by the nineteenth century, they were nonexistent. Since American textbooks were based on nineteenth-century European textbooks, the contributions of Arab scientists never entered the American educational system at all; perhaps more importantly, they never entered into the psyche of the generations of Americans to come.

Although we think of the eighth and ninth centuries as the Dark Ages, this era was actually the Golden Age of science from a global perspective. While Europe was reeling from the decline of the Roman Empire and entrenched in religious extremism, the Islamic civilization was the keeper of enlightenment and progress.

## A New Dark Age

While early Muslims were immersed in culture, science, and philosophy, they took their eyes off the defense of their empire—specifically the looming invaders coming from the East. The Mongols, under the command of Hulagu Khan, the grandson of Genghis Khan, laid siege to the city of Baghdad from January 29 to February 10, 1258. On February 10, Baghdad surrendered, and the Mongols sacked the city and destroyed its vast libraries, including the House of Wisdom. Ian Frazier of the *New Yorker* estimates the death toll ranged from 200,000 to 1 million. Grand mosques and hospitals were destroyed. According to survivors' accounts, the waters of the Tigris ran black with ink from all the books thrown into the river and red from the blood of scientists and philosophers killed. Luckily, some of the books that survived destruction were later translated from Arabic to Latin and seeded key aspects of the Renaissance in Europe.

Islamic and Arab civilization never truly recovered following the destruction of Baghdad by the Mongols.

As the Western world now revels in scientific and cultural progress, the "Middle East" has reverted to its own dark age, one that is most reflected by the two hegemonic powers of the Muslim world: Saudi Arabia and Iran.

Education and intellectual thought were the key elements of the Islamic Renaissance of the eighth and ninth centuries in Baghdad, yet only three of the seven Wahhabi Saudi kings from 1932 to present could read or write legibly. While openness to opposing political views was a hallmark of eighth-century Islamic culture, today in Tehran, Iran, the main purpose of cranes is not to build libraries and universities; rather, they are used to publicly hang political dissidents. While the Abbasid Caliphs brought scholars and artists from both Arab lands of the Arabian Peninsula and the Levant and from Persia (current-day Iran) under one umbrella to advance civilization, the current-day Saudi and Iranian anti-intellectual regimes peddle in hate to deepen the divide among the two ethnic groups (Arabs and Persians)

The accomplishments of the Islamic civilization at the end of the first millennium would not be possible in today's Muslim countries. In both Saudi Wahhabism Islam and Iranian Ayatollah Islam, the culture and thought process that led to those discoveries would be labeled blasphemous. Young kids growing up in the "Middle East" today are keenly aware that it was great once, yet they now live in societies that greatly limit the possibility for innovation and progress.

## Coffee!

Your history textbook may not have mentioned it, but something many of us drink daily—coffee—was introduced to the West by Arabs! Coffee was first introduced in Yemen around AD 1400, and the first coffeehouse in the world was established in the city of Mecca around 1500. Soon, coffee became popular in the larger Muslim Ottoman Empire; it is said that by the mid-1550s there were hundreds of coffee houses in the capital city of Constantinople (Istanbul—in current-day Turkey). The Ottoman Turks called it *khave* (from Arabic *qahwa*). The word was adapted as *koffie* in Europe, where it was introduced to the Republic of Venice via trade with the Ottoman Empire in the sixteenth century.

In his book *Uncommon Grounds: The History of Coffee and How It Transformed Our World*, Mark Pendergrast explains that before coffeehouses were introduced, many Europeans were drunk on alcohol most of the day, as water was not particularly safe to drink. Therefore, cafés had a significant impact on culture; it was much more than a pleasant drink. The founding of many newspapers and large businesses (like Lloyd's of London) took place at coffeehouses. The inception of the iconic works of Beethoven and Bach took place in coffeehouses.

Coffee had an impact on American history as well. When the American revolutionaries raided the British tea ships and threw crates of tea into the harbor in 1773, Americans largely switched to drinking coffee. One of America's Founding Fathers, John Adams, wrote in a letter to his wife Abigail, that despite his love for tea, he has switched over to drinking coffee to be patriotic. Let that sink in: a Founding Father switched from British tea to Arabic coffee in order to feel more patriotic (Figs. 1-15a and 1-15b)!

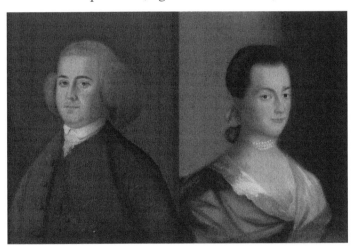

**Figures 1-15a and 1-15b:** Second US President John Adams (left) and his wife Abigail Adams (right). Both paintings by Benjamin Blyth.

Coffee isn't the only Arabic contribution that revolutionized American taste buds. I went to college and medical school and developed my career as a neurosurgeon in the City of St. Louis, in America's Midwestern state of Missouri. St. Louis hosted the 1904 World's Fair, which was opened by President Theodore Roosevelt and attended by nearly 20 million people. While the fair introduced

Americans and the world to some new inventions like the X-ray machine and private automobiles, it also introduced the ice-cream cone! The fair had exhibitors from all over the world, including two Syrians (Ernest Hamwi and Abe Doumar) who were introducing people to a popular Syrian dessert, a flat grid-like pastry called *zalabia*. One day, an ice-cream salesman next to their stand ran out of plates. Doumar came up with an idea: why not roll up the zalabia and place the ice cream inside it? It became a hit at the fair, and the ice-cream cone was born.

## The Narrative

The invention of civilization, writing, our number system, the concepts of algorithms, light, modern medicine, philanthropy, the official state funding of research, and the first university in history were all created by Arabs and Muslims in Arab lands. Not coincidentally, these seminal historical events have ALL been omitted from Western school curriculums. It is inconceivable that these profound omissions happened by chance.

Representative Steve King's question, "Where did any other subgroup of people contribute more to civilization?" reflects an idea that the academics and the media in the West never challenged. It mirrors the prevailing notion that for about 900 years—from approximately the seventh to the fifteenth century—Europe fell into the coma of the Dark Ages as the rest of the world lay dormant, and when it woke up, humanity could advance again.

Implicit in this belief is the notion that when white Westerners are not active on the world stage, no one else is capable of or interested in advancing humanity. It would be easy to just say this is just an ethnocentric xenophobic narrative, but this narrative has a complex political motive that will be discussed in this book. The truth is that during those 900 years, the world continued to evolve, and the Islamic civilization provided a wealth of knowledge and discoveries, that were the cornerstone of the European Renaissance and Enlightenment movements, the credit to the Islamic civilization has intentionally been omitted from the global historical memory.

# Chapter 2
# Invaders from the West:
# Ultimate Betrayal

**W**hile regulars in the French café **Bonne Biere were drinking** wine and having dinner on Friday, November 13, 2015, terrorists of the so-called Islamic State (ISIS) walked in with the sole purpose of massacring civilians. At the end of that deeply sad evening, they managed to kill 130 innocent people while wounding some 400 more in multiple sites in an organized attack across Paris.

This recent strike carries echoes of a more insidious attack in France nearly a century earlier, when secret maps were being drawn by British and French agents, also while having wine in Paris. A tangled web of allegiances during World War I left a trail of secret agreements and broken promises. This attack, however, was not the result of Islamic extremism but rather a result of Christian extremist ideology. For me to be able to explain what happened, I need to take you back where we left off in the last chapter after the fall of the Islamic civilization following the Mongol invasion.

The countries we associate with the "Middle East" today—such as Iraq, Jordan, Lebanon, and Saudi Arabia—did not exist until recently; instead, from the fourteenth century, following the fall of the golden age of the Islamic civilization (Chapter 1) to the early twentieth century, the "Muslim World" existed as one country—the Ottoman Empire which was much like the federal government that oversees each state in the United States. At its peak, the Ottoman Empire extended from current-day Hungary in the north to current-day Yemen in the south, and from current-day Iraq in the east to current-day Algeria in the west. The Ottoman fleet dominated the Mediterranean and Red Seas as well as the Persian Gulf.

The Ottoman Empire's capital city of Constantinople is the present-day Istanbul, capital of Turkey; however, in its day, Constantinople was a multilingual and multicultural metropolis that served as a meeting point that connected the Muslim East and the Christian West (Fig. 2-1).

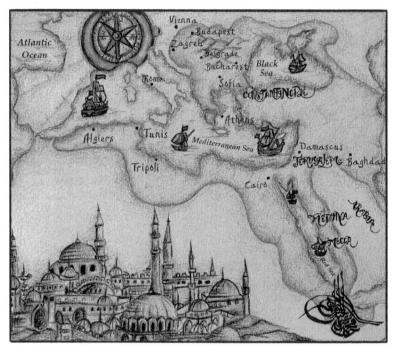

**Figure 2-1:** A map of the Ottoman Empire depicting its greatest extent in AD 1638. It spanned across three continents: Asia, Africa, and Europe.

## Christendom, Islam, and Queen Elizabeth

When I was in college at Washington University in St. Louis, I was invited to Thanksgiving dinner by one of my friends. Over dinner, my friend and I told his parents of our plans to visit Europe the next summer.

As soon as my friend and I listed Istanbul on our travel itinerary, both his mother and father asked us to reconsider; they brought up a movie they had seen about the "Turks" being "unsavory" characters.

They were referring to the 1978 Hollywood hit *Midnight Express* (Columbia Pictures). The film is based on a nonfiction book by Billy Hayes about his own experience as a young American student who escaped from a Turkish prison after being convicted of smuggling drugs. However, the movie deviated from his original account and characterized Turkish men as "evil." Hayes later criticized the film-makers for doing so. The power of Hollywood: a single movie ruined Turkey's image for an entire generation of Americans.

From media and popular culture, it is often thought that the deep military encroachment of the Ottomans into Central Europe translated into a cataclysmic clash between Christendom and Islam, but the reality was not so! There were three dominant world players at this time: the Muslim Ottoman Empire, the Catholic Church and the resulting Holy Roman Empire, and the emerging Protestants (the naming stems from "protest" against the Catholic Church).

The Ottomans were more tolerant of other faiths compared to Europeans of their time. In the fifteenth century, the German-born Chief Rabbi of Edirne wrote a message circulated to Jewish communities in Europe in an effort to convince Jews to move to the Ottoman Empire in order to escape persecution in Christian Europe:

> I have heard of the afflictions, more bitter than death, that have befallen our brethren in Germany—of the tyrannical laws, the compulsory baptisms and the banishments, which are of daily occurrence. I am told that when they flee from one place a yet harder fate befalls them in another . . . on all sides I learn of anguish of soul and torment of body; of daily exactions levied by merciless oppressors. The clergy and the monks, false priests that they are, rise up against the unhappy people of God . . . for this reason they have made a law that every Jew found upon a Christian ship bound for the East shall be flung into the sea. Alas! How evil are the people of God in Germany entreated; how sad is their strength departed! They are driven hither and thither, and they are pursued even unto death . . . Brothers and teachers, friends and acquaintances! I, Isaac Zarfati, though I spring from a French stock, yet I was born in Germany, and sat there at the feet of my esteemed teachers. I proclaim to you

that Turkey is a land wherein nothing is lacking, and where, if you will, all shall yet be well with you. The way to the Holy Land lies open to you through Turkey. Is it not better for you to live under Muslims than under Christians? Here every man may dwell at peace under his own vine and fig tree. Here you are allowed to wear the most precious garments. In Christendom, on the contrary, you dare not even venture to clothe your children in red or in blue, according to our taste, without exposing them to the insult of being beaten black and blue, or kicked green and red, and therefore are ye condemned to go about meanly clad in sad colored raiment . . . and now, seeing all these things, O Israel, wherefore sleepest thou? Arise! And leave this [European] accursed land forever!

Sure enough, King Ferdinand II of Aragon and Queen Isabella I of Castile issued a decree (the Alhambra Decree—also known as the Edict of Expulsion) in March 1492 to expel Jewish people from Spain by the end of July; the Spanish expulsion of the Jews, in combination with the Spanish Inquisition that followed, is considered one of the most traumatic events in Jewish history in the second millennium in addition to the Holocaust.

In contrast, the Ottoman Empire welcomed the Jewish people. In fact, the sultan sent Ottoman ships to Spain to carry Jewish passengers to safety (Fig. 2-2). When speaking of the expulsion, Ottoman Sultan Bayezid II said to his courtiers that Ferdinand "has impoverished his own country and enriched mine." Some 40,000–100,000 Jews settled in the Ottoman Empire and went on to become citizens and contributors to its culture and civilization.

**Figure 2-2:** Sultan Bayezid II sent Admiral Kemal Reis to bring Jews from Spain to the Ottoman Empire. Shown is Reis's flagship *Göke.*

The Catholic Holy Roman Empire was intolerant of Protestants as well as Jews; therefore, Protestants saw themselves as more similar to Muslims than to Catholics. In his book *The Sultan and the Queen: The Untold Story of Elizabeth and Islam,* Jerry Bolton provides an exquisite glimpse into this unusual alliance. The book includes correspondence between the Protestant Queen Elizabeth I of England (Fig. 2-3) and the then sultan of the Ottoman Empire, Sultan Murad III. In this letter, written on October 25, 1579, Queen Elizabeth aligns herself with the sultan by naming a common enemy:

> Elizabeth by the grace of the mighty God, the only Creator of heaven and earth, of England, France, and Ireland Queen, the most invincible and most mighty defender of the Christian faith against all idolatries, of all that live among the Christians, and falsely profess the name of Christ, unto the most imperial and most invincible prince, Zuldan Murad Chan . . .

By calling Catholics "idolaters" and "false," she assured Murad of their shared antipathy toward the Catholic Empire.

Queen Elizabeth's religious convictions played out on the battlefield as well. One of England's greatest military victories, which occurred during her reign, was the defeat of the Spanish Armada

(Catholic Empire) in 1588. There is evidence of military cooperation between England and the Ottomans in the lead-up to this historic victory (Fig. 2-3).

**Figure 2-3:** Queen Elizabeth I, *The Rainbow Portrait*, c.1600 by Isaac Oliver (oil on panel). The queen is wearing recognizable "Middle Eastern" jewelry, reflecting a close relationship with the Islamic world.739819 Queen Elizabeth I, \'The Rainbow Portrait\', c.1600 (oil on panel) by Oliver, Isaac (c.1565-1617); 128x102 cm; Hatfield House, Hertfordshire, UK; (add.info.: Queen Elizabeth I (1533-1603) queen of England and Ireland. Elizabeths holds a rainbow with the inscription "Non sine sole iris", "No rainbow without the sun", reminding viewers only the Queen\'s wisdom can ensure peace and prosperity. A jeweled serpent is entwined along her left arm, and holds from its mouth a heart-shaped ruby. Above its head is a celestial sphere. Her gown is embroidered with wild-flowers and her cloak with eyes and ears.)

## Vienna

Historically and strategically, the two biggest military campaigns undertaken by the Ottomans in Europe were the capture of Hungary and the siege of Vienna.

In Hungary, thousands of Protestants endured forced conversions by the fanatical Catholic Church during much of the sixteenth and seventeenth centuries. Hundreds of Protestant pastors were enslaved if not sent to the gallows. The Ottomans were able to conquer Hungary largely because the average person did not trust the leading aristocratic class; many Christian peasants therefore joined the Ottomans to fight against their own leaders. It's worth noting that this distrust is quite similar to the attitude many in the "Middle East" hold toward their present-day political leaders, which has contributed to some young people joining external militarized movements in recent decades.

In his book *Two Faiths, One Banner: When Muslims Marched with Christians across Europe's Battlegrounds*, Ian Almond provides an excerpted letter from a Hungarian military commander to his superior which illustrates the disconnect between the peasants and the ruling class:

> The serf hates his lord . . . there is no one in the peasantry to learn the word of God from; they indeed believe the Ottomans are the people of God and the true faith is theirs, and so God is on their side. I am afraid they will not run against the Ottomans but turn against their lords . . .

Sure enough, when the Ottoman Empire clashed with the Kingdom of Hungary, the Ottomans had an army of 80,000 men, about a third of whom were Christian Romanians, Serbians, Bulgarians, and Greeks. The Ottomans won control of the region through the Battle of the Mohacs in 1526 and ruled Hungary for the following 150 years. Similarly, when the Ottomans laid siege to Vienna in 1683, according to most estimates, about half of the 100,000–120,000 men in the Ottoman army were Christian. Vienna, however, did not fall, and this Ottoman loss signaled the empire's diminishing control in Europe and beyond.

## The Sick Man of Europe

Just like the Roman Empire before it, the sun began to set on the Ottomans by the eighteenth and nineteenth centuries. The Ottomans were increasingly threatened by an emerging empire to their north: the Russian Empire.

It became most clear that Russia posed a threat when it invaded and occupied the large region of land inhabited by Turkic tribes in Central Asia. Throughout the latter half of the nineteenth century, as Russian conquest spread, the land became known as "Russian Turkestan." Although most of this area has since become independent, the easternmost part of this region and home of the Uyghurs, known as East Turkestan or Uyghurstan, was incorporated by China (Fig. 2-4).

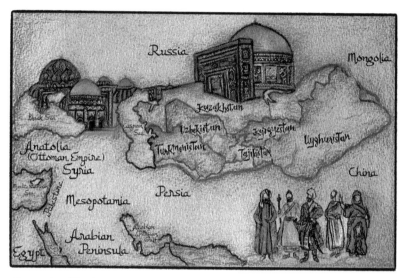

**Figure 2-4:** The historical Islamic central region of Asia, or Turkestan, is indicated in the central part of the map. Once Turkestan gained its independence from the Soviet Union, it became a set of Islamic Central Asian countries—Kazakhstan, Kyrgyzstan, Tajikistan, Turkmenistan, and Uzbekistan—depicted in the map. Uyghuristan (also known as East Turkestan), however, was occupied by China and renamed Nanjiang. The concentration camps for Muslims China created in Uyghurstan in early twenty-first century are intended to suppress aspirations of independence. The historic Silk Road, which connected the Eastern and Western civilizations for centuries, wound through this region. Turkestan also gave rise to the families that formed the Ottoman Empire in Anatolia, the Mughal Empire in India, and the Timurid Dynasty of Central Asia (named for Timur or Tamerlane, the founder).

By the early twentieth century, the Ottoman Empire was in decline as a result of multiple shortcomings; the Russian threat to the north was consuming much of the empire's resources, it remained agrarian and did not invest in building factories like the emerging European powers, and it had lost the visionary leadership of its founders. It was mocked and labeled by Tsar Nicholas of Russia as "The Sick Man of Europe," and the threat of collapse felt imminent to many Ottomans. As a result, a political reform group called the

Young Turks emerged; they advocated for changes that they believed would prevent the eventual collapse of the empire. Chief among their attempts to salvage the empire was a push to eliminate the monarchy and install a constitutional government. Through a fast-spreading rebellion which culminated in the Young Turk Revolution of 1908, they successfully instituted the country's first multi-party democracy.

## Divide & Conquer

The Ottoman Turks, while essentially on their knees by the 1910s, were faced with conundrum! As tension within the Ottoman Empire boiled over during the early twentieth century, so too did conflict on the world stage. The Ottoman Turks, still reeling from recent political upheaval, understood that not entering the dawning world war or choosing the wrong alliance could spell out the death of the empire.

Their calculus, or more accurately their gamble, was that if they were to align themselves with the winning side, they may have a chance to stay alive.

The Allies of World War I, which consisted of Great Britain, France, and Russia (known as the Triple Entente) made for a risky option. Both the British and the French were eager to expand into the territory that is now the "Middle East," a direct threat to the Ottoman Empire's geographic domain. In contrast, the Germans who, along with Austria-Hungary, comprised the Central Powers, primarily sought opportunities to expand in Europe. Moreover, it would have been difficult for the Turks to join the Allied Powers with their archenemy of the past two centuries, the Russians. As a result, the Ottoman Empire reluctantly entered World War I as a member of the Central Powers in 1914.

What Britain did next to weaken the Ottomans would change history for a century to come. Britain had achieved tremendous success in India in the 1850s using its colonial model of "divide and rule" by creating animosity between Hindus and Muslims. To explain how Britain used this model to target the Ottomans, allow me to set the scene as follows:

Hejaz, the region along the Red Sea in western Arabia, was a strategically and politically sensitive region for the Ottoman leaders (sultans) as it was the birth place of Islam and the location of the two holy cities of Mecca and Medina (Fig. 2-5).

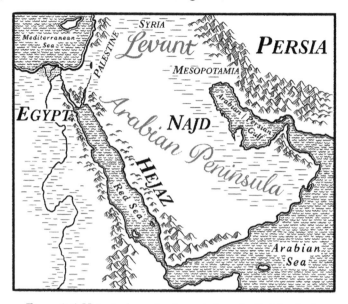

**Figure 2-5:** Hejaz is the region located along the Red Sea in the western part of the Arabian Peninsula.

The Ottoman sultans were very shrewd in how they governed this region. It is important to note that while they shared the same religion, the Ottomans were Turks (language: Turkish) and were ethnically distinct from the Arabs (language: Arabic). Instead of placing an Ottoman Turkish governor, they upheld the centuries-old principle that the governor of Hejaz be a member of the Arab Hashemite Clan (descendants of the Prophet Muhammed). The title given to the governor of Hejaz was Al-Sharif (meaning *noble* in Arabic, a title only given to the Prophet's descendants). This gave significant credibility to the Ottomans in their rule over Hejaz throughout the rest of the Islamic Empire. Neither the terms *sultan* nor *Al-Sharif* are synonymous with the term *caliph*. The term *caliph* has specific meaning in Arab and Muslim cultures, but its meaning has largely been botched in the West. It is important for the purposes of this book and this chapter that I explain it.

# The Caliph

The term *caliphate* has been used by politicians (especially US Secretary of State Mike Pompeo) and the mainstream media completely inaccurately. This is due to the fact that the terrorist organization, the so-called "Islamic State" (ISIS), declared it was establishing a caliphate. Given the lack of education and historical knowledge among the leadership of ISIS, as well as among many decision-makers like Mr. Pompeo, it is highly unlikely they understood the term *caliphate*. When the Prophet Muhammed died in the seventh century, the people around him set about to elect a successor, a steward with both political and religious authority to steer the larger Islamic community. There were four caliphs: Abu Bakr, Umar, Uthman, and Ali, all highly pious, honorable, and egalitarian men who believed in meritocracy and embodied the ultimate concept of the term *caliph*. The combined rule of the four caliphs was a mere 29 years. Thereafter, from the late seventh century to the early twentieth century, there were a number of Muslim empires with leaders that were appointed to their positions based on pure nepotism, and with very few exceptions did not uphold the principles of the original four caliphs, and therefore were not considered "caliphs" in the true sense.

From a macro point of view, the true caliphs were men who held wide visionary views that embodied the concepts of egalitarianism, meritocracy, and philanthropy. At a personal level they were pious and humble. Let me quote a sentence from Caliph Umar ibn Abd al-Aziz (AD 682–720) to illustrate my point: "Spread wheat on the tops of mountains so it cannot be said that a bird went hungry in the land of the Muslims."

It is important to note that the term *caliph* was not used operationally to refer to the Ottoman sultans in Istanbul; they realized they did not live up to that standard. However, at the periphery of the Ottoman Empire, some Muslim populations, for example in India, conceptually viewed the Ottoman sultan as a "caliph." The British from their colonial experience in India were very aware of this fact.

ISIS was not the first to attempt to use the "caliph" title for nefarious purposes. Great Britain beat them to it!

How and why the British would attempt to recreate the concept of the seventh-century "caliphate" is both nefarious and ingenious! At the outset of WWI, in 1914, Britain would appoint its highly decorated hero, Horatio Herbert Kitchener (Fig. 2-6), as its secretary of state for war. He was very clever and one of his goals was to map out the southern desert area of Palestine (the reasons for which will become clear later in the chapter).

How could a British military general get permission from an enemy nation to map out their territory? He used religion! Kitchener said that Britain requested permission to map the area as a Christian nation, based on the biblical account in the book of Exodus of the path taken by Moses and the Jews to Egypt, an account that

**Figure 2-6:** Field Marshal Horatio Herbert Kitchener, 1st Earl Kitchener, had a legendary reputation as a military leader in the early part of the twentieth century among the British population. He served as the secretary of state for war for Britain during WWI.

is also present in the Qur'an. Under the auspices of the "Palestine Exploration Fund," he reported that the government wanted to do an archeological study of potential scientific evidence for the Exodus. Due to the religious nature of the request, the Ottomans gave permission.

The core team for the mission were British intelligence officers disguised as archeologists, including a young intelligence officer named T.E. Lawrence. The team mapped out the desert region connecting Egypt to the habitable inner region of Palestine, now known as the West Bank.

Before his appointment as the secretary of state for war, Kitchener had spent years in military leadership positions for Britain in Egypt, Sudan, and India; he knew that the original caliphs were Arab, while Ottoman sultans were Turkish.

Therefore, Kitchener believed if they could come up with an Arab "caliph" that answered to the British crown, and if the Allies were to win the war, Britain would be able to control the Arab and Muslim peoples and lands through its personal caliph.

For Britain, the most obvious candidate to serve as its "vassal caliph" was the Sharif of Hejaz, an Arab who came from the lineage of the Prophet Muhammad. At the time, the Sharif in Mecca was Hussein ibn Ali al-Hashimi (Fig. 2-7).

The Sharif was the 38th generation in the lineage of the Prophet Muhammad, specifically, the lineage of the Prophet's grandson— Al-Hasan ibn Ali. Although he has essentially been omitted from Western historical memory, his is the quintessential story which explains how and why the current "Middle East" was created.

The British strategy to "divide and rule" Hindus versus Muslims, which had been effective in India 60 years earlier, was again employed to divide Turks and Arabs. The British knew that if they were to win the Sharif's allegiance away from the Ottomans, with his status as the spiritual leader of Islam and the figurehead of Arabs in the region, they would wield a tremendous amount of influence. The British were already aware there had been a long-standing, tenuous relationship between the Ottoman sultan in Istanbul and the Sharif in Mecca, so the British secretary of state for war, Horatio Herbert Kitchener, would appeal to the Sharif to make a deal.

Sharif Hussein was in his early 60s at the inception of WWI when he received a message from the British high commissioner, Sir Reginald Wingate, telling him that he was "the right man to take over his rightful heritage and verify the hopes of his people—the Mohammedans [term used by the West at the time for Muslims] and Arabs to recover their stolen Khalifate."

The stakes were high for the Sharif; he was being asked to revolt against the Ottoman sultan, who would surely exact revenge against him if the Allies lost the war. Also at stake were over a thousand years of tradition for the Arabic people and descendants of Muhammad governing the holy sites.

Therefore, the Sharif's request of the British was equally bold: he asked that if he fulfilled the British request and the Allies won the war, Arabs would get their long-standing dream of an independent Arab nation. This land would encompass the Arab lands of the Ottoman Empire that would include (by today's terminology) the Arabian Peninsula, Iraq, Syria, Jordan, Yemen, and Palestine.

**Figure 2-7:** The Sharif of Mecca Hussein ibn Ali al-Hashimi. His last name refers to the Hashemite clan, which comes from Hashim ibn Abd Manaf, great-grandfather of the Prophet Muhammad.

At the insistence of the British, the Sharif made one concession: he agreed to "special administrative arrangements" for the provinces of Baghdad and Basra, which the British would lease from the Arab nation for a short period of time. This agreement was further solidified during meetings between the Sharif and his sons with senior

British officials in the port city of Jeddah (Hejaz), as well as by written documents exchanged between the Sharif and Sir Henry McMahon (the senior diplomat assigned by Britain to confirm the deal with the Arabs). The 10 letters exchanged from July 1915 to March 1916 documenting the agreement between the British and the Arabs are known in the literature as the McMahon–Hussein Correspondence.

Unfortunately for the Sharif, there was a secret he was not privy to. The British leadership, should they win the war, never planned to deliver on their promise—they never truly intended to create an independent Arab country. Instead, through Horatio Herbert Kitchener's plan, they would have a figurehead "caliph" who would be subservient to London after the war.

## Revolution & Betrayal

With the agreement in hand, Sharif Hussein ibn Ali al-Hashimi declared the Arab rebellion against the Ottomans in June 1916. The rebel army received financial and logistical support from the British and was commanded by Feisal, one of the Sharif's three sons (Fig. 2-8).

The British planned to attack the Ottomans in Palestine once Feisal fought his way up north from Hejaz; they wanted Feisal to protect their right flank, which moved north from Hejaz toward the Jordan Valley. The British assigned intelligence officer, T.E. Lawrence, who had mapped southern Palestine for Kitchener a few years earlier, was appointed to serve with Feisal as a liaison between the Sharif's army and the regional British forces (Figs. 2-9, 2-10, and 2-11).

**Figure 2-8:** Prince Feisal (1883–1933). He was from the lineage of the Prophet Muhammad (38th generation). He commanded the Arab Revolt against the Ottomans during WWI. (Painting by the British artist Eric Kennington.)

The 1962 epic Hollywood movie *Lawrence of Arabia* (Columbia Pictures) depicts T.E. Lawrence's role in the Arab Revolt during

World War I. Although intended as a historical drama, the film erroneously overemphasizes Lawrence's role in the victories achieved by the Arab Army. The terms "savages," "greedy," and "barbaric" are used and portrayed by the actors to depict Arabs.

The classic theme in Hollywood movies with two opposing sides is that one is "good" (protagonist) while the other is "bad" (antagonist). However, that does not apply when the two sides are Arab or Muslim—in that case, they are both bad! In this specific movie, there are two sides in the conflict: the British and the Muslim Arabs against the Ottoman Muslim Turks. The British are

**Figure 2-9:** T.E. Lawrence, the British intelligence officer who joined Feisal as a liaison, and who later published his memories of the "Arab Revolt" campaign in his book *Seven Pillars of Wisdom*.

depicted as the heroic "good" side, while the Arabs fighting alongside them are depicted as "bad" by conflating them with the Turks!

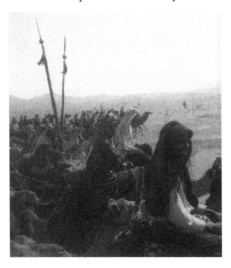

**Figure 2-10:** Historic photograph: Feisal leading his 5,000-strong army from Hejaz to Syria. He can be seen in the middle, wearing a white robe.

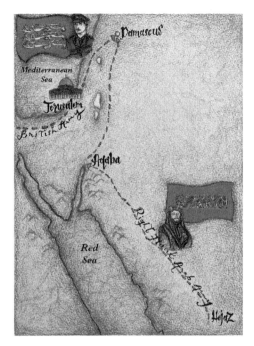

**Figure 2-11:** Feisal's advance from Hejaz (green
dotted line) to protect the right flank of the
Allenby-British Army advance from Egypt (red
dotted line). Feisal defeated the Ottomans and
captured the strategic port city of Aqaba before
proceeding to Damascus.

Consider *Lawrence of Arabia*'s depiction of one of the commanders of the Arab Army, Auda Abu Tayi, who was a hero of the Arab
Revolt and a legendary figure known for his bravery and chivalry
(Fig. 2-12). In the movie, he is portrayed as a greedy, self-centered,
barbaric individual.

The battle to capture the strategic port city of Aqaba was won
due to the bravery of Auda Abu Tayi and his men, not T.E. Lawrence
as the movie would have you believe. The only memorable action of
T.E. Lawrence during the Aqaba invasion was that he accidently
shot his own camel in the head and was fortunate enough to survive
the ensuing fall! In the movie, T.E. Lawrence is seen valiantly leading
the forces into Aqaba on his horse.

Auda's descendants were so distraught by the intentional nefarious portrayal of their ancestor that they sued Columbia Pictures, but this was a David versus Goliath battle—a family of modest means from Jordan's desert versus a mammoth Hollywood studio—and the case was dropped.

The movie *Lawrence of Arabia* won seven Oscars at the 35th Academy awards in 1963, including best picture and best director. It has since been recognized as one of the greatest and most influential movies in the history of cinema. The film's commercial success illustrates the pervasiveness of such nefarious depictions of Arabs and Muslims, which form stereotypes and memories that viewers retain for a lifetime.

**Figure 2-12:** Auda Abu Tayi, a brave hero of the Arab Revolt, is depicted as a vile character in the film *Lawrence of Arabia*. (Painting by the British artist Eric Kennington.)

WWI had two fronts, a Western (the main European front) and an Eastern (the subject of this chapter). The highly acclaimed 2019 WWI Western-front film *1917* (DreamWorks Pictures) also presents the British officers as heroes. In keeping with Hollywood's long-standing use of the good-versus-evil theme, the Germans in the movie, who were the enemy of the Allied powers, are notably still depicted as less nefarious than the Arabs in *Lawrence of Arabia*, who were allies of the British!

## Jerusalem

The alliance with Sharif Hussein worked as planned for the British. Under the command of General Edmund Allenby and with Feisal protecting their right flank, British forces successfully invaded Palestine, defeating the outnumbered Ottoman troops (Fig. 2-13).

**Figure 2-13:** General Edmund Allenby enters Jerusalem on December 11, 1917. The Crusaders had historically entered Jerusalem using violence; Allenby chose to show respect for the land by entering on foot.

What maps did Allenby use to invade Palestine? The maps created by Horatio Kitchener under the guise of the "Biblical Expedition" with T.E. Lawrence as one of the archaeological team members! Why did the British choose to invade Palestine and capture Jerusalem, while Feisal went around through Jordan to meet them in Damascus?

Allenby invaded Jerusalem on December 11, 1917. Up until that point, Muslims had ruled Jerusalem since AD 638 for a total of 1,176 years. This period of Muslim rule had only been interrupted once before, by Christian occupation 673 years prior, for 103 years in the twelfth and thirteenth centuries by the Christian Crusaders.

The final push to completely defeat the Ottomans entailed the conquest of Syria, as it was the last Arab frontier bordering historic Anatolia (Turkey)—the home of the Ottomans. The British and Arab armies entered Damascus on October 1, 1918, heralding the end of Ottoman rule over the Arab regions of the "Middle East."

Once in Damascus, the two military leaders, Allenby and Feisal, met for the first time face-to-face at the Victoria Hotel on October 3, 1918. Feisal, who had been fighting the Ottomans for two years, asserting military dominance all the way from Hejaz to Damascus, walked into that meeting fully expecting the British, as promised, would now support the creation of an independent Arab country extending from the western part of the Arabian Peninsula (Hejaz) to northern Syria. What he was told at that meeting in Damascus would forever sow the seed of hatred of the "Arab" peoples toward the "West"; Allenby informed Feisal that Britain would not uphold the agreement and none of the promises made would be fulfilled (Fig. 2-14).

**Figure 2-14:** Photograph from Damascus in October 1918: Prince Feisal was received jubilantly by crowds everywhere he went; they saw him as the hero who would give them the long-awaited "Arab Nation." This specific photograph was taken on October 3, right outside of the Victoria Hotel after Feisal had finished his meeting with Allenby. The weight of the world was on him; he knew he would no longer be able to deliver the promised land.

What Feisal had not known, and would soon find out, the British had three secrets that would forever change the world, secrets that his trusting father, the Sharif sitting in Mecca, had no idea about.

# Secret Number 1: The Puritan & The Messianic Vision

Britain's internal politics had been far from static during the two years Feisal fought for the British. The religious agendas of political and military leaders in London would go on to shape the future of the "Middle East."

Horatio Kitchener, the British secretary of state of war who designed the plan to create a modern "caliphate" and initiated the negotiations with Sharif Hussein, died in June 1916 when his naval boat struck a German mine; at this time, the Arab Revolt was already underway. Only a few months later, in December 1916, British Prime Minister H. H. Asquith stepped down under pressure as British casualties mounted in the Western front. Asquith's cabinet had approved Kitchener's deal with the Sharif, but his replacement, Lloyd George, had differing political views: he saw the "Middle East" as a war prize if Britain were to emerge victorious.

Lloyd George grew up a devout Anglo-Saxon Christian Zionist evangelical and would routinely use biblical terms in his conversations about the "Middle East" region. He believed in the evangelical interpretation of returning Jews to Zion, or biblical Israel. When elected to the post of prime minister, he made it clear to his cabinet that Palestine would be captured by the British, and it would in no way be part of the territory promised to the Sharif by his predecessor.

George demanded that Britain occupy Palestine from the town of Dan to the town of Beersheba (towns that had been mentioned in the Bible). Beersheba was known to the British officers based on the maps generated by the Kitchener intelligence operation of southern Palestine; Dan, however, was a mystery for the officers, and George searched for it in his biblical nineteenth-century atlas without success. A year later, however, the British Military did manage to locate it: it is known as Tel Qadi in Arabic and Tel Dan in Hebrew. Once located, the British adjusted their borders to satisfy the prime minister's wishes, basing their occupation on the prime minister's biblically motivated choice of location!

The prime minister's fixation with the town of Dan is not unlike the terrorist group ISIS's 2014 invasion of a small town northeast of Aleppo, Syria, by the name of Dabiq. ISIS chose Dabiq based on a Hadith, a saying by the Prophet Muhammed, in which he mentions Dabiq as a site of a battle that would occur around the time of Armageddon.

The stars were aligned for Prime Minister George. A man by the name of Theodor Herzl, a Jewish Austrian journalist, founded the Zionist Congress at the turn of the twentieth century (Fig. 2-15). Herzl was concerned about the persecution of Jews in Russia and the fervent anti-Semitism in Germany and France; he made it his mission to get Jews out of harm in Europe and identified a number of regions as candidates for a Jewish homeland, including Cyprus, El-Arish strip of the Sinai in Egypt, Argentina, and Uganda in Africa.

**Figure 2-15:** Theodor Herzl, the father of modern political Zionism.

Herzl is recognized as the father of modern political Zionism; the definition is based on his own words: "Zionism strives to create for the Jewish people a home in Palestine secured by public law." It is important to note that Herzl was talking about a "homeland" and not an official governmental "state" in Palestine. He presented Palestine as the ideal location given the connection to Jewish culture and history. However, for Herzl and Jewish political Zionism, Palestine was not a requirement for this homeland. It is important to note that for Christian Zionism, then and now, Palestine as the location is an absolute requirement. At the Sixth Zionist Congress in Basel, Switzerland, in 1903, Herzl presented his case for a Jewish homeland in Uganda, Africa. Herzl died in 1904, and with him died the Uganda plan.

Regardless, Uganda was not going to work for Lloyd George or the evangelical Puritan upper class in Britain; for them, as we will discuss later, only Palestine could be the site. It is important to note that among the same upper class there were sentiments of anti-Semitism. The coexistence of holding anti-Semitic views while providing strong support for the creation of a Jewish state in Palestine may on its face seem like a contradiction, but in reality it is a pattern we will see so frequently in the journey of this book that I have named it the "duplicitous syndrome." This double-dealing will be addressed in detail later. At about the same time as Herzl's death, Lloyd George became a lawyer for the Zionist movement and became very entrenched in it for a decade before he would go on to become the prime minister of Britain.

Zionism, the movement to establish a Jewish state in Palestine, was not uniformly supported by European or American Jews at the beginning of the twentieth century. The converse is true when it came to extreme messianic Christian evangelicals; they strongly supported the creation of a Jewish homeland in Palestine.

Prime Minister Lloyd George assembled a strongly pro-Zionist cabinet, including Arthur Balfour as its Foreign Secretary. In the summer of 1917, while Feisal was leading the Arab Army through the desert to protect the British advance into Palestine, Balfour was working with the president of the British Zionist Federation, Chaim Weizmann, to produce a document which pledged Palestine as the site for a Jewish nation in violation of Britain's existing deal with Sharif Hussein (Fig. 2-16).

This pledge, known as the Balfour Declaration, was issued as a letter to Lord Rothschild, a leading figure in the British Anglo-Jewish community (Fig. 2-17). Only 67 words long, the Balfour Declaration declared that Britain would "view with favour the establishment of a national home for the Jewish people" in the Holy Land. The declaration was the gift of the century to both Jewish and Christian Zionists.

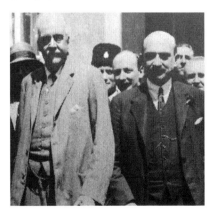

**Figure 2-16:** Arthur Balfour (left) and Chaim Weizmann (right), the two architects of the Balfour Declaration. This picture was taken during Balfour's visit to Tel Aviv in 1925.

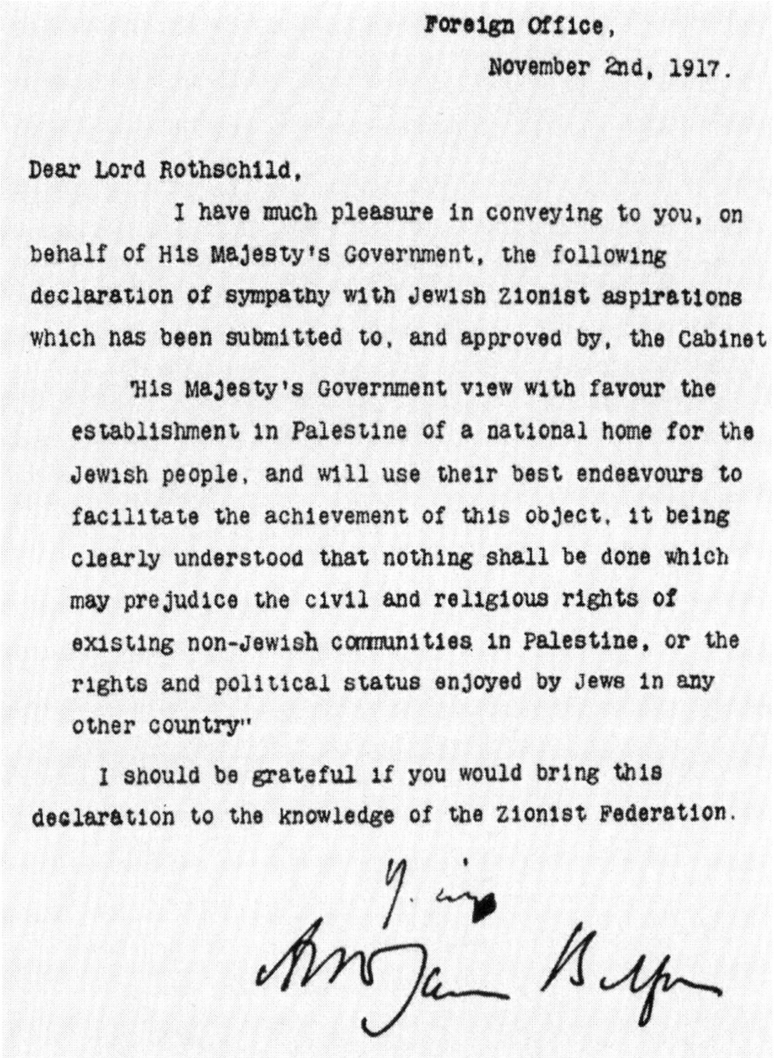

Foreign Office,
November 2nd, 1917.

Dear Lord Rothschild,

I have much pleasure in conveying to you, on behalf of His Majesty's Government, the following declaration of sympathy with Jewish Zionist aspirations which has been submitted to, and approved by, the Cabinet

"His Majesty's Government view with favour the establishment in Palestine of a national home for the Jewish people, and will use their best endeavours to facilitate the achievement of this object, it being clearly understood that nothing shall be done which may prejudice the civil and religious rights of existing non-Jewish communities in Palestine, or the rights and political status enjoyed by Jews in any other country"

I should be grateful if you would bring this declaration to the knowledge of the Zionist Federation.

**Figure 2-17:** The Balfour declaration of 1917.

While recent religious extremist movements have originated from the "Middle East," the first major extremist religious act in modern history was the creation of a new country, Israel, on a land inhabited by Palestinian Muslims and Christians. Why this should be defined as an extremist religious act is the fact that the Christian Zionist promoters used interpretations of the Bible rather than political strategy or colonial expansionism as the rationale.

As I traveled throughout the Arab world and spoke to local people in cafés, university campuses, and people's homes during the past 10 years, I was surprised to learn that most were not aware of the history of Sharif Hussein and his son Feisal, but the name "Balfour Declaration" was familiar to each person I came across. In contrast, during similar conversations in the US, Latin America, Europe, Africa, and Asia, I learned that most people had heard of neither the Sharif nor the Balfour Declaration.

I was struck by a comment from the late Palestinian American academic Edward Said, who commented that the Balfour Declaration was "made by a European power . . . about a non-European territory . . . in a flat disregard of both the presence and wishes of the native majority resident in that territory." The Balfour Declaration represents the far-reaching colonial influence of the West; so powerful that they could declare, based on religious extremist interpretations, the gifting of a land that was already populated by another group of people. To today's Arabs, this declaration marks not only a blatant betrayal, but a clear refusal to honor the homes, livelihoods, and beliefs of their people.

What also became clear to me is that in the Arab world, the impression across the board is that the Balfour Declaration was a Jewish conspiracy. There is no doubt that there was lobbying by powerful Jewish Zionists like Chaim Weizmann and Lord Rothschild, but the declaration was ultimately the work of evangelical Christian Zionists. Whether evangelical Christians used Zionist Jews or vice-versa, Palestine was no longer in the future of the Arab people.

## Secret Number 2: Sykes and Picot

Unbeknownst to the Sharif of Mecca, the Balfour declaration was not the only secret negotiation that the British were involved in. At the same time that Britain was making promises to the Sharif, they entered into secret negotiations with the French to divide up the Ottoman Empire among themselves—including the same lands promised to a future Arab nation. The French, for their part, initially had no idea that the British had secretly committed those lands to the Arabs in return for their allegiance.

While the British raised biblical interpretations as justification for their decisions, the French rationalized division of the post-war territory based on historical connections to the Crusade routes from the twelfth and thirteenth centuries. As French commanders had passed through Syria (and present-day Lebanon) while on their way to the holy land, they built castles; the French therefore laid claim to the Syrian and Lebanese territories based on these structures and routes. French politicians used the term "mission historique" to assert their claim to Syria based on the Crusades almost a millennium before. In the West today, it is common to hear in popular culture that the peoples of the "Middle East" are stuck in historic wars and animosities, but the ironic truth is that it was the British and French who used medieval religious fervor to create the present-day "Middle East."

Mark Sykes, a conservative British politician, and Francois Georges-Picot, a French diplomat and lawyer, were put in charge of the secret negotiations between Britain and France. In their meetings, the two men redefined the map of the "Middle East," dividing it between Britain and France (Fig. 2-18).

Please note that the map was signed by Picot and Sykes on May 8, 1916. This was exactly two months after the British finalized the deal with the Sharif of Mecca in March 1916 promising the same land for a future Arab nation.

No Arab scholar, historian, politician, or leader was consulted on where the borders were drawn to create the "Middle East" as we know it today.

The secret Sykes-Picot Agreement was ratified by both the British and French governments in May 1916, one month before the Sharif of Mecca was instructed by Britain to start his fight against the Ottomans.

All three of Britain's negotiations—the promise to the Sharif in Mecca, the Balfour Declaration, and the Sykes–Picot Agreement—took place in parallel. Additionally, Sykes was also intimately involved with the Balfour discussions, strongly believed in Zionist ideology, and was working closely with Chaim Weizmann and Lord Rothschild!

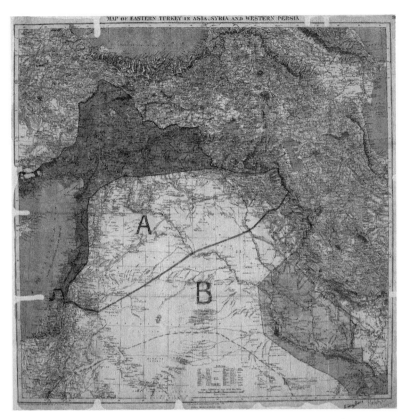

**Figure 2-18:** Map of the Sykes–Picot Agreement; the area designated *A* was to go to France, while the area marked *B* would go to Britain. The signatures of both Sykes and Picot can be seen in the bottom-right corner of the map (signed on May 8, 1916).

Once Palestine was captured, Prime Minister George made it clear that the territory would not be shared with any other Western powers. Although the French were allies in the war, George told French Prime Minster Georges Clemenceau, "Except for Great Britain no one had contributed anything more than a handful of black troops to the expedition in Palestine . . . the other governments [meaning the French] had only put in a few nigger policemen to see that we did not steal the Holy Sepulchre!" It goes without saying that just like the duplicitous syndrome involving the Jews, the Christian

Zionist extremism movement was also deeply prejudicial toward people of African descent.

Meanwhile, in the months that Feisal was fighting the Ottomans and moving north toward Damascus, he heard rumors about possible British double-crossing. He wrote to his father of his concerns, but the Sharif, a man who believed in the old ideals of honor, admonished Feisal. In a letter dated May 1917, Sharif Hussein told his son: "Never doubt Great Britain's word. She is wise and trustworthy; have no fear."

It was not until their meeting on October 3, 1918, at the Victoria Hotel in Damascus that General Allenby informed Feisal of the fact that he and his father had been betrayed: Palestine had been promised away to the Jews of Europe. Furthermore, he was told that the Arab lands that were promised to his father as the site of the future independent Arab nation would instead be divided between Britain and France. Scott Anderson, in his book *Lawrence in Arabia* provides in exquisite detail the history of this historic deceit.

Next, the British tried to bribe the Sharif into endorsing their newly created "Middle East." They offered £300,000 (equivalent to £13,200,000 today, or $16,734,000). He categorically refused.

The British were asking something totally new, something never seen in Arab culture before. They were looking for "puppet" leaders to run those lands as vassals for Western powers. The Sharif's categorical refusal meant he had to be disposed of. (The next chapter will explain his demise.)

This left a potentially dangerous vacuum in the area. If the Sharif was not going to be the puppet leader over the holy places (Mecca and Medina) in Hejaz, who could the British install as the custodian who would be willing to act as the protectorate of the Islamic faith and secretly be subservient to Britain? The British would look eastward to the deep deserts of Arabia to find their man. This is Secret #3, and for that I devote the next chapter.

## Artificial Lines & Internal Divisions

Muslims lived in a federal system for over a thousand years, from the fourteenth century until World War I. Although it was not a perfect system, the Ottoman Empire allowed Arabs, Turks, and Jews to live together in overall peace with respect for minority rights. The small Jewish communities in Palestine and North Africa were treated with respect. So where does the sectarian hate and violence we see in the current "Middle East" come from?

The Balfour Declaration by the British, the creation of artificial borders to divide up the "Middle East" by the British and French, and the deceit and betrayal of Sharif Hussein fertilized the seeds of distrust and anti-Western sentiments of the present-day "Middle East." In 2016, the then vice president of the United States, Joe Biden, accurately attributed the problems of the "Middle East" to "artificial lines, creating artificial states made up of totally distinct ethnic, religious, and cultural groups."

George and Balfour acted based on their biblical interpretations from an extremist Anglo-Saxon evangelical (Christian Zionism) standpoint, not out of concern for the Jewish suffering in Europe.

In fact, George and Balfour were not necessarily representative of mainstream Christendom of the time. France, a majority Catholic nation, had historical "Crusader" nostalgia, but at no point supported the Christian Zionist point of view. The other major block of Christendom, the Eastern Church, was similarly opposed to Christian Zionism. The president of a highly respected France-based organization called Œuvre des Écoles d'Orient, which was the main custodian of the interests of Eastern Christianity in the Orient, called the British plans for Palestine "inadmissible." He warned that "the country of Christ [Palestine] should become the prey of Jewry and of Anglo-Saxon heresy [Christian Zionism]."

Similarly, Weizmann and Rothschild did not represent the mainstream Jewish thinking of the time. David Fromkin, an American scholar best known for his historical account of Europe's role in shaping the "Middle East" in the early twentieth century, notes that "Zionism had attracted little support among France's Jews" in his classic book covering the events described in the chapter "A Peace to End All Peace." In Britain, he recounts, there was also a lack of support amongst Jewish people; in fact, the primary political opposition to Zionism came from the only Jewish member of Lloyd George's cabinet, Edwin Montagu.

Likewise, there is no evidence that there was widespread support for Zionism among Jews in the United States at the turn of the twentieth century. It was not until the first Jewish Supreme Court justice, Louis Brandeis (for whom Brandeis University is named), lent his support to the movement in the 1910s that it gained momentum amongst American Jews. From an international standpoint, Fromkin reports that "only about one percent of the world's Jews had signified their adherence to Zionism."

## A Reflection on the Betrayal

The betrayal by the British of the Arab's hopes and dreams to establish a nation of their own set in motion the creation of a "Middle East" that would be embroiled in conflict for generations to come. This will become even more clear when I share with you the third secret in the next chapter. Betraying the peoples of this region would go on to become a standard rather than an exception. Kurds—who are Muslims but ethnically distinct from Arabs, Turks, and Persians, and who are indigenous to the Mesopotamian plains and highlands (now southeastern Turkey, northeastern Syria, northern Iraq, northwestern Iran, and southwestern Armenia)—made a deal with the US to fight ISIS in return for America's protection of their towns. They became the biggest force to weaken ISIS. The Kurds lost thousands of their fighters in the process, but were able to declare territorial victory over ISIS in March 2019. In October, once the Kurds delivered ISIS, US President Donald Trump, in an about-face, pulled the rug from underneath the Kurds and discontinued US protection. General Joseph Votel, former commander of US Central Command, expressed his disappointment by stating, "It doesn't seem very honorable to step away from your partners." That is a very similar sentiment I observed during my research for this chapter among many British commanders following WWI, when the British government betrayed the Sharif of Mecca.

"You are leaving us to be slaughtered," said General Mazloum Kobani Abdi, commander of the Kurdish-led Syrian Democratic Forces (SDF), to the top American diplomat in northern Syria. That exact statement could have been said to British diplomats 100 years prior, when Britain turned Arabs over to vassal dictators. To illustrate my point, all we need to do is look at the dictatorship of the Al-Assad family in Syria. In 1982, Hafez al-Assad massacred 20,000

Syrian Arabs in the town of Hama (west-central Syria). Fast forward to the early twenty-first century, when his son, Bashar al-Assad, killed over 200,000 Syrian Arabs (including torture and the use of chemical weapons). The Kurdish general's statement, "You are leaving us to be slaughtered," echoes the perpetual betrayal of the people of the region that was set in motion 100 years ago.

While Islamic extremism has tainted the reputation of today's "Middle East," as made all too clear by horrific attacks like those on the Paris café in 2015 at the opening of this chapter, it is primarily Christian extremism and fundamentalist readings of the Bible (Christian Zionism) that shaped the geography of the region and created the resulting religious and political tensions of the twentieth century.

# Chapter 3
# Invaders from the East 2.0: False Kings

In Chapter 1, we discussed "Invaders from the East," the Mongols who destroyed Baghdad in its golden age and thus extinguished the Enlightenment Era of the Islamic Civilization. In Chapter 2, we discussed the "Invaders from the West," the British and French, both of whom betrayed the Arabs and divided their lands. There would be a third invader, this time again from the East!

Once the British and French had a foothold in the Arab lands, they needed vassal kings to do their bidding. The Sharif of Mecca categorically refused all attempts by the British to bribe him to remain in his position and serve as their puppet/vassal king/vassal caliph for them over the holy places in Hejaz (Mecca and Medina). They had to come up with a plan to remove him from Hejaz and insert a subservient vassal king. How did they do that? Allow me to explain in this chapter.

Let's start with an orientation of the Arabian Peninsula (commonly referred to as "Arabia" in the west). For our purposes, the two main regions of Arabia are 1) Hejaz-on the western side along the red sea and 2) Najd, the central desert region (Fig. 3-1).

Najd, due to its desert terrain and sole occupancy by Bedouin tribes since recorded history, was never incorporated by any civilization. The Roman, Persian, and not even the Islamic Empires of the first and second millennia ever saw the strategic need to incorporate this land. From a religious standpoint, dating back to the seventh century, Najdi tribes adopted the Islamic religion, which had emerged from Hejaz. For religious guidance, the people of Najd relied on ulama (religious leaders) educated in the scholarly centers in Hejaz (Mecca and Medina), Cairo, and Damascus. In 1703 a man by the name Mohammad ibn Abd al-Wahhab was born in Najd and he would go on to challenge the orthodoxy of Islam. He declared that all Muslims in the Ottoman Empire, the flag bearer of the Islamic religion, were not true Muslims! The only true Islam, according to him, was how he defined it. He then advocated militancy to spread his ideas.

**Figure 3-1:** Arabian Peninsula: The western region, Hejaz, is of major historical significance for the Arab and Muslim civilization as it contains the holy cities of Mecca and Medina. The central region is known as Najd. The town of Al-Diriyah (shown) in Najd is a significant location in the history of the Wahhabi movement.

Following the September 11, 2001, terrorist attacks on the United States, America's intelligence apparatus zoomed in on the Kingdom of Saudi Arabia, specifically to analyze their efforts to spread the extremist "Wahhabi" philosophy into countries extending throughout Asia to North Africa. The agencies were particularly interested in looking at the money flow from some the Kingdom's ruling class that facilitated the emergence of thousands of "jihadists" (self-proclaimed holy warriors) in multiple countries. French President Emmanuel Macron stopped other countries from sending imams (Muslim religious leaders) to France in order to curb the influence of extremist Wahhabi ideology on its young Muslims. Countries like Pakistan and Afghanistan do not have the financial nor the political power to be able to stop Saudi Wahhabi imams from doing the same. What is this extremist Wahhabi philosophy? And how did it start? The answers lie in a marriage of convenience that took place on the Arabian Peninsula.

## A Marriage of Convenience

Ibn Abd al-Wahhab (the Father of Wahhabism) emerged from Najd in the early part of the eighteenth century. He lacked the scholarly background in Islamic jurisprudence that was the basis for the ulama (religious scholars) of the time. Both his father and brother were scholars and served as judges, and they both categorically denounced him and his ideas, as did the religious scholars of the Arabian Peninsula at the time. It is important to note that although he did not have official education in jurisprudence, he did make educational trips which included the holy places (Mecca and Medina). His most influential educational stint occurred in Basra (current- day Iraq). Basra and the Iranian cities where he spent time were mostly of the Shia sect of Islam, while the Arabian Peninsula was predominantly Sunni Muslim, as it is to this day. Much like in Christianity, in which there are the two main divisions (Catholics and Protestants), in Islam the two main divisions are Sunni and Shia. (The difference between the two will be described in a later chapter.)

For the remainder of this book, when I mention "traditional" or "orthodox" Islam, I am referring to Sunni Islam. When I speak of "Wahhabi" Islam, I am referring to the extremist movement within Sunni Islam.

Today, it is believed in much of the Arabian Peninsula and the larger Muslim world that the premise of the Wahhabi movement was based on Ibn Abd al-Wahhab's strong stance against the idol-worshipping that he believed was being practiced by Muslims in Najd. There is, however, no reliable historical evidence suggesting that the Muslim Bedouin tribes were worshipping idols anywhere at that time in Najd. The last time there was documented polytheism in Najd was in the seventh century, before the introduction of Islam.

It is important to note to the non-Muslim reader that in orthodox Islam, any images or physical objects representing God, the Prophet Muhammad, his family and companions, and other prophets (including Abraham, Moses, and Jesus) are strictly forbidden. The key concern is that the use of visual images and objects can encourage idolatry (the worship of a physical object as a god). In pre-Islamic Arabia, the Bedouins were polytheistic and were idol worshipers, which the new religion of Islam replaced with monotheism and worship through prayer.

The Wahhabis used propaganda to claim that the Bedouins of eighteenth-century Najd, after more than 1,000 years of practicing Islam, were so backward, uneducated, and naive that they easily reverted to idol worship. This is deeply insulting to the true history of the proud Najdi tribes. This propaganda, however, did help the Wahhabis spread their message over the ensuing 200 years.

The Muslims of the time were practicing their religion based on the original tenets of Islam and were not using images or statues in any way. The Wahhabis, however, had a deeply fanatical interpretation of "idol worship." For example, Wahhabis are averse to using the names of noted Islamic historical scholars when naming schools.

Furthermore, Ibn Abd al-Wahhab and his followers declared that a "true" Muslim (meaning Wahhabi Muslim) could not live in the same community or do business with orthodox Muslims, who they defined as idolaters. Even to live in the holy places of Mecca and Medina, or in the populous cities of Cairo or Damascus, made one an infidel! This philosophy effectively declared that the entirety of the Ottoman Empire was full of idolaters.

This created a major divide in Islam. It explains why non-Wahhabi Muslims were the primary victims of ISIS, the jihadist terrorist group that emerged at the turn of the twenty-first century.

David Commins, in his book, *The Mission and the Kingdom*, provides an exquisite and detailed account of the history of Wahhabism.

Ibn Abd al-Wahhab, due to his extreme views, was expelled from a number of towns in Najd, where many scholars considered him to be a heretic. After he was expelled from the town of Al-Uyayna, he went to a small oasis town some 25 miles away called Al-Diriyah. This move from one small town to another in the middle of the Arabian desert on that day in 1744 would change the course of history in the "Middle East" and would go on to have a global impact.

The town of Al-Diriyah had a very astute clan leader, Mohammad ibn Saud (referred to as Ibn Saud for the remainder of the chapter), who was but one of the numerous tribal leaders who had been raiding each other for centuries for financial gains, territory, and status. Ibn Abd al-Wahhab, who had no family support nor endorsement from the religious establishment, was seeking a local tribal chieftain to lend him the support he needed to spread his message. What was Ibn Abd al-Wahhab willing to give the tribal chief in return? He was offering the ultimate prize for any tribal leader; he and his followers would pledge their wholehearted allegiance to the chief as their political and military leader. It is this 1744 covenant of categorical deference to Ibn Saud—in return for his adoption of the new religious philosophy—that gave Ibn Saud a unique advantage in Najd. In other words, Ibn Saud believed that Ibn Abd al-Wahhab's philosophy (whether he believed in it or not is hard to know) gave him an edge against the other tribal chieftains and could propel him to expand his tiny oasis rule into the wider Najd. Abd al-Wahhab's declared that any "Muslim" who did not ascribe to his exclusionist interpretation of Islam would be labeled as an idolater and would be deprived the immunity of his "property and life." This gave Ibn Saud the basis to invade cities in Najd and beyond. He now had a religious rationale for raiding and looting: a proclaimed holy war or jihad. Some two-and-a-half centuries later, this covenant between the Wahhabis and the Saudis still stands. By this pledge of allegiance, Ibn Abd al-Wahhab would give Ibn Saud the "deal of the century" or perhaps historically more accurately, as we will see, "centuries" (Fig. 3-2).

It is important to state that had the chance encounter in the mid-eighteenth century between Ibn Abd al-Wahhab and Ibn Saud not happened and had a pact not been made, there would be no Al-Qaeda nor ISIS some two centuries later. Wahhabism is at the core of both Sunni terrorist organizations.

Over the next 200 years, the Ibn Saud family gained footholds in Najd under the Wahhabi flag. Instead of traveling to the holy places of Mecca and Medina or Cairo and Damascus that had formerly been standard in Islamic education to become a religious scholar, Najdi students travelled to Al-Diriyah (and later Riyadh) to study Wahhabi philosophy. Over time, Wahhabism, once a fringe fundamentalist movement, became a central belief in the Arabian Peninsula.

**Figure 3-2:** Where it all Happened—a contemporary picture of the town Al-Diriyah, where the covenant between the Abd al-Wahhab and Al-Saud families was pledged in AD 1744.

The superpower in the region at the time was the Muslim Ottoman Empire. They were initially slow to act on what they assessed to be a heretic with a few followers deep in the deserts of Arabia. But after the death of Ibn Abd al-Wahhab by the early nineteenth century, the Ottoman leadership in Istanbul became alarmed by the expanding extremist cult movement in the middle of the Arabian Peninsula. The Ottomans decided to lay siege to Al-Diriyah by sending "federal" troops from Egypt and Hejaz in 1818.

With the approaching Ottomans, the Saudi–Wahhabi group invoked jihad against the Ottomans that they regarded as "infidels." After a five-month standoff at the Diriyah compound, the Saudi–Wahhabi ruler Abdullah Ibn Saud, great-grandson of Mohammad Ibn Saud, surrendered and was deposed to Istanbul. The Ottoman sultan ordered Ibn Saud's public execution and display.

The reaction of the "federal" Ottomans to the Wahhabis was very similar to the US Federal government's response to the Branch Davidians (an extremist offshoot of the Seventh-day Adventist Church), who under their inspirational leader, David Koresh, were holed up in a compound in Waco, Texas, that federal agents sieged and then stormed in 1993.

The animosity between the Saudis and Turks was reignited in October 2018 over the extrajudicial torture, premeditated killing, and dismemberment of the US-based journalist Jamal Khashoggi in the Saudi Consulate in Istanbul by a hit team belonging to the Saudi government. On social media, Khashoggi's violent killing was likened by some to the public execution of Abdullah ibn Saud in Istanbul in 1818 (Fig. 3-3).

After deposing the Saudi ruler, the Ottomans rounded up all of the Al-Saud and Ibn Abd al-Wahhab family members in Al-Diriyah and deported them to Cairo and Istanbul for religious rehabilitation. The Ottomans then leveled the whole compound of Al-Diriyah, believing they had forever defeated the extremist fringe group.

**Fig 3-3:** A handmade image of Abdullah ibn Saud, who was executed by the Ottomans in Istanbul in 1818. Abdullah, based on Wahhabi doctrine, had banned all music in Najd. Just prior to his execution in Istanbul, a lute was played by the Ottomans.

## The Outsiders—The Exchangers

Allow me, before we move on in this story, to share with you the context of fundamentalist movements in the history of Islam. The Wahhabis were not the first fringe militant group to emerge in this faith. Early on after the death of the Prophet Muhammad in the seventh century, a fundamentalist sect would emerge that would threaten the leadership of the young and emerging Muslim empire. Known as the Khawarij (meaning those who have left) or ash-Shurah (meaning the Exchangers), they were responsible for the first act of sedition (known as *fitna* in Arabic) in the history of Islam. They assassinated two of the four original caliphs, Uthman and Ali. Throughout their history, the Kharijites, much like the Wahhabis, rationalized the indiscriminate killing of other Muslims (non-Kharijite Muslims). The city of Basra (current-day Iraq) was a central location for the advances of Khawarij ideology in the seventh and eighth centuries, and it is the same city where Ibn Abd al-Wahhab spent a significant amount of time for his religious studies (Fig. 3-4).

**Figure 3-4:** The blood-soaked Qur'an of Uthman ibn Affan (AD 583–656), Islam's third caliph. Uthman was reading this Qur'an when he was attacked and killed by the Kharijites in his home in Medina in the mid-seventh century. It is believed that this Qur'an was then sent to Mesopotamia (present-day Iraq), where it was kept for hundreds of years, until Tamerlane, the founder of the Timurid Empire, invaded the region in the fourteenth century. He took it to his hometown of Samarkand, Uzbekistan. The Russians who invaded the Muslim lands of central Asia in the nineteenth century took the Qur'an and placed it in the Imperial Library in St. Petersburg. Following the Russian revolution in the early twentieth century, in a rare gesture of goodwill, Lenin sent it back to Central Asia, where it is currently housed in a museum in Tashkent, Uzbekistan. I took this picture during my visit to this museum in June 2018.

Did the colossal defeat of the Saudi–Wahhabi group by the Ottoman Empire have an impact on future events to come?

I often wondered why Osama bin Laden, the founder of the Wahhabi-based terrorist organization Al-Qaeda, selected the date of September 11 for the massive terrorist attack on the US in 2001. Dates of terrorist attacks often have historical significance to those that plan them.

The 1995 Oklahoma City bombing, committed by the white supremacist Timothy McVeigh, was planned as a revenge against the US federal government for the 1993 Waco siege mentioned above. McVeigh chose the anniversary of the Waco siege for his act of terror.

Gavrilo Princip, a Christian Serb extremist, assassinated Archduke Franz Ferdinand of Austria and the archduke's wife, Sophie, Duchess of Hohenberg, in Sarajevo on June 28, 1914. It is thought that that date was important to Princip because it corresponded to the fourteenth-century defeat of the Serbs by the Ottomans. The assassination of the archduke was the catalyst for World War II (Figs. 3-5 and 3-6).

**Figure 3-5:** Archduke Franz Ferdinand and his wife, Sophie, were assassinated after leaving the Sarajevo Guildhall on June 28, 1914.

**Figure 3-6:** The first page of the edition of the *Domenica del Corriere*, an Italian paper, depicting Gavrilo Princip killing Archduke Francis Ferdinand and his wife in Sarajevo. (Drawing by Achille Beltrame.)

Bin Laden was well versed in the history of the Arabian Peninsula, and he was a devout Wahhabi. The insulting historical defeat and surrender of Abdullah ibn Saud and the Wahhabi clan to the Ottoman Empire, whom he would have considered non-Muslim idolaters, occurred on September 11, 1818. While it is ultimately speculation, I believe this may be why Bin Laden selected this date for his attack on the United States.

## The Ikhwan (the Brethren)

We left off in the central Arabian Peninsula with the Ottomans scorched-earth policy toward the Al-Saud–Wahhabi group and the execution of their leader in Istanbul in 1818. By leveling Al-Diriyah, the Ottomans thought that they had exterminated the menace of the Wahhabi cult. This was not so. Some members of the Al-Saud family escaped capture and fled to the nearby small town of Riyadh. Riyadh, however, was ruled by the Al-Rashid family, who were traditional orthodox Sunni Muslims that were fundamentally opposed to the Wahhabi ideology. As a result, the Al-Saud family struggled and by the second half of the nineteenth century went to live in exile in Kuwait (Figs. 3-7a and 3-7b).

During their time in exile the bond between the Al-Saud and Ibn Abd al-Wahhab clans would significantly strengthen by a number of intermarriages.

**Figures 3-7a and 3-7b:** In the mid-nineteenth century, the Saudi–Wahhabi alliance moved to Riyadh, a small town 12 miles southeast of Al-Diriyah. On the left is an early-twentieth-century aerial photograph of Riyadh. On the right is a view of the Sahat al-'Adl (the Justice Square) in Old Riyadh in the same period. In 1902, the town's population of 14,000 was enclosed by city walls and was one square kilometer in area. The walls were built of mud and bricks, had a height of almost eight meters, and incorporated towers and defended gates.

In 1901, a 27-year-old member of the Al-Saud family, Abdulaziz, not satisfied with living in exile in Kuwait, returned to Najd with a small group of raiders. Within a year, he and his followers defeated the Al-Rashid family and took over the city of Riyadh (Figs. 3-8 and 3-9).

The Ottomans, who were quite weakened by this time and dealing with the looming WWI, did send a force into Najd to again try to exterminate the Al-Saud–Wahhabi movement, but Abdulaziz was successful in his guerrilla warfare against them and was able to gain

**Figure 3-8:** The last of the Al-Rashidi ruling princes in Najd, Saud al-Rashidi, before the takeover by the Al-Saud clan. The Al-Rashidi family fought Wahhabism, believing it was a cult philosophy that endangered traditional Islam.

momentum. Over the next decade he was able to control much of Najd and restored the Wahhabis to their roles of political and religious power.

With the Wahhabis back in control of Najd in the early part of the twentieth century, what is their goal for this region? As mentioned before, the Wahhabis saw the Muslims living in the cities of Hejaz and throughout the Ottoman World as non-Muslim. Ironically, they looked down on their own people as well, meaning other nomads, the Bedouins. Wahhabi ulama would embark on a novel mission, never before seen in the history of Islam, to create "reeducation" camps for the Bedouins to be indoctrinated into Wahhabi philosophy. These camps had both religious and military missions, to create Wahhabis that would then become a zealous militant group. The idea was to take the Bedouins out of their traditional nomadic lifestyle and put them in agricultural settlements formed in desert oases. (Each settlement was called a *hijra*). Each hijra was provided with living quarters, a mosque, weapons, and perhaps most importantly, rigorous teaching.

They were strict in their teachings: if one were to consider Ottomans or any traditional Muslim to be a true Muslim, that would make one an infidel as well. To give assistance to or ally with anyone but a Wahhabi Muslim would make one an infidel. Perhaps the most dangerous of the beliefs was that taking the life of infidels (traditional Muslims and non-Muslims) is permissible. Groups like Al-Qaeda and ISIS later based their principles on the same ideology that the Bedouins were taught in these camps.

**Figure 3-9:** Abdulaziz ibn Saud (1910).

The Bedouins converted in these settlements became collectively known as *Ikhwan*, which means "brethren" in Arabic. (Note that although the words appear similar, this term is not related to the social-religious movement "Islamic Brotherhood" that emerged in Egypt in the 1920s.)

The Ikhwan did not disappoint; by all definitions, the Ikhwan were trained into a terrorist organization. They soon invaded neighboring Bedouin tribes, who had been traditional Sunni Muslims, and gave them the option of converting to Wahhabism or be killed, just as ISIS would do 100 years later. Again, foreshadowing the twenty-first-century ISIS, they had a reputation for killing captives without mercy, a practice categorically prohibited in traditional Islam. When the Ikhwan became overly violent and began massacring known tribes with no apparent reason, Abdulaziz purportedly tried to tame them.

## The King Maker: Winston Churchill
## "I am a Zionist"

As Wahhabism sprang forward from the deserts of Arabia in Najd, the Sharif in Mecca and his son Feisal fought from Hejaz to Damascus for an independent Arab nation. At the end of the last chapter, General Allenby delivered the news to Feisal that there would be no Arab nation and Palestine would instead be made into a home for a future Jewish nation. According to the British, the Sharif of Mecca had to go. He had turned down their bribes to accept the new "map" of the "Middle East" they had created, and he had refused to serve as their vassal leader. They needed to come up with their own "man" who would overthrow the Sharif and serve as the British vassal ruler over Islam's holy places.

Back in London, in now the post–WWI era, the British Prime Minister George needed a like-minded new dynamic individual to help plan the future. Just a few short months after the Victoria Hotel meeting in Damascus (in January 1919), he selected a 45-year-old politician who strongly shared his Christian Zionist views to become the new secretary of state for war for Britain. His name was Winston Churchill.

Churchill is well recognized for his monumental role as British prime minister in the Allied victory over Nazi Germany during World War II. However, Churchill's role in creating the "Middle East" after World War I has been omitted from the limelight, perhaps for a reason.

Like George and Balfour, Churchill was an emphatic Christian Zionist, but he was not sympathetic toward the Jewish people. He spoke somewhat accusatorily of "the Jews, whom we are pledged to introduce to Palestine and who take it for granted that the local population will be cleared out to suit their convenience." It appears strange that Christian Zionists continued to act on behalf of the Jewish people without a true interest in their well-being, a "duplicitous syndrome" explored throughout this book.

Soon after taking the post of secretary of state for war for Britain, Churchill announced his strategy for filling the power vacuum after they would remove the Sharif in Mecca: "My ambition is that the Arabs should be our first brown dominion, and not our last brown colony."

My use of the term *vassal* has a deep historical meaning in this context. A vassal is a person who has an obligation to a lord or king. The term comes from a Celtic word that means "boy." In medieval Europe, the concept developed with teenage gangs who would carry out nefarious tasks for their lords in return for financial support. It further evolved under the reign of Charlemagne (the ninth-century iconic king of France mentioned in Chapter 1) when it became standard that in return for allegiance to the king, the vassal would be given land. Churchill, who was a student of history and the most astute politician, would embark on the most comprehensive and ambitious "vassalage" program in history that would go on to create the political system of the modern "Middle East" as we know it today. Churchill would later become the "King Maker"; he would give land (Middle Eastern territories) and appoint the vassal kings, who then in return would bend the knee to the real throne, Britain!

The stars were aligned; Churchill was looking for "candidates" for vassal kings in the "Middle East" and Abdulaziz was becoming powerful in Najd. Churchill had a litmus test for any would-be kings in the vast Arab lands it occupied following WWI. First, the candidate had to support a homeland for Jews in Palestine (Christian

Zionist demand), and second, he had to categorically reject Sharif Hussein's concept of an "independent Arab nation" ruled by a leader independent of Western control. It goes without saying, the Sharif of Mecca had failed both tests.

The views of Abdulaziz on these two critical requirements are best explained in his communication of February 10, 1920, with H. R. P. Dickson, the British Attaché to Bahrain, who documented, "[Abdulaziz] was so unconcerned with the question of Arab nationalism," and "He implored Britain and France to ensure that the Arabs would never be given independence in Palestine, Syria, Lebanon or Iraq and declared his wholehearted support for the imposition of the projected mandates [meaning the Sykes–Picot division and occupation of Arab lands]." In another communication, Abdulaziz himself stated "both Britain and France should never grant them [meaning Palestinians, Syrians, Lebanese, and Jordanians] *hurriya* ['freedom' in Arabic]." As part of the larger issue of an independent Arab nation, the freedom of Egypt was also at stake. On this Abdulaziz is quoted as saying, "On no account should they listen to the demands of the Egyptians," whom he added had "been disturbers of the peace ever since the days of the Pharaoh." On the specific issue of Palestine, which was one of the core concerns for Churchill, Abdulaziz would say the Palestinians were "not true Muslims" and therefore asserted his support of the Balfour Declaration.

Abdulaziz passed the litmus test with flying colors, but Churchill felt the need to disclose the extreme beliefs and violence of the Wahhabis. In his speech to the House of Commons on June 14, 1921, he warned the British government:

> They [Wahhabis] hold it as an article of duty, as well as of faith, to kill all who do not share their opinions and to make slaves of their wives and children. Women have been put to death in Wahhabi villages for simply appearing in the streets. It is a penal offense to wear a silk garment. Men have been killed for smoking a cigarette. . . . Austere, intolerant, well-armed, and bloodthirsty, in their own regions the Wahhabis are a distinct factor which must be taken into account, and they have been, and still are, very dangerous to the holy cities of Mecca and Medina.

Despite that admission he would add about Abdulaziz, "He has always shown himself well disposed towards Great Britain."

From a historical context, the above description of the Wahhabis by Churchill fits to a tee that of ISIS 100 years later.

The first public acknowledgment by the British government that they were paying Abdulaziz as a vassal of Britain (of course this was before the discovery of oil in Arabia) was as follows, "We have arranged to continue the subsidy which Ibn Saud [Abdulaziz] has hitherto received from the British Government of £60,000 a year, together with a lump sum of £20,000." The detailed information regarding the payments to Abdulaziz by the British government are documented in the British Parliament discussion notes between Lord Lamington, Belhaven, and Stenton on March 7, 1923 (Fig. 3-10).

**Figure 3-10:** Winston Churchill (left) and Abdulaziz ibn Saud (right). The Churchill–Abdulaziz covenant became the model for the vassalage program in all countries of the newly created region of the world known as the "Middle East."

The reader may be wondering why Abdulaziz was so open to becoming a vassal king for Britain. It was not just for the money; he was actually vehemently opposed to the freedom of Arabs in the Levant, Palestine, and North Africa (see map, Figure 2-5), as in his mind they posed a potential threat to his rule. He grew up in a very insular world in the deep deserts of Arabia; he could not relate to the Palestinians in any way and therefore had no reason to oppose the

Balfour Declaration. For him, Palestine might as well have been on Mars! Similarly, the language of an "independent Arab nation" was not only totally foreign to him but he perceived it as a threat to his leadership in the Arabian Peninsula. To him, the concept of Arab freedom and an Arab nation belonged to intellectuals in metropolitan cities like Cairo and Damascus, and he detested all that. Perhaps most importantly, he was a devout Wahhabi, which created his world view. The Wahhabi view of the world was and has always been directed totally inward. Their first targets were the Bedouin tribes of Najd, whose orthodox Sunni Islam they considered to be an apostasy. With the sword they converted these tribes into Wahhabism. Once their world enlarged beyond Najd, their target became the next geographic layer of Muslim communities; the Sharif of Mecca and the Arabs of the Levant and Egypt. For the Wahhabis, the British and the French were never the enemy; the Arabs and the traditional Muslims were. The Wahhabi concept of the "enemy within" persists to this day in the Saudi kingdom as well as all Arab dictatorships that were created by Britain using the Saudi prototype.

**Figure 3-11:** St. John Bridger Philby, British intelligence officer and key advisor to Abdulaziz ibn Saud during World War I. He served on the British Secret Intelligence Service in Palestine following the end of the war and later worked with Israel's first prime minister, David Ben Gurion, to try to create a back-door connection between Ben Gurion and Abdulaziz. Author Stephen Schwartz labeled Philby the "British Godfather of Saudi Arabia."

Beyond their decision not to live up to the pledge made to the Sharif of Mecca prior to WWI, besides being the default option, what was it about Wahhabism in particular which so appealed to the British? The answer is best summarized by St. John Philby, a British intelligence officer and a close advisor to Abdulaziz during WWI, according to whom there were two key principles: first, the Wahhabis were deeply hateful of Muslims who were not Wahhabis and considered them infidels, while they were essentially neutral toward Christian (British and French) forces in the region. This also explains the policy of the Saudi ruling family to host American troops in Arabia some 100 years later. Philby would write to his superior (Major Percy Cox) on June 2, 1918, that Wahhabis "viewed all non-Wahhabi Muslims as polytheists and unbelievers liable to jihad, and that the Ottomans and the Hashemites led by Sharif Hussien topped the list." He added, "the more their hatred for other Muslims intensified the more it converged with our own interests." Second, "[Wahhabis] display an absolute devout obedience to their leader," which was music to the ears of the British, who were looking for vassals with absolute authority over their people (Fig. 3-11).

## Secret Number 3: Double Crossing

From June 1916, when the Sharif of Mecca finalized his deal with the British to establish an independent Arab nation, to October 1918, when he was dealt the blow that the British had reneged on the agreement, he knew that the British were in diplomatic contact with key tribal chiefs in the Arabian Peninsula including Abdulaziz. What he was completely unaware of, however, was that from the start of their agreement with him in 1916, the British were already grooming Abdulaziz to become the leader of the Arabian Peninsula, as they had never intended to honor the agreement.

After the end of WWI, the Sharif, lamenting the Balfour Declaration becoming a reality in Palestine, reached out to Abdulaziz. He sent a confidential letter to Abdulaziz with the request to keep it secret from the British. Abdulaziz, however, immediately sent a letter to Major Percy Cox on September 4, 1922, disclosing the Sharif's correspondence. Abdulaziz told the British that the Sharif "talked a lot about Palestine" and that he asked him to stop being a "tool" for the British, which the Sharif told him was weakening the Arabs and hurting the dignity of the Islamic civilization. The Sharif declared in his letter to Abdulaziz that he would be willing to abdicate his own position in favor of whomever would best protect Palestine. Abdulaziz was very astute; by sharing the contents of this confidential letter with the British, he knew he would get what he had been waiting for: British support for him to personally overthrow the Sharif. He was right!

The Sharif of Mecca was double-crossed twice, by the British and by Abdulaziz (Figs. 3-12 and 3-13).

**Figures 3-12 and 3-13:** As part of the British vetting of Abdulaziz as candidate to serve as their vassal in Arabia, he met in 1916 with Major Percy Cox (picture on left) and Ms. Gertrude Bell (both pictures), a senior British political officer and policy maker. She was the first woman in modern history to graduate from Oxford with a first class honours degree. She went on to become a respected archeologist who was the first to detail the Arabian deserts for the British. Note the two ironies: 1) The Wahhabi ideology (for which Abdulaziz was the leader) categorically stated that a Muslim (according to their definition) could not collaborate (in business or otherwise) with idolaters (which for them the Christian British would be!) and 2) Percy Cox was a devout Christian Zionist, so he and Abdulaziz were in agreement about both the Balfour Declaration and the Sykes–Picot agreement. Gertrude Bell was not; she would state that she viewed the Balfour Declaration with "the deepest mistrust" and that "It's like a nightmare in which you foresee all the horrible things which are going to happen and can't stretch out your hand to prevent them." Mark Sykes, in a letter to his wife, would say about Bell: "Confound the silly chattering windbag of conceited, gushing, flat-chested, man-woman, globe-trotting, rump-wagging, blethering ass." Bell would go on, a few years later, to play a critical role in the creation of the country of Iraq. Sykes was not alone in his chauvinistic attitude toward Bell—Hollywood did the same to her. In the much acclaimed 1996 movie *The English Patient*, some British soldiers were studying a desert map when one asks, "But can we get through those mountains?" Another replies, "The Bell maps show a way," to which the response comes, "Let's hope he was right." However, in the 2015 film *Queen of the Desert*, despite typical Hollywood negative depictions of Arab culture in the movie, the actress Nicole Kidman provided an elegant portrayal of Bell for the intelligent officer, writer, archaeologist, and explorer she was.

## Invasion of the Holy Places

Churchill was aware that bringing the Saudi Wahhabis to Islam's holy places would not come without significant bloodshed. Therefore, he gave the Sharif of Mecca one last chance to accept the new reality that there would be no independent Arab nation and Palestine would no longer be under Arab guardianship.

Churchill implored the Sharif's sons to speak to their father. First, he sent a message via his son Abdullah, Feisal's older brother, asking the Sharif to sign a treaty that accepted the Balfour Declaration; Churchill warned Abdullah that otherwise, his father would be "under the mercy of the Ikhwan." Churchill added that Abdulaziz was "very dependent" on the British financially, and therefore could be stopped if the Sharif would acquiesce to the British. Churchill sent a similar message to Feisal, warning that Abdulaziz would "accomplish the ruin of his [the Sharif's] house" unless his father would bend the knee to the British. However, the Sharif castigated both sons for even considering such an agreement.

In a final attempt, Churchill sent T.E. Lawrence to meet with the Sharif. Lawrence met the Sharif in Jeddah, Hejaz, on July 29, 1921. The Sharif compared the potential loss of Palestine to his own limbs: it was, he said, "like the palm and fingers of one hand, and I could not [consent] to the amputation of any finger."

After reminding the Sharif of Britain's influence over the Wahhabis, Lawrence offered him another bribe of £300,000. The Sharif categorically refused.

With the final seal of approval from the British, Abdulaziz mobilized westward toward Hejaz (Fig. 3-14).

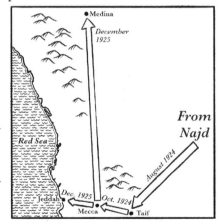

**Figure 3-14:** Invaders from the East 2.0: Abdulaziz ibn Saud's invasion of Hejaz and the occupation of Islam's holy cities of Mecca and Medina.

Abulaziz's forces, the Ikhwan, first attacked the mountain city of Taif in August of 1924. After a short siege, the Sharif's Hashemite forces stood down and the Saudi Ikhwan overtook the city. They then proceeded to slaughter 300–400 civilians (traditional orthodox Sunni Muslims) in an incident known as the Taif massacre, sparking fear in the other large cities of Hejaz: Mecca, Medina, and Jeddah.

**Figure 3-15:** Black & white picture from 1910 of pilgrims in the grand mosque in Mecca. The cube-shaped structure in the middle is called the Kabba ("cube" in Arabic). Based on Islamic history, it was built by Abraham and his son Ishmael around 2000 BC.

Sure enough, the Ikhwan invaded Mecca next; the city fell on October 16, 1924. This marked the first time in Islamic history in which Mecca was no longer under the custodianship and rule of the Prophet Muhammad's descendants, and the first time in its 4000-year history in which it was ruled by people from outside of Hejaz (Fig. 3-15).

Although Abdulaziz wanted his relationship with the British to be kept secret—he did not want the larger Muslim community to be aware that he was invading Islam's holy places in collaboration with a Christian power (the British)—the Hashemite government of Hejaz was now fully aware of the alliance. While Abdulaziz's forces were invading Hejazi towns, Palestinian intellectuals published excerpts of the secret agreements, known as the 1915 Anglo–Saudi Protectorate Treaty. This angered Abdulaziz, who asked the British representative, "Are there no state secrets in England?"

The Prophet's city, Medina, was the next to fall on December 3, 1925. In the port city of Jeddah, the business and cultural center of Hejaz, a group of 140 business and civic leaders sought the help of the British government to protect Hejaz from Abdulaziz, perhaps still unaware of the alliance. Of course, the request was denied. After a one-year siege, Jeddah fell on December 23, 1925. Jeddah had been a vibrant multicultural city, but following the Wahhabi takeover, all music was banned. The Wahhabis were also opposed to cars, radio, and telegrams, believing these technologies were the devil incarnate (Fig. 3-16).

**Figure 3-16:** Richard Burton, a nineteenth-century British geographer and explorer, visited Medina in 1853. The image shows his drawing of the Prophet's Mosque (Al-Masjid an-Nabawi). The central larger dome (known as the green dome) is above the tomb of the Prophet Muhammad. All surrounding domes above the tombs of the Prophet's closest companions and family members seen here have since been destroyed by the Saudi Wahhabi group.

Under the official auspices of the British government, Abdulaziz was inaugurated as king of Hejaz on January 8, 1926. Within weeks, official recognition of Abdulaziz as the ruler of Hejaz came from the Soviet Union, France, and the Netherlands. No such recognition came from any Arab or Muslim country.

A few years later, in 1932, the territories invaded by Abdulaziz were unified as "The Kingdom of Saudi Arabia." This name, which came from London, was devised by George Rendell, the head of the "Middle East" desk of the British Foreign Office.

## The Destruction of the House of Prophet Muhammad

By controlling the holy cities of Mecca and Medina, and as a result of the wealth that came from the 1938 discovery of oil in the new country of Saudi Arabia, the Wahhabis transformed the culture of the Arabian Peninsula. They mainstreamed Wahhabism in the Arabian Peninsula and beyond. They exported their philosophy by building mosques in poor communities in Asia and Africa, and each mosque came with a Saudi Wahhabi imam. Almost all future Islamist terrorists were a product of this indoctrination. The various intellectual schools of thought within Islam that had existed under the rule of the descendants of the Prophet Muhammad for over 1,000 years were erased and replaced by one cult mentality.

In a 2014 *Time* magazine article titled "Saudi Arabia Bulldozes Over Its Heritage," it was estimated that 98 percent of the Arabian Peninsula's historical and religious sites had been destroyed by the Saudi government. One of the benefits of Islamic cultural history, given that it emerged some 600 years after Christianity, had been the preservation of historical religious sites, including the homes of the Prophet and his family members, for over 1,000 years. However, under the Saudi Wahhabis, the house of one of the Prophet's closest confidants and one of the most highly revered figures in Islamic history, his uncle Hamza, was flattened. The same fate met the house of Abu Baker, the Prophet's closest friend and Islam's first caliph; his house was replaced by a Hilton hotel!

They did not even spare the house of the Prophet Muhammad and his wife Khadija. Allow me to tell you the story of the honorable lady Khadija. She was the daughter of a leader within the tribe of Quraysh (the ruling family of Mecca in the sixth and seventh centuries). She was a very successful businesswoman who owned and managed one of the biggest trading caravans in Mecca. She had been widowed twice, and at the age of 40, through her family, would ask a young man whose name was Muhammad (who later would become the Prophet) to consider marrying her. Muhammad was 25 years old and he initially hesitated as he was poor and she was wealthy, but ultimately, he proposed to her and they married. They would go on to have a number of children and would live a harmonious monogamous life for 25 years until Khadija died at age 65. The Prophet Muhammad would call the year of her death the "Year of Sorrow." He would go on to marry again, but only after the death of Khadija.

What did the Saudis do the house of the Prophet Muhammad? The house that witnessed the earliest stories of the emergence of Islam as a religion, in which Khadija became history's first Muslim convert and organized the feeding of the poor and persecuted early

Muslims of Mecca, was demolished and turned into public toilets by the Saudi government (Figs. 3-17 and 3-18).

Khadija's leadership as a historical pioneering businesswoman was well known and respected in Christian Europe as such roles for women were unheard of at that time. In the publication *Promptuarium Iconum Insigniorum* (France, AD 1553), which showcased 950 most notable figures of human history, she was one of the very few women figures selected; to the best of my knowledge, she was the only person from outside the biblical and European realms to be selected.

**Figure 3-17:** (left) Mecca AD 1778. Also spelled *Makkah* (which is closer to the Arabic pronunciation). The ancient name of the city is *Bakkah*. Older Arabic literature names the mountains surrounding Mecca *Faran* (or *Pharan*). Some scholars contend that is the desert of Paran mentioned in the Old Testament Genesis 21:21. The twelfth-century Syrian geographer, Yaqut al-Hamawī, wrote that *Faran* is "an arabized Hebrew word, one of the names of Mecca mentioned in the Torah." When Malcolm X, the American human rights activist, visited Mecca in 1964, he was mesmerized by its historic beauty, which he said was "as ancient as time itself" and believed would "surpass the architectural beauty of India's Taj Mahal."

**Figure 3-18:** (right) Mecca in the twenty-first century (aerial view). The grand mosque and the Kabba are now dwarfed by skyscrapers built on hundreds of millennium-old historical sites.

The Saudi demolition of historical sites was driven by financial incentives as well. After seeing the sheikhs of Abu Dhabi and Dubai make billions by building hotels and skyscrapers and developing a global tourist trade, the Saudi Wahhabis sought a similar fortune. There is an insatiable desire by Muslim pilgrims to visit Mecca from all over the world; seeking to capitalize on this tourism, the Saudis in the early twenty-first century sent bulldozers in the middle of the night to flatten some 400 sites of Islamic historical significance, including the few remaining 1,000-year-old buildings.

The Saudi government assigned the project to the Bin Laden group (the family of Osama Bin Laden). If I may remind you, in Chapter 1 we discussed the Abbasid Empire (named after the Prophet's uncle, Abbas), the era that saw the greatest scientific advances in the world during the Middle Ages. The Saudi Wahhabi group destroyed the physical signs of the Abbasid's contributions to Mecca. Pillars built by the Abbasids in the eighth century on the eastern side of the grand mosque (Al-Masjid al-Haram) were demolished. In 2012, they raised a group of behemoth structures, including the Makkah Royal Clock Tower, in place of these ancient sites. Saudi financial leaders are very proud of the fact that, in their competition with their cousins in Abu Dhabi and Dubai, the clock tower stands at 1,972 feet, one of the world's tallest buildings.

While oil exports, valued at $111.1 billion in 2018, make up 42 percent of Saudi Arabia's GDP, tourism may soon surpass the value of the country's oil. According to a Saudi government-controlled newspaper, the pilgrimage "revenues are poised to exceed $150 billion by 2022." Both the country's oil and tourist sites are resources derived from lands not part of Najd but were invaded by Abdulaziz with the help of the British, and a large portion of the profits are thought to be funneled to the royal family.

Not only does the Saudi Wahhabi leadership profit financially from the tourism of Muslims, but by the destruction of the ancient sites they have achieved the "Wahhabization" and the "Saudization" of the ancient cities of Mecca and Medina. In addition to the deeply seated hatred the Wahhabis have toward Islam's historical sites, their destruction also serves a strategic and political purpose. By destroying these sites, they effectively removed all physical connections to the descendants of the Prophet, who were the custodians of these sites for over 1,000 years. Although the Saudi Wahhabi group, with the backing of the British, invaded the holy places only recently (in the 1920s), someone visiting Mecca and Medina today, unaware of the actual history, would get the impression that the Saudi Wahhabis have ruled forever (Figs. 3-19 and 3-20)!

Medina, the second-holiest city in Islam, did not fare any better. Medina is a holy site because it is where the Prophet lived the last ten years of his life and was then buried. There, the Saudi Wahhabis leveled the resting places of the Prophet Muhammad's family members and his companions at the Al-Baqi Cemetery. Then they turned their attention to the Prophet's Mosque in Medina. After destroying the surrounding domes, there were proposals to demolish the green dome atop the Prophet's burial place. Moreover, in a 2007 letter from the Saudi Grand Mufti Abdulaziz al-Sheikh (also a descendant of Ibn Abd al-Wahhab), he called for the burial place of the Prophet Muhammad to be leveled. In 2014, another senior Saudi Wahhabi cleric proposed in a 61-page document that the Prophet's remains be relocated to the Al-Baqi Cemetery, where they would be interred anonymously.

**Figures 3-19 and 3-20:** Ajyad Fortress, which stood in the hills overlooking the mosque in Mecca, was built by the Ottomans (with the cooperation of the Prophet's descendants) in AD 1780. The picture on the left is from the nineteenth century. It was demolished by the Saudi government in 2002. (The picture on the right is from the twentieth century prior to its demolition). Turkey, one of the few Muslim countries willing to criticize the Saudi government, called the demolition of the fortress an "act of barbarism."

When these proposals were seen in countries with freedom of press, a number of newspapers in Britain raised an alarm. Understanding the potential for global backlash, the Saudi government denied any plans to further alter the Prophet's burial place (Fig. 3-21).

The Wahhabis' hate for history has one key exception: their own history! In November of 2019, under the direction of King Salman and his son Mohammad bin Salman (MBS), the Saudi government announced a $17 billion "Diriyah Gate Project" that will include eight museums to showcase the "history" of Al-Diriyah (the town where the covenant of the Ibn Saud and Ibn Abd al-Wahhab was

**Figure 3-21:** The central "Green Dome" in the Masjid an-Nabawi (the Prophet's Mosque) in Medina is artistically depicted. It was built above the tomb of the Prophet in AD 1279. The actual dome that exists today was added in 1818 by the Ottoman Sultan Mahmud II and it was painted green in 1837. The Wahhabis, who have destroyed the surrounding domes over the tombs of the Prophet's companions and family members, have sought to demolish this dome as well and to flatten the Prophet's tomb. However, due to international criticism and backlash from the larger Islamic world community, Saudi authorities have not done so.

sealed). An official Saudi newspaper called it "one of the most important projects in the Kingdom"!

In another telling example of the Saudi Wahhabi's priorities, the country did not open its doors in the wake of the humanitarian crisis created by the Al-Assad regime of Syria (yet another example of an Arab dictatorship) in the early twenty-first century. While countries like Jordan, Lebanon, and Turkey welcomed Syrian refugees, Saudi Arabia, with its vast wealth, kept its door closed, choosing instead to spend heavily on Wahhabi mosques around the world in an attempt to convert traditional Muslims. Their top priority has been to mainstream Wahhabism.

Although it is Saudi Wahhabi actions around the world that have fanned the flames of hatred toward Islam, it is non-Wahhabi Muslims who have borne the brunt of the resulting Islamophobia. While the Saudi Wahhabi leaders live in their palaces in the Arabian Peninsula, average working-class Muslims living in the US and Europe are the ones that suffer the consequences of Islamophobia. In 2020, 44 percent of Germans have said that they see a fundamental difference between Islam and their values; 53 percent have said the same in Italy. This tiny minority of Islam within the Arabian Peninsula, the Wahhabi extremists, with the power of the bully pulpit—and the massive financial clout from oil and pilgrims—have managed to create a negative image of the religion that has led to Islamophobia all over the world. The overwhelming majority of the close to two billion Muslims in the world do not only reject the alternative Islam of the Wahhabis, but actually have been the main target of both Wahhabism and Islamophobia.

## What Happened to the Sharif of Mecca?

Once Abdulaziz invaded Hejaz, the Sharif wanted to leave for Jerusalem, but the British would not allow it. The Sharif was then exiled to Aqaba, a northern port city on the Red Sea (the city that was used as base by his son Feisal during his advance up north to Damascus). Abdulaziz let the British know he was displeased with the Sharif living in a city where he was physically so close to his supporters, the Palestinians. The British then forcibly exiled the Sharif to the island of Cyprus (the place for political prisoners at the time). He would spend the last few years of his life in captivity until he suffered a major stroke at age 78 and was then sent to Amman, Jordan, where he died a few months later. At that point, the British acquiesced for him to be buried in Jerusalem.

The title of the last chapter, "The Ultimate Betrayal," is meant to represent the life and death of the Sharif of Mecca. He was betrayed three times: first by the British, for whom he fought a war and they reneged on their part of the deal. Next, he was betrayed by Abdulaziz ibn Saud, who schemed with the British against him. He was finally betrayed by his sons, who ultimately chose to bend the knee and become vassal kings.

The Sharif cut ties to his sons, labeling them "puppets." He was especially hurt by Feisal, the commander of his troops. It has been said that he did not talk to Feisal again so long as he lived.

## Kings Galore!

In Europe, once Churchill selected Abdulaziz to represent the interests of the West in the Arabian Peninsula, the "vassalage program" was launched. In my review of the original cables and records from 1915–1923, there was a clear concern among some British diplomats and military leaders that the betrayal and double-crossing of the Sharif of Mecca was not in keeping with British ideals and honor. On June 21, 1922, a motion in the House of Lords calling the Balfour Declaration "unacceptable" was carried by 60 votes to 29. The risk of a backlash from the British public was becoming a concern in the Christian Zionist Cabinet.

Churchill responded by recommending to the Cabinet "the removal of all anti-Zionist civil officials, however highly placed." He also believed that working with the Sharif's sons would restore the perception of British honor, as it would show respect for the Hashemite descendants of the Prophet Muhammad.

The Arabian Peninsula was now the hands of Abdulaziz ibn Saud (as a custodian of British interest), Palestine was in the hands of the British (as a result of the Balfour Declaration), and Syria was in the hands of the French. This left three primary newly created regions that needed "vassal kings": Iraq, Jordan, and Egypt.

The two older sons of the Sharif, Abdullah and Feisal, were offered a clear-cut choice. They could acquiesce to the British demands and live like kings, with all the grandiose trappings of that title, but be vassals of the British Government; alternatively, they could face the same fate as their father and live in exile. Both, as mentioned above, sold out to the British and accepted to serve as vassal kings.

Churchill made the older son, Abdullah, the king of the newly created country of Jordan, known as Transjordan at the time. As T.E. Lawrence explained, Abdullah fit the profile of the "ideal British agent" because he was "not too powerful, and who was not an inhabitant of Transjordan, but who relied upon his Majesty's Government for the retention of his office" (Fig. 3-22).

Churchill made Feisal the king of the newly created country of Iraq. Feisal was a more problematic figure from the British perspective; he had been a wartime commander and had not reacted well when General Allenby retracted his pledge for Arab freedom. Therefore, placing Feisal geographically further away from Palestine was important.

The final piece to the puzzle of the "Middle East" was Egypt. The British had occupied Egypt since 1882,

**Figure 3-22:** With his father in exile, the new leader of Jordan, Abdullah (left) with the leader of Saudi Arabia, Abdulaziz (right).

and it had served as the base of all their operations in the Arabian Peninsula and the Levant. The British accordingly had already had a vassal king in Egypt: Fuad I.

The initial pledge for an independent Arab nation had included Egypt. Therefore, at the end the war, Saad Zaghloul, a former Egyptian minister of justice and leader of the legislative assembly, officially asked Britain to keep her promise and allow Egypt's freedom. His fate was no better than that of the Sharif of Mecca; he was arrested by the British and sent to exile in Malta, another island on which the British kept political prisoners. Fuad I (and later his son Farouk) then served as kings. They passed both parts of the British litmus test: they served under the authority of Britain, and that they did not discuss Palestine or the Balfour Declaration (Fig. 3-23).

In a cable from the British Foreign Office dated February 23, 1922, the "obligations" of the British to Sharif Hussein and the Arabs were declared "satisfied" when his two sons were crowned kings; of course, the term "vassal" was not used. The memo explained why Hashemite rule in Hejaz was out of the question: it could threaten British

**Figure 3-23:** Abdulaziz of Saudi Arabia (left) and Farouk of Egypt (right).

plans in Palestine. Jerusalem housed the third-holiest site in the Islamic faith, the Al-Aqsa Mosque. The Christian Zionist demand of turning Palestine over to the Jews was the cornerstone for all decision-making regarding Palestine. Beyond that, from a British strategic standpoint, they could not allow a single Arab Muslim country to rule over all three of Islam's holiest sites, Mecca, Medina, and Jerusalem. In their view that would consolidate too much power in Arab Muslim hands, essentially making it similar to the Ottoman and the Abbasid Empires.

## Making Sense of Churchill

I grew up looking at Winston Churchill as a truly heroic figure, a man who saved Western civilization during World War II. With words like "We shall not flag nor fail. We shall go on to the end . . . We shall fight on the beaches, we shall fight on the landing grounds, we shall fight in the fields and in the streets . . . We shall never surrender," he was a skilled orator and a powerful figurehead who in some ways embodied the resiliency and steadfastness of the West. The historian Isaiah Berlin called him "the largest human being of our time," and it's hard to argue (Fig. 3-24).

**Figure 3-24:** Statue of Winston Churchill in front of the British Parliament.

But then why would Shashi Tharoor, chair of the Indian Parliament's Foreign Affairs Committee, say that Churchill was "one of the great mass murderers of the twentieth century, yet is the only one, unlike Hitler and Stalin, to have escaped historical odium in the West"?

Well for a start, Churchill called Indians "a beastly people with a beastly religion." Perhaps the most sensitive issue for Tharoor and other Indian scholars is the 1943 famine that killed some three million people in the region of Bengal. This famine has largely been attributed to Churchill's decision to have food from India exported in order to feed British military units in Asia and Europe. Churchill justified the famine by saying that the Indians had been "breeding like rabbits." During the British campaign in the Indian subcontinent he said, "The dominant race [white European Christians] resent the slightest suggestion of inferiority . . . This is the material for empirebuilding."

Similarly, during the British invasion of Afghanistan, he said that the Pashtuns (powerful tribe that resisted the invasion) "needed to recognize the superiority of [the British] race." He would boast about what the British troops had done to the civilian population in Afghanistan: "We proceeded systematically, village by village, and we destroyed the houses, filled up the wells, blew down the towers, cut down the great shady trees, burned the crops and broke the reservoirs in punitive devastation. . . . and every tribesman caught was speared or cut down at once." From the larger context of this book, none of these actions by Churchill have ever been documented as acts of terrorism in Western literature.

Iraq also protested the heavy hand of Britain after the installation of Feisal as the new vassal king. In response to the civilian outcry, Churchill responded, "I am strongly in favour of using poisoned gas against the uncivilized tribes; it would spread a lively terror." He himself used the word "terror," but Hollywood and the mainstream media choose not to represent his actions as such because it does not fit the narrative of terror and terrorism as purely an Arab and Muslim phenomenon.

Churchill once said, "History will be kind to me, for I intend to write it myself." And that he did. After seeing movies like *Darkest Hour* and *Lionheart*, if I didn't know better, I would have thought he wrote all of the Hollywood screenplays about himself, too!

## An Oasis in the Desert

The Lloyd, Balfour, and Churchill Christian Zionist plan for the "Middle East" continued to work through the vassal kings, but ironically, it was a son of Abdulaziz named Faisal (not be confused with Feisal, the son of Sharif Hussein) who nearly brought it all toppling down (Fig. 3-25).

**Figure 3-25:** Faisal ibn Abdulaziz, known for the type of humility not seen before or after him in Saudi Arabia. When he became king in 1964, he said, "I beg of you, brothers, to look upon me as both brother and servant. 'Majesty' is reserved to God alone and 'the throne' is the throne of the Heavens and Earth."

Faisal ruled Saudi Arabia from 1964 to 1975. Although his mother (Tarfa) was from Ibn Abd al-Wahhab's family, Faisal started to challenge the extremist Wahhabi thinking.

Faisal was quite different from his father Abdulaziz, who was more insular and focused on Najd. Faisal was highly educated and spoke English and Turkish and was said to know French. He questioned the main tenet that allowed the establishment of the Saudi Kingdom: the Balfour Declaration. This was a lifelong issue for Faisal. He knew that his father had supported the Balfour Declaration at the founding of the country, so he did not initially engage Western powers on the issue. Instead, Faisal made changes within his own domain in the years following Abdulaziz's 1953 death. Many of his family members owned enslaved people, but Faisal abolished slavery in 1962 when he was a crown prince under his brother King Saud. There is some evidence that US President John F. Kennedy, someone Faisal respected, had strongly pushed this issue (Fig. 3-26).

**Figure 3-26:** President John F. Kennedy hosting the then Crown Prince Faisal in the US (1962).

Two years later, in 1964, his brother King Saud abdicated the throne and Faisal became king.

As mentioned above, the Wahhabis were opposed to television, believing it was of the devil! Faisal established TV broadcasting in the Kingdom in 1966. This did not go over well with the Wahhabis. A nephew of his by the name of Khaled led a group of Wahhabi zealots in an attack on the newly established Saudi TV headquarters; he was killed by the security forces on site.

Faisal and his wife Effat advocated education for women. Together they established the first school for girls, Dar al-Hanan ("House of Affection") in Jeddah, and the first women-only university, Kulliyat al-Banat in Riyadh. For this to happen, Faisal had to confront the Wahhabi control in the judicial and education branches who opposed women's education (Figs. 3-27 and 3-28).

**Figure 3-27:** Queen Effat was the wife of King Faisal. She is very connected to the history of Najd, as her great-grandfather came from a branch of the Al-Saud family (Al-Thunayan). He was taken captive by the Ottomans during their incursion into Najd to quell the Saudi Wahhabi extremists in the 1800s (discussed in detail above). He and his family were exiled to Istanbul where Effat was born in 1916.

Her father died when she was young, and she was raised by her aunt. Despite growing up very poor, she excelled in school. Faisal met her when he was a prince during an official visit to Istanbul. She taught Faisal Turkish and he taught her Arabic. She was a devout Muslim and covered her head (hijab) in public as is the standard in traditional Islam, but not her face (niqab) as required by the Wahhabi version of Islam. As queen, she became the doyenne of philanthropy for Saudi Arabia and developed the first social welfare organization for the country in the 1960s.

**Figure 3-28:** On the right she is shown with young girls in a classroom. It was her mission to develop girls' education in Saudi Arabia. Her own children would become the most highly educated within the Al-Saud clan. The girl who grew up a poor orphan would go on to become the most respected and influential queen in the history of Saudi Arabia. If there is ever a diamond that can be found in the desert, then that diamond would have to be Effat.

Saleem I. Abdulrauf

In October 1973, a major war broke out with Egypt and Syria on one side and Israel on the other. It is known as the Ramadan War (in the Arab and Muslim worlds) and as the Yom Kippur war (in Israel). The problem for United States, the Western superpower which had carried the torch of Britain's inherited vassalage program, was that they were no longer dealing with Abdulaziz; he had died in 1953. This was the first test of the West dealing with one of its "vassal" kings who was not willing to bend the knee—not this time, not when it came to this issue.

Conversely for Faisal, this was not the JFK administration he was dealing with. President Richard Nixon, who in October 1973 was deeply embroiled in the Watergate scandal, which threatened his presidency. The US secretary of state was Henry Kissinger, a Jewish refugee who had fled Nazi Germany with his family, an ardent supporter of Israel. Early in his presidency, Richard Nixon had pushed Israel on its nuclear program and attempted to enact an evenhanded policy toward the "Middle East" conflict. Based on his concerns about Kissinger's strong bias toward Israel, he had asked that Kissinger be kept "out of play" when it came to decisions about the Palestinian–Israeli issue. But, at the peak of the Watergate crisis, which also corresponded to the October 1973 war, Kissinger became the key US decision maker during the Arab–Israeli war.

From Faisal's perspective, he proposed that both the US and Saudi Arabia stay out of the war. That was exactly what took place, until around October 18, when Israel took heavy losses and it became apparent that Israel may lose the war. Kissinger at that time authorized urgent US military support for Israel on an epic scale. There were more sorties flown by the US Air Force to Israel in October 1973 than were flown during the Berlin Airlift of 1948–49. These decisions by Kissinger were not uniformly acceptable to national security advisors and the military leadership. US Chairman of the Joint Chiefs of Staff (JCS) General George Brown would remark that the massive urgent military support of Israel was due to Jewish control over the US government, which led to his near-resignation.

The above Kissinger military effort, code-named "Operation Nickel Grass," would go on to become the biggest military re-supply mission in history. This crossed the line in the sand that Faisal had drawn. Faisal would take an action that would have a global impact that he could not have envisioned. He declared an oil export embargo on the United States. At that time, 83 percent of US oil imports came from Arab lands.

From the US perspective, this a was a "vassal" king who had just confronted the master. For the first time in the history of the Saudi–US relationship, Kissinger indicated that the US could invade Saudi Arabia to secure the oil supplies. In response, Faisal made a statement that to this date is quoted among nostalgics for Arab pride in the region: he said that "we the people" who came from living in tents, eating dates, and drinking camel milk, and if we had to, we can go back to that. For the first time, a "vassal" king challenged the superpower. Faisal was no Abdulaziz.

Secret documents released by the British National Archives in 2004 (after the obligatory 30-year rule for the release of intelligence classified reports) revealed that the US, in the wake of the oil embargo, had clear-cut plans to invade Saudi Arabia, Abu Dhabi, and Kuwait in 1973. The plan was to employ two brigades to seize eastern Saudi Arabia (where the oil fields are located) and one brigade to take over Kuwait and Abu Dhabi.

Before committing to military action, a serious diplomatic effort was undertaken by the United States. American officials knew full well that in Faisal's worldview there were two main enemies of the wider Arab and Muslim worlds: Zionism and Communism. In private meetings with Faisal, American officials insinuated that the US would take a more evenhanded approach in the future when dealing with the Palestinian issue, and informed him that the oil embargo was having a significant negative impact on the US efforts in its war against communists, including in Vietnam. The oil embargo was then lifted. Faisal was named the *Time* magazine person of the year in 1974.

The long-term impact of the embargo would change the world's economy forever. The price of a barrel of oil throughout the 1960s was $1.80, and the average price of gasoline Americans were paying per gallon did not exceed 35 cents. The October war oil embargo brought to an end the longest period of unprecedented economic prosperity in US and modern European history which extended from 1945 to 1973, one that was driven by cheap oil prices. Those some 30 years would go on to be called by the French the *Trente Glorieuses*

("Glorious Thirty"), and the end of which the *Financial Times* would describe in a 1973 headline "The Future Will Be Subject to Delay." The long-term impact of the October war oil embargo led to an increase in the price oil by 400 percent.

In the context of this book, I would like to posit, this major negative impact on the Western economy and on the pocketbook of the average citizen from the oil embargo, at its core, is a direct result of Christian Zionism's actions in Palestine at the end of WWI.

About a year later, on March 25, 1975, at 10:00 a.m., Faisal was holding court (known as *Majlis* in Arabic) hosting a Kuwaiti delegation. As per standard, he was greeting guests lined up to shake his hand. A young prince, a nephew of his named Faisal ibn Musaid, joined the line. They shook hands and as it is an Arab custom to show the highest respect to an elder by kissing their forehead, Ibn Musaid proceeded to do so and the king leaned his head forward toward his nephew. At that moment, Ibn Musaid pulled a gun from his robe and shot the king in the head three times. The king fell on the floor immediately and was pronounced dead in the hospital shortly afterward.

Standing next to the king at that moment was Ahmed Zaki Yamani, the oil minister of the Kingdom who steered the country and the world during the oil crisis. Yamani, holding one of the key positions in the country, was a commoner who came from an average family in Hejaz. He was mentored by Faisal throughout his career, and this reflected an aspect of Faisal that was very different from all Saudi monarchs: he believed in meritocracy.

Queen Effat died in February 2000. Her daughter Lolowah would quote her mother some years later as saying, "Women are the builders of nations."

For a generation of Arabs and Muslims, Faisal was akin to John F. Kennedy for a generation of Americans. Faisal, next to president Gamal Abdel Nasser of Egypt, was the most popular figure ever to emerge in the modern history of the Arab world. He was also seen with reverence by millions of Muslims in Asia. His assassination was a major public relations issue for the Al-Saud family, given that the assassin came from within. The first reports that came out indicated that Ibn Musaid was mentally unstable, but that was not true. The story that was peddled and stuck in the minds of the peoples of the

"Middle East" and still persists to this day was that the US Central Intelligence Agency (CIA) was responsible for the assassination.

In the process of writing this book, I had the opportunity to meet with a group of Saudi businessmen and intellectuals in Washington, DC. I asked the question as to who they believe was responsible for Faisal's assassination. Across the board the answer was the US, specifically, the CIA. According to them, the CIA had mentally "programmed" the young prince to do the deed. When I asked the same question to individuals throughout the Muslim parts of Asia, I got the same answer, the CIA.

**Figure 3-29:** Ibn Musaid pictured with his girlfriend, actress Christine Surma.

Why did Ibn Musaid kill King Faisal? Ibn Musaid went to the US to study at age 22. He assimilated very well into American college life and was at best an average student academically. He dated actress Christine Surma when he was a student at the University of Colorado Denver in 1968. During his stay in the US, he received the news that his brother, Khaled, was killed by King Faisal's security forces. You may recall that a group of Wahhabi zealots attacked the TV station headquarters in protest of making TV available in the Kingdom, and they were led by a nephew of the king by the name of Khaled. Khaled was Ibn Musaid's older brother; he killed Faisal in act of revenge (Fig. 3-29).

Interestingly, when I told the group of Saudi businessmen and scholars the reason why Ibn Musaid assassinated Faisal, it was all news to them!

The court found Ibn Musaid guilty in the king's murder on June 18, 1975. He was publicly executed hours later. He was one of three brothers, and the remaining brother Bandar was arrested and was released after a year in jail. There was no evidence that there was a larger conspiracy to kill the king.

After Faisal's death, his sons established the King Faisal Foundation, which is considered to be one of the largest philanthropic foundations in the world. In my travels around the world as a visiting professor, I have had the opportunity see some of the world's top academic institutions, and the King Faisal Specialist Hospital and Research Centre in Riyadh is the best I have seen in the "Middle

East." Pakistan's third-largest city, Lyallpur, was renamed Faisalabad (meaning the "City of Faisal").

On a lighter note, the Grateful Dead, the band known for its eclectic style, eulogized King Faisal in the title track of its 1975 album *Blues for Allah* (Fig. 3-30).

**Figure 3-30:** The Grateful Dead (from a 1970 photoshoot). They eulogized Faisal in their 1975 album as they heard he had been a fan!

Faisal tried to subdue the monster—the Wahhabi ideology—and he paid his life for it.

A bigger picture of the character of the "Kingdom of Saudi Arabia" can be seen by analyzing the eras of three of its kings: Abdulaziz (reign 1932–1953), Faisal (reign 1964–1975), and Fahad (reign 1982–2005). Abdulaziz was the founder and the insular thinker who did not concern himself with the larger issues affecting the Arab and Muslim peoples. Faisal was a paragon of honor, a visionary who believed in improving the lives of people throughout the Arab and Muslim worlds. Fahad was deeply corrupt and lacked the respect of the populace.

The future direction of Saudi Arabia will be defined by the current crown prince and power behind the throne, Mohammed bin Salman (MBS). He, much like Abdulaziz, does not subscribe to the idea of standing up for larger issues affecting Arabs and Muslims. He does share Faisal's attitude toward modernizing the country and limiting the power of extremist Wahhabism. In clear contrast to Faisal, however, and in similarity to classic "Middle Eastern" autocratic dictators, he believes in the power of using fear to control his peoples.

The Churchillian vassalage program is dependent upon the fact that there would be no open societies with freedom of the press in the "Middle East." Consequently, Arab dictators are afforded umbrella protection from Western powers for actions against their populations that they would not tolerate in other parts of the world. MBS has made full use of this protection. For example, on his second day of an official visit to Saudi Arabia, Lebanon's prime minister, Saad Hariri, was summoned by MBS. He was separated from his bodyguards and his cell phone removed. He was given a prewritten resignation letter which he read live on Saudi TV telling his people in Lebanon that he was resigning! Western powers remained silent. Had a non-Arab dictator taken such a nefarious action toward the head of state of an independent country (like Lebanon in this case) there would have been an international outcry and major consequences. So why can an Arab autocrat get away with it? The answer to this question is a fundamental aspect of this chapter. It goes back to the covenant between Churchill and Abdulaziz (MBS's grandfather). To keep the Arab populations muzzled, the Arab dictators would be allowed to rule as they please. This resulted in the conspiracy of secrecy and fear that the Arab people have been subjected to for some 100 years now.

## A Deal with the Devil

At the end of this section, I would like to share a few observations. The "Middle East" today is not what the Sharif of Mecca envisioned, but rather is what Churchill and Abdulaziz created.

I am sure you have noticed that I have used the term "Middle East" with quotations throughout this book. The reason is because it is purely a colonial term. The term most likely originated in the colonial British India Office in the 1850s. The American naval strategist Alfred Thayer Mahan used the term in 1902 to "designate the area between Arabia and India." It did not become widely used until Winston Churchill created the "Middle Eastern Department" to define the lands within his vassalage program. It is at its core a pejorative term. Later in the book I propose some ideas for the people of the "Middle East" to consider in place of this term.

For George, Balfour, and Churchill's Christian Zionist grand plan in Palestine to work, they had no option but to forbid "free" Arab nations. They reasoned that Arab countries with freedom of speech and press would question their grand plan. Therefore, having puppet dictators was the only viable option. The dictators are actually the gift that keeps on giving. To hide the shady story of how they got into power, the dictators themselves have suppressed historical data from the early twentieth century (disclosed in this chapter) from their populations. The facts presented in this chapter will be new information for most people of the "Middle East." Not only did the people of the "Middle East" suffer from historical omissions and revisions at the hands of their own leaders, but the West, as outlined throughout this book, have also revised their history. This dual betrayal of the Arab and Muslim peoples by their own vassal leaders on one hand and by "Western" societies on the other, is crucial in understanding this region and its volatility.

US President Abraham Lincoln once said, "You can fool all the people some of the time, and some of the people all the time, but you cannot fool all the people all the time." So how do you then fool all of the people all of the time? How do you get whole populations in Western countries to turn a blind eye to the actions of dictators in the "Middle East" who are known to abuse and massacre their own peoples? You do it by dehumanizing Arabs and Muslims and then normalizing that dehumanization for it to carry through from generation to generation. How do you achieve that? I will give the answer in the next section of the book!

# The Heist
# of the Century

# Chapter 4
# Are Blue-Eyed People More Violent?

The following is a true story: a teacher named Jane Elliott walked into her third-grade class and told them research has shown that blue-eyed people are inferior to brown-eyed people; they are more prone to violence, less intelligent, messier, and less active. She added, "If you give them something nice, they just wreck it."

She explained that brown-eyed people have more of a special chemical called melanin in their eyes, hair, and skin. She told her students that research proved the more melanin, the smarter the person.

These were smart kids growing up in America in the 1960s, the new space age. One brown-eyed boy, feeling good about what he had learned, said "Hey, Mrs. Elliott, how come you're the teacher if you've got blue eyes?" Before she could answer, another brown-eyed boy piped up, "If she didn't have blue eyes, she'd be the principal or the superintendent!"

Mrs. Elliott set the rules for the day, saying blue-eyed kids had to use paper cups when they drank from the water fountain. "Why?" one blue-eyed girl asked.

"Because we might catch something," a brown-eyed boy said. All the students turned to the teacher for affirmation, and she nodded. Throughout the morning, brown-eyed kids made fun of their blue-eyed classmates. "Well, what do you expect from him, Mrs. Elliott," a brown-eyed boy said as a blue-eyed boy got an arithmetic problem wrong. "He's a bluey!"

In another area of the classroom, a smart blue-eyed girl who had been excellent in math started making mistakes. She felt down. During the break, three brown-eyed girls ganged up on her: "You better apologize to us for getting in our way because we're better than you are," one of the brown-eyed girls said—and the blue-eyed girl did.

This social psychology exercise took place on April 5, 1968, in the town of Riceville, Iowa, the day after the assassination of America's iconic civil rights leader, Dr. Martin Luther King Jr. The all-white students, aged eight and nine, had recently made Dr. King their "Hero of the Month," and they couldn't understand why someone would kill him. Elliott wanted to show them how discrimination can be created and how it could create false feelings of inferiority and superiority.

On the second day of the exercise, Elliott reversed the groups and made the brown-eyed kids the "inferior" ones. After experiencing humiliation the day before and knowing what it felt like, the blue-eyed kids, now in the dominant position, were less aggressive and less derogatory toward the "inferior" brown-eyed ones. She went on to apply this exercise to teenagers and adults and had similar results with far more passionate and emotional responses. Each study demonstrated the same inherent and powerful principle that discrimination is taught (Fig. 4-1).

**Figure 4-1:** Jane Elliott's discrimination exercise began on April 5, 1968, in Riceville, Iowa. These third graders were the heroes who taught all of us amazing lessons.

What Elliott showed in this exercise was that the "superior" brown-eyed students, who were just as sweet and tolerant as the blue-eyed students before the exercise, became mean-spirited toward their "inferior" blue-eyed classmates once their teacher (by creating a stereotype) told them they were better. "I watched what had been marvelous, cooperative, wonderful, thoughtful children turn into nasty, vicious, discriminating little third-graders in a space of fifteen minutes," Elliott later said.

Verla, who was a student subject in Elliott's exercise, said of her experience, "Nobody likes to be looked down upon. Nobody likes to be hated, teased or discriminated against." In my "exercise" of writing this book, these are exactly the type of sentiments I heard from young Muslims around the world. After all, if it's this easy to make children turn against peers in their own classroom, how easy must it be to create discriminatory beliefs against people of a different religion and complexion who live halfway around the world? Yasmeen, a 22-year-old student at Cairo University, said to me in a group discussion, "They [Hollywood/the West] always make us look evil."

Prejudice and generalizations are potent tools in the demonization of the "other." In the hands of those with authority, like politicians, movie directors, and reporters, they can foster a herd mentality. Daniel Kahneman, an Israeli American psychologist and world expert on behavioral economics, was awarded the 2002 Nobel Memorial Prize in Economic Sciences (shared with Vernon L. Smith) for establishing the cognitive basis for human errors, best explained in his book *Thinking, Fast and Slow*.

According to Kahneman, cognitive bias arises from *heuristics*, shortcuts we use to form judgments. *Priming* is one phenomenon that can guide thinking by creating artificial associations between various ideas and images. He gives an interesting example to explain the phenomenon: if you are asked to fill in the blank in *SO_P* and had just been exposed to the word *EAT*, you are more likely to fill the blank with a *U* and create the *SOUP*. But if you were shown the word *WASH* just beforehand, you are more likely to add the letter *A* and create the word *SOAP*.

I started this book by sharing my experience of watching Steven Spielberg's *Back to the Future*, set in America's 50s. Although the movie otherwise has nothing to do with the "Middle East," when the villain shows up, he is an "Arab" character. When you prime the population with such examples which closely associate Arab appearances with violence and villainy, viewers develop a bias, or stereotype. Priming, Kahneman explains, operates entirely subconsciously and involuntarily, which of course makes it all the more dangerous.

The second heuristic Kahneman speaks about is *cognitive ease*, meaning we find things that are familiar to us to be more acceptable or true. He gives the example of why dictators keep repeating the same messages over and over; once repeated enough, people start to believe them in a process called normalization—a concept I ended the last chapter with, the two-step process of dehumanizing Arabs/Muslims and then normalizing it. How has Hollywood utilized these concepts? By repeatedly presenting negative stereotypes about Arabs and Muslims. In his book *"Evil" Arabs in American Popular Film: Orientalist Fear,* Tim Jon Semmerling presents essays on five movies which create negative stereotypes and biases of those in the East. Semmerling delineates each movie and uncovers an "assault" by the Arabs/Muslims on some aspect of American/Western life presented at the core of each film. His essay subtitles reveal the way in which each film positions Arabs as a fundamental threat to a different American value:

- *The Exorcist* (1973): Assault on American Confidence
- *Rollover* (1981): Assault on the American Economy
- *Black Sunday* (1976): The Loss of Frontier Heroism
- *Three Kings* (1999): Assault on Victory Culture
- *Rules of Engagement* (2000): Attack from the Multicultural Front

Through repeated depictions of Muslims and Arabs as a threat to American life, Hollywood creates the notion that they are the enemy. With repeated exposure to such films, this idea becomes more normalized to audiences each time.

Kahneman's concept of *causes trumping statistics* explains why the film industry has been so successful in driving the American public's perception of Arabs and Muslims. This idea refers to the tendency to overlook data-based stories, real historical facts, in favor of stories that we find emotionally or personally moving, which is the heart of moviemaking.

Another concept that Kahneman talks about is the *halo effect*, which has to do with how we perceive others. In general, if someone makes a good first impression on us, we view them and everything they do in a positive way, whereas, if the first impression is bad, then we tend to be more critical of them afterward. Hollywood has monopolized the first impression that people around the world have of Arabs and Muslims. For most people, especially in the US, their first impression of Arabs and Muslims is their depiction in Hollywood movies.

Films don't have to be explicit about who is "good" or "bad"; instead, the subtleties of casting and visuals do lots of heavy lifting in influencing our subconscious impressions. Consider the discrepancies between the Arab Revolt and the historical Sharif of Mecca as opposed to the historical drama *Lawrence of Arabia* (Figs. 4-2, 4-3, 4-4, and 4-5).

**Figures 4-2 and 4-3:** On the left is the real T.E. Lawrence; on the right is how he is portrayed in the movie *Lawrence of Arabia*. A young Peter O'Toole plays Lawrence as a dashing blue-eyed protagonist, his rounded facial structure and gentle expression creating a much softer and more sympathetic portrayal.

**Figures 4-4 and 4-5**: In contrast, on the left is the real-life Feisal, who was known to be a handsome and kind gentleman, and on the right is his depiction in the movie *Lawrence of Arabia*, with actor Alec Guinness portraying him as a harsh and shifty character.

Not only are Arabs and Muslims dishonest, violent, and evil, according to the film industry, but they are also ugly! We subconsciously assume the best of good-looking people and the worst of those who are less attractive (by Hollywood's standards), and Hollywood exploits this fallacy in movies for children and adults alike.

It is important to note that Hollywood has negatively depicted other groups as well over the decades, including American Indians and African Americans; Arabs are not alone in being portrayed as different from the white, Anglo-Saxon American "default." In the years following World War II, the explosion of movies in which Nazis and Japanese characters served as antagonists directly speaks to the tendency of fiction to mirror real-life cultural tensions, which are in turn exacerbated by these exaggerated dramas.

However, the American portrayal of Arabs is not limited to one period in history, although there have certainly been times during which Arabs were particularly demonized, such as the decade following 9/11. Jack G. Shaheen's book *Reel Bad Arabs: How Hollywood Vilifies a People* identifies 1,100 movies which vilify Arabs from before 9/11! Beyond the sheer volume, there is something more sinister at play in the insidious way that Arabs are criticized in popular media which doesn't even focus on race or religion. Instead, these criticisms are slipped into conversation, normalized through the dialogue. For example, in the 1966 classic movie *Who's Afraid of Virginia Woolf*, starring the beloved actors Richard Burton and Elizabeth Taylor, an American professor tells his wife in the heat of an argument, "You can go on like a pumped-up Arab, slashing at everything in sight, scarring up half of the world if you want to." The quote, which takes up only a few seconds of the movie's screen time, nonetheless reinforces the stereotype of Arabs as violent, dangerous people and assumes a sympathetic white audience.

What is the impact of such subliminal messaging? It feeds into the *availability heuristic*, the mental shortcuts we all make based on previous impressions when forming our opinions. For example, let's say you plan to fly from Los Angeles to London. The night before your plane takes off, you see a plane crash on TV. Now you are scared of taking that flight, because that example is readily available in your mind; it's memorable, but it's not actually representative of what happens to most flights. Although the car ride from your house to the Los Angeles airport is statistically more dangerous, your flight is the scary part because it more readily sticks in your mind.

Similarly, every exposure people have with the terms "Middle East," "Arab," or "Muslim" has been primed by Hollywood and popular media, forming repeated impressions that easily come to mind when we hear these terms or we see a person of "Middle Eastern" heritage. Although the history and lives of Arabs differ from the pop-culture depictions, generations of Americans have been primed to think of all Arabs and Muslims as the "blue-eyed kids" of Jane Elliott's third-grade class.

# Chapter 5
# Are Arabs Scam Artists?

**I**n 1979, Angelo Errichetti, the very popular mayor of Camden, New Jersey, walked into a dimly lit room. He was greeted by a tall, bearded man dressed in a traditional Arabic head covering and robe. The man introduced himself as Kambir Abdul Rahman, an Arab Sheik interested in making considerable investments in America. He then offered Errichetti a considerable amount of money in exchange for an illegal casino license in Atlantic City for his company, Abdul Enterprises Ltd.

In the months that followed, Abdul Rahman offered similar bribes to a number of officials, including Senator Harrison "Pete" Williams (Fig. 5-1) and Representatives Raymond Lederer, Frank Thompson, and Richard Kelly. All of the bribes were accepted.

**Figure 5-1:** Senator Harrison Williams (left) and Sheik Abdul Rahman (right).

Here's the catch: Kambir Abdul Rahman was no Arab Sheik. He was a Federal Bureau of Investigation (FBI) agent of Lebanese descent. The FBI operation, which took place from 1978 to 1980, was conducted to expose the corruption of the mayor and a number of congressmen and was code-named "Abscam" (short for "Arab Scam"). Arabs, however, had nothing to do with it; they were just used to create an image of con artists! At the time, this was the largest political corruption probe in the bureau's history. The FBI paid a real convicted conman, Melvin Weinberg, to plan the whole operation. Weinberg later said, "There's only one difference between me and the congressmen I met on this case: The public pays them a salary for stealing."

As part of my research for this chapter, I went through many articles in major newspapers from that time period. Much to my dismay, I could not find one article raising the issue as to how this operation would further perpetuate the negative stereotype of Arabs—who had nothing to do with these politicians nor the sting operation. I started to wonder how, among all the reporters writing about this historic sting operation, not a single one would raise this issue. But the answer lies in what this book is attempting to establish; it is not that these reporters were inherently prejudiced individuals, it was the fact that they all grew up primed for normalizing Arabs and Muslims as nefarious.

The effects of negative stereotyping go beyond people's thoughts; they have very real, concrete consequences. As an extreme example, in Nazi Germany, one of the most successful propaganda operations which normalized the vilification of Jews among the larger German populace were the caricatures depicting Jews as "evil" (Fig. 5-2).

Once Abscam became public, it exploded in popular culture. *Saturday Night Live* parodied the scandal in a skit titled "The Bel-Airabs" (a spoof of *The Beverly Hillbillies* in which the characters are "Arabs"). The Grammy-winning folk singer Tom Paxton wrote and recorded the song "I Thought You Were an Arab" (pronounced "Ay'-rab"). In an episode of the 1980s TV hit show *Dallas*, an FBI agent tells the main character, J.R. Ewing, "I even nailed a couple of those ABSCAM guys."

Of course, Hollywood was not going to be left out. A 1982 movie about Abscam had to be canceled after the early death of John Belushi, who was supposed to play the role of Melvin Weinberg. A fictionalized film version of Abscam was ultimately released, the 2013 Academy Award–nominated movie *American Hustle.* The undercover FBI agent on the Abscam operation was a consultant for the movie.

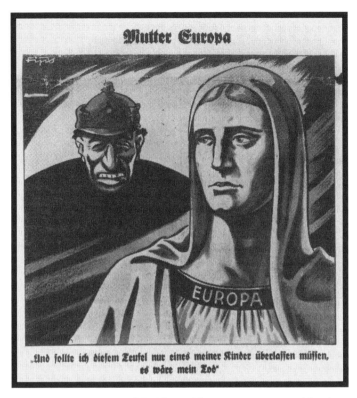

**Figure 5-2:** Front page of the Nazi publication, *Der Stuermer* (October 1937) depicting the Jew as the devil (left) threatening the white Christian woman representing "Mother Europe" (right). The caption reads, "Mother Europe. If I had to leave even one of my children to this devil, it would be my death."

The government-based stereotyping in the FBI Abscam operation, combined with the stereotypes in popular culture, fit with the concept Daniel Kahneman calls cognitive ease. Most of us do not go and investigate every interaction we have nor piece of media we consume; instead, we often trust what feels familiar. It is easier for our brains to process information when it already has a foundation; therefore, the more often we are exposed to stereotypes, the less likely we are to challenge them. The FBI, the TV shows *Saturday Night Live* and *Dallas*, and the actors in the movie *American Hustle* (Amy Adams, Jennifer Lawrence, Bradley Cooper, Christian Bale) are all familiar to us. As a result, the cumulative repetitive narrative in which they present "Arabs" leads us to accept those stereotypes as truth.

For years I have been puzzled by the question of where this deep hatred came from. More movies have been directed toward vilifying Arabs and Muslims than Nazis—America's WWII enemy and the committers of the Holocaust. More movies have been made that vilify Arabs and Muslims than Russians—America's Cold War enemy (1947–1991). To avoid any confusion, all of the examples I have mentioned occurred before the terrorist acts of September 11, 2001. It is not just Hollywood; the mainstream media have played along, as well as the US government, as demonstrated by the FBI example above.

One of America's largest vilification campaigns in its 244-year history has been against Arabs and Muslims. As a scientist, I knew this could not possibly be solely attributed to cultural differences (e.g., their customs, the way they pray, their past civilization, etc.), as peddled in the popular culture by such phrases as "They hate our way of life." Allow me to illustrate using the example of another "foreign" ethnic group who also happens to be "Brown," also number over a billion in the world, also have significant cultural differences, also from the same part of the world, also worship differently (even more differently as they worship deities)—the Hindus—yet there has rightly been no vilification campaign against them by Hollywood and the media.

I became convinced that there had to be a much deeper reason for targeting Arabs and Muslims.

# Chapter 6
# Longing for Armageddon

I ended the last chapter with the pivotal question: where does the hate, the propaganda, and the historical revisionism about Arabs and Muslims in Western culture come from? To answer this question, it is critical to look at the history of a small region along the eastern Mediterranean Sea called Palestine, and specifically the city of Jerusalem. Therefore, I will start by taking you on a historical journey of Palestine's interaction with the West. This journey will lead us to the answer to this vexing question!

## The Persian Messiah

Palestine was conquered by the Neo-Babylonian Empire (based in Mesopotamia—present-day Iraq) in 589 BC. They destroyed the temple in Jerusalem referred to as Solomon's Temple in biblical literature. There is, however, no archaeological evidence for the existence of Solomon's Temple, and the structure is not mentioned in surviving contemporaneous extra-biblical historical sources. The Babylonians exiled the Jews from Palestine. The Persians, under the command of Cyrus the Great, defeated the Babylonians in 539 BC, occupied Palestine, and freed the Jews to return to live and rebuild in Jerusalem. This act by Cyrus would give him a special place in Jewish history. According to the Hebrew Bible (Isaiah 45:1), God anointed Cyrus for this task, even referring to him as a messiah (meaning the savior/liberator) and he is the only non-Jewish figure in the Bible to be called so. After this the Persian Empire would enter an extended period of time (499 to 449 BC) fighting the Greeks (what is known as the Greco–Persian Wars).

*Saleem I. Abdulrauf*

## An Evil People

The 2007 fictionalized period action movie *300* (Warner Brothers) dramatized the Greco–Persian Wars (Fig. 6-1). From a historical perspective, in response to the Greeks burning down the Persian regional capital of Sardis, the Persian king, Darius the Great, vowed revenge. However, he died before doing so, and his son Xerxes (the grandson of biblical Cyrus mentioned above) took on the mission. The movie is about the battle of Thermopylae where the two forces met.

**Figure 6-1:** Greek hoplite and Persian warrior fighting each other. Depiction in ancient kylix, fifth century BC.

The Greeks/Spartans were led by King Leonidas and the Persians by King Xerxes. In the movie, Leonidas is portrayed as the valiant, muscular hero and Xerxes as the effeminate, beastly villain (Fig. 6-2).

**Figure 6-2:** A still from the movie *300*: King Leonidas (left) played by Gerard Butler and King Xerxes (right) played by Rodrigo Santoro. The movie attempted to display Xerxes as a homosexual. The director of the movie, Zack Snyder, would say about his depiction of Xerxes: "What's more scary to a 20-year-old boy than a giant god-king who wants to have his way with you?"

This movie is in many ways a classic Hollywood portrayal of the peoples of the "Middle East." The journalist Steven Rea said the movie "successfully tapped into a certain militaristic, xenophobic mind-set." He added "*300* does make allusions to the war in Iraq." In this movie, which would go on to have a cult following, Hollywood was priming yet another generation of Americans and young people around the world; "Middle Easterners" are evil enemies!

## A Miraculous Birth

**Figure 6-3:** Alexander the Great. A mosaic in an ancient Roman floor in Pompeii showing Alexander fighting King Darius III of Persia in the Battle of Issus in 333 BC.

Moving away from fictionalized accounts and going back to real history: Alexander the Great, from the ancient Greek kingdom of Macedonia, defeated the Persian Empire and occupied Palestine in 332 BC (Fig. 6-3). This marked the first time in history that Palestine was occupied by a Western power. For the purposes of this book, the Greek, Roman, and all other European Empires are designated as the "West," while the Persian, Arab, and Ottoman Empires, given the familiarity with the term, are designated as the "Middle East."

The Greek rule over Palestine was, from a historical perspective, relatively short lived and did not make a major social nor cultural impact. In contrast, the Romans took Palestine in 63 BC, marking the start of a centuries-long rule over the land with significant cultural impact. Therefore, the relationship of Palestine with the West truly began with the Roman occupation. The Romans named the province *Palaestina*.

This paragraph is based on religious rather than documented scientific historical data. During the Roman rule of Palestine, according to both Christian and Muslim traditions, the miraculous birth of Jesus from the Virgin Mary would occur. It is estimated that this happened at some point between 7 and 4 BC. Jesus, as a young boy growing up among the poor in Galilee in northern Palestine, was exposed to a difficult environment; one in which peasants were significantly taxed and could get evicted from their land. He would go on to preach about justice, equality, love, and resistance to corrupt authorities. He would challenge the established religious authority—the Pharisees (Jewish leaders). He called them hypocrites for teaching the law to others without practicing it themselves, especially some of the most important parts of it—justice, mercy, and faithfulness to God. By labelling the religious leaders as unscrupulous, he, by extension, challenged the governing authority—the Romans. Jesus was arrested and taken to the house of Joseph ben Caiaphas, the Jewish high priest, where he was mocked and physically beaten. He subsequently underwent a trial before the Sanhedrin (Jewish judicial body). Jesus is said to have been mostly quiet during the trial and did not mount a defense, but he did make some statements that angered the high priest and they concluded he was guilty. Jesus was then taken to the Roman governor Pontius Pilate, who issued the sentence of death by crucifixion. Biblical scholars estimate this took place between 26–30 AD. Mark, the author of the first Gospel in 65–75 AD, blamed the Jews for the "execution" of Jesus rather than the Roman governor. The assignment of responsibility of Jesus's Crucifixion to the Jews was a watershed moment that would forever impact the relationship between Christendom and Judaism. It is an integral part of the duplicitous syndrome I describe in this book.

The Pharisees had hoped that by eliminating Jesus, his message would likewise be eliminated forever. However, history had other plans. Christian missionaries started to spread Jesus's message over the next few decades by traveling along trade routes throughout the Roman Empire. Christianity would go on to have the most followers of any religion in the world.

In AD 70, in response to a Jewish revolt in Jerusalem, the Romans destroyed the Jewish temple known as the Second Temple in biblical literature, also known as Herod's Temple in Jewish religious literature.

## Helena, the First Pilgrim

The Roman Empire was pagan until Emperor Constantine (AD 272–337) said he saw a vision, "I saw with my own eyes of a cross of light in the heavens, it bore the inscription 'by this sign you will conquer.'" He became convinced God was on his side and converted to Christianity. Historians differ on his motives for converting, some cite possible political reasons. His mother Helena, who became Christian and is believed to have had an influence on her son's conversion, would go on to become the first consequential figure in the West's relationship with Palestine (Fig. 6-4). She traveled to Palaestina in AD 326 to undertake the effort to find the actual sites mentioned in the Gospels. She is said to have found the true cross on which Jesus was placed for crucifixion immediately outside Jerusalem's walls. Helena also identified a rock-cut tomb said to be that of Jesus at the site right next to where Jesus is said to have been resurrected. On that site, known as Golgotha, Constantine ordered

**Figure 6-4:** Seated statue of Helena (in Musei Capitolini, Rome).

the building of a church, the Church of the Holy Sepulchre. He went to Jerusalem in AD 335 to oversee the dedication ceremony of the newly built basilica at the Church of the Holy Sepulchre.

It is also said that Helena found the nails that were used on the true cross. To protect her son—Emperor Constantine—she placed one in his helmet and the other in the bridle of his horse. Saint Ambrose (AD 339–397), the then bishop of Milan, would write about the Jews, "They thought they had defeated Christianity by killing Christ, but through the finding of the Cross and the nails, as a result of which Christ and Christianity had come to life again, they [Jews] themselves were defeated."

The whole concept of pilgrimage by Christians to the holy places started with Helena. A woman in her seventies, she continued to travel throughout Palestine and erected memorial churches on the holy sites that she identified.

Constantine relocated the capital of the Roman Empire from Rome to the city of Byzantium in AD 330, which was then renamed "Constantinople." It is known today as Istanbul.

## The Messenger of God

The next historical event that would go on to have a major impact on the history of Palestine and the world would occur in AD 570. Another boy was born, but this time in the city of Mecca, in Hejaz (Fig. 6-5). The boy, who came from a noble family but was orphaned at a young age, was named Muhammad. As a young man he was known for his

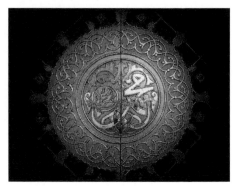

**Figure 6-5:** "Muhammad the Apostle of God" inscribed on the gates of the Prophet's Mosque in the city of Medina in Hejaz.

integrity and was given the nickname "al-Amin" (meaning the "honest one" in Arabic). He was described as handsome, eloquent, and kind. He rebelled against the polytheistic pagan practices in Mecca, in which the Kaaba housed some 360 idols. This made Mecca a financial center based on the idol-worshipping pilgrims coming from all over Arabia. Muhammad would go on to preach about justice for the weak, support for the poor, care for the orphans, and rights for women. His words threatened the status quo and the way of life of the ruling establishment—the Quraysh tribe. The Meccan aristocracy first tried to appeal to Muhammad with wealth but he declined; they then offered him to become "king" of Mecca, and in response to these offers he made his historic statement, "By Allah [God], if they put the sun in my right hand and the moon in my left on condition that I abandon this course, until Allah [God] has made me victorious, or I perish therein, I would not abandon it." They subsequently attempted to assassinate him but failed.

While the central core of Christianity is Jesus, the central core of the new religion, Islam, would become the Qur'an. In Islamic tradition, the Qur'an is the word of God as spoken by the archangel Gabriel to Muhammad. Muhammad repeated these words verbatim to his companions who then directly transcribed them. Therefore, the Qur'an that exists today is identical, letter by letter, word by word, to the words of Gabriel as repeated by Muhammad and transcribed in the seventh century (Fig. 6-6). This was critical for early Muslims, as it was known that the Bible had been altered over time.

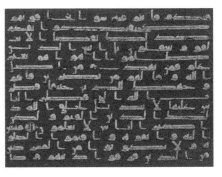

**Figure 6-6:** A folio from a ninth- to tenth-century Qur'an (Metropolitan Museum of Art, New York City).

Muhammad would tell his people that he held no higher status than any of the prophets mentioned in the Qur'an and the Bible. Islam regards Jesus as a blessed prophet who was persecuted by the Jews, and over time his message was altered and politicized by Christian leaders. Over the centuries to come, Muslims would witness a lack of understanding of their reverence for Jesus by Western Christendom. The Muslim standard greeting in Arabic, "as-salamu alaykum" ("peace be upon you"), is the same greeting Jesus used; "Then said Jesus to them again, peace be unto you" (John 20:21). Muslim prayers, which involve prostration with the forehead touching the ground, are the same as how Jesus prayed: "And he went a little farther, and fell on his face, and prayed" (Mathew 26:39).

Mary, the mother of Jesus, would become the most exalted woman in the Islamic faith. She is mentioned more times in the Qur'an than in the Bible. The following is the archangel Gabriel's salutation to Mary in the Qur'an (3:42):

> O Mary, God has chosen you, and purified you; He has chosen you above all the women of creation.

About the immaculate conception of Mary, the Qur'an (21:91) states:

> Remember the one who guarded her chastity. We breathed into her from Our Spirit and made her and her son a sign for all people.

While Christianity and Islam share the belief of the story of Jesus, Judaism considers him a false prophet. On the other hand, Judaism and Islam share the principle of the absolute singularity of God as opposed to the principle of the Trinity in Christianity.

Early Muslims believed that Islam was not a new religion but rather a continuation of the Abrahamic messages (including those revealed by Moses and Jesus), and that Muhammad was to be the final Prophet. According to Islamic beliefs, Muhammad was foretold in the Bible (Deuteronomy 18:18):

> I will raise up a prophet from among their countrymen like you, and I will put My words in his mouth, and he shall speak to them all that I command him. It shall come about that whoever will not listen to My words which he shall speak in My name, I Myself will require it of him.

Islamic tradition is based on the core principle that the Qur'an contains the actual "words" of God as spoken by the Prophet Muhammad.

Within a few short decades, Hejaz and the entirety of the Arabian Peninsula converted from polytheism to Islam. Islam defined its three holiest religious sites: the Grand Mosque in Mecca, the Prophet's Mosque in Medina (Al-Masjid an-Nabawi), and the Al-Aqsa Mosque (literally, the "Farthest Mosque" in Arabic) in Jerusalem.

## An Epic Battle

After the death of Muhammad (AD 632), the new "Muslim Empire" continued to expand in every direction. Just north of the Arabian Peninsula, in the Levant (this term has traditionally referred to the region encompassing lands in Syria, Jordan, Palestine, and Iraq), the Arabs were being ruled by a "foreign" Empire, the Romans. A clash was inevitable.

The Roman emperor at the time was Flavius Heraclius (Fig. 6-7).

Anti-Jewish sentiments were ubiquitous at that time within the Christian Roman Empire. In AD 630, Heraclius decreed that all Jews

**Figure 6-7:** Solidus of Emperor Heraclius (aged 35–38). Constantinople mint. Struck AD 610–613. Helmeted and cuirassed facing bust, holding a cross.

must convert to Christianity. Heraclius, who was deeply religious, committed massacres against the Jews in Palestine. By massacring Jews, Heraclius broke an earlier oath he had made to them. The monks, to protect Heraclius, provided an atonement for the violation of this oath by pledging themselves to a yearly fast called the Fast of Heraclius, which is still observed by Coptic Christians to this date.

The Roman Army, which numbered between 100,000 to 400,000 men, was commanded by Vahan, who was of Armenian origin and a highly trusted field commander of Heraclius. The Muslims were outnumbered multifold, with an army size of between 24,000 to 40,000. The Muslim Army was commanded by the legendary Khalid ibn al-Walid; everyone in his army would have heard stories about his courage and valor. When Khalid was a young commander, he had been bestowed the title "Sword of God" by the Prophet Muhammad (Fig. 6-8).

Khalid both tactically and strategically outmaneuvered the Roman generals and on the sixth day of fighting, he was able to win a decisive victory at the Battle of Yarmouk on August 20, AD 636. The British historian David Nicolle would say that winning this battle cemented Khalid's reputation "as one of the greatest tacticians and cavalry commanders in history."

Khalid was welcomed into Damascus by cheering crowds on the streets. Damascus would remain under Arab Muslim rule for the next 1,282

**Figure 6-8:** The location of the epic battle between Heraclius and Khalid ibn al-Walid in an area east of the Sea of Galilee that is today between the borders of Syria, Jordan, and Israel, along the banks of the Yarmouk River. Romanticized depiction of Heraclius (upper left) and Khalid (upper right).

years, until the day yet another general entered it in October 1918; General Allenby (as part of the British occupation of the Levant discussed in Chapter 2: Invaders from the West).

Heraclius, who received the news of the loss at his palace in Antioch (in present-day Southern Turkey), was devastated. In reflecting on the situation, he would do something unheard of from emperors and kings; he would blame himself for the mistakes he had made in his life, mainly his incestuous marriage to his niece Martina. Based on his deep religious beliefs, he accepted this defeat as an act of God. After observing a solemn service of intercession at the Antioch Cathedral, he took a ship to Constantinople (the Roman capital). In his historic farewell message, he would say, "Farewell, a long farewell to Syria, my fair province. Thou art an infidel's now. Peace be with you, O Syria—what a beautiful land you will be for the enemy."

I would like to share the story of an experience that served as a tremendous lesson for Khalid. During the lifetime of the Prophet Muhammad, Khalid, as a young commander, was on a military mission dealing with a conflict with a tribe named Banu Jadhima in Ta'if (a city in Hejaz) in January AD 630. Khalid ordered his soldiers to kill some of the captives to avenge the killing of his uncle some years earlier. When this news reached the Prophet Muhammad, he raised his hands and twice said "O Allah [God], I am free from what Khalid has done." He immediately sent Ali (a future caliph) to make every possible reparation to the family members of those who had been killed. Khalid was taught a major lesson by the Prophet Muhammad, as the killing of prisoners of war is categorically forbidden in Islam. The actions of groups like Al-Qaeda and ISIS in the early part of the twenty-first century prove their categorical lack of knowledge of Islamic history, ethics, and jurisprudence.

The Battle of Yarmouk was one of the most consequential battles in human history and an epic event in the relationship between the East and West. It has been sidelined by historians and the popular culture in the West. Despite a classic David and Goliath storyline of a small army, led by a charismatic young commander (Khalid), defeating the mammoth Roman army, Hollywood has never touched it!

As we end this section about this epic battle, I would like to share an interesting backstory I came across while researching the topic. Heraclius was a deeply devout Christian but also listened to his astrologers. It is said that astrologers revealed to him that a circumcised people would conquer his empire, which became an impetus for him to target the Jews. Looking back at it, I am wondering if his astrologers were right—he just got the circumcised people wrong!

## The Savior of the Church of the Holy Sepulchre

With the Roman Empire defeated in the Levant, the capture of Jerusalem was imminent. To set the stage of what would happen next, let me introduce you to two very honorable men.

The patriarch of Jerusalem was Sophronius, who was appointed to that position by Pope Honorius just two years before the Battle of Yarmouk (AD 634). Prior to that he had been a monk, scholar, and theologian. He is venerated as a Saint by the Eastern Orthodox and Catholic Churches.

On the Muslim side was Caliph Umar ibn Al-Khattab, who oversaw his army's wins under the command of Khalid in the Levant. He was a paragon of honor and humility. He walked around the capital city of Medina in the evenings to see if any child was crying, concerned that if a child went to bed hungry, he would be negligent in his duty as the leader. Let me use a quote from Umar to illustrate the point: "If a dog dies hungry on the banks of the River Euphrates, Umar will be responsible for dereliction of duty."

The Muslim forces had Jerusalem surrounded. However, they were under strict orders from Umar not to attack and spill blood in the holy city. Sophronius, faced with the knowledge that Jerusalem was about to fall, would send a letter to the commander of the Muslim forces (Abu Ubaidah ibn al-Jarrah). Sophronius had heard about Umar's honorable character and stated that he would not turn the city over to anyone except Umar in person. Umar, honoring his request, accepted the terms of the patriarch and traveled to Jerusalem.

What followed was an iconic interaction between the two honorable men in February of AD 638. When they met, it was prayer time in the Islamic faith. Sophronius showed the ultimate respect to Umar by offering to let him pray inside the Church of the Sepulchre (Fig. 6-9). Umar politely declined the invitation and walked to an open area close to the church to perform the prayer. The patriarch was bewildered and would ask the caliph about it after the prayer. Umar explained that if he had prayed in the church, some overzealous Muslims may someday in the future use the rationale that the first site in Jerusalem where Umar prayed should be converted into a mosque. Based on Umar's stand that day, no Muslim ruler of Palestine would ever transgress that principle, and the Church of the Holy Sepulchre was forever defended by Muslims. Grypeou, Swanson, and Thomas, in their book *The Encounter of Eastern Christianity with Early Islam*, wrote "The seventy-eight year-old Patriarch must have been impressed by the humility of the forty-six year-old warrior and caliph."

**Figure 6-9:** Interior view of the Church of the Holy Sepulchre. Shown in the center is the somber burial chamber that was built around the rock-cut empty tomb identified by Helena (the mother of Emperor Constantine) in AD 326 as that of Jesus. The church also includes the site where Jesus is said to have been resurrected, making this church the holiest site in Christendom.

Umar would make a historic decision during his short stay in Jerusalem. Jews had been evicted from the city by consecutive Roman Emperors including Heraclius. Umar welcomed Jews back into Jerusalem. This act by Umar was no less than what Cyrus the Great had done some 1,000 years earlier which memorialized his name in the Bible as a "messiah."

What Umar did next would have a direct impact on what is happening in Israel/Palestine today. He wanted to build a mosque on a holy site described by the Prophet Muhammad in his lifetime. The

Prophet had designated a specific site on top of a hill in Jerusalem to be the third most sacred site in the Islamic faith after the Kaaba in the Grand Mosque in Mecca and the Al-Masjid an-Nabawi in Medina. Up to that point, Jerusalem had been under Roman occupation, and Umar being the first Muslim ruler to capture the city would define it to be his responsibility to establish this mosque, the Al-Aqsa Mosque. He went to the site described by the Prophet Muhammad and found that it was being used as a rubbish heap for the city. There was no existing temple at the site. Christians and Jews helped the Muslims clean the site so the mosque could be built (Fig. 6-10).

**Figure 6-10:** The Dome of the Rock in the Al-Haram al-Sharif (from Arabic: "the Noble Sanctuary") in Jerusalem is a UNESCO World Heritage Site. It is the earliest religious monument to be built by a Muslim ruler that has been archaeologically confirmed. It was initially completed in AD 691. The art historian and archaeologist, Oleg Grabar, described the Dome of the Rock as a "unique monument of Islamic culture in almost all respects."

Why has the historically significant encounter between Umar and Sophronius been mostly omitted from Western historical texts and popular culture? What I am trying to establish in this book is that the intentional omissions of positive actions of the Islamic civilization, combined with the fictionalized negative depictions, have set the stage for the manufactured prejudice toward Arabs and Muslims over the past 100 years.

The patriarch was so impressed by Umar's decision not to pray inside the Church of the Holy Sepulchre that day that he gifted him the keys to the church. Umar gave the keys to a local Muslim Palestinian family with strict orders to protect the church. Saladin and all Muslim leaders to follow would issue similar decrees honoring the principle of protecting the church. To this date, over 1,380 years after the day Umar ordered the protection of the church, descendants of that Palestinian family still hold the keys and open and lock the church every day!

In closing this section about Umar, the "savior of the Church of the Holy Sepulchre," I would like to mention how his character compares to the kings and dictators in the "Middle East" today, who were created by Churchill and Britain as part of their Palestine-focused vassalage program following WWI. Umar made sure he did not benefit financially from the government he was ruling. As an example, when the wealthy Persian Empire sent an envoy to Medina to meet the caliph of the emerging Muslim Empire, he was looking for a palace in Medina but found none. When he inquired, he was led to Umar sitting under the shade of a tree with some of the city's poor. The envoy was astonished. The kings and dictators of the "Middle East" today live in massive palaces and have similarly massive Swiss bank accounts with money that was generated on the backs on their people. Umar had a principle of not appointing anyone related to him to public office even if they were qualified, while today's "Middle East" leaders almost exclusively appoint only family members to key positions. The young generation throughout the Arab and Muslim worlds look at their leaders with deep resentment and frustration, which extremists have used to recruit young minds to join their nefarious movements.

## The Holy Warriors:
## Christendom's Jihadis

The next major interaction Palestine would have with the West was the Crusades (AD 1099–1244). This holy war had such a cataclysmic impact on the relationship between the West and the "Middle

East" that rather than discussing it here, I have dedicated an entire section of the book to it entitled "The Three Invaders of Jerusalem." I mention it here so that the chronology of the events is made clear.

## The Birth of a New Christianity

We have traversed over 1,200 years of Christendom, and the term "Zionism" had not been mentioned by any Christian leader so far.

In this book, I have posited that the key principle behind the creation of the "Middle East" as we know it today was "Christian Zionism." Zionism refers to the movement that compels Jews from around the world to establish a homeland in Palestine. The Christian Crusaders, who were the mantle holders of Christendom at the beginning of the second millennium and occupied Jerusalem for long stretches of time between AD 1099–1244, never had an interpretation of the Bible that could lead to the concept of Zionism. The Crusaders, as we will see in the next section of the book, were deeply devout Christians, and had they had any such interpretation of the Bible, it would have been at their fingertips to create a Jewish homeland in Palestine.

"Zionism" is therefore a relatively recent term. It was coined in the late nineteenth century (AD 1892) by Nathan Birnbaum in Vienna, Austria, who wrote a book titled *The National Rebirth of the Jewish People in its Homeland as a Means of Solving the Jewish Problem.* Birnbaum was referring to the persecution of Jews in Christian Europe. Zionism and its purposes and philosophies are not the same for Zionist Jews and Zionist Christians. Evangelical Christian Zionism is an eighteenth- and nineteenth-century British–American extremist political ideology that had not previously existed in Judaism nor Christendom. It has had a massive impact on the lives of millions of people in the "Middle East" for some 100 years now. However, when I have spoken to Arabs and Muslims around the world about their understanding of "Christian Zionism," they, across the board, had no idea of its existence nor its meaning. More surprisingly, when I spoke to mainstream Christians in the US and Europe, most also had no real understanding. Therefore, most people have no idea why the "Middle East" was created in its current fashion following WWI.

To find the answer of the central question of this chapter, I must next explain the origins of Christian Zionism.

## The German Rebel

A sixteenth-century German priest, Martin Luther, rebelled against the Catholic Church, which led to the most significant change in Christendom in the second millennium (Fig. 6-11). By advocating for a reformation, he created a splinter group that is now known as the Protestants. While Luther had legitimate claims against the Catholic Church, especially when it came to corruption related to monies collected from believers to wash away their sins (a practice known as indulgences), he opened a door for uneducated laypeople to question the teachings of the Bible. The Catholic Church regarded Luther as an extremist heretic. Joan Acocella, a reporter for the *New Yorker* wrote, "A representative of the Vatican once claimed that Luther was conceived when the Devil raped his mother in an outhouse."

**Figure 6-11:** Engraving of Martin Luther from 1530.

Luther's views of Muslims and Jews would go on to play an important role in relation to the pivotal question posed at the beginning of this chapter.

Luther lived at a time when the Muslim Ottoman Turks were a power player in Europe. Although he wrote, "The person of the Antichrist is at the same time the pope and the Turk," he gave tacit support for Protestants across Europe who allied themselves with the Ottomans against the Catholic Empire. (An example of such alliance is provided in Chapter 2 of Queen Elizabeth I with Sultan Murad III.)

When it came to the Jews, Luther was an unapologetic deep anti-Semite. In his 1543 treatise *On the Ineffable Name and the Generations of Christ*, he talks about the devil and the Jews:

> He [the Devil] stuffs and squirts them [the Jews] so full, that it overflows and swims out of every place, pure Devil's

filth, yes, it tastes so good to their hearts, and they guzzle it like sows.

In reference to Judas, the disciple who—according to the four canonical Gospels—betrayed Jesus, he wrote,

> When Judas Schariot hanged himself, so that his guts ripped, and as happens to those who are hanged, his bladder burst, then the Jews had their golden cans and silver bowls ready, to catch the Judas piss . . . and afterwards together they ate the shit.

In another writing he would advocate for the burning down of synagogues.

Martin Luther, the founder of Protestantism, would have a significant impact on evangelical preachers that would lead the movement after him about their views of Muslims and Jews. The massacre of six million Jews during the Holocaust in the twentieth century may also have a link to Luther. In 1946, at the Nuremberg trials, the founder and publisher of the anti-Semitic newspaper *Der Stürmer* (an illustrated example of which I provided in the last chapter, Fig. 5-2), Julius Streicher, would say Martin Luther was his inspirational figure.

A French pastor who was influenced by Luther's ideas, John Calvin (1509–1564), would go on to become one of the scions of the Protestant Reformation movement against the Catholic Church. He shared Luther's views about Jews and the end-of-days prophecies.

## Christianity *Reinterpreted*

Christian scholars estimate that the Crucifixion of Jesus occurred between AD 30 to 33. The earliest known list of the 27 books which make up the New Testament dates to the fourth century; however, there is no concrete information as to when the 27 books were actually written. There are some estimates regarding the earliest writings of the New Testament—the four canonical Gospels. The Gospel of Mark most probably dates from AD 66–70, Matthew and Luke around 85–90, and John from 90–110. All four were written anonymously, and Christian scholars agree that none of the Gospels were written by eyewitnesses of Jesus. All of the New Testament books, including the four canonical Gospels, were written in Greek. The interpretation of the teachings of the Bible during the first 1,500 years of Christianity was provided by highly learned Greek-speaking Christian scholars. A pivotal point in Christianity's history occurred when the Bible was translated into English for the first time in 1526 by an Englishman, William Tyndale. This made the Bible vulnerable to distortions. Tyndale was a strong supporter of Martin Luther, and incorporated Luther's ideas in his Bible. While Christian religious scholars across Europe considered Tyndale a heretic and condemned him for his personal edits of the Bible, it was too late. The process of making the Bible available to English-speaking people in Britain and the new colonies in North America was already in motion. The unsuspecting English speakers would have no way of checking the authenticity of the translations since they did not know Greek. Tyndale's Bible would become a major contributor to the AD 1611 publication of the King James Bible, one of the most widely read Bibles in the world today. It has been suggested that a significant portion of the King James Bible comes word for word from Tyndale's version.

## "Road Map to Armageddon"

Tyndale had set the stage for extremist Christians to alter the Bible and its interpretations. This 200-year period (1700–1900) would see tremendous activism in editing and reinterpreting the Bible among evangelical puritanical preachers in Britain and the US (where this period of religious revivalism has been called the Great Awakening). These extremist evangelicals were inexplicably fixated with the end of days—Armageddon.

In the New Testament Romans 11:25, "a part of Israel has become resistant." The Protestant disciples of John Calvin, Beza in Geneva and Bucer in Strasbourg, believed that this verse referred to unbelieving Jews. Accordingly, the new edition of the Geneva Bible in the seventeenth century added the concept of "conversion" into Romans 11: "He sheweth that the time shall come that the whole nation of the Jews, though not everyone particularly, shall be joined to the Church of Christ." This version of the Bible, with the idea of the need to convert Jews to Christianity, became highly circulated in Britain and the early American colonies in the seventeenth century, and idea of converting Jews to the Church of Christ became entrenched among Protestants on both sides of the Atlantic. Jonathan Edwards (1703–1758), considered to be one of America's most important and original philosophical theologians, would declare the need for Jews to repent:

> Jewish infidelity will be overthrown. Jews will cast away their old infidelity. They shall flow together to the blessed Jesus. Nothing is more certainly foretold than this national conversion of the Jews in Romans 11.

In this new reinterpretation movement in evangelical Protestantism, activist preachers would also introduce another concept they believed to be linked to the required Jewish repentance and conversions; they called it *millennialism*. They focused on the verse in Revelation 20:1–6 "They came to life and reigned with Christ a thousand years." In the some 1,700 years in the history of Christendom, the interpretation of this verse had been a symbolic thousand rather than a literal thousand years on Earth, as espoused by the new evangelical preachers of Britain and the US.

The Second Coming of Jesus Christ is mentioned both in the Bible and the Qur'an. However, the evangelical preachers in the eighteenth and nineteenth centuries would tie Jewish conversion and millennialism to the Second Coming. There is not a consensus among the various Protestant evangelical groups regarding the chronological order of these three phenomena: conversions, millennialism, and the Second Coming of Christ. However, there was clear cut-agreement about the fact that for all of these to happen, evangelical Christianity must create a way for Jews to be brought to Palestine (a concept they termed *Restoration*)—thus the birth of Christian Zionism. To these evangelical preachers, Jews merely existed as a means to an end in order to accomplish the Christian vision of end-of-days prophecies: the concept that they can expedite the day they will be risen into the clouds where they will meet Jesus Christ—known as the Rapture in evangelicalism. Christians will go to heaven, while all others, including the Jews, will be left behind on Earth where they will spend seven dreadful years, ultimately annihilated and ending up in hell.

British nineteenth-century evangelicals formed the London Jews Society (LJS) in 1809, a missionary group with the aim of converting the Jews of London. In 1813, the LJS constructed a multi-building structure next to the Jewish community in East London for its proselytizing activities that was named Palestine Place. By 1841 the LJS had expanded its activities into wider Europe and Russia.

The evangelical movement was not limited to preachers. Powerful politicians in Britain got on board. The influential Lord Shaftesbury, considered to be one of the historical scions of Christian Zionism, wrote in 1839 (Fig. 6-12):

**Figure 6-12:** Lord Shaftesbury (1801–1885), known in English history as a philanthropist, was the founder of the concept that Christian Zionism should be more than just a religious idea. He integrated it into the British government ethos. Later this merger would also take a foothold in the US.

> The Jews must be encouraged to return in yet greater numbers and become once more the husbandman of Judea and Galilee . . . though [the Jews] admittedly a stiff-necked, dark hearted people, and sunk in moral degradation, obduracy, and ignorance of the Gospel . . .

The condition I termed the duplicitous syndrome is well illustrated in Shaftesbury's words, deep anti-Semitism combined with the ruse of caring about the Jews' well-being. Lord Shaftesbury would go on to become the founding president of the Palestine Exploration Fund (PEF). The innocent- and scientific-sounding name had a sinister purpose, as Shaftesbury himself would declare in 1865:

> Let us not delay to send out the best agents [spies] . . . to search the length and breadth of Palestine, to survey the land, and if possible to go over every corner of it, drain it, measure it and, if you will, prepare it for the return of its

ancient possessors, for I believe that the time cannot be far off before that great event will come to pass.

One of the first major goals of the PEF was to map the Al-Haram al-Sharif, which contains the Al-Aqsa Mosque (Fig. 6-13). Why would the evangelical powers in Britain be more interested in fully mapping this Muslim holy site in Jerusalem rather than the Church of the Sepulchre—the holiest site in Christianity? The answer will become clear as we dig deeper into this new interpretation within Christendom.

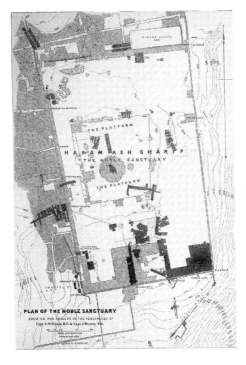

**Figure 6-13:** Plan of the Al-Haram al-Sharif—sketched in detail by the PEF as part of their survey of Palestine in 1884. They detailed every gate leading to the Dome of the Rock.

Let me take you back to Chapter 2, when the senior British general Horatio Kitchener sent a PEF expedition to Palestine in the early part of the twentieth century. To obtain permission from the Ottomans, the expedition was proposed under the guise of a religious mission to find scientific evidence of the biblical account of the Exodus. He followed Shaftesbury's directions mentioned above and sent British intelligence "agents" to map out southern Palestine in preparation for a future invasion, which ultimately took place when General Allenby invaded Palestine in 1917.

The Ottomans and Palestinians were victims of naivete and excessive trust of the British prior to WWI in the early twentieth century, as are most Arabs in countries ruled by vassal leaders today. The Ottomans and Palestinians should have suspected foul play when the British evangelical PEF was more interested in the Islamic Nobel Sanctuary than the Christian sites of Jerusalem! Similarly, many Arabs throughout the "Middle East" today continue to trust their vassal dictators despite the many red flags, as outlined in this book, that they are not working in their best interest.

The British architects of WWI, discussed at length in Chapter 2—Lloyd George, Arthur Balfour, and Winston Churchill—all students of the above evangelical interpretation of the Bible, found themselves in key governmental positions which enabled them to enact their extremist ideations. Lloyd George, who grew up in an evangelical Welsh Baptist home, was the British prime minister at the end of WWI who reneged on the promises made to the Sharif of Mecca. He would later (in 1925) say before the Jewish Historical Society:

> I was brought up in a school where I was taught far more about the history of the Jews than about the history of my own land. I could tell you all the kings of Israel. But I doubt whether I could have named half a dozen of the kings of England . . .

One of Prime Minister George's biographers, Christopher Sykes (ironically the father of Mark Sykes, who coauthored the secret maps used to divide Arab lands), described why it was impossible to brief George on the cultural realities of Palestine:

> Largely because he could not move beyond the Christian Zionist worldview of his youth. When briefed repeatedly on the contemporary geography of Palestine, Lloyd George insisted on reciting from his memory of childhood Sunday school lessons biblical cities and lands of Bible times, some of which no longer existed.

Arthur Balfour (for whom the Balfour Declaration was named) grew up in an evangelical Scottish Presbyterian home and saw his role as the British foreign secretary (akin to the title secretary of state in the US) as an instrument to fulfill divine evangelical biblical prophecies. In a letter to his niece in 1906 (10 years before the British government made a deal with Sharif Hussein to fight on their side in return for the liberation of the Arab nation which would include Palestine), he wrote, "no political difficulty about obtaining Palestine [for establishing a Jewish State]." Winston Churchill's Zionist ideations were equally strong, as discussed in detail in Chapter 2.

Stephen Sizer, whose book *Christian Zionism: Road-map to Armageddon?* served as a key reference for me in my research for this chapter, has said of Balfour and George, "Their support for the World Zionist movement was a direct result of their evangelical upbringing."

George, Balfour, and Churchill, by acting on their fanatical religious convictions via their governmental powers, created a reality we know today as the "Middle East."

While scholars and pundits in the West routinely criticize the literal interpretation of the Qur'an by Islamic extremists, I have yet to find any such harsh criticisms in the mainstream media about the literal interpretation of the Bible within the evangelical community in the West.

## The Americanization of Evangelicalism

While Luther in Germany and Calvin in France both had significant influence throughout Europe, the most profound impact of their interpretations of the Bible was in Britain, especially in England. Both men defined the enemy to be the Catholic Church and Islam. America's first immigrants in the early seventeenth century, who settled in colonies on the northeast coast of the US, came from England and were rebels who believed that the Church of England had not purified itself enough from the Catholic Church—thus they would go on to be known as Puritanical. Puritanism was considered a pejorative term, since it was borne out of religious extremism. They held deeply Calvinist views about Christianity. By the early eighteenth century, Jonathan Edwards, the American evangelical preacher and one of the leaders of the Great Awakening, preached that the destruction of both the Catholic Church and Islam was necessary to usher in the Judgment Day foretold in the book of Revelation of the New Testament.

The hatred for Islam within the Catholic Church in Europe over the centuries stemmed from the Ottoman Empire's success in expanding within the continent. The hatred for Islam in the evangelical community, especially in the formative years of the US, was based on the fact that Muslims had sovereignty over Palestine, which they saw as anathema to realizing their manufactured concepts related to the end-of-days prophecies.

A clear example of the evangelical extremist philosophy is demonstrated in the question raised by Elias Boudinot, who was president of the Second Continental Congress (1782–1783) and had served under President George Washington as director of the US Mint, "Who knows but God has raised up these United States, in these latter days, for the very purpose of accomplishing his will in bringing his beloved people [Restoration] to their land [Palestine]?" A congressman from essentially the time of the creation of the US was already asking questions about evangelical biblical philosophy and indirectly targeting the Muslim land of Palestine for a future occupation.

It did not take long. In 1891, the evangelical preacher William E. Blackstone presented to the then US President Benjamin Harrison a petition calling for establishing a Jewish state in Palestine. The petition was endorsed by 413 American leaders who represented key aspects of society and culture at the time. The signers included future US President William McKinley, Supreme Chief Justice Melville Fuller, giants of America's industry including J.P. Morgan and John D. Rockefeller, and as has been outlined throughout this book, the insidious involvement of the mainstream media, as it was signed by the editors of dozens of newspapers.

The twentieth century would see an advance of the evangelical Zionist agenda that Calvin, Shaftesbury, and Churchill could only have dreamt of. The movement took a foothold deep within the US government.

The moment that launched this leap occurred at the noon cabinet meeting in the White House on May 12, 1948. The question at hand was whether the US would give its blessing to do something which had never been done in modern human history: to establish a country for religious purposes inside another country against its will.

Would the US proceed with what the evangelical preacher Blackstone had proposed some 60 years earlier, to establish a Jewish state inside Palestine? President Harry Truman would do something uncharacteristic: he brought a low-level non-cabinet member political player, Clark Clifford, into the meeting. Clifford was an ardent Christian Zionist. He quoted verses from Deuteronomy during this most sensitive cabinet meeting to push for US support. Within 48 hours, for the first time in 2,000 years, a new Jewish state in Palestine was declared at 6 p.m. EDT on May 14, 1948. While Israel is a reality today, it is important to get a sense of what the decision of establishing a state based on religion sounded like at the time. The renowned American author David McCullough would write about the response of the American delegation that evening in the United Nations on May 14, upon the announcement of the establishment of a Jewish state in Palestine, "Some American delegates broke into laughter, thinking the announcement must be somebody's joke." They thought the creation of a country on the basis of religion in someone else's country sounded like a hoax!

The Christian Zionist leaders in the US were very shrewd; in the second half of the twentieth century they actively sought to get entrenched within the United States' highest political and military institutions. Ronald Reagan, when governor of California in the 1970s prior to becoming president, said "Libya has now gone communist, and that's a sign that the day of Armageddon isn't far off." President Reagan did attack Libya militarily, and whether his religious views were part of that decision is not known. President George W. Bush, in the run-up to the Iraq War in 2003 (which we now know was based on fabricated data claiming Iraq possessed weapons of mass destruction), reached out to French President Jacques Chirac to convince him to join the US in the invasion of Iraq and in the conversation referred to "Gog and Magog." Chirac did not understand what President Bush was talking about and consulted religious scholars in France for help. Gog and Magog refer to a nefarious peoples with whom a war has been mentioned in the end-of-days prophecies of Judaism, Christianity, and Islam. It appears President Bush may have believed that the Iraqis were Gog and Magog. President Reagan and the evangelicals of his era believed the Russians to be Gog and Magog.

Evangelical Zionists started to recruit inside America's most prestigious military schools, academies which produce future leaders. The American author and former priest James Carroll spoke of the dangers of combining political and military power by a single extremist movement in his book 2001 book *Constantine's Sword: The Church and the Jews—A History* and his 2007 documentary movie by the same name directed by Oren Jacoby.

Carroll went to the prestigious US Air Force Academy in Colorado Springs, Colorado, to investigate reports that extremist evangelicals were trying to recruit air force cadets. He also interviewed the renowned evangelical pastor Ted Haggard, who had established a church in Colorado Springs. Haggard stated, "Evangelicalism is growing and developing. There is a new megachurch, a megachurch being two thousand people in attendance or more. There is a new megachurch in America every two days, and they are all evangelical." He added that the George W. Bush White House communicated with evangelical leaders weekly via phone call every Monday. He said it was his mission to convert non-believers at the US Air Force Academy. A young cadet (Casey Weinstein) in the academy spoke about personal insults hurled at him for being Jewish, and a number of other cadets believed that "the academy was putting its full-fledged stamp on conservative Christian ideology [evangelicalism]." This explains the duplicitous syndrome I introduce in this book; while Christian Zionists take a Judeo-centric view of the end of days, they are at the same time deeply anti-Semitic.

At the United States' oldest and most iconic of the five service academies, West Point, in the state of New York, there is an evangelical campus ministry—the Officers' Christian Fellowship. In 2012, a West Point cadet, Blake Page, quit just months before graduating to bring attention to the evangelical proselytizing that exists at the academy.

Another cadet, however, had a different experience: he became an ardent evangelical while at West Point. His name was Mike Pompeo, who would go on to become the US secretary of state under Donald Trump (Fig. 6-14).

The Trump administration became a bastion of extremist evangelicalism and Christian Zionism. A key leader representing these extremist ideas was the vice president, Mike Pence (Fig. 6-15). Michael D'Antonio and Peter Eisner, in their book *The Shadow President: The Truth About Mike Pence*, argued that Pence's central goal was to change the US government to be based on biblical law, or Christian Dominionism.

Author Anne Applebaum has provided a deep insight into the world of Pence and Pompeo. Speaking with a confidential source (a former member of the Trump administration), she was told that both Pence and Pompeo "have convinced themselves that they are in a biblical moment." The source added that Pence and Pompeo believed that "we are approaching the Rapture, and this is a moment of deep religious significance."

**Fig. 6-14:** Mike Pompeo, the 70th US secretary of state, pictured in Jerusalem on the roof of the King David Hotel to get the optic of the Dome of the Rock in the background for his speech at the Republican National Convention on August 25, 2020. Pompeo was sending a message to the evangelical Zionist audience that their dream of someday taking over this Islamic sacred site to convert it into a temple is alive and well.

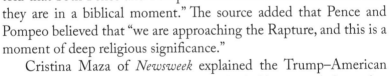

Cristina Maza of *Newsweek* explained the Trump–American evangelism connection: "Many evangelical Christians believe that Trump was chosen by God to usher in a new era, a part of history called the 'end times.'" Trump capitalized on this relationship. Robert Jeffress, the renowned evangelical pastor, in a statement in the White House in December 2019, described Trump as "the most pro-faith president in history" and that God will "bless those who bless Israel and curse those who curse Israel." It is important to note that Jeffress is also on record as saying that Jews will go

**Figure 6-15:** Mike Pence, 48th vice president of the US. An evangelical spokesman, Johnnie Moore, called Pence the "most influential evangelical ever in American public life."

to hell, which is consistent with the duplicitous syndrome described in this book.

Donald Trump, not himself a religious man, would go on to capitalize on his deep support within the evangelical community. In December 2019, Trump became the first US president to recognize Jerusalem as the capital of Israel. The move was intended to end the long-held aspirations of Palestinians for East Jerusalem, which was invaded by Israel in 1967, to become the capital of a future Palestinian state. Religious historian Neil Young told *Newsweek*, "At this point, Trump's decision to recognize Jerusalem as the capital of Israel is the only concrete thing his evangelical supporters can point to as part of fulfilling biblical philosophy to bring about the second coming of Christ."

While American evangelicals are not a monolith, a poll conducted by LifeWay Research in 2017 found that 80 percent of evangelicals believed that the 1948 creation of the State of Israel fulfilled the biblical prophecy that will lead to the Second Coming of Christ. Moreover, evangelical end-of-days prophetic beliefs have become mainstream ideas within American culture; in response to the same question by the Pew Research Center in 2003, about one third of *all* Americans said the existence of Israel fulfilled biblical prophecy. In a 2010 Pew poll, 41 percent of Americans expected that Jesus will be returning before 2050; meaning in their lifetime. Apparently, the only entity in America who did not get the memo is the mainstream media; they understandably vigorously examine Islamic extremism, but evangelical Christian Zionism is not an area they deem worth exploring!

### Jewish Zionism: "Palestine or Argentina?"

The evangelical push for the conversion of Jews was and is deeply insulting to Jews. Conversely, for the persecuted Jews in Europe, the evangelical concept of Restoration did understandably seem appealing. But even that was not an easy sell.

The evangelical preacher William Blackstone (mentioned above for petitioning the US president to occupy Palestine to create a Jewish state) also sought to convince Jews to leave the US to take part in making Restoration a reality. He arranged a meeting with Jewish leaders in Chicago in 1890. Rabbi Emil Hirsch would tell him, "We modern Jews do not wish to be restored to Palestine . . . the country wherein we live is our Palestine . . . we will not go back . . . to form a nationality of our own." We heard this same sentiment in Chapter 2, as the author-historian David Fromkin noted that the only opposition to creating a Jewish nation inside Palestine in Prime Minister Lloyd George's Zionist cabinet at the end of WWI came from the only Jewish member, Edwin Montagu. The reality is that at the end of the nineteenth and beginning of the twentieth century, the overwhelming majority of Jews in Europe and the US were opposed to Zionism, while evangelical leaders were pushing for it. Two factors ultimately led to garnering Jewish support: the persecution of Jews in Europe and the emergence of charismatic leaders within the Jewish community who would campaign for Zionism. I am sure the convenient irony is not lost on the reader; the same people who, for their own prophetic ideations, pressed the Jews to move to Palestine were the same people who were persecuting Jews in Europe!

Theodor Herzl, whom we discussed in Chapter 2, emerged to address the anti-Semitism in Europe. Contrary to popular depictions of Herzl, especially in the Arab and Muslim worlds, he was no religious extremist. He called for political Zionism not based on end-of-days prophecies but rather as a potential solution to the treatment of Jews in Europe. In his monograph *The Jewish State* he posits, "It is foolish to revert to old stages of civilization, as many Zionists would like to do." Furthermore, in a chapter titled "Palestine or Argentina?" he proposed Argentina as a potential homeland for the Jews: "Argentina is one of the most fertile countries in the world . . . The Argentine Republic would derive considerable profit from cession of a portion of its territory to us." As discussed in Chapter 2, he also suggested Uganda in Africa as a homeland for the Jews. It goes without saying that for the evangelical Zionists, there could be only one place: Palestine.

Two Jewish leaders, one in the US and the other in Britain, would work with the evangelical movement to solidify the location to be Palestine. Supreme Court Justice Louis Brandeis partnered with William Blackstone and worked diligently to convince American Jews to support Zionism. Around the same time, in Britain, Chaim Weizmann worked closely with Arthur Balfour to do the same there.

*Saleem I. Abdulrauf*

Once the Jewish state was created in Palestine in 1948, consecutive Israeli prime ministers have partnered with Zionist leaders in American government, religion, and the entertainment industry to impact public opinion in the United States. Let me share an example with you. Jerry Falwell Sr., the evangelical preacher who founded the Baptist Liberty University in Lynchburg, Virginia, promoted Israeli policies in the US at a grand scale. When Israel bombed the Iraqi nuclear plant in 1981, the first phone call Prime Minister Menachem Begin made was to Falwell before calling President Reagan. Similarly, when Prime Minister Benjamin Netanyahu visited the US in 1998, his first meeting was with Falwell before meeting with President Clinton.

**Figure 6-16:** Jared Kushner, an ardent Jewish Zionist who became the chief architect of the US "Middle East" foreign policy during his father-in-law's (Donald Trump's) presidency.

In the early part of the twenty-first century, the son-in-law of President Donald Trump, Jared Kushner, became the mantle holder of Jewish Zionism in the United States (Fig. 6-16). Although he delivered to the evangelical Zionists what they had sought for so long—for Jerusalem to be recognized by the US as the capital of Israel—he was not immune from the duplicitous syndrome. Some evangelicals believe him to be the Antichrist! End-of-days prophecies in Judaism, Christianity, and Islam speak of the emergence of a false prophet; based on the descriptions of the "beast" provided in Revelations in the New Testament, some evangelicals believe he would be Jewish, charismatic, falsely claim to bring peace to the "Middle East," and be represented by the number 666. Kushner, Jewish, owning the 666 Fifth Avenue complex in New York City, and being a close friend with Israel's Prime Minister Benjamin Netanyahu—for some evangelical Zionists that makes him the ideal candidate for the Antichrist title!

136

## The Third Temple

Earlier in the chapter we discussed that based on biblical sources the Neo-Babylonians destroyed Solomon's Temple in Jerusalem in 589 BC. The Romans destroyed the Second Temple (Herod's Temple) in AD 70 in response to a Jewish revolt. Unlike Solomon's Temple, there is archaeological evidence of the existence of Herod's Temple. Jewish *eschatology* (end-of-days philosophy) includes the belief that Herod's Temple will be replaced by a Third Temple. The Hebrew Bible calls for the construction of this temple just prior to or during the Jewish Messianic age—when the Jewish Messiah will reign on Earth. While Christian and Muslim eschatology contend that the coming Messiah will be Jesus the son of Mary, Jewish eschatology contends that he will be someone other than Jesus.

When Israel invaded the West Bank in 1967 and occupied East Jerusalem, the chaplain for the Israeli Defense Force (IDF), Rabbi Shlomo Goren, blew the *shofar* (a horn historically used for Jewish religious services) and performed a religious ceremony near the Dome of the Rock. According to historian Stephen Sizer, the rabbi "was criticized by both the secular Israeli press and Orthodox Jews." The reason for this is that within Orthodox Judaism, the concept of the Third Temple and any religious ceremonies related to it are reserved for the Messianic age.

Where does Orthodox Judaism and evangelical Christianity believe the Third Temple must be built? According to both, it must be right on the exact spot of the Dome of the Rock, a sacred site in Islam. The only way to build the Third Temple is to destroy the Dome of the Rock. This explains why extremist evangelicals are fixated on this site, and also explains why the Palestine Exploration Fund (PEF) created such a detailed map of the Al-Haram al-Sharif where the Dome of the Rock is located (Figs. 6-10 and 6-13). The Dome of the Rock is shown as the centerpiece on the cover of this book.

The Third Temple did not become a prophecy in evangelicalism until the twentieth century! Nineteen hundred years of Christianity never mentioned it as part of its prophecies. The concept of a Jewish temple had ceased to have any significance for Christianity following the statement attributed to Jesus in John 2:19, "Destroy this temple," combined with the building of the Church of the Holy Sepulchre in the fourth century by Emperor Constantine at a higher ground than that of the temple. Moreover, there is no mention in the New Testament that a Third Temple would be built.

Earlier in the chapter we witnessed that when Caliph Umar took control of Jerusalem from the Christians in AD 638, he identified the place for Islam's holy sanctuary on a desolate hill that was used for the garbage collection of the city. The gate of the city that led to this area was called "Dung Gate" by the population of Jerusalem when Umar arrived there. If the early Christians, who were close to the time of Jesus and spoke the language of the original biblical writings, in any way felt that building a Third Temple was important to their faith or to its prophecies, they would have done so during their 300-year reign of the city prior to the arrival of Umar. Similarly, if the very extreme Christian zealots, the Crusaders, had any such interpretations, they would have built the Third Temple during their 103-year rule over the city in the twelfth and thirteenth centuries.

In the twentieth century, the extremist reinterpretation of the Bible within American evangelicalism went into overdrive. They linked all of the phenomena that they had generated over the previous 300 years (conversions, Restoration, millenarianism, the Second Coming of Christ) to the building of the Third Temple. Hal Lindsey, the renowned American evangelical Christian pastor would say, ". . . rebuilding of the great temple, the most important sign of Jesus Christ's soon coming is before us." He would add that building the temple would put Judaism and Islam "on an inevitable course of war over the site, a war that will start Armageddon." While it is commonly believed that religions advocate for peace, that is not so in the Christian Zionism philosophy of evangelicalism; war is a necessary occurrence for the prophecies to be realized. Mike Pompeo, the zealot evangelical secretary of state, opposed any peace deals with Iran, a country viewed to be deeply antagonistic toward Israel. When Pompeo was asked the question referring to the Old Testament Persian Queen Esther (the wife of the Persian King Xerxes mentioned in the beginning of the chapter) who saved Jews from a massacre, whether Trump had been "raised for such a time as this, just like Queen Esther, to help save the Jewish people from the Iranian menace?" His answer was "As a Christian, I certainly believe that's possible."

Perhaps the most telling statement by Pompeo was in 2015 when he said, "We will continue to fight these battles," because there is a "never-ending struggle" until "the Rapture."

As a secretary of state, he has been clear about the fact that he does not separate church from state: "In my office, I keep a Bible open on my desk to remind me of God and his word, and the truth." Pompeo declared the Bible "informs everything I do."

## How to Create an Enemy: The Precursor of Hollywood

I started this chapter with a question: where does the hate, the propaganda, and the historical revisionism about Arabs and Muslims in Western culture come from?

In everything I have shared with you so far there has been a missing link. Yes, there were powerful evangelical leaders within the US government, but for a democratic nation based on the consent of the governed, to enact major acts of war against other nations and peoples to fulfill religious prophecies, there needs to be acquiescence by the general public. Therefore, for Christian Zionism to succeed in expediting perceived prophecies, an enemy had to be made of the Palestinians, Arabs, and Muslims.

For the war against Nazi Germany during WWII, there was no need for a large-scale vilification campaign targeting the Germans, as the threat posed by the Nazis was obvious. For the war against Japan during WWII, there was no need for a large-scale vilification campaign targeting the Japanese as the American people were fully aware that Japan had attacked Pearl Harbor in Hawaii. For the Cold War against the Soviet Union in the latter half of the twentieth century, there was no need for a large-scale vilification campaign targeting the Russians because the Soviet nuclear threat was obvious.

Now let's look at Palestinians, Arabs, and Muslims. They posed no threat in the twentieth century (prior to the recent advent of the global Islamist terrorist organizations). Historically it has been quite the contrary; they were loyal allies during WWI. Moreover, their religion reveres Jesus and his mother Mary. Therefore, there would be no math or physics by which the American population would support the killing of innocent Arab and Muslim civilians, let alone the large-scale violence that would be required to capture Palestine and sustain that occupation over the long haul just to fulfill an extremist prophetic ideation. What would be necessary would be a campaign like no other to make the American people hate Arabs and Muslims—thus began the largest vilification campaign in modern history.

The fervor for extremist evangelical Zionism in early American history peaked in the era of the Revolutionary War in the latter part of the eighteenth century. This would witness in 1780 the first play about Islam on American soil titled *Mahomet the Imposter* (Mahomet refers to the Prophet Muhammad), a play based on fictitious accounts of Islamic history using fictitious characters aiming at depicting the Prophet as a villain (Fig. 6-17). This was the first exposure Americans had to Islam. It played in the US for 16 years. Prior to opening in the US, it played in London under the direction of the Zionist evangelical minister James Miller.

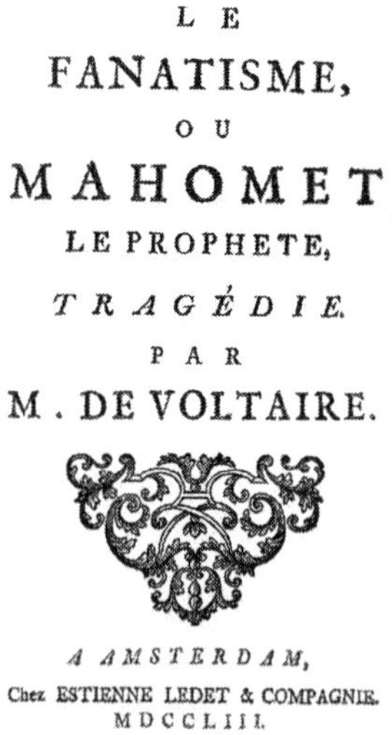

L E

FANATISME,

O U

MAHOMET

LE PROPHETE,

*TRAGÉDIE.*

P A R

M . DE VOLTAIRE.

*A AMSTERDAM,*

Chez ESTIENNE LEDET & COMPAGNIE.

M D C C L I I I.

**Figure 6-17:** Title page of the five-act play *Le Fanatisme ou Mahomet le Prophète* by the French philosopher Voltaire. The play was ironically banned in France by the Catholic Church after its premiere in Paris. This was not done out of love for Islam, but rather the church was concerned that it could open the door for possible fictionalized plays about Jesus and the Apostles.

Since that play in the late eighteenth century, the overwhelming majority of Americans have formed their opinions of Palestinians, Arabs, and Muslims based on what they see in Hollywood movies and what they hear on mainstream media. Not only has this been one of the largest vilification campaigns, but perhaps also the most successful in modern history.

## Expediting the Rapture

While the British created the "Middle East" to fulfill the evangelical end-of-days prophecy, American evangelicalism would take it one step further. To accomplish the vision of the prophecy, they would identify the enemy as Palestinians, Arabs, and Muslims in general, the custodians of Islam's sacred sites in Jerusalem. There is no written memo declaring this enemy, but it is well understood, especially among evangelicals who pursued major leadership positions within the US government. For evangelical Christian Zionism to accomplish such an ambitious plan of creating a state within a state half the world across and then sustain it by setting up vassal dictators throughout the region, a buy-in by the masses over generations was pivotal. Without vilifying Arabs and Muslims in popular culture, it would be impossible to achieve such goals. The only entities capable of impacting the feelings and emotions of the populace—Hollywood and the mainstream media—did their part.

In my review of the New Testament to write this chapter, and admittedly I am no religious scholar, I could not find any mention of Christian Zionism nor the concept of taking over the actual land of Palestine to create a Jewish state. Additionally, I spoke to a number of evangelical preachers in the US who told me that Christian Zionism is nothing but a cult movement and they do not believe it has a biblical basis. I believe the cult designation makes sense. It is not unusual for cult leaders to fool their followers for personal gains while they themselves may not necessarily believe in the concepts they are peddling. Let's look at some of the evangelical Zionists discussed in this chapter. Clark Clifford, the evangelical Zionist who persuaded President Truman to give the green light to establish a Jewish state in Palestine in 1948, ended his career facing federal charges of criminal fraud, conspiracy, and accepting bribes. Ted Haggard, former president of the National Association of Evangelicals and the preacher who focused on the US Air Force Academy in Colorado, had to step down after he was exposed for having extramarital homosexual affairs. Mr. Grant Hass, on whom Haggard made sexual advances, reported that Haggard told him, "You know what, Grant, you can become a man of God, and you can have a little bit of fun on the side." Jerry Falwell Jr. resigned from his post as president of Liberty University following a sex scandal. One of the mainstream evangelical preachers I interviewed for this chapter described the Zionist evangelical leaders as "snake oil salesmen." Regardless of whether this whole Christian Zionism movement has been nothing but a cult, it has been the largest and most influential cult in American history.

There has never been so much made out of so little. The Christian Zionist movement within evangelicalism has created manufactured concepts using words from translated and edited verses of the Greek New Testament, which was written decades after Christ's death, and none of the authors are believed to be Christ's contemporaries. The imaginary concepts that were generated regarding the end-of-days prophecies would go on to have a deep impact on both British and American foreign policies; thousands of Palestinian civilians have been killed, hundreds of thousands of Arab and Muslim civilians have been killed in wars and conflicts, and millions of Arabs today live under brutal vassal Arab dictators, *all* in the name of fulfilling the evangelical manufactured end-of-days ideations.

# Three Invaders
# of Jerusalem

# Chapter 7
# Deus Vult

At the end of Europe's first millennium, life was hard for most people except the aristocracy. Everyday functions revolved around the concept of "sin." The peasant class, which comprised most of the population, was poor and had no political power. Rather than science and math books, most Europeans were exposed to religious textbooks, much like in Afghanistan under the Taliban rule or in the religious schools funded by the Saudi–Wahhabi missions in Asia and Africa at the turn of the twenty-first century.

The aristocracy, too, lived a life enveloped in religion, but they were continually engaged in feudal fighting as well. Today, violent leaders who claim to be deeply religious are most strongly associated with the "Middle East," but there was no shortage of ruthless Christian nobles. One such aristocrat was Fulk Nerra, or Fulk III, who in AD 1000 ruled a county called Anjou in western France. Thomas Asbridge's book *The Crusades* provides a detailed account of Fulk's life: he was a brutal landlord who regularly engaged in plundering and violence. Fulk burnt his own wife at the stake for adultery, but he also self-identified as a devout Christian; for him, religion and violence were entwined. He went on a pilgrimage to Jerusalem where he is said to have been, upon his own request, led naked by his servant into the Church of the Holy Sepulchre. There, he asked his servant to beat him while he wept and asked Jesus for forgiveness.

Beyond the behavior of their leaders, the geopolitical landscape of Christian Europe at the end of the first millennium mirrored the twentieth-century developments in the Arabic world. The great Roman Empire of the early first millennium had fractured into smaller states throughout Europe, similar to the division of the Muslim Empire, which was divided into smaller vassal states following WWI.

The Arab Muslim Empire, at the start of the second millennium, viewed Europe as a collection of warring and backward tribes. In contrast, the Arab Muslim Empire was perceived as the seat of the world's cultural and scientific advances. Of course, a thousand years later, the reverse was true (Fig. 7-1). In the twentieth century, the United States and Europe dismissed the "Middle East" with an attitude best exemplified by a phrase I have heard a number of times, even from some politicians: "These people have been fighting each other for thousands of years." Europe, at the turn on the first millennium, was just like the "Middle East" at the turn of the second: ripe for an extremist militant religious movement.

**Figure 7-1:** Cordoba, Spain (in the background is the mosque of the old town). The Christians of Europe witnessed the advances of the Arab Muslim Empire even closer to home in Southern Spain, which was part of the Islamic Empire at the time. Author James Wasserman said, "Cordoba in the tenth century was considered the most sophisticated city in Europe with paved sidewalks, lighted streets, bridges, a large freshwater aqueduct, beautiful gardens, and a renowned university."

## A Pope Takes a Stand

In European culture, which was centered around Christianity, the most powerful person was not any of the multiple kings of the scattered states, but rather the pope.

In March 1088, a new pope was elected, a man named Odo of Chatillon, born from a noble family in the Champagne region of France. Odo's papal name was Urban II. Urban was both astute and shrewd; he made it his life's mission to channel all of the religious zealotry, feudal infighting, and the sense of cultural inferiority toward a larger mission.

He called for a council to be convened in Clermont, a city located in the central Auvergne region of France, in November of 1095. The 60-year-old pope selected France not only to revisit his ancestral land, but also ostensibly to deal with a problem with the king of France, Philip the Amorous. The king had fallen in love with the wife of one his counts and subsequently decided to divorce his own wife, who had just given birth to their child. He then abducted the count's wife and refused to return her.

It was not unexpected that the pope would be involved in this issue of divorce and abduction; what was unusual, however, was that the pope invited twelve archbishops and eighty bishops to convene in Clermont. The issue of a king acting out would not require the largest clerical assembly of Urban II's papacy!

In the book *Distant Lands*, Lars Brownworth provides an exquisite account of the Clermont Council. According to Brownworth, the king's behavior was dealt with in private meetings. The king was asked to return his mistress to the count, but he refused and was therefore excommunicated. Urban then requested that the local cathedral be opened to the public for a major announcement. As word of the cathedral's opening spread, people from surrounding towns traveled to Clermont.

On November 27, 1095, Pope Urban II gave an address. The French monk Robert of Reims recounted Urban's speech:

> This land which you inhabit [Europe], shut in on all sides by the seas and surrounded by the mountain peaks, is too narrow for your large population; nor does it abound in wealth; and it furnishes scarcely food enough for its cultivators. Hence it is that you murder one another, that you wage war, and that frequently you perish by mutual wounds. Let therefore hatred depart from among you, let your quarrels end, let wars cease, and let all dissensions and controversies slumber. Enter upon the road to the Holy Sepulchre; wrest that land from the wicked race [Muslims], and subject it to yourselves . . .

With Urban's speech, the Crusades were born.

What Urban was doing here fits very well with a concept defined by a twentieth-century French anthropologist, René Girard. He developed a concept called *mimetic theory*. Essentially, he was saying that we want things (e.g., security, food supply) because other people (other Europeans) want them too. And when more and more people want the same thing, it becomes scarce, creating a conflict (*mimetic conflict*)—and Europe was in mimetic conflict. Girard suggested that human societies manage this mimetic conflict through scapegoating—the process by which "others" get targeted—Urban wanted to channel this crisis to achieve his goal. Urban also fully understood that Christians of his time would do anything to seek redemption. Essentially, what Urban was saying to the French was that he had a solution for all their problems: to deal with your earthly (food, life security) and eternal (redemption) struggles, you must go and kill the infidels (the scapegoat/the Muslims). Scapegoating allowed Urban to turn attention away from the failings of European leadership and create an external source of blame, and in the process, occupy the holy land.

Beyond scapegoating Muslims, Pope Urban also suggested that European Christians must act as saviors. Fulcher of Chartres quoted the following from Urban's speech: "I, or rather the Lord, beseech you as Christ's heralds to publish this everywhere and to persuade all people of whatever rank, foot-soldiers and knights, poor and rich, to carry aid promptly to those Christians and to destroy that vile race [Muslims]." Throughout his speech, Urban called his people "Soldiers of St. Peter," stressing that by participating in this holy war, they were defending Christendom itself and becoming *militia Christi*, a knight of Christ.

Through his rhetoric, Urban suggested that the Crusades were divinely inspired. Despite his depiction of Muslims as violent and vile, Pope Urban appealed to the religious fervor of his followers by implying that they would be martyrs if they died during the Crusades: "All who die by the way, whether by land or by sea, or in battle against the pagans [Muslims], shall have immediate remission of sins. This I grant them through the power of God with which I am invested" (Fig. 7-2).

The historian Thomas Asbridge noted that "[Urban's] accusations bore little or no relation to the reality of Muslim rule in the Near East," but despite the lack of factual basis, "his explicit dehumanization of the Muslim world served as a vital catalyst to the 'crusading' cause."

**Figure 7-2:** Pope Urban II calling for the First Crusade at the at the synod of Clermont, France. Steel engraving made around 1800.

The promise of forgiveness and redemption of past sins of those who would fight to reclaim the holy land was a key element in the "holy wars." The opportunity to reach heaven in return for committing mass killings helped justify the extreme violence that would be required. We would witness the same justification 1,000 years later, when extremist Muslim militant leaders such as Osama bin Laden promised "paradise" to their foot soldiers for committing acts of mass terror, including the September 11, 2001, attacks which killed thousands of innocent civilians on US soil.

By the end of Pope Urban's speech, grown men were weeping and cries of "Deus vult" ("God wills it") were chanted. Historian Philip Hitti called Urban's words that day "probably the most effective speech in all history." It was a speech that sparked a fire of hatred that would last for centuries and that ultimately led to France's claim over Arab lands at the end of WWI, which they termed *mission historique*.

Although Pope Urban gave his rousing oration in 1095, he set the date on which the European crusading army would set off for Palestine as August 15, 1096. This allowed time for landlords who would be leading the crusading army to settle their affairs before leaving. Urban hoped that his call would attract the participation of the highly trained knights of Europe who had been fighting each other for years. However, given the dire economic situation in Europe and the promise of "paradise," thousands across Europe's social classes heeded the call. Former priest and author James Carroll observed in his book *Constantine's Sword* that the Crusades attracted "many serfs, but also landowners, from desperate economic straits." Not only did a crusader get to leave his worldly problems, but he also got eternal salvation.

## On the Way to Palestine

The word *crusade* comes from the Latin "crux," meaning "cross." All crusaders were to sew a cross-shaped piece of cloth on their tunics. Asbridge estimates that up to 100,000 individuals heeded the call for the Crusade; approximately 7,000 to 10,000 were knights, 35,000 to 50,000 were infantry, the remaining tens of thousands were foot soldiers from the poor serf classes. There was no central command or a single leading general for the crusaders. The European nobility each commanded their own military contingency. Due to the aristocratic nature of the leadership, the First Crusade is also sometimes referred to as the Princes' Crusade.

The first victims of the crusaders were not the Muslims; they were the Jews. One of the aristocrats leading his own contingency was Count Emicho of Leiningen; as his contingency traveled along the Rhine, they attacked Jewish communities. Once they reached the city of Mainz, they massacred another 700 Jews. Author Susan Jacoby said, "They killed the women also, and with their swords pierced tender children of whatever age and sex." In one of the most horrible accounts I read in researching for this book, Jewish mothers, using knives, cut the throats of their own nursing infants, preferring that over the murder of their children by the weapons of the "uncircumcised." According to historian David Nirenberg, these massacres in Germany planted the seeds for the twentieth-century Holocaust.

Why would the crusaders massacre Jews? One of Emicho's soldiers said it outright when talking to a rabbi on the day of one of the massacres: "You are the children of those who killed the object of our veneration [Jesus Christ]" (Fig. 7-3).

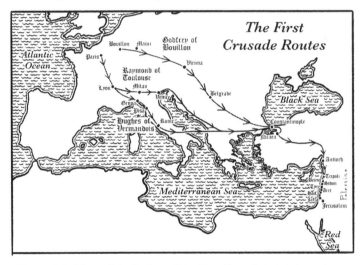

**Figure 7-3:** Many of the leaders of the First Crusade led their armies to Constantinople, where they combined into one large army before marching forth toward Palestine. The four primary leaders of the First Crusade were Hugh, count of Vermandois; Godfrey of Bouillon; Raymond of Toulouse; and Bohemond of Taranto. Hugh, count of Vermandois, was the younger brother of King Philip of France. Godfrey of Bouillon, the duke of a large territory that encompassed parts of what is now Belgium, the Netherlands, and northwestern Germany, was a descendant of the iconic French King Charlemagne mentioned in Chapter 1. Raymond of Toulouse ruled over a vast territory in southern France and already had experience fighting Muslims in Spain. Bohemond of Taranto was Norman (a descendant of the Vikings who settled in France); he traveled from Italy's Amalfi coast across the Adriatic Sea.

## Holy Deeds in the Holy Land

The crusaders began their siege on Jerusalem in June 1099. The Fatimids, the Muslim dynasty that ruled Palestine, completely underestimated the crusaders as backward European tribal gangs. They were unprepared.

After a five-week siege, the crusaders broke into the fortified city of Jerusalem on July 15, 1099. Many Muslims took refuge at the Al-Aqsa Mosque and the Dome of the Rock, the combined area known as Al-Haram al-Sharif. This area has been a venerated site in Judaism, Christianity, and Islam for thousands of years; the following are accounts of what happened there on that day:

> In the Temple and porch of Solomon, men rode in blood up to their knees and bridle reins.
>
> —Raymond of Aguilers

> In this temple, 10,000 were killed. Indeed, if you had been there, you would have seen our feet colored to our ankles with the blood of the slain. But what more shall I relate? None of them were left alive; neither women nor children were spared.
>
> —Fulcher of Chartres

> [Our leaders] also ordered all the Saracen [Arab Muslims] dead to be cast outside because of the great stench, since the whole city was filled with their corpses; and so the living Saracens dragged the dead before the exits of the gates and arranged them in heaps, as if they were houses. No one ever saw or heard of such slaughter of pagan people, for funeral pyres were formed from them like pyramids, and no one knows their number except God alone.
>
> —Gesta Francorum

Only the Muslims who were able to pay ransom survived; they were driven from their homes and forced to leave the city.

Jews who fought side by side with the Muslims in defending the city were also targeted. Ibn al-Qalanisi wrote, "The Jews assembled in their synagogue, and the Franks [Europeans] burned it over their heads."

The massacres were not just based on hunger for blood; as Asbridge writes, the crusaders were "also empowered by heartfelt piety and the authentic belief that they were doing God's work." Filled with religious fervor, they overtook the city (Fig. 7-4).

**Figure 7-4:** *Taking of Jerusalem by the Crusaders, 15th July 1099.* Oil on canvas by Emile Signol. Note the Dome of the Rock in the upper left and the slaughtered Muslim civilians on the ground.

Nearly a thousand years later, the brutal violence of the First Crusade went unacknowledged by Pope Benedict XVI (Joseph Aloisius Ratzinger), who served as pontiff from 2005–2013. He delivered the Regensburg lecture at the University of Regensburg in Germany on September 12, 2006. The German-born pope had previously served as a professor of theology after graduating from the university. In his lecture, he quoted the little-known fourteenth-century Byzantine Emperor Manuel II Palaiologos: "Show me just what Muhammad brought that was new and there you will find things only evil and inhumane, such as his command to spread by the sword the faith he preached" (Fig. 7-5).

**Figure 7-5:** Pope Benedict XVI (Joseph Ratzinger), a scholar of the history of the Catholic Church, in his Regensburg lecture in 2006, omitted referencing the mass killings of Muslim and Jewish civilians during the Crusades, but rather focused on an unsubstantiated account of violence committed by Muslims in the seventh century. This photograph was taken during my visit to the Vatican in 2007. I had read about the history of the papal ring and the pontiff was kind enough to show it to me when I respectfully asked to see it (as shown in the photograph).

It is important to note that Pope Benedict was a student of Christian history, fully aware of the atrocities committed by Pope Urban II and Christendom using the "sword" during the Crusades. The pope's use of the quote drew international backlash from those who found it a misrepresentation of Islamic beliefs and culture. Although he later claimed that the quote did not reflect his own views toward Islam but was instead meant to "draw out the essential relationship between faith and reason," it is notable that he looked toward Islam, and not Christianity's own Crusades, for the association between violence and religious fervor.

## "It Isn't Even the Past"

In 1901, historian William Stearns Davis noted that the crusaders "sought no worldly gain, but to wash out their sins in infidel blood." This idea holds true not only for the Christian crusaders, but also for Islamist terrorists some thousand years later. The combination of unspeakable violence and deep faith defines both sets of "holy warriors" who justified killing in the name of God as an act of devotion—the crusaders at the turn of the first millennium, and the Islamist terrorists at the turn of the second.

Writer William Faulkner said, "The past is never dead; it isn't even the past." The 1099 massacre by the crusaders in Jerusalem, the largest massacre at the holy site in recorded history, became etched in the psyche of the "Middle East" for centuries to come. This explains why, when President George W. Bush referred to his war on terrorism as a "crusade" in 2001, his words raised the specter of a larger war on Islam. This is especially relevant in the context of Bush's rush to invade Iraq in 2003, claiming "God told me to end the tyranny in Iraq." Deus vult, which has become a rallying cry for white supremacists in the US and Europe, has lived on for a thousand years (Fig. 7-6).

**Figure 7-6:** Located in France, this statue of Pope Urban II memorializes the Christian idea of a righteous war. Although the pope's words launched the First Crusade a thousand years ago, they have been echoed to justify repeated Western intervention in the Arab and Islamic worlds for centuries. Cathedral of Clermont Ferrand. Puy de Dome in Auvergne, France.

# Chapter 8
# Clash of the Holy Warriors

The First Crusade was a success from the perspective of the pope and the church. Urban II did not live long enough to see his dream come true; he died fourteen days after the fall of Jerusalem on July 29, 1099, but the news had yet to reach Italy. Four hundred and sixty years after Caliph Umar took Jerusalem without killing a single person in the city, it was now in the hands of the crusaders.

The Crusades resulted in the occupation of five territories in Arab and Turkish lands (Fig. 8-1). Combined, these territories were known as the *Outremer*, which in French means "overseas." The Outremer states were ruled by the French aristocracy and it was this nostalgic connection to Outremer that led to the French to stake a claim over Arab lands after World War I, as discussed in Chapter 2.

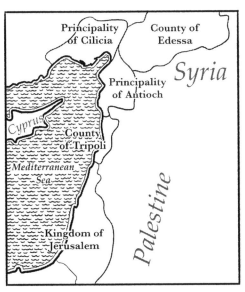

**Figure 8-1:** Outremer: The five regions occupied by the French crusaders. The largest and most strategic was the creation of the Kingdom of Jerusalem in Palestine. To its north was the County of Tripoli (in current-day Lebanon); further north was the Principality of Antioch (in current-day Syria and Turkey), to the northeast was the County of Edessa (in current-day Turkey), and to the northwest was the Principality of Cilicia.

The response from the Muslim Empire did not come quickly; the empire was divided with no central command. It wasn't until 45 years later that the Muslim Turkish Seljuk Sultanate retook the County of Edessa in 1144. In response, Pope Eugene III issued a papal bull (*Quantum praedecessores*) calling for a Second Crusade. This effort was led by King Louis VII of France and King Conrad III of Germany.

As Christian extremism escalated in preparation for the Second Crusade, so did anti-Jewish propaganda, just like it did during the First Crusade. A Cistercian monk from northern France, Radulf, began preaching against the Jews, which led to massacres committed against Jews in a number of German cities.

It is interesting to note that, since it took months to travel to Palestine, much of the crusading nobility took their wives on the mission with them. This created several intriguing stories! Louis VII was a pious Christian who was willing to die for the cause; his wife, Queen Eleanor of Aquitaine, came from a wealthy family in southern France and grew up in the public eye. She was the most eligible bachelorette in Europe when she married Louis VII at age 17.

At 25, she was smart and accomplished in her own right and did not buy into the Crusade ideals. Louis VII was deeply in love with her, but some scholars suggest that she was already bored of him and considered him a weak leader. She reluctantly agreed to join Louis on the mission, but the relationship deteriorated throughout the trip.

It reached a boiling point once they arrived in the Outremer state of Antioch. In those days, royals needed papal approval to get divorced, and in order to receive it, they needed a convincing reason. Queen Eleanor threatened Louis with a divorce on the grounds that they were too closely related; they were third cousins. Louis did not tolerate her public threats and insults; he had her arrested and she was then forced to travel to Jerusalem against her will (Fig. 8-2).

Upon Queen Eleanor's return to France, she requested an annulment of her marriage, but her request was rejected by Pope Eugene III. She began an affair with Henry II, the duke of Normandy, and was subsequently able to attain an annulment. She married the duke and when he became the king of England, she became a queen for the second time.

**Figure 8-2:** Queen Eleanor of Aquitaine depicted in an 1858 oil-on-canvas painting by Frederick Sandys. The painting is displayed at the National Museum Cardiff.

On a political level, the Second Crusade was a monumental failure. The largest Christian army to ever assemble in Outremer was unable to win a single victory against the Muslims. Both King Louis and King Conrad returned to Europe, embarrassed by their failures.

## A Warrior is Born

Some ten years before the Second Crusade, a boy named Yusuf (which is Arabic for Joseph) was born in 1137 to a Kurdish family. Kurds are a proud people who are Muslim and ethnically distinct from Arabs. Yusuf was born in the town of Tikrit, located in Mesopotamia (present-day Iraq).

Yusuf came from a noble family; both his father and grandfather had served as governors of Tikrit. Yusuf grew up in a loving family and spent his early childhood in Damascus, which was not part of the Outremer but rather within the Islamic Empire. Damascus, Baghdad, and Cairo made up the Islamic Empire's centers of education and civilization.

Yusuf grew up in the heart of the city, right next to the Great Mosque (the Umayyad Mosque) with its courtyards, arches, and elegant dome. The Great Mosque, which now is one of the oldest and largest in the world, contains the shrine of John the Baptist, where it is said his head is buried. Although John the Baptist is primarily a Christian figure, he is also revered in Islam as a prophet.

In this cosmopolitan city of Damascus was a large pioneering hospital. The concept of doctors making morning teaching rounds on patients was established there, a concept which later was adapted in Europe and subsequently in the US. It is the standard practice by which I and generations of physicians have been trained.

Growing up, Yusuf loved Arabic poetry and history. He also learned all about the pedigrees of Arabian horses and became an excellent horseman. In school, Yusuf learned that Damascus had been liberated from the Roman Empire some 500 years earlier by a heroic warrior by the name of Khalid ibn al-Walid. Yusuf learned about recent history as well, including the brutal massacre of Muslims in the city of Jerusalem about 50 years earlier by what his people considered fanatic extremist Christian invaders (the First Crusade).

Yusuf was but 11 years old when Louis VII came to the edge of Damascus on his way to Jerusalem as part of the Second Crusade. Damascus was too formidable for Louis to conquer, but in the three-day battle for the city, Yusuf's beloved older brother, Shahanshah, was killed by the crusaders.

Yusuf would later be known by his bestowed name, Salah ad-Din (Saladin). In these formative years, Saladin came to the conclusion that the Muslim Empire was weak and therefore an easy target for external invaders due to the internal divisions among the self-serving leaders within the once-glorious empire. Teenage boys, like Saladin, wondered where brave men like Umar and Khalid had gone.

Instead of lamenting the past, Yusuf decided to take action in the name of his homeland. His story is well documented by the French historian Anne-Marie Eddé in her biographic book *Saladin*. According to Eddé, Saladin accompanied his uncle, a military commander, to Cairo. There, his character, intellectual curiosity, and bravery were noticed by the leadership of the time.

By the age of thirty, Yusuf became a governing leader in Egypt. His meteoric rise in Egypt is comparable to that of the biblical and

Qur'anic Joseph in Egypt. The Muslim Empire's Abbasid Caliph, based in Baghdad, benefitted from Yusuf's counsel, as Egypt was under constant threat of being invaded by the crusaders. Walking around Cairo today, you can still see the fortification walls which Saladin built in the twelfth century to protect the city from crusader invasions (Fig. 8-3).

**Figure 8-3:** Shown are fortifications around the city of Cairo, built during Saladin's rule.

In Cairo, Yusuf became beloved by the people for his austerity programs for the poor. The most respected Jewish scholar, physician, and philosopher of the time, Maimonides, who was facing discrimination in Spain, moved to live in Cairo under Saladin's protection.

In his mid-thirties, Yusuf became the governor of the entire region from Syria to Egypt, abutting right up to the Outremer. This unification of the Muslim Empire, under the leadership of the Abbasid Caliphate power in Baghdad, was a game changer. It was after this reunification that the Caliph bestowed upon Yusuf the title of "Salah al-Din," (meaning "Righteousness of the Faith") and from which the westernized version "Saladin" was adapted (Fig. 8-4).

The historian John Man provides an exquisite account of Yusuf's life as a young man and later as a commander in his book, *Saladin*.

**Figure 8-4:** A romanticized portrait of Saladin by
the nineteenth-century French artist Gustave Dore.

Saladin spent the next decade under the aegis of the Caliph in
Baghdad, unifying the other disparate regions within the Muslim
Empire from Morocco all the
way to Yemen, including the
Hejaz region. During this time,
there were a number of skir-
mishes between the Muslim
Empire and the Kingdom of
Jerusalem, ruled by King Baldwin
IV. Baldwin was known as the
Leper King, as he suffered from
a severe form of the disease. In
one of these skirmishes, Baldwin
was almost killed, and in May
1180 he asked for a truce, which
Saladin accepted (Fig. 8-5).

**Figure 8-5:** Image of the Leper King
(played by actor Edward Norton) in
the 2005 movie *Kingdom of Heaven*. In
a fictionalized version of the Crusades,
Director Ridley Scott gave more of a
fair and balanced view of Muslims than
is standard in Hollywood.

## The Original Terrorist

The man who emerged as Saladin's true enemy was Raynald of Châtillon, a French crusader who traveled with Louis VII in the Second Crusade. Raynald was not the typical "holy warrior," purely driven by a willingness to kill and die for God; he had a particular hunger for power, looting, and blood. The author John Man described Raynald as "brutal, deceitful, vengeful and shameless."

In Outremer, the second-most important state after Jerusalem was Antioch. Antioch was a historic city of the Roman Empire; it was where the Roman Emperor Heraclius was based during the Battle of Yarmouk (discussed in Chapter 6).

Antioch's princess, Constance, had been married at 8 years of age and was widowed at 22 when her husband was killed. Raynald knew that it was critical for each of the Outremer states to have a male lord, so he schemed and got the support of the king of Jerusalem (the Leper King's uncle at the time) to go to Antioch and marry the noble Constance. Soon, he eyed the Christian island of Cyprus in the Mediterranean, not far from Antioch.

For Raynald to travel to and attack Cyprus, he needed significant funding. The wealthiest person in Antioch was the patriarch of the state, Aimery, who was not initially willing to commit his money to Raynald's quest. According to the historian William of Tyre, Raynald had Aimery arrested, stripped naked, and beaten; he then had him placed in the sun with honey put on his wounds so that insects would attack him. The old man ultimately relented, and Raynald soon had the money for his voyage.

In Cyprus, Raynald and his men looted monasteries and abused nuns. They kidnapped citizens and demanded large sums of money in return, their pillaging akin to that of ISIS at the turn of the second millennium. Historian Lars Brownworth summarized Raynald's acts in Cyprus as "a three-week-long spree of murder, rape and carnage across the Christian island."

Once Constance died, Raynald was no longer welcome in Antioch; his violence had become widely known, and he soon fell out of favor. However, the royalty in Jerusalem, who had always supported Raynald, came to his aid once again. Fortunately for Raynald, there was another young widow! Stephanie of Milly (Etiennette de Milly) lived in Kerak, a castle located east of the Dead Sea in what is now Jordan. Kerak was along the route of Muslim pilgrims traveling from Damascus to Mecca. By marrying Stephanie, Raynald became the master of the castle, a title indicative of early Christianity's dismissal of women and treatment of marriage as a financial transaction.

Displeased with the truce between Saladin and King Baldwin IV, Raynald developed a terrorist group with the aim to travel south to Hejaz and attack Islam's holiest sites, Mecca and Medina. He specifically planned to target the tomb of the Prophet Muhammad in Medina. Raynald planned this attack during the Muslim pilgrimage season in the spring of 1183. He and his men took ships down the Red Sea to enter Hejaz. The ships were primarily built at Kerak and then transported to the port city of Aqaba by camel. Aqaba, you may recall from Chapter 3: Invaders from the West, was the staging ground for Feisal when he was traveling in the opposite direction, up north to the Levant as part of British attack.

Historical accounts document the arrival of three ships in the town of Aydhab on the west coast of the Red Sea, directly across from Hejaz (Fig. 8-6).

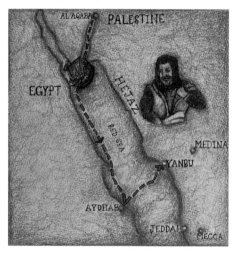

**Figure 8-6:** Map depicting the route that Raynald of Châtillon took with the aim of attacking the burial place of the Prophet Muhammad in the city of Medina. The artist's depiction of Raynald in the upper right corner is based on available accounts.

Aydhab was the primary port city in Egypt that pilgrims from Africa departed from en route to Hejaz. The Raynald crusaders plundered and looted the city of Aydhab; they killed some pilgrims and took others as hostages for ransom. The terrorists also burnt sixteen ships that were carrying pilgrims who had just returned from Jeddah. A few days later, they crossed the Red Sea and arrived in Rabigh, a small port town north of Jeddah. Most likely they were aiming for Jeddah, where the loot would have been much larger, but it is possible that poor navigation led the crusaders off course. Jeddah, you will recall from Chapter 2, is where British officials, including T.E. Lawrence, met with the sons of the Sharif of Mecca to strike a deal in the beginning of the twentieth century.

John Man estimates that it took Raynald's force approximately six weeks to travel from Aqaba to Rabigh. Saladin, who was in Harran (now southern Turkey), received intelligence about the attacks and dispatched immediate orders to his admiral in Cairo, Husam al-Din Lu'lu. The admiral intercepted the crusader force in Rabigh, preventing Raynald from reaching the holy sites. While Lu'lu's force was able to kill or capture the crusaders and free the Muslim captives, Raynald escaped to Kerak. Afterward, Saladin took an oath that he would never forgive Raynald.

A few months later, in November 1183, Saladin arrived with a military force looking for Raynald at the Kerak Castle. The timing of his arrival was interesting—a wedding ceremony was taking place inside the castle (Fig. 8-7)!

Stephanie of Milly's 17-year-old son from her first marriage was getting married to the 11-year-old Isabella, the younger half-sister of the Leper King. Saladin's forces bombarded the castle using mangonels, but once Saladin found out about the wedding, he instructed his troops not to target the tower that housed the newlyweds.

**Figure 8-7:** A contemporary picture of the Kerak Castle, located in Jordan.

Raynald, once again, narrowly escaped; in my research for this book, I have not come across a man with as many lives as he! Once Saladin got word that Raynald had escaped the castle, he ended the siege.

## Fourth of July

By the summer of 1187, Saladin had completed the unification of the Islamic Empire. However, the Leper King Baldwin of Jerusalem, with whom Saladin had a truce, had died in March 1185 and Raynald was again committing acts of mass terrorism against Muslims throughout the newly rejoined Islamic Empire.

Raynald's atrocities again brought Saladin to action. In the spring of 1187, as of hundreds of Muslim pilgrims were returning from Mecca, Raynald attacked them, and those who survived were taken as prisoners to Kerak Castle. Raynald received a letter from Saladin demanding that the hostages be released but he refused. According to Saladin's secretary and biographer Imad ad-Din al-Isfahani, "The sultan swore he would take [Raynald's] life with his own hand."

Because King Baldwin of Jerusalem had no children, his sister Sibylla (Sibylle in French) became queen; she quickly married a newly arrived French knight, Guy of Lusignan, so that Jerusalem would have a king. King Guy, Raynald, and the other leaders of the Outremer states combined their forces to face Saladin. Their armies met near a small town called Hattin, just west of the Palestinian city of Tiberias. The crusaders had some 20,000 troops; Saladin had close to 30,000. Saladin, who was by now a veteran general, outmaneuvered the Crusading forces and overpowered their men. On the Fourth of July, 1187, in an area known as the Horns of Hattin, the crusader army was decisively defeated. Historian Thomas F. Madden called it "the greatest defeat in crusading history." The battle of the Horns of Hattin would become the second-most consequential battle between the so-called "East" and "West," just after Yarmouk (Chapter 6).

The Fourth of July would be celebrated as a day of liberation in many Muslim lands for centuries to come; some 600 years later, they were joined by another group of proud people who also defeated their occupiers to celebrate on the same date: the Americans!

At the end of the battle, the crusading commanders were brought to meet Sultan Saladin; King Guy was the first one into his tent. Guy was scared and wobbly on his feet; Saladin, known for his magnanimity, spoke to him calmly through an interpreter and treated him with honor and respect. Raynald, however, did not receive such courteous treatment. When questioned about his violation of past promises, Raynald defiantly replied, "Kings have always acted thus, I did nothing more." Raynald may have stood his ground, but I am not sure that he could have done anything to save his life that day. Raynald was escorted outside the tent, and Saladin, living up to his twice-sworn oath, beheaded him with his own sword.

After the beheading, a frightened King Guy was reassured by Saladin: "Kings do not kill kings." After a short imprisonment and an oath that he would return to Europe, never to fight Muslims again, King Guy was released.

## The City on the Hill

Saladin entered the city of Jerusalem on October 2, 1187. The city's residents expected a total massacre of the Christian population, just as the crusaders had committed 88 years earlier when they massacred the Muslim population. But just like the Caliph Umar in the seventh century, Saladin prohibited violence when he took the city.

Women whose husbands were taken prisoner at Hattin came to Saladin asking for his help and he in turn freed their husbands. For the women who had lost their fathers or husbands in that battle, he provided financial assistance. Queen Sibylla was allowed to join her husband, King Guy. Stephanie, the widow of Raynald, was treated respectfully, and her son Humphrey, who had been taken prisoner at Hattin, was freed so that he could join his mother. Echoing the biblical Cyrus the Great and the historical Caliph Umar, Saladin allowed the Jewish people to resettle in the city of Jerusalem.

Whereas the crusaders had taken over the Al-Haram al-Sharif (the Temple Mount) and defiled the Al-Aqsa Mosque by turning it into a stable for horses, Saladin respected the Church of the Holy Sepulchre. He remembered the oath that Caliph Umar had given to the patriarch Sophronius some 550 years earlier, a promise that this church, the holiest in Christendom, would always be protected by Islam. Saladin had entered Jerusalem on a Saturday and the next day, Sunday services were conducted at the Church of the Holy Sepulchre.

Historian John Man noted that in the reconquest of Jerusalem, "Islam was victorious twice over, militarily and morally." The historical novelist, Percy Newby, added that "The crusaders were fascinated by a Muslim leader who possessed virtues they assumed were Christian" (Fig. 8-8).

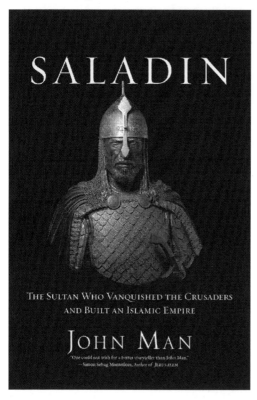

**Figure 8-8:** Cover image of the book *Saladin* by author John Man. Jonathan Phillips, professor of history at the University of London, wrote of Saladin that it was "impossible to think of another figure from history who dealt such a deep wound to a people [Christians] and a faith [Christendom] . . . and yet became so admired."

## Chivalry

As a young boy, my favorite book was the nineteenth-century historical adventure novel *The Three Musketeers* by the French author Alexandre Dumas. I was fascinated by the culture of chivalry, honor, and bravery exhibited by the knights in the book.

*Chivalry*—the informal code of piety, manners, honor, and nobility—that was developed in twelfth-century France was directly linked to the Christian institution of knighthood. However, author James Wasserman wrote that chivalry developed from a "combination of Germanic military codes, Muslim warrior ideals, and Christian devotion," indicating that its origins may be grounded in Islam as well.

The roots of chivalry in Europe harken back to the eighth century, when the Muslim Empire ruled Spain. Abd al-Rahman al-Ghafiqi, originally from Yemen, climbed the leadership ladder to become governor of the Islamic Empire in Spain. Across the Pyrenees Mountains, the natural border between Spain and France was Aquitaine, at that time the ancestral homeland of Queen Eleanor. A regional conflict with Duke Odo of Aquitaine led Ghafiqi to cross the Pyrenees and invade Bordeaux, Aquitaine's largest city. The local French people saw in Ghafiqi's army "the first armored knights in all of Europe, the first armored cavalry," according to author Michael Hamilton Morgan. He added, "It will soon be lost to history that one of European courtly mythology—the armored knight on horseback, and his weaponry and tactics—will soon come from this fearsome 'alien' invader. Mounted knights and armor are really Muslim imports to Europe."

The renowned Spanish author, Vicente Blasco Ibáñez, later added that "Europe did not know chivalry, or its adopted literature or sense of honor before the arrival of Arabs in Andalusia [term used for Spain during Muslim rule] and the wide presence of their knights and heroes." The concept of the armored knight on horseback as an Arab Muslim import is another historical omission from Western popular culture.

In Arabic the word for chivalry is *Adab*. In Arab families around the world, every young boy hears that word from his mother perhaps a few times a week, and to some boys it is said daily! Within the Arab desert tribal life in the early first millennium, the concepts of honor, bravery, and generosity were lauded as core values of who they were as people. The only entertainment that existed for them was poetry. These values represented the ethos of the poems said in tents and under the shining light of the moon in cool desert evenings.

Enter into this formula the Arabian horse, the symbol of Arab identity and prowess. Many young men protected their horses by keeping them in their own tents; it is said that this close connection between a horse and his rider led to the development of both the intelligence and affinity for humans that are the hallmarks of the Arabian horse.

All pure Arabian horses are thought to descend from the blood-lines of five mares: Ekhailan, Ebian, Saqlawi, Hmadani, and Hadban. The legendary story of these five mares dates back to the Prophet Muhammad, who himself was a great lover of horses. It is said that the Prophet Muhammad led his entire herd of horses loose at an oasis while they were thirsty. Before the herd reached the water, he called them back; only five mares returned. It is the trait of loyalty that made these five mares the Prophet's favorites and earned them the name Al Khamsa, meaning "The Five" in Arabic.

Just as the bloodline of the Arabian horse can be found in almost every modern breed of horse in the world today, so had the virtues of the original Arabian knight (*faris* in Arabic) been instilled in the formation of the knights of Europe. The culture of the Arabian horse would later also arrive in America; George Washington, who can only be described as the "Father of the United States," rode a gray Arabian horse by the name of Blueskin during the American Revolutionary War. However, Arab and Muslim contributions to European and American culture would soon be omitted from the American consciousness by generations of writers, filmmakers, jour-nalists, and politicians, and consequently the larger global popular culture (Fig. 8-9).

Let me share with you a classic story about the virtues of Arabian knights which is passed from generation to generation in Arab households. It is about a sixth-century knight and poet, Hatim al-Tai, who lived in the town of Ha'il in northern region of the Arabian Peninsula. He was the faris who defined the concept of generosity as part of the knighthood culture and he is touted in the classic *One Thousand and One Nights* for his benevolence. One day, hungry and tired travelers approached Hatim's tent looking for a place to stay during their travels. Hatim did not have enough food to feed them, but out of the obligation to fulfill his duty of hospitality, he sacrificed his horse that he had loved so much so that his guests did not go hungry.

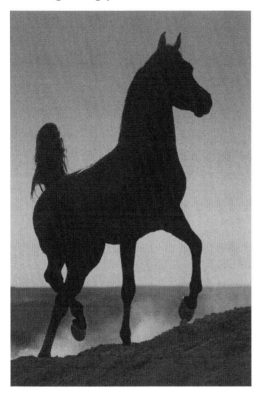

**Figure 8-9:** There is no horse more beautiful than the desert Arabian horse with their characteristic chiseled head, large eyes, long arching neck, and high tail carriage. Known for their endurance and intelligence, the breed originated in the Arabian Peninsula but became the progenitor of the classic American racehorse, the thoroughbred. All thoroughbreds have ancestry that traces back to three Arabian stallions exported in the seventeenth and eighteenth centuries.

To this date, it is a proverbial phrase in Arab culture that someone who is overwhelmingly kind is "more generous than Hatim." The knight and poet was mentioned by the Prophet Muhammad for his altruism, setting the standard of bravery, honor, and piety that Arabian knights took with them to foreign lands during the massive expansion of the Islamic Empire in the seventh century. One of those lands was Spain, where Arab and Spanish poets intermingled and romanticized these traits for centuries, giving rise to the concept of chivalry.

I started this book with my experience of watching the movie *Back to the Future* as a young boy with my friends, and how embarrassed I felt by the nefarious depiction of "Arabs." There was another movie experience that had a similar impact on me. I have loved horses since I was little boy, so when I got to see the 1979 movie *The Black Stallion* with my friends, I was beyond excited. In this movie, based on the 1940s Walter Farley book by the same name, the renowned Francis Ford Coppola wasted no time peddling the classic Hollywood agenda—the "Arab" as the villain. An "Arab" man abuses the titular black stallion and then physically attacks the young American boy who loves the horse, which had nothing to do with the storyline. Its only function was to generate contempt for the "Arab" character. This is part of the ongoing decades-old Hollywood narrative of propagating negative imagery of Arab and Muslim peoples and cultures.

This generalization and cultural stereotyping in *The Black Stallion* are also seen in the film's credits. Instead of naming the character who attacks the boy and abuses the stallion, the character is simply listed as "Arab"!

Through films like *Back to the Future* and *The Black Stallion*, both of which were made for a family audience, directors prey on impressionable minds. As a neuroscientist, I am particularly aware that the human brain is very impressionable at a young age. Hate, prejudice, and racial stereotyping can indeed be "uploaded." The impact on a whole generation of children to perceive Arabs and Muslims as "evil" through Hollywood's intentional depictions cannot be underestimated. To quote author William Greider, "Hollywood is our great national entertainer and also the most effective teacher of our young."

## A Lion Roars

Unlike a movie, Saladin's story does not end after his valiant recapture of Jerusalem. Pope Urban III is said to have died from the shock of the news that Jerusalem had been captured by Muslim forces; some theologians in Western Europe proclaimed it a sign of the apocalypse.

It only took the new pope, Gregory VIII, nine days to issue his papal bull (*Audita tremendi*) calling for the Third Crusade. He ordered a seven-year truce throughout Europe, commanding kings to stop fighting each other and prepare for a holy war against Arabs instead. Three primary crusading kings emerged: German Emperor Frederick I of Barbarossa (also known as Redbeard), King Philip Augustus of France, and King Richard I of England.

Frederick I of Germany was the first to depart for Palestine. He led 20,000 knights and thousands of additional soldiers; no single army so large had ever left Europe before. Frederick left Regensburg, Germany, in May 1189. As he and his forces approached the Outremer state of Antioch in June 1190, the seventy-year-old emperor fell from his horse while crossing a river and died as a result. Frederick was not forgotten. Hitler's invasion of the Soviet Union during WWII was nicknamed "Operation Barbarossa." In this invasion, soldiers were told to target "Jewish Bolshevik sub-humans," the "Asiatic flood," and the "Mongol hordes." Such language fuels the doctrine of White supremacy and continues to drive nostalgia for the Crusades in Europe and the United States.

Richard of England had just been crowned at age 32. He was the son of Queen Eleanor of Aquitaine, who had gone on the Second Crusade as a newly wedded wife of Louis VII and later married Henry II of England. Richard was the product of this remarriage. In many ways, he bore similarities to Saladin: he was intelligent, charismatic, and loved both poetry and horses. Just like Saladin, he entered the army at a very young age; Richard began his military service at 16, only two years older than Saladin had been when he entered the armed forces. During his time in the army, Richard was bestowed the title *Coeur de Lion* ("Lionheart") for his skills in combat.

Before coming to England for his coronation, Richard lived most of his life in Aquitaine, France, in his mother's ancestral land. He spoke French, and based on the sources I reviewed, he most likely did not speak any English (Fig. 8-10).

Richard the Lionheart was crowned king of England at Westminster Abbey in London on September 3, 1189, exactly a month before Saladin's recapture of Jerusalem. English tradition barred Jews from his investiture ceremony, but some Jewish leaders arrived with gifts for the new king. According to

**Figure 8-10:** Richard I, anointed during his coronation in Westminster Abbey. Image from a thirteenth-century chronicle.

the twelfth-century archdeacon of Middlesex, Ralph de Diceto, courtiers stripped and flogged them. When rumors spread that Richard had ordered the killing of Jews, the Jewish population in London was targeted by angry mobs. Among those killed was the noted Jewish scholar, Jacob of Orléans. Within a few months, in the middle of the religious fervor surrounding the Third Crusade, Jews in the city of York had to hide within the keep of York Castle, commonly called Clifford Tower. The crusaders who surrounded York Castle demanded that the Jews be baptized or be killed. Rabbi Yom Tov of Joigny and the other men killed their own wives and children and then set fire to the wooden structure of the tower, choosing to burn alive rather than leave their fates to the crusaders. The few who survived the fire were killed by the mob, again demonstrating the anti-Semitic fervor of Christian extremism.

To fund the Third Crusade, a new tax of 10 percent on all revenue and movable properties was levied on the English people; the tax was called the Saladin tithe. It was collected by bishops, priests, and heads of local churches. Those who refused to pay were imprisoned. The so-called Saladin tithe was the largest tax ever collected in the history of England up to that point.

Across the English Channel, in France, the 24-year-old King Philip Augustus was at the helm. The two leaders could not have been more different. Philip of France was a prototypical politician, while Richard of England a warrior. Richard had inherited the Angevin region of France, which included his mother's Aquitaine, increasing political tension between the monarchs. The decision of the two kings to travel together to Palestine projected an image of unity between the crusaders for the masses, but it had more implicit political implications as well; it ensured that neither could stir up trouble in the other's absence. To consolidate an optic of the alliance, Richard was engaged to Philip's sister, Alys.

## On the Way to Palestine

While the crusaders before them had taken land routes, Philip and Richard decided to travel by sea. They traveled separately to the Italian island of Sicily as the first stop on the way to the holy land.

At the time, Sicily's former queen had been Richard's sister, Joan, whose husband William II, died in 1189. After the king's death, Sicily was conquered by his illegitimate cousin, Tancred, who stripped Joan of her lands. When Richard arrived, he insisted that Tancred repay Joan's dowry; after Richard spent months in Sicily laying siege to Messina, Tancred submitted to the demands.

During this time, the relationship between Richard and Philip only deteriorated. Richard's mother, Queen Eleanor, joined them in Sicily, but with a surprise; displeased with her son's engagement to Philip's sister, she brought with her Princess Berengaria of Navarre (from northern Spain), whom she had selected to be Richard's future wife. Consequently, Richard broke his engagement to Alys. Joan grew close to Berengaria during the stay in Sicily. With her work accomplished, Queen Eleanor returned to France. At their next stop, the island of Cyprus, Richard and Berengaria were married.

In Cyprus, Richard received another guest: Guy, the former king of Jerusalem that had been freed from imprisonment by Saladin on the condition that he would return to Europe, never again to take arms against Muslims. As it turned out, Guy broke his promise as soon as he was released. King Guy joined a crusading army (formed of men that had also been freed by Saladin following the Hattin battle!) as the commander and laid siege to the Palestinian port city of Acre (*Akka* in Arabic). Guy traveled to Cyprus to ask Richard for reinforcements to topple the city; consequently, Acre became Richard's point of attack on Palestine.

Richard, with some 150 ships holding 6,000 to 8,000 men, arrived at Acre on June 7, 1191. It was easy for him to conquer the city with the help of Guy and his forces. Subsequently, negotiations through envoys ensued between Richard and Saladin on the exchange of prisoners of the Acre battle. Apparently during these negotiations, Richard, who was known for his temper, would commit an act that is seared in crusader history. He ordered 2,600 Muslim civilians (men, women, and children) to be escorted outside the city wall and then executed. The mass killings occurred on August 20, 1191, on a hilly area outside Acre called Ayyadieh (and therefore the Christian and Islamic chronicles refer to it as the *massacre at Ayyadieh*). This was the second largest mass killing of Muslims by the crusaders since the Jerusalem genocide during the First Crusade 92 years earlier. A number of the accounts presented in this chapter are based on the *Itinerarium Peregrinorum et Gesta Regis Ricardi*, which is said to be a first-hand contemporary (1189–1192) Latin narrative of the Third Crusade that has been translated to English by the Irish-born historian Helen Nicholson.

These massacres would have a deep impact on the psyche of the Arab and Muslim consciousness for centuries to come. Leaders like Saladin, who were well versed in Islamic literature and jurisprudence, understood that Islam placed clear-cut limitations on reciprocating with barbarity. The concept of jihad in Islam involves killing from a purely military standpoint but within explicit boundaries as defined in the Qur'an: "Fight in the Way of Allah those who fight you, but transgress not the limits. Truly, Allah likes not the transgressors" (2:190). Saladin commanded his army to abide by the Qur'anic words. He would also tell his commanders, "I warn you against shedding blood, indulging in it and making a habit of it, for blood never sleeps." Let's fast forward 1,000 years to the current "Middle East," which definitely lacks leaders of Saladin's character and virtue; allowing the emergence of terrorist groups such as Al-Qaeda and ISIS, whose actions resemble that of the fanatical crusaders.

At this point it had become clear to the French king, Philip, that the soldiers of the crusading army viewed Richard as their main leader, and consequently, with the excuse of health issues (he did have intermittent health issues the whole time), he decided to return to France. Richard was wise to political maneuvering and obtained an oath from Philip that he would not make any moves on acquiring his lands in France in his absence. Given the intensity of the early campaign in Palestine, Richard also sent his wife Berengaria back home to France, but his sister, Joan, remained with him.

## March to Jerusalem

Richard was too seasoned of a general to head directly to Jerusalem from Acre straightaway. Over the next few months, he marched his army south along the coastline under the protection of his ships as they advanced by sea.

Saladin's army tracked him all along. During this time, a number of battles ensued; the most notable took place in a forest area close to the seaside village of Arsuf. There, Richard landed a major victory against Saladin before overtaking the port city of Jaffa and continuing his march toward what is now the Gaza region (Fig. 8-11).

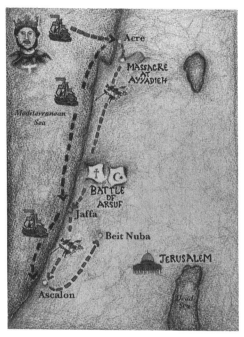

**Figure 8-11:** Richard the Lionheart's military advance in Palestine. He arrived in Acre from Cyprus in June 1191. His strategy was to march south, hugging the coast to protect his right flank while waiting for the right opportunity to go inland and attack Jerusalem. After a major win at the Battle of Arsuf, he captured Jaffa and subsequently Ascalon. He next headed toward Jerusalem and reached as far as the town of Beit Nuba in June 1192. In the upper left quarter is an artist depiction of Richard based on available accounts.

Although they were enemies, a mutual respect developed between the two opposing commanders. During one battle, Richard the Lionheart fell from his horse and was left on the battlefield; Saladin sent him two Arabian horses so that the fight would be fair. On another occasion when Saladin received news that Richard had fallen ill, he sent his own doctor to attend to Richard.

Despite his victories, Richard began to realize that venturing inland toward Jerusalem away from the coastal protection provided by his ships was going to be much more challenging. To avoid defeat, Richard made an interesting proposal; he suggested that his sister, Joan (initially without her knowledge), marry Saladin's brother, Saif al-Din, and that after the marriage, the couple would rule Palestine. There were significant discussions about the marriage proposal, but Richard's insistence that Saif al-Din convert to Christianity ended the arrangement.

Richard finally ventured inland and reached the Palestinian village of Beit Nuba, just twelve miles from Jerusalem, in January 1192. At this point he realized that the conquest of Jerusalem, the reason for his Crusade, would be a formidable undertaking; he then made the most consequential decision of his Crusade: he decided not to proceed and extended a truce offering to Saladin. Through envoys, he entered into negotiations with Saladin, hoping to achieve a face-saving settlement.

The leaders agreed upon a three-year truce. Many in the crusading army were dissatisfied by Richard's decision, feeling that their quest had been in vain. However, Saladin allowed them to enter Jerusalem and go to the Church of the Holy Sepulchre. Richard did not join his men; his honor stood in the way, as he had sworn to return Jerusalem to Christendom.

Despite their extensive negotiations, and contrary to depictions in popular culture, Richard and Saladin never met in person. On October 9, 1192, Richard boarded a ship home, never to return to Palestine again.

A month later Saladin returned home to Damascus. At the end of February of the following year, Saladin became ill. He developed a fever that lasted days, lost his appetite, and became very lethargic. He died at home at dawn on March 4, 1193. The sultan had given all of his wealth to the poor throughout his life and had no fortune to his name when he died, unlike the corrupt leaders of the "Middle East" today. There were not even enough funds to pay for his funeral, so it was paid for by family members. He is buried where he grew up as a child, right next to the Umayyad Mosque in Damascus.

Saladin's chivalry and honor would not be forgotten, even in the West. In the fourteenth century, Dante's *Divine Comedy*—a core text of the Western literary canon—includes Saladin as the most lauded non-Christian right next to the likes of Homer, Plato, and Caesar as a "great hearted soul." His legacy in the West is best summarized by the words of Karen Armstrong, the former Catholic religious sister turned renowned author: "Saladin's career reminds us that moral charisma and integrity can be recognized and honored by people on both sides of a vicious conflict."

As far as Europe's leading crusader, Richard the Lionheart would never see his wife again; he did not seek out Queen Berengaria upon his return to Europe. It is said that she remained in France, which engendered her reputation as "the only English queen never to set foot in the country."

In March 1199, Richard was hit by a crossbow in his shoulder in an attempted assassination; soon, the wound became gangrenous. On April 6, 1199, he died in the arms of his mother, Queen Eleanor, in Châlus, France. His heart was buried in Normandy, France, while his body was buried next to his father at Fontevraud Abbey in Anjou, France, where Eleanor was also later buried (Fig. 8-12).

**Figure 8-12:** Richard the Lionheart had a deep connection to the history of England and its people. This image shows his statue outside the Palace of Westminster, Houses of Parliament, London. The symbol of the three lions, depicted on the cover of this book on the leftmost warrior, is the Royal Arms of England (the Royal Banner). It comes from King Richard's seal which depicts three lions, most likely representing Richard's three principal positions as king of England, duke of Normandy, and duke of Aquitaine.

## The Day When Constantinople Cried

After the Third Crusade, Jerusalem was still in the hands of the Muslim Empire. In 1198, a new pope, Innocent III, was elected; he soon called for a Fourth Crusade to reclaim the holy lands. Based on the failures of the Second and Third Crusades, there emerged a popular thought that the Byzantine Roman emperors in Constantinople had not given their maximum support during the previous Crusades. All Crusades except Richard's had taken land routes which traveled through Constantinople. Although the intellectual and artistic hierarchy in Constantinople felt the crusaders were doing God's work by fighting the Muslims, they viewed them as backward fundamentalists. The crusaders on their part felt that the half-hearted support from the Orthodox Christians of Constantinople contributed to the failures of the previous crusades. Therefore, the crusaders elected to attack Constantinople itself. For the first time in crusading history, Christians attacked a Christian city!

Beginning on April 12, 1204, the crusaders terrorized the city of Constantinople for three days. Women, young girls, and even nuns were raped. Inside the grand Church of the Holy Apostles, the tombs of former emperors were attacked, and once their rings and jewelry had been stolen, the bodies were thrown out.

Other churches throughout the city were also looted. Grand artistic works of the first millennium were stolen, then melted for their gold and silver. One of the grandest works of antiquity, the large bronze statue of Hercules, suffered the same fate, as did the beautiful statue of Helen of Troy. Fortunately, one major work of art survived: the famous bronze horses adorning the hippodrome in the city; these were sent to Venice (Fig. 8-13). Like the future terrorist group ISIS's vandalizing and looting multiple cities in northern Iraq and Syria, the crusaders destroyed multiple historical pieces of art and monuments in the name of their holy mission.

After ransacking Constantinople and stripping the city of its wealth, the men of the Fourth Crusade decided to go back home rather than proceed to Palestine. The legacy of the Fourth Crusade is not that they failed to go and capture Jerusalem—Richard the Lionheart also failed in that regard—but rather they created a schism in Christianity that lasts to this date. There was no Protestantism in Christendom at this point in history; it was, broadly speaking, a unified religion. But the crusaders came from Latin churches, while those in Constantinople spoke Greek. The Crusade of April 1204 would forever separate Roman Christianity from the followers of the Eastern Orthodox church based in Constantinople.

**Figure 8-13:** The Horses of Saint Mark (Triumphal Quadriga) dating back to the second or third century. In this photo, the horses are located inside St. Mark's Basilica in Venice, where they were taken from Constantinople during the Fourth Crusade. They were forcibly removed from the Basilica by Napoleon in 1797 and taken to Paris for the design of the Arc de Triomphe du Carrousel. They were returned to Venice in 1815.

The Christians in Constantinople wondered how men bearing the cross of Christianity could kill other Christians so violently; a thousand years later, Muslims wondered the same of ISIS. One Constantinople senator who witnessed the violent takeover contrasted it to the fall of Jerusalem to Saladin, saying it would have been better for the city to have been conquered by the Muslim "infidels." He did not regard the crusaders as true representatives of Christianity; instead, they were "exposed as frauds . . . trampling on the cross for the sake of little gold."

## A Children's Crusade

The failure of the Fourth Crusade to conquer Jerusalem further incited religious zeal in western Europe, especially in northern France and parts of Germany. The knights, who were of the highest class, had failed, which led some men in the working class to believe that they, not the aloof and out-of-touch nobility, were better suited to achieve victory.

The subsequent Crusade, a collection of attempts by laymen to take Jerusalem, none of which ever actually reached Palestine, are collectively known as the "Children's Crusades." The most well-known of these efforts was undertaken by Nicholas of Cologne, a shepherd boy from Germany. Nicholas had a vision that he must travel to southern Italy and there, at the Mediterranean, the sea would part as it had done for Moses. Nicholas believed that his followers would then be able to walk to Jerusalem, where they would convert all Muslims to Christianity.

Nicholas quickly became a public figure, and thousands joined him on the journey. Unfortunately, large numbers died during the crossing of the Alps to Italy. Those who made it were disappointed to find that the sea did not part; they returned home in humiliation.

This was the second major disappointment for Pope Innocent III. Seeking redemption, he called for the Fifth Crusade. His new strategy was a plan that Richard the Lionheart had considered after his failure to capture Jerusalem. Innocent and his church recognized that Palestine was straddled by two strongholds of the Muslim Empire, Syria and Egypt. The Muslim army's resources during the previous crusades had all been imported through Egypt, so Innocent suggested a surprise attack on Egypt instead of a direct bid for Palestine. Capturing Cairo, he believed, would surely lead to the capture of Jerusalem.

In the spring of 1218, the crusaders of the Fifth Crusade successfully captured the Egyptian port city of Damietta. As they marched forth, the army confronted the sultan of Egypt, Al-Kamil (a nephew of Saladin) at the small town of Mansoura, just north of Cairo. The crusaders made a major military strategic error: they camped in an exposed area right next to the Nile. Al-Kamil, whose forces controlled the dam which regulated water levels, simply flooded the area, trapping the crusaders. Despite the advice of his commanders to destroy the invading crusaders, Al-Kamil let the opposing forces return back to Europe.

# An Emperor's Crusade

Emperor Frederick II of Germany was blamed for the failure of the Fifth Crusade, although he had not been part of the Crusade at all. Frederick was an unusual leader for his time in Europe; he was an intellectual who supported scientific advances and was cynical of the church. Author Lars Brownworth reported a conversation in which Frederick referred to Christians as the "swine" who had polluted Jerusalem. Needless to say, there was a confrontational relationship between Frederick and the popes who had served during his tenure. Frederick had initially agreed to participate in the Fifth Crusade and sailed from Brindisi, Italy, but he fell ill from an epidemic and soon returned home to recover. Because he had not contributed to the Crusade, Frederick was blamed for its failure and was officially excommunicated by Pope Gregory IX in September 1227, the first of his three eventual excommunications.

Jerusalem remained under Muslim control but continued to have a nominal Christian "king"—an honorary title given to the descendants of King Baldwin IV's family. Frederick took the thirteen-year-old Yolande of Brienne as one of his numerous wives; Yolande's father was John of Brienne, king of Jerusalem. Frederick and Yolande were married in Germany, which officially allowed Frederick to claim the title of Christian king of Jerusalem. Frederick had to travel there to be anointed, thus launching an unusual Sixth Crusade.

While Frederick embarked to Palestine with his loyal German military, he had no support from the pope or followers of the Roman Church since he had been excommunicated. Once he arrived in Palestine (at Acre), he entered negotiations with Sultan Al-Kamil.

Al-Kamil and Frederick were seasoned diplomats. Yolande had just died in childbirth, weakening Frederick's claim to Jerusalem; however, Al-Kamil saw that if he could give Frederick entrance into Jerusalem as a "Christian king," a war could be avoided.

The pair came to a truce, the terms of which were that the Muslim holy places of the Al-Haram al-Sharif (Al-Aqsa Mosque and the Dome of the Rock) would remain in Muslim hands as well as the governance of the Muslims in the city. All Christian sites would be governed by the Christians. This was no different from the city's existing reality—the Muslim Empire had already allowed for Christian control over all Christian sites—but for Frederick, this saved face, since he could enter Jerusalem and claim the title of "king."

On March 18, 1229, Frederick entered Jerusalem and went to the Church of the Holy Sepulchre, which was deserted. The patriarch of the Church of the Holy Sepulchre saw the title of "king" as bogus and refused to conduct an inauguration ceremony for Frederick. The Christian population of Jerusalem wanted nothing to do with Frederick. Although he was bedecked in his imperial crown, there would be no coronation ceremony.

Soon afterward, Frederick sailed back to Germany. The pope did not see Frederick's Crusade as a success for Christendom. According to the pope, the excommunicated Frederick was no longer a "real" Christian, and the Muslim holy places of Jerusalem were still in Muslim hands; that was not acceptable.

## The King & the Mongols

In France, the young, pious King Louis IX was likewise not content with the Sixth Crusade; seeing that Jerusalem was not truly in Christendom's hands, he vowed to go on a Crusade at age eighteen.

Louis was a deeply devout Christian who would be remembered in Western literature as one of the greatest crusaders right next to Richard the Lionheart. He was a believer in Egypt as the entry point for the Crusades and studied the failures of the Fifth Crusade, assessed the mistakes made, and decided that he would go to Egypt to conquer Cairo before heading to Palestine.

He arrived in Damietta in 1249, some thirty years after his predecessors of the Fifth Crusade. After taking the port city, he headed to Mansoura, intending to enter Cairo. There, he faced a similar defeat as the men of the Fifth Crusade and retreated to Damietta, where he and the French crusading knights were all taken as prisoners of war, only to be freed after a significant ransom was paid.

Any other king would have immediately returned home, but not Louis; he headed to Palestine. In Acre, he helped the Christian force by building new fortifications. During this renewed effort, however, he came to the same conclusion as Richard the Lionheart: he could not invade Jerusalem. He returned to France after a six-year campaign.

As Louis was returning home, however, there was a much larger storm gathering in the East. In February 1258, the Mongols, led by Hulagu Khan (the grandson of Genghis Khan), invaded Baghdad, killing the caliph and destroying all libraries and historical landmarks. This brought to an end the Golden Age of the Islamic civilization, and an end to its preeminence as the world leader in science and the arts (Chapter 1).

The destruction of the Islamic Empire was celebrated throughout Europe as a great victory. Soon, the Mongols continued westward and entered Syria; they captured Damascus and Aleppo. They made it clear that they intended to march south toward Palestine and Egypt.

In Egypt, with no central command from Baghdad, a hardened group of Muslim fighters, the Mamluks (former slaves of the elite who rebelled against their enslavers), were now in power. The name *Mamluk* translates to "one who was previously owned." The Mamluk sultan executed the Mongol envoys who demanded that he turn over control of Palestine and Egypt. The Mongols had met their match! Commanded by the ruthless and intelligent General Baibars, the Mamluks not only refused to surrender; they wanted revenge.

The two forces met on September 3, 1260, in southwestern Galilee at an area called Ayn Jalut. There, Baibars won a decisive victory, marking the first time that anyone had been able to defeat the formidable Mongols. It was a historic event, one that is also lost from Western historical and popular consciousness. If the Muslims had lost that day, all the great religious sites in Jerusalem, including the Church of the Holy Sepulchre, would have been nothing but figments of our historical imagination today.

Baibars had requested the assistance of the crusaders in the remaining Outremer states to fight the Mongols with him, but they refused. So, after his victory, he turned his sights on them. He attacked their remaining city-states and acted with violence more reminiscent of the crusaders rather than that of Saladin; he killed troops and civilians alike. He destroyed one of the historical cities of the first millennium, Antioch. However, Baibars did not cross the line drawn by Umar and Saladin before him: he did not attack the Christian population of Jerusalem nor destroy Christian landmarks in the holy city (Fig. 8-14).

Back in France, King Louis was by this time in his mid-fifties, but he never relinquished his dream of taking Jerusalem from the Muslim infidels. Louis, by today's definition, was a pure fanatic. For example, his punishment for blasphemy was mutilation of the tongue and lips. Predictably, with his crusading zealotry came anti-Jewish sentiments; he ordered some 12,000 manuscript copies of the Talmud (the central text of Rabbinic Judaism) burned in Paris in the year 1243.

**Figure 8-14:** Bronze bust of Sultan Baibars in Cairo at the National Military Museum of Egypt.

Against the wishes of his nobles, Louis decided to launch another Crusade (the Eighth Crusade—the "Last Crusade" as termed by some historians). His strategic decision was to attack the Muslim state of Tunisia, weakened after the fall of the Abbasid Empire. From my review of original documents, it seems that in selecting Tunisia, Louis hoped to draw the Mamluks of Egypt into a confrontation further away from their stronghold of Cairo.

Louis's forces arrived in Tunisia on July 18, 1270, at the historic area of Carthage. There, while camping in the sizzling summer heat of North Africa, an epidemic of dysentery swept through the troops and many fell sick. Louis died from the illness on August 25, 1270. The last words out of his mouth as recorded by his advisors were "Jerusalem, Jerusalem." On the sands of Tunisia, at Carthage, the last Crusade ended.

**Figure 8-15:** The statue of the crusading French King Louis IX sits in Forest Park in St. Louis, Missouri. I took this picture in July 2020.

Louis was canonized by the Catholic Church in 1297, the only French monarch in history to become a saint. The city where I attended university and medical school, St. Louis, Missouri, is named for the fanatical crusading king of France (Fig. 8-15)!

## The Knights Templar

Throughout the Crusades there was an interesting phenomenon happening in the background. There was a secret society. A society of some of the most violent warriors of the Crusades known as the Knights Templar. They believed their mandate came directly from God. They arguably were the most powerful secret society in the world during the roughly 200-year span of the Crusades. The Knights Templar was founded by the French knight Hugues de Payens in the aftermath of the bloody massacre of the Muslims and Jews in Jerusalem during the First Crusade in July 1099. De Payens and other like-minded knights felt that after the slaughter, there would be significant anger within the local Islamic and Jewish populations, and therefore it was necessary to have a group of crusaders to protect European pilgrims traveling to Jerusalem.

The Templars were given residence inside the then conquered Al-Aqsa Mosque at the Al-Haram al-Sharif (the Temple Mount), the third-holiest site in the Islamic faith, which the Templars also used as a stable for their horses. The name *Templars* comes from the biblical Temple of Solomon, which is believed to be where the Al-Aqsa Mosque compound is located.

The order gathered funds quickly; as their reputation spread in Europe, wealthy families contributed funds and property to what they believed to be the valiant nature of their cause. Within short order, the Templars had properties in countries throughout Europe including France, England, and Spain. The author Conrad Bauer calls the Templars "the first multinational corporation in the history of the world." The group that formed as fighters of Christ under the claim of humility and piety had quickly become a major financial power and the largest independent army of the time.

The Templars acted as warrior monks; they wore white robes, which later had a red cross added to them by Pope Eugene in 1147. Their main claim to fame, however, was their brutality in battle and crimes against Muslim civilians. They also used a unique military tactic known as the squadron charge, a suicide attack. The knights would gather in a tight formation and charge the enemy as fast as possible, knowing that a number of them would die in the maneuver.

Although the Knights Templar have gone into relative obscurity in our historical memory of the Crusades, they have had a lasting impact. On July 22, 2011, a 32-year-old Norwegian man, Anders Behring Breivik, left his mother's flat in Oslo and parked a van containing a bomb outside the Regjeringskvartalet, the government buildings in the center of Oslo; he lit the fuse and left the scene. As Norwegians watched in horror the news of the eight people who died in the explosion, Breivik headed to a summer camp for a youth league on the island of Utøya and shot dead 69 people. Six hours before the attacks, Breivik had posted a video on YouTube depicting himself as a modern-day member of the Knights Templar.

Breivik believed in the need for a modern-day Crusade against Muslims; similar to the Templars, he believed every Muslim should be given the opportunity to convert to Christianity or be killed. He also blamed feminism for eroding the fabric of European society; instead, he advocated for a total restoration of patriarchy. He went on the killing spree to bring attention to his manifesto opposing the rights of Muslims and women; despite his extremism, the court psychiatric evaluation determined that he was not psychotic.

While unusual, Breivik was not alone in his radical contemporary resurrection of the Knights. Several years after his attacks, a 28-year-old Australian man named Brenton Tarrant, who was captivated with the historical battles between Christendom and Islam and saw Anders Breivik as his hero, shot and killed 50 worshippers in two mosques in Christchurch, New Zealand, on March 14, 2019.

A more well-known connection to contemporary politics exists between the Knights Templar and the Ku Klux Klan (KKK). Beyond their eerily similar uniform of white robes, the KKK was also a secret fraternal White nationalist terrorist organization. The KKK, however, emerged in America's South in the 1860s and primarily targeted African Americans. While the first wave of the KKK died out in the early 1870s, it saw a sudden resurgence in 1915. What was the impetus for this second wave? Like so many other foundations of bias and prejudice, the answer can be found in Hollywood.

In February 1915, director D. W. Griffith released the movie *Birth of a Nation* that presented a nostalgic view of the KKK as valiant defenders against "unintelligent" Black men, who were portrayed as sexually aggressive toward White women. The movie was a massive commercial hit; it was shown in the White House East Room to President Woodrow Wilson, his family, and the US cabinet. The movie sparked incidents of violence against African Americans in cities around the country, and within a span just a few months, it inspired the re-birth not of a nation, but of the KKK.

The movie also benefitted a former Methodist minister from Georgia, William J. Simmons. He was already a member of a White supremacist fraternity, the Knights Templar! Once the movie came out, Simmons found documents from the original Klan and accounts from members of the first wave. The look the new twentieth-century KKK adopted was based on the images from the original nineteenth-century KKK as displayed in the movie, which in turn came from the European crusading Knights Templar. Simmons named his group the Knights of the KKK. When the movie played in Atlanta, Simmons and his Klansmen paraded in white robes—many on robed horses—just like in the movie. Within months of the movie's release, the membership of the new KKK reached an estimated 85,000. In 1921, the Klan founded the Gates City Manufacturing Company in Atlanta and produced regalia imitating *Birth of a Nation*'s designs.

The KKK was now here to stay. In 1918, Georgia Governor Hugh M. Dorsey wrote to the National Association for the Advancement of Colored People (NAACP), "I believe that if the Negroes would exert their ultimate influence with the criminal element of their race and stop rapes that it would go a long way towards stopping lynchings." The governor's words illustrate the way in which the KKK's atrocities were permitted by government officials.

Hollywood had stoked the flames of racism, legitimizing public vitriol toward minority populations. The African Americans who were lynched by the KKK in America's South, the young Norwegian victims on the island of Utøya, and the Muslim worshippers shot dead in Christchurch may not have ever heard of the Knights Templar from the twelfth century, but they were all victims of their philosophy. Hollywood was the middleman between the Knights Templar of the twelfth century and the KKK of the twentieth century (Figs. 8-16 and 8-17).

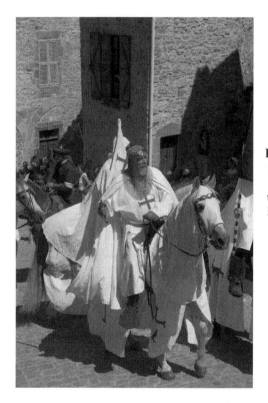

**Figure 8-16:** Annual celebration of the Knights Templar at the Medieval Festival in the town of Cordes-sur-Ciel in Tarn, France, showing the white robes of the men and their horses.

**Figure 8-17:** Photograph from January 1, 1900, of KKK members on horseback showing the same attire as seen in Figure 8-16.

## The Two Prophecies

While the Abbasid Caliphate had a great culture of science and innovation, it lacked a military leader of Saladin's caliber when the Mongols attacked and sacked Baghdad in February 1258.

From its ashes, another Islamic Empire emerged: the Ottoman Empire. The Ottomans knew that in order to stop the continued European Crusades, they needed to do something that had been unachievable for over 1,000 years: capture the Roman Empire's capital, Constantinople.

Mehmed (Mohammad in Turkish), a boy prince, was the heir apparent to the sultan throne. In school he learned a seventh-century hadith (a saying of the Prophet Muhammad): "Verily you shall conquer Constantinople. What a wonderful leader will her leader be, and what a wonderful army will that army be." Mehmed believed the prophecy was speaking about him. When he became sultan at age 21, he would plan to do something that 23 massive armies had failed to do over the previous 1,000 years: conquer the most highly defended city in Europe. Following an eight-week siege and the largest artillery attack in human history to date, he did just that: Mehmed captured Constantinople on May 29, 1453. This marked the end of the Roman Empire's 1,123-year rule of the city that Constantine, the son of Helena (discussed in Chapter 6), had established as the capital of the empire in the fourth century.

There was a second prophecy worth mentioning related to the conquest of Constantinople, this one from Christian orthodox theological literature. It stated that Constantinople would fall just like it was founded, during the reign of an emperor by the name of Constantine who also would have a mother by the name of Helena. Constantinople fell to Mehmed during the reign of Emperor Constantine XI, whose mother's name was Helena Dragaš.

The battle between Mehmed and Constantine was very similar to that of Saladin and Richard the Lionheart—all valiant men. Constantine, it can be argued, was braver than Lionheart who chose to return to Europe. Constantine had the opportunity to escape when Mehmed entered the city, but he chose to fight alongside his soldiers. He reflected back on an ancestral Greek hero, Leonidas (from Chapter 6), who had said, "I would rather die on my feet than live on my knees." Constantine chose to die fighting as a brave man.

The entrance into Constantinople, first by the crusaders in 1204 and then by the Muslims in 1453, each provide a unique glimpse into the differences between the leadership of Western Christianity and Eastern Islam. When the city fell to Sultan Mehmed's forces, there was plundering by the front-line soldiers. However, when the sultan witnessed this, he came to tears and said, "What a city we have given over to plunder and destruction."

**Figure 8-18:** The story of Mehmed the Conqueror as portrayed in the 2020 historical docudrama, *Rise of Empires: Ottoman*. Pictured is Turkish actor Cem Yiğit Üzümoğlu, who played Mehmed the Conqueror. The emergence of alternative moviemakers outside of the traditional Hollywood studios has opened the door for more fair depictions of Arab and Muslim figures, as demonstrated in this series produced by Karga Seven Pictures and distributed by Netflix, Inc.

The Roman historian George Sphrantzes, who was an eyewitness to the fall of Constantinople, described the sultan's magnanimous actions as follows: "Citizens of all ages who had managed to escape detection were to leave their hiding places throughout the city and come out into the open, as they were to remain free and no question would be asked." Sultan Mehmed also ordered the restoration of houses and property to those who had abandoned the city before the siege. Sphrantzes further described the sultan's orders, "If they returned home, they would be treated according to their rank and religion, as if nothing had changed." The Hagia Sophia was converted into a mosque, but the historic Greek Orthodox church was untouched, and Gennadius Scholarius was appointed patriarch of Constantinople.

The 21-year-old sultan ended the great 1,700-year-old Roman Empire. He put an end to the Crusades. Turkish history would go on to remember him as Mehmed the Conqueror (Fig. 8-18).

After the fall of Constantinople, the Ottomans ruled the "Middle East" from the thirteenth century until World War I, but religious fervor did not die in Europe. The emergence of a new form of Christianity in the sixteenth century, Protestantism, resulted in one of the most brutal wars in human history: the conflict between Catholic and Protestant states known as the Thirty Years' War lasted from 1618 to 1648. This war was mainly fought in Central Europe and resulted in some eight million casualties.

Two peace treaties, together known as the Peace of Westphalia, were signed in 1648 to end this war. However, exactly 533 years to the date after Urban II's declaration of the First Crusade in Clermont, Pope Innocent X—who had considered war to be God's work—issued a proclamation on November 26, 1648, which declared the peace treaty "null, void, damnable, and empty of meaning and effect for all time." However, this was a different Europe than Urban's time. People were sick of killing in the name of religion.

It can be said that the Crusades were a monumental failure; they failed to accomplish their two key goals: long-lasting occupation of the Al-Aqsa Mosque/Dome of the Rock, and the forced conversion of Muslims into Christianity. Yet, the Crusades changed Christianity itself. Priests, who started as the successors of the apostles in early Christianity, walked Jews to their death along the Rhine River in Germany during the first two Crusades. Warrior priests (Knights Templar) committed unspeakable massacres in the holy land while bearing the cross.

A few centuries later, priests sanctioned massacres of the indigenous populations of South America by the Spaniard invaders. The Crusades did not change other religions nearly as much as they changed Christianity itself. It had now become a militarized belief system, totally foreign to the teachings of Jesus, Prince of Peace.

# Chapter 9
# Birth of a Nation

I n the previous two chapters of this section we witnessed the Christian and Muslim invaders of Jerusalem. In this chapter we will look at the third and final invader of Palestine, the Jews.

The earliest record of the invasion of Palestine comes from the Hebrew Bible, in which God commanded the Jews to conquer Palestinian cities by putting them "under the ban"—meaning that every man, woman, and child was to be slaughtered. This is specifically stated in Deuteronomy 20:16–18: "do not leave alive anything that breathes. Completely destroy them." An example of such actions is Joshua's conquest of the Palestinian city of Jericho, in which all people were slaughtered and the city was burned to the ground (detailed in the book of Joshua in the Hebrew Bible). Such violent actions committed in the name of religion, whether it be Judaism, Christianity, or Islam, have laid the foundation for ongoing acts of violence by their respective believers to this day.

## Historical Treatment of Jews by Christianity vs. Islam

In AD 70, Jews revolted against the pagan Roman rulers of Palaestina Prima (the name of Palestine as a province of the Roman Empire) and were then expelled from Jerusalem. In the early seventh century, a much larger Jewish revolt against the Romans, who had become Christian by that time, would ensue. The Jews allied themselves with the Roman's archenemy, the pagan Persian Empire. According to the Armenian bishop and historian Sebeos, 17,000 Christians were slaughtered by the Jews in the attack on Jerusalem. Some Christian sources put the extent of the massacre closer to 90,000. This Jewish revolt was the most organized and far reaching. A surprise attack on the city of Tyre to massacre Christians on Easter was discovered and stopped. The response to the actions of the Jews brings us to Emperor Heraclius, whom we met in Chapter 6; in AD 630 he retook Jerusalem and massacred the Jews. After Khalid ibn al-Walid had his monumental victory over Heraclius/the Roman Empire at Yarmouk in 636, Caliph Umar took the city of Jerusalem without any killings in 638. Umar allowed Jews to return and resettle in the city. Muslims would go on to rule Palestine for 461 years until the first crusaders invaded in 1099 (Chapter 7). The crusaders expelled the Jews from Jerusalem, only for them to be allowed back in once Saladin retook the city in 1187 (Chapter 8).

Similarly, Jews were treated far better by Muslims than Christians not only in the "Middle East" but also in Europe. The Iberian Peninsula (Spain) was under Muslim rule from the eighth to the fifteenth centuries, during which time Jewish communities thrived. However, things changed quickly once Spain was reconquered by Christian forces. Queen Isabella and King Ferdinand issued the Alhambra Decree in 1492 to expel the Jews, many of whom boarded ships sent by the Ottoman Empire to offer protection and immigration to Muslim lands (Chapter 2).

Over the next 600 years, the Ottoman Empire would allow Jews to live and flourish in Jerusalem by having an "open-door policy" in Palestine and throughout the empire for Jews who had been persecuted in Europe. Those Jewish communities, all the way from Morocco to Iraq, thrived for centuries under Muslim rule.

For over a thousand years (from 638 until the start of twentieth century), Jews were routinely persecuted by Christians while Muslims routinely protected them. Therefore, the oft-used statement by politicians and mainstream media that "those people have been fighting each other for thousands of years" when referring to the Arab–Israeli conflict is categorically false.

## Betrayal 2.0

The above synopsis brings us to the beginning of the twentieth century. The Ottomans believed they had developed a trusting relationship with Jews after protecting them for centuries on Muslim lands. That set them up for being completely unaware when covert sinister acts were taking place. The best example of this was the case of

Aaron Aaronsohn. Aaron was a Jew from Romania with significant expertise in agriculture who immigrated to Palestine in 1909 and was funded by Jewish philanthropists in the US. He worked for the Ottoman government as a scientific advisor on agricultural matters in Palestine. However, he had an ulterior motive. He was a spy who envisioned a Zionist takeover of Palestine. Under the guise of carrying out his job for the Ottomans, he mapped Palestine over the span of a few years. This brings us back to Chapter 2 when General Allenby invaded Jerusalem on December 11, 1917. Allenby's invasion of Palestine was based on two sets of maps: one made by T.E. Lawrence under the guise of being an archeologist and the other made by Aaronsohn under the guise of being a botanist! It was Aaronsohn's maps of the oases in the Palestinian desert that led Allenby to take the route to Jerusalem through Beersheba rather than entering the Ottoman military strongholds in Gaza. Years later the director of British intelligence went as far as saying that Allenby's victory would not have been possible without the information provided by Aaronsohn. The Arabs and Muslims were victims of naivete and excessive goodwill toward Jews that had been passed down for centuries from Caliph Umar and Sultan Saladin.

## A Land Without a People for a People Without a Land

The renowned Israeli historian Ilan Pappé labeled the early twentieth-century Jews who immigrated to Palestine, such as Aaronsohn, *settler colonialists*, and he defined Jewish Zionism as a settler colonialist movement.

As discussed in Chapter 2, the first shot across the "Palestinian" bow was the Balfour Declaration issued by the Christian Zionist British government which conveniently coincided with Allenby's invasion of Palestine in 1917. Although the British government stated in the Balfour Declaration that their objective to establish a national home for Jews in Palestine was major, it alone was not going to be enough to bring it to fruition. The facts on the ground could not support such an edict. In the 1880s, the community of Jews in Palestine amounted, based on the most generous estimation of the data, to no more than three percent of the population. (I will use the three percent rather than the less than one percent mentioned by some sources for the purposes of this book.) They were known as the Yishuv Jews and were well assimilated in Palestinian life and never called for or aspired to create a Jewish nation. That was the typical situation for Jews in countries around the world; they were productive, assimilated citizens of their respective nations. They were *biblical* Zionists (as opposed to *political* Zionists). We discussed Christian Zionism in detail in Chapter 6, and below I will outline the concept of Zionism in Judaism (both biblical and political).

In biblical Zionism, the term *Israel* was used to refer to the descendants of the 12 sons of the patriarch Jacob (who was also known as Israel) that made up the Jewish people. The creation of Israel as a nation in Orthodox Judaism is associated with the end-of-days eschatology; it cannot happen until the Messiah comes, which in Judaism has not yet occurred. The idea of having an actual physical country of Israel in the twentieth century is a newly invented concept that is called political Zionism. You may recall from Chapters 2 and 6, Theodore Herzl, the father of this new movement, promoted the idea of creating a homeland for the Jews based on the persecution they were suffering in Europe, not based on the end-of-days philosophy. Proof of this was his recommendation to look at Argentina and Uganda as possible sites for the creation of a Jewish homeland. It was the Christian Zionists, based on their fanatical end-of-days interpretations of their faith, that demanded the Jews to go to Palestine and establish an Israel. The only power that could deliver a Jewish state at the end of WWI was the Christian Zionist British cabinet. For the Jewish political Zionists (like Chaim Weizmann and Lord Rothschild in England), the stars could not have been better aligned. These machinations were happening behind the scenes, unbeknownst to the Ottoman governing authority in Palestine, who continued to welcome Jewish immigrants. The Jews who were immigrating in the early twentieth century from Europe to Palestine, the colonial settlers, had a different goal in mind; they were not the austere Jewish immigrants the Ottomans had been used to for centuries.

Based on the American historian and demographer Justin McCarthy's review of the original data, in 1914, Palestine had a population of 657,000 Palestinian Muslim Arabs, 81,000 Palestinian Christian Arabs, and 59,000 Jews. (The Jewish Zionist immigration had now increased the subset of Jews in Palestine from 3 percent to

9 percent.) The British government interim report of 1920 on the Civil Administration of Palestine estimated the total population of Palestine at 700,000. It stated, "The Jewish element of the population numbers 76,000. Almost all have entered Palestine during the last 40 years. Prior to 1850 there were in the country only a handful of Jews." Therefore, the Jews who entered Palestine with a Zionist colonial settler agenda had increased the Jewish element in Palestine from 3 to 10 percent by 1920. By the time the Palestinians figured out what was going on, it was too late; the Christian Zionist British government was in charge in Palestine. The Zionist movement at that point recognized that even 10 percent was not enough to declare a Jewish state in Palestine. Chaim Weizmann, the architect from the Jewish side working with the Christian Zionists (Lloyd George and Arthur Balfour) to create a Jewish state, would then further rev up the Jewish immigration from Europe to Palestine to make it in his own words "as Jewish as England is English."

Besides an immigration movement on steroids, the Zionist movement came up with an ingenious plan, a plan to create an alternative reality! Most Palestinians, the historical saviors of the land of milk and honey, were simple farmers with no real contact to the outside world and especially not with Europe and the US. The Ottoman Empire was busy with WWI. Therefore, the Zionist plan was to carry out a propaganda campaign to impact the public opinion where it really mattered, Europe and the US. They used the slogan "A land without a people for a people without a land." They tried to omit the presence of the Palestinian people.

This became a long-term slogan, as future Israel Prime Minister Golda Meir would say:

> There were no such thing as Palestinians.

## Irgun ארגון

Following WWI, Palestine was officially under the total control of the British—a British Mandate. While that was great for the Jewish cause, in the ensuing years in the 1920s, however, the Christian Zionist monopoly over the cabinet in London started to weaken, and with that emerged voices in the British government and public that started to raise questions about the Balfour Declaration. Lord Sydenham Hansard said in the House of Lords on June 21, 1922:

> If we are going to admit claims on conquests thousands of years ago, the whole world will have to be turned upside down.

The renowned English author H.G. Wells would pose the question:

> If it is proper to "reconstitute" a Jewish state which has not existed for two thousand years, why not go back another thousand years and reconstitute the Canaanite state? The Canaanites, unlike the Jews, are still there.

As predicted, the massive Jewish immigration became a source of tension and skirmishes between the Palestinians and the Jews. To add context, in the early twenty-first century, the impact of immigrants coming into the US from its southern border or those arriving into Europe in boats pale in comparison to that of the Jewish immigrants from Europe into Palestine in the first half of the twentieth century. The Jewish migration into Palestine was admittedly focused on changing the population demographics of the country. The same right-wing groups in the US and Europe who are vehemently opposed to any immigration into their countries were and are some of the biggest supporters of Jewish immigration into Palestine!

This massive migration under the watch of the British government resulted in many English intellectuals and the public becoming critical about their now historic role in suppressing the identity and the rights of the Palestinian people. Under this mounting humanitarian pressure, the British government issued a white paper (an authoritative policy report) in 1939 that limited Jewish

**Figure 9-1:** Irgun emblem. The left side depicts a map of Palestine, on the right is that of Jordan. Fanatic Zionists believed that both countries must be conquered to form the new state of Israel.

immigration to 75,000 for five years and ruled that further immigration would then be determined by the Arab majority.

These were fighting words as far as the Zionist movement was concerned. This led to the formation of the Zionist terrorist organization named Irgun (Hebrew: אצ״ל‎) (Figs. 9-1 and 9-2). The founder, Vladimir Jabotinsky, would provide a very honest assessment:

> Has any People ever been seen to give up their territory of their own free will? In the same way, the Arabs of Palestine will not renounce their sovereignty without violence.

**Figure 9-2:** The *Falastin* newspaper, owned by Palestinian Arab Christians, featuring a caricature on its June 18, 1936, edition showing Zionism as a crocodile under the protection of a British officer telling Palestinian Arabs: "Don't be afraid!!! I will swallow you peacefully. . ."

The Irgun decided to send a lethal message to the British government following their limitations on Jewish immigration into Palestine following the release of the white paper. The King David Hotel in Jerusalem was where the central offices of the British Mandate of Palestine known as the Secretariat of the Government of Palestine were located. Irgun terrorists disguised as Arab work-men and as hotel waiters planted a bomb in the basement of the main building of the hotel. On July 22, 1946, during the busiest time of day at 12:37 p.m., the bomb was detonated, killing 91 people (Fig. 9-3).

**Figure 9-3:** Picture of the King David Hotel from 1946, following the Jewish terrorist bombing which killed 91 people. The picture shows the bombing-related collapse of the western half of the southern wing of the hotel.

In the consciousness of the public in Western countries, acts of terrorism are uniquely linked only to Arabs and Muslims; this phe-nomenon is purely a result of decades of historical omissions by the political establishment and mainstream media.

The King David Hotel attack was ordered by an Irgun leader by the name of Menachem Begin, a man who would go on to become a hero and the prime minister of Israel (Fig. 9-4)!

The acts of terror committed by Begin made him the most wanted man in Palestine, and MI5 (United Kingdom Military Intelligence Section 5) placed a "dead-or-alive" bounty of £10,000 on his head. He grew a beard and changed his identity to a lawyer named Yisrael

Halperin, and once the British anti-terrorism police unit got closer to his location, he moved again and assumed a new identity, Yisrael Sassover, masquerading as a rabbi! Begin was a master at hiding, as once the police unit figured out his alias, he took yet another identity, this time as a doctor, Yonah Koenigshoffer. He was never caught and only emerged once the British left Palestine in 1948. He would never be tried for his acts of terrorism.

**Figure 9-4:** A wanted poster distributed by the British authorities in Palestine searching for terrorists. The top left picture is that of Menachem Begin.

In July 2006, the Menachem Begin Heritage Center organized an event celebrating the sixtieth anniversary of the King David Hotel bombing! A plaque commemorating the bombing was unveiled. In attendance was former and future prime minister of Israel, Benjamin Netanyahu, as well as many former Irgun terrorists. The reason

I chose to mention Netanyahu has to do with the irony, given his stance on terrorism. Let me quote him:

> The root cause of terrorism lies not in grievances but in a disposition toward unbridled violence. This can be traced to a world view which asserts that certain ideological and religious goals justify, indeed demand, the shedding of all moral inhibitions.

Netanyahu's definition of terrorism in his quote fits Irgun completely.

When the British government heard of the ceremony commemorating the King David bombing, the British ambassador issued the following statement: "We do not think that it is right for an act of terrorism, which led to the loss of many lives, to be commemorated."

It is important to note that Irgun was not the only Zionist terrorist organization operating in Palestine. A separate terrorist organization known as Lehi (often called the Stern Gang) also existed. Lehi believed that the sooner the British left Palestine, the sooner a Zionist state could be established. In that regard, it initially sought an alliance with Fascist Italy and Nazi Germany in order to weaken the British and expedite their exit from Palestine. One of the key leaders of Lehi was a man by the name of Yitzhak Shamir, who was no less brutal than Menachem Begin. He ordered the assassination of the British minister of state in the "Middle East," Walter Edward Guinness. Shamir was subsequently arrested under the command of British Sergeant T.G. Martin. Shamir was sent to a detention camp in Africa (in Eritrea). Lehi tracked down T.G. Martin and assassinated him. Shamir was able to escape from prison and remained in hiding until the State of Israel was declared and he returned. He went on to become Israel's seventh prime minister. He would never be tried for his acts of terrorism.

## A US President Intervenes

Within weeks of the King David Hotel bombing, Zionist organizations in Europe and the US started to put significant pressure on the leaders of their respective countries to give them part of Palestine to create a new country. Leaders allied with the Zionist cause took the matter to the United Nations (UN). The resolution to give half of Palestine to the Zionists was dead on arrival as it violated the UN Charter's principles of national self-determination (granting the people of a country protection from a hostile entity trying to take over their land without their permission). That did not deter the Zionist forces from pushing for it. They needed the most powerful man in the world, the US president, to support the resolution and to twist the arms of other nations to vote for it. The thirty-third president of the United States, Harry Truman, did both, and on November 27, 1947, the UN General Assembly adopted Resolution 181 to recommend the partitioning of Palestine. Truman would tell a close Jewish friend, Eddie Jacobson, that "he [Truman] and he alone was responsible for swinging the votes of several delegations." This was historic; it was the first and only time in the history of the UN that half of a country was recommended to be taken away and given to an external force. It was also historic for another reason: it marked the passing of the baton from Britain to the US to take the lead role in continuing the Christian Zionist agenda in the "Middle East" as it was first set forth by Lloyd George, Arthur Balfour, and Winston Churchill in the first half of the twentieth century (Chapters 3 and 6).

As you can imagine, President Truman is lionized as a hero in Zionist circles, and he is not remembered fondly in the larger "Arab world" for what he did. But I believe it is important to peel the curtain back a bit to understand the context of what the president was going through. Truman, a Democrat, was running for his second term in 1948. Tremendous pressure was put on him by Zionists in the US for him to deliver that UN vote. It is perhaps best to use his own words from his personal diary that was declassified by the Truman Presidential Museum & Library in Independence, Missouri, in 2003:

> The Jews, I find are very, very selfish. . . . They care not how many Estonians, Latvians, Finns, Poles, Yugoslavs or Greeks get murdered or mistreated as DP [displaced persons] as long as the Jews get special treatment. Yet when they have power, physical, financial or political neither Hitler nor

Stalin has anything on them for cruelty or mistreatment to the underdog.

By the underdog, Truman meant the Palestinians. I hope this sheds some light for Arab people to understand that Truman was no religious fanatic; he did what he had to do in the world he was living in. Some may argue that he did not have to cave to political pressure. There was a WWII hero, larger than life in the American consciousness, who took that view—Truman's secretary of state, General George Marshall Jr. Marshall, who was known for his deep adherence to core principles, humanitarianism, and prioritization of US national security, categorically disagreed with Truman in his support of the Zionist agenda (Fig. 9-5).

**Figure 9-5:** General George Marshall (1880–1959). He was the chief of staff under President Franklin D. Roosevelt during WWII. Winston Churchill would say that Marshall was the "organizer of victory," referring to the Allied Victory during WWII. He advocated for significant US support to rebuild post-war Europe—a strategy known as the Marshall Plan. He served as secretary of state and secretary of defense consecutively. Marshall was awarded the Nobel Peace Prize in 1953.

As mentioned, this was the most unusual resolution ever voted on at the UN. There had not been another instance of a resolution to strip people of their land up to that date and there has not been ever since. Massive pressure was put on countries to vote for it, and smaller countries caved quickly under US financial threats. I want to share an anecdote about India, not a small country and more importantly, a very proud country. India's prime minister was a Hindu who was considered the paragon of Indian democracy, Jawaharlal Nehru. He spoke about the unethical ways the votes were being influenced with contempt and disgust. Not only was India being bribed with millions of dollars, but Nehru's sister, Vijaya Lakshmi Pandit, the Indian ambassador to the UN, had received daily death threats unless "she voted right." India voted against the resolution, but most other countries caved under the pressure.

## The Mythical Democracy

Irgun, following the UN recommendation, was now further invigorated as it would be taking half of Palestine. However, the Zionist movement was then faced with the hurdle of a math issue! Imagine their predicament: they had promised the "West" that they would create the first democracy in the backward "Middle East," but the overwhelming population on either half of the would-be partitioned Palestine would be Palestinians! That would create the dilemma of what a real democracy would require—one person, one vote. This would guarantee that the government would be overwhelmingly Palestinian. The Zionists were not going to have any of that, so they came with a plan to terrorize the Palestinian population to the point that they would leave their homeland.

Irgun launched a terror campaign by attacking villages and committing massacres. One major joint attack by Irgun and Lehi led to the most massive fear campaign in the history of the Palestinian people. On April 9, 1948, 120 members of the combined terrorist groups entered the 600-person Palestinian village of Deir Yassin, near Jerusalem. Men, women, and children were slaughtered. According to a count conducted by the International Red Cross, besides the bodies left lying in the streets, 150 more corpses were found in one cistern alone, including people who had been either decapitated or disemboweled. The Israeli historian Benny Morris wrote that there were also cases of mutilation and rape. The massacre at Deir Yassin accomplished its intended goal; news of the killings sparked terror in village after village of Palestinians. Because there was no Palestinian army to protect them (as they ostensibly were under the British Occupation protection), they started fleeing Palestine. This achieved the main purpose of the terror attacks and massacres: Palestinians fled in droves.

## The Bible and the Cabinet Meeting

Back in the White House, President Truman was struggling with a major decision he would have to make. It was clear based on what was happening on the ground in Palestine that the British would withdraw soon, leaving a vacuum for Irgun and Lehi. That would mean that they would declare the formation of a Zionist state in Palestine. It was one thing to help a conceptual vote in the UN, it was another to recognize a nation borne out of terrorism. American credibility was on the line.

The renowned American historian and author David McCullough, in his book *Truman*, provides an exquisite and detailed account of what the president was going through in making this decision.

There were two camps. General George Marshall, the secretary of state, vehemently opposed US recognition of a Zionist state based on national security, ethical, and humanitarian grounds. On the other side was the lawyer turned Washington, DC political operative, Clark Clifford. Clifford was a staunch evangelical Christian Zionist and a political advisor to President Truman. Clifford masterfully used the cards of the Jewish vote and Zionist financial backing of his campaign during the 1948 election to influence the president to recognize the Zionist State of Israel.

Truman clearly had a deep sympathy for the suffering of the Jews, especially as victims of the horrendous crimes of the Nazis during WWII, but the political Zionist movement was getting under his skin. He wrote, "The action of some of our United States Zionists will eventually prejudice everyone against what they are trying to get done." At a cabinet meeting, he angrily said, "Jesus Christ couldn't please them when he was on earth, so how could anyone expect that I would have any luck."

Chaim Weizmann, the grand old wizard of the Zionist movement, traveled from Britain to Washington, DC, to put pressure on the president to recognize the new Zionist state. Truman categorically refused to meet him. Clifford, with the help of Truman's old Kansas City Jewish friend and business partner Eddie Jacobson, was able to twist the president's arm to see Weizmann. As there was a concern in the State Department that the president was under undue pressure from the Zionists, Truman met with Weizmann secretly in the White House without informing the State Department. In a follow-up letter to Truman, Weizmann wrote, "The choice for our people, Mr. President, is between statehood and extermination." The irony, of course, is that the only people at risk of extermination at that point were the Palestinians.

Four weeks after the Deir Yassin massacre and exactly two days before the British had planned to pull out of Palestine, on May 12, 1948, a meeting took place in President Truman's office with cabinet members to chart America's next step. Present in the meeting was a non-cabinet member—Clifford. General Marshall, known for his reserved and respectful attitude, said, "I don't even understand why Clifford is here. This is not a political meeting." Clifford gave an impassioned speech about the Holocaust and the Old Testament, specifically quoting from Deuteronomy. My citation from Deuteronomy in the beginning of this chapter ("Do not leave alive anything that breathes. Completely destroy them"), did in fact come alive thousands of years later, in the White House that day. The historic impact of bringing extremist religious ideologies into the decision-making of the world's superpower on that day cannot be underestimated.

Marshall stressed that domestic political considerations must not impact foreign policy; looking right at Truman, he said that "the great office of the President" was on the line. Truman sided with Clifford rather than Marshall. Two days later, on Friday, May 14, 1948, the same day the British announced their withdrawal, for the first time in modern history, an announcement was made to create a country inside another country. It was named Israel. It took only minutes for the White House to recognize the new state. General Marshall, based on his military code of ethics of respecting the chain of command, in this case the president, did not resign. However, he never spoke with Clark Clifford again. Clifford, as a result of this achievement, had a meteoric rise in Washington, culminating in his service as secretary of defense under President Lyndon B. Johnson in the late 1960s. His last stand was in the 1980s when he served as the chairman of Washington, DC's largest bank, First American Bankshares, and faced federal charges of criminal fraud, conspiracy, and taking bribes.

Chaim Weizmann was named the first president of Israel.

Irgun went on to officially become the Israeli Military (Israel Defense Force or IDF).

While well-known evangelical Christian Zionists Lloyd George, Arthur Balfour, and Winston Churchill had their impact on the creation of the "Middle East" as we know it today, Clark Clifford, though not well known in history books, had a significant impact on the creation of the State of Israel. Clifford injected two new key principles to US foreign policy in the "Middle East,": US domestic political considerations (funding for campaigns), and extremist evangelical Christian ideations. To this date, those two variables are core to the US decisions involving Arabs, Muslims, Palestinians, and Israel. It is important to contextualize this. The prevailing and accurate view among the mainstream media and public in the West is that Islamist terrorists are using antiquated religious interpretations to push their agenda. What is never said—or perhaps is forbidden to be mentioned—is that the whole basis of creating a Zionist state and then protecting it by placing vassal Arab dictators in the "Middle East," was and continues to be based on extremist evangelical Christian religious edicts and ideations. For the mainstream media to never mention this is nothing short of abdication of journalistic standards.

## "The Ethnic Cleansing of Palestine"
## Ilan Pappé, Renowned Israeli Historian

The Arab dictators who were British vassalage regimes, had now become American vassals, and found themselves in a very difficult bind with the events in Palestine. Abdulaziz ibn Saud was always able to muzzle his Saudi population, but for the dictators in Egypt, Jordan, and Syria, it was a more difficult problem. They had to publicly show that they were helping their Palestinian brethren and sent troops into Palestine to fight the Zionists. The Arab forces were categorically defeated. These outside Arab troops had zero chance against the Zionists who had been funded by Europeans and spent decades studying the Palestinian landscape and entrenching themselves in it. Among the men fighting the Zionists in 1948 was a 20-year-old idealist by the name of Yasser Arafat, a man who years later would lead an organization by the name of the Palestine Liberation Organization (PLO) with the purpose of the "liberation of Palestine" through armed struggle, which included acts of terrorism. This book is not encyclopedic, and the acts of terror committed by Palestinians against Jewish civilians are well documented in the West and within popular culture. This book intends to uncover omitted historical facts by the mainstream media.

Ehud Barak, who spent most of his life as a member of the IDF, went on to become Israel's tenth Prime Minister. He told a television interviewer,

> If I was [a Palestinian] at the right age, at some stage I would have entered one of the terror organizations and have fought from there, and later certainly have tried to influence from within the political system.

The PLO was considered by the United States to be a terrorist organization until 1991, and has since accepted it, just as the UN does, as the sole legitimate representative of the Palestinian people. It has for the most part morphed into the entity known as the Palestinian Authority (PA).

While intellectuals often say that terrorism does not pay, the above example contradicts that view. Without acts of terrorism, there is no path that would have led to the creation of the State of Israel in 1948.

Israel's first prime minister, David Ben-Gurion, would provide an honest assessment:

> Why should the Arabs make peace? If I was an Arab leader I would never make terms with Israel. That is natural: we have taken their country. Sure God promised it to us, but what does that matter to them? Our God is not theirs. We come from Israel, but two thousand years ago, and what is that to them? There has been antisemitism, the Nazis, Hitler, Auschwitz, but was that their fault? They only see one thing: we have come here and stolen their country. Why should they accept that?

In creating a new state, the Zionists would face the ultimate dilemma. They knew this was a fragile state, since it lacked real legitimacy in the eyes of the peoples of the world and given the atrocities that were committed to achieve the goal. They knew their main audience is and forever would be the American public, and as long as they had US backing (financial and military), they would not have to worry about what anyone else thinks. And, therefore, a "democratic" country in the midst of Arab dictatorships would appeal to the psyche of the American public. But how do you create a democratic country when the people you hate, the Palestinians, are the overwhelming majority? The answer to this question will go on to become one of the saddest stories of the past 100 years. There were a number of options: continue to massively increase Jewish immigration, kill as many Palestinians as they could get away with, forcibly evict Palestinians, or use terror and fear tactics to drive them out en masse. They utilized all four!

The UN Commission on Genocide Prevention describes *ethnic cleansing* as "a purposeful policy designed by one ethnic or religious group to remove by violent and terror-inspiring means the civilian population of another ethnic or religious group from certain geographic areas." Ethnic cleansing is defined as a "crime against humanity" under the statute of the International Criminal Court (ICC). While the term *ethnic cleansing* has been raised around the world when discussing the Zionist state, it has been heavily restricted in the US. The irony of that cannot be understated given that the First Amendment of the Constitution guarantees freedom of speech. The forums in which sensitive issues are widely debated in American life have traditionally been university campuses. President Donald Trump, with his ardent Zionist son-in-law, Jared Kushner, standing next to him, signed an executive order on December 11, 2019, which would penalize US universities if they fail to prevent speech that is critical of Israel. This fits the original Israeli strategic thinking; as long as the US public has limited information about Zionist crimes, Israel cannot be held accountable.

Going back to Palestine and the newly created State of Israel, by mid-1949, *half* of the Palestinian population was forcibly expelled or fled in fear of Zionist terror attacks. More than 700,000 Palestinians were driven out. (The total Arab population of Palestine in 1947 was 1.4 million.) There has been no other such atrocity in the world in recent memory where half of the population of a country has been ethnically cleansed, yet this fact does not exist in the American public consciousness; they have been purposefully denied exposure to these facts.

In the span of a few months, more than 400 Arab villages disappeared. Once bustling centuries-old Palestinian cities like Haifa and Jaffa are almost exclusively Jewish now. The overwhelming majority of the Palestinians driven out ended up in refugee camps in Lebanon, Jordan, Syria, Egypt, and Iraq. The Saudi regime, which claims to be the mantle holder of the Islamic faith and calls itself the custodian of the two holy mosques, and the one which was financially most capable among the countries mentioned, took no refugees.

This Palestinian exodus is known in Arabic as Al-Nakbah (meaning "catastrophe"). It is remembered officially by Palestinians on May 15 every year, which also marks the day on which the State of Israel was announced by Zionist forces in Palestine. On the same day, one group of people celebrate the creation of a new country, while another mourns the loss of theirs (Fig. 9-6).

**Figure 9-6:** Palestinians in 1948, five months after the creation of Israel, leaving a village in Galilee. Note the young children having to walk hundreds of miles barefoot. Among the families fleeing Galilee, specifically the town of Safed, was a 13-year-old boy by the name of Mahmoud. He would later become a leader of his people—Mahmoud Abbas.

There is a principle in international law that guarantees the rights of refugees to return to their home following expulsion. For example, we discussed in Chapter 2 that Jews who were being persecuted in Spain in the fifteenth century were brought to safety by the Muslim Ottoman Empire to live in Arab Muslim lands. In 1924, through a royal decree, the Spanish government provided the opportunity for the descendants of those Jews who were expelled or fled out of fear to obtain Spanish citizenship. The Israeli government has categorically denied the right of Palestinian refugees to return to their homes. The issue of the "right of return" has been one of the key hurdling blocks in all Israeli–Palestinian peace negotiations.

The question is, why are the Israelis willing to break all ethical and international standards over this issue? The answer is simple: the Israelis have gotten themselves into a difficult corner—the democracy ruse. Let me explain. Let's take the current situation for example. The Israel Central Bureau of Statistics estimated that the collective Palestinian Arab population in the region of historic Palestine (the 1947 Palestine) amounted to 5.79 million people in 2017. The CIA estimated the population of Israel (excluding the West Bank and Gaza) to be 8,424,904 as of July 2017, with the Jewish population being 74.4 percent, Palestinian 20.9 percent, and other 4.7 percent. That calculates into a Jewish population of 6.31 million. Although the 6.31 million Jews compared to the 5.79 million Palestinians shows a slight majority of the Jewish population, there is some opaqueness by the Israeli government regarding the true number of Palestinians, which is likely under-reported. As the US State Department report from 2015 stated, "In the combined areas of Israel, Jerusalem, the West Bank and the Gaza Strip, Jews no longer represent the majority." Regardless, looking at both reports (Israeli government data and the US State Department), there is an overall parity of the two populations. With a free and fair election, therefore, you would have quite a mixed government both in the cabinet posts and the Knesset (the parliament). Clearly that does not exist nor would be allowed; no such election has ever been held. The national elections eliminate 4.7 million Palestinians (who live under Israeli total control with no voting rights) in the West Bank and Gaza, while the Jews who live in the same regions get to vote!

The answer to the question asked above is that if refugees were allowed to return, the overwhelming majority of the population would be Palestinian, and that is something Israel can never allow. So, being a legitimate pluralistic democracy, according to Zionists, can never be an option. It is best stated by Israel's longest-serving prime minister, Benjamin Netanyahu: "Israel is not a state of all its citizens. According to the Nation-State Law that we passed, Israel is the nation-state of the Jewish People—and them alone," An admission by the leader of Israel that it is not a legitimate democracy.

Israeli democracy is akin to us taking a town in America, and saying White people can vote, but Black people cannot. It technically would be a democracy as there is voting taking place, but it would be a ruse!

It is important to note that when I use the terms *Palestinians* or *Arabs* in Palestine, it includes both Christians and Muslims. They are deeply connected when it comes to their struggle against what they both label as the "Zionist invasion." The pictures and videos from Bethlehem (from the Church of the Nativity) on Christmas Day seen around the world are Christian Palestinian Arabs. Bethlehem is an Arabic word, the first part, *beit*, means house and the second part, *laham*, means meat ("House of Meat").

## "Palestine: Peace Not Apartheid"
## The Thirty-Ninth President of the US, Jimmy Carter

Over the decades, Israel, with the help of the US, would develop a formidable military force far superior to the combined militaries of the surrounding fledgling Arab states. Hostilities between the Israelis and the Arab states were commonplace throughout those years. On the morning of June 5, 1967, Israel launched a sudden air assault that destroyed 90 percent of Egypt's air force on the tarmac. A similar fate was had by Syria. With no Arab air force, Israel had complete command of the skies and sent ground forces that captured what had been Palestinian territory under the UN partition plan of 1947 (the West Bank and Gaza) and thus captured its golden target, East Jerusalem. (West Jerusalem was already in Israel's hands.) It captured the Sinai Peninsula of Egypt, and the highly strategic Golan Heights of Syria. The whole effort took just a few days—it is known as the Six-Day War or the 1967 War. The Sinai is no longer under Israeli occupation. The occupation of East Jerusalem has never been recognized by the international community.

The whole Israeli philosophy since its inception, in a nutshell, has been simple but extremely nefarious—taking land by force and then asking the people they took the land from what they are willing to give in return to have it back. Israel has used this strategy in Lebanon, Syria, Jordan, and Egypt—every land that borders it (Fig. 9-7).

Why did Israel feel so emboldened to carry out such a massive surprise attack in June 1967? The answer has never been publicly disclosed. Israel had just succeeded in developing a nuclear weapons program on the eve of its attack on Egypt. According to Avner Cohen, a nuclear historian at the Middlebury Institute of International Studies at Monterey, it had three nuclear devices by then. Despite all the military aid the US gives Israel, nuclear weapons were never part of that arrangement. Quite the contrary—it was a point of friction when US intelligence became aware of the Israeli's efforts to build a nuclear bomb at the nuclear complex in Dimona (an area 19 miles southeast of Beersheba and 22 miles west of the Dead Sea in the Negev Desert). Every US administration since Truman's, despite all the public accolades they bestow on Israel, has known it to be an unpredictable militant inciter, and for it to possess nuclear weapons poses a risk to regional and global security. By the time Richard Nixon became president in 1969, it was a fait accompli, and all administrations since have accepted this reality and kept it top secret.

The Israelis understood that they needed every newly elected US president to sign a letter agreeing not to pressure it into signing the international Nuclear Non-Proliferation Treaty (NPT) and for the US not to inspect Israeli nuclear sites. This became especially critical for the Israelis in the past decade, when they have been putting pressure on Iran to undergo international inspections, and they have been worried that this issue would be raised with regards to Israel. The process is, once a new president takes power in Washington, DC, a high-level Israeli delegation visits the White House and demands utmost secrecy in getting the presidential signature. This happened most recently when President Donald Trump took office in January 2017. The Israeli delegation arrived at the White House on February 13, 2017. While Trump is the most pro-Zionist president in US history, I was surprised to find out from the work of Adam Entous, a reporter for the *New Yorker*, that even his closest aides knew nothing about the existence of such letters and they clearly felt uncomfortable pressure from the Israelis.

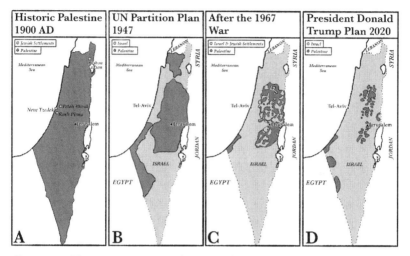

**Figure 9-7:** The expansion of Israel (light color) from the early twentieth century to present time.

**A)** Palestine (dark color) at the beginning of the twentieth century. The first Jewish settlements in Palestine were Petah Tikva (1878), Rosh Pina (1882), Rishon LeZion (1882), and Neve Tzedek (1887).

**B)** The 1947 UN partition of Palestine.

**C)** Following the 1967 War until the present day. Note the Israeli settlements shown inside the Palestinian territories.

**D)** The 2020 Donald Trump Peace Plan, as devised by his ardent Zionist son-in-law, Jared Kushner. It envisions Palestinians living in an "archipelago" setting surrounded by Israeli lands without the right for refugees to return.

(More detailed description of the "archipelago" concept is provided in Figure 9-8).

After the 1948 and 1967 wars, there was one more, the Ramadan/ Yom Kippur War in 1973—which I discussed in detail in Chapter 3.

That brings us to what is touted as the most complicated and most unattainable peace in the world—the "Middle East" peace between Israelis and Palestinians. The reality is, it is quite simple and very attainable if both sides want it.

Allow me to explain. It depends on Israel returning the West Bank, Gaza, and East Jerusalem to Palestine with illegal settlements removed, returning the Golan Heights to Syria, and allowing the Palestinian refugees to return home. On the other side, the Palestinians and all Arab states must recognize the legitimacy of Israel. Those are the elements on the table at every peace negotiation to date. Palestinians would sign that tomorrow. Israel has not agreed to a single one of those points, let alone all of them. So where does the widely held view in the US among the public at large that it is the Palestinians who do not want peace, and that the Israelis seek it?

The mainstream media would have us believe that the Palestinians, who for generations now have been living under cruel occupation within an apartheid system, apparently do not want a peaceful solution. The mainstream media would also have us believe that the Israelis, who receive the largest amount of foreign aid from the US taxpayers compared to any other country in the world—a large portion of which is military support and therefore something that would naturally decrease if there is peace—and would have to share Jerusalem as a capital with the Palestinians, are apparently eager for peace.

The most ingenious plan to solve the problem would come from none other than President Trump! He gave the job of solving the "Middle East" problem to his trusted advisor, the ardent Zionist Jared Kushner, a man with zero experience in foreign policy. Kushner came up with a plan termed the "deal of the century." His plan was unveiled on January 28, 2020, proposing that all illegal Jewish settlements on Palestine's West Bank and Gaza remain intact and be protected. Jerusalem would be the sole property of Israel. No Palestinian refugee would be allowed to return home. He tried to solve the Israeli democracy conundrum like no one before, by putting Palestinians in a scattered patch (archipelago) of territories—not a contiguous state, thus assuring that not only would they have no right to vote in the country they live in (the so-called one-state solution), but also that they do not get their own real country! When the Palestinians did not jump at this "great" deal offered to them, Kushner's response is best summarized by the article from *Vanity Fair* reporter Bess Levin: "Jared Kushner: Palestinians Have Never Done Anything Right in their Sad, Pathetic Lives." Ms. Levin summarized Kushner's disappointment: "The first son-in-law has warned Palestinians not to 'screw up this opportunity' at peace that he's so graciously given to them"!

I would like to illustrate Jared Kushner's ignorance and deep bias when it comes to the Palestinian issue. During an appearance on CNN on August 17, 2020, Kushner commented on the status of the Al-Aqsa Mosque in Jerusalem: "There has been this myth in the Arab world that Muslims are not allowed to go to pray at the Al-Aqsa Mosque; it has been a symbolic gesture used by the radicals and the Islamic jihadists for *hundreds of years* to basically rile up the populace." The fact is, Israel invaded East Jerusalem in 1967; prior to that, Jerusalem had been under Muslim control for hundreds of years and Muslims prayed openly in the Al-Aqsa Mosque. So for him to declare that Muslims claim that Israel did not allow Muslims to pray at the Al-Aqsa mosque for "hundreds of years" when it has only been 53 years since Israel occupied Jerusalem either reflects significant ignorance or he is intentionally "riling up the populace" to vilify Muslims; either way it reflects his lack of credentials to represent America in these very serious and strategic negotiations.

The concept of putting Palestinians in an archipelago in the West Bank surrounded by Jewish settlements (which are illegal based on international law) is nothing new; this Israeli policy has been going on for years and Trump and Kushner are trying to make it official. Adam Entous of the *New Yorker* gave us a unique glimpse into this issue. Toward the end of Barack Obama's presidency, Frank Lowenstein, the Obama administration's special envoy on Israeli–Palestinian negotiations, came across US government intelligence maps of the West Bank and wanted the president to see them. When the president was shown the maps, he was "surprised" to see how "systematic" the Israelis had been at cutting the Palestinians off from each other. These maps showed that Israeli illegal settlements and outposts totaled 60% of the West Bank! Frank Lowenstein shared his findings with the Israelis, and they did not challenge the veracity of the data. What Lowenstein was bringing to the forefront is that while the Israelis have been sitting at negotiating tables accepting the premise of a two-state solution, in reality they never intended to do so. They had already strategically encircled all Palestinian towns in the West Bank with Jewish settlements, assuring that there could never be a contiguous Palestinian state. Lowenstein was indeed correct, as evidenced by the 2020 Trump Peace Plan in which Kushner and Netanyahu removed all hopes of a contiguous Palestinian state and assured that Palestinians would live on "islands" encircled by Israelis. The plan essentially mimics the "open-air prison" model that the Israelis have employed for decades in Gaza and applies it to the rest of the Palestinian population (Figs. 9-8 and 9-9).

Despite everything, I believe it is possible to achieve peace to end the Israeli–Palestinian conflict. The US is the only world power that both sides would listen to. The problem is, the US has declared it cannot and will not be impartial; it will always side with the Israelis. To quote the highly respected former US Secretary of State James Baker, "You cannot be Israel's lawyer and expect to solve the Palestinian–Israeli dispute."

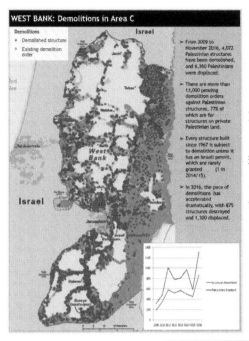

**Figures 9-8 and 9-9:** Maps displaying the long-standing Israeli strategy of separating the Palestinians in the West Bank from one another by creating an "archipelago," which normally refers to a group of islands. The key purpose of this strategy has been to change the facts on the ground so that the Palestinians could not have a future contiguous state. The US State Department map on the left shows the demolitions of Palestinian homes and villages by the Israelis.

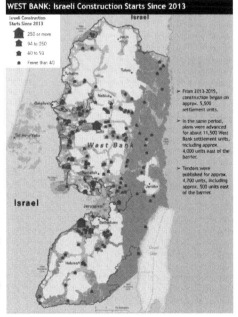

The map on the right shows the building of Israeli settlements on top of the demolished Palestinian homes and villages, thus creating the separated Palestinian "islands" (shown as white regions in the two maps). For Palestinians to go from one "island" to another (e.g., going from home to work, or children going from home to school), they must pass through Israeli check points. The plan also blocks the Palestinians from having any geographic connection with the outside world. This was the core principle of the Kushner–Netanyahu initiative, known as the 2020 Trump Peace Plan.

## Fair and Balanced News: American Media Coverage of the Arab–Israeli Conflict

Imagine if a foreign power attacked a US naval ship in international waters killing dozens of American sailors; of course we would expect extensive media coverage of the event, perhaps for weeks, and there would be cries from politicians and the public to retaliate.

As mentioned above, there was friction between the US and Israel in the 1960s over Israel's development of nuclear weapons. During the 1967 Six-Day War, the USS *Liberty* was in international waters in the Mediterranean. It may well have been gathering intelligence on the Israelis, which is something the US has the right to do without permission. On June 8, 1967, Israel carried out an air and sea attack on the *Liberty*, killing 34 crew members (naval officers, seamen, two marines, and one civilian), wounding 171 crew members, and severely damaging the ship.

The Israelis claimed that they mistook the *Liberty* for an Egyptian ship. The survivors, including the ship's commander who was injured during the attack, William L. McGonagle, categorically refute that claim and insist it was deliberate (Fig. 9-10).

I will not get into the possible motives that have been suggested as to why Israel carried out this attack. The US mainstream media was totally silent. No mention in the evening news nor in the morning newspapers!

President Lyndon B. Johnson, known to be very pro-Israeli, also kept silent. The official US records of the *Liberty* incident were designated top-secret and closed to the general public. Given Commander William

**Figure 9-10:** The US Navy's electronic reconnaissance gathering ship, the USS *Liberty*, after the attack by Israel in international waters on June 8, 1967, which killed 34 Americans and seriously damaged the ship.

L. McGonagle's heroic actions on board the ship that day to protect his men, he received the Medal of Honor, the most prestigious military medal. The Medal of Honor is presented by the president of the United States in the White House, but not on this occasion, as the public would have found out about it. It was awarded instead at the Washington Navy Yard by the secretary of the navy in a secret ceremony. For Lyndon B. Johnson, protecting the Israelis was more important than the legacy and honor of America's heroes on board the USS *Liberty*.

Twenty-four-hour cable news did not exist in 1967, but in 2017, at the commemoration of the fiftieth anniversary of the attack, it did. These networks, who claim the highest standards in fairness and transparency, remained silent.

Let me pose another scenario: a young American girl gets killed in broad daylight by a foreign military. Surely that would become the biggest news story of that day and the weeks to come.

Rachel Aliene Corrie, who was born and raised in Olympia, Washington, was touched by the plight of Palestinians living under Israeli occupation (Fig. 9-11). For a senior college project (independent-study program), she traveled to Gaza to initiate a "sister city" project between Olympia and Rafah (a refugee camp in southern Gaza). While in Palestine she became outspoken about the Israeli practice of collective punishment—a tactic in which the punishment for any Palestinian boy suspected to be associated with militant acts against Israel is to bulldoze the home of the boy's family.

**Figure 9-11:** Rachel Aliene Corrie, since she was a young girl, dreamt of making the world a better place.

I want to share with you excerpts from e-mails Rachel sent to her family from Palestine:

*February 7, 2003*

> Hi friends and family, and others,
>
> I have been in Palestine for two weeks and one hour now, and I still have very few words to describe what I see. It is most difficult for me to think about what's going on here when I sit down to write back to the United States.

*February 20, 2003*

> Mama,
>
> . . . Know that I have a lot of very nice Palestinians looking after me. I have a small flu bug, and got some very nice lemony drinks to cure me. Also, the woman who keeps the key for the well where we still sleep keeps asking me about you. She doesn't speak a bit of English, but she asks about my mom pretty frequently – wants to make sure I'm calling you.
>
> Love to you and Dad and Sarah and Chris and everybody. Rachel

*February 27, 2003*

> [To her mother]
>
> Love you. Really miss you. I have bad nightmares about tanks and bulldozers outside our house and you and me inside. Sometimes the adrenaline acts as an anesthetic for weeks and then in the evening or at night it just hits me again – a little bit of the reality of the situation. I am really scared for the people here. Yesterday, I watched a father lead his two tiny children, holding his hands, out into the sight of tanks and a sniper tower and bulldozers and Jeeps because he thought his house was going to be exploded. . . .
>
> This is in the area where Sunday about 150 men were rounded up and contained outside the settlement with gunfire over their heads and around them, while tanks and

bulldozers destroyed 25 greenhouses – the livelihoods for 300 people. . . .

Honestly, a lot of the time the sheer kindness of the people here, coupled with the overwhelming evidence of the willful destruction of their lives, makes it seem unreal to me. I really can't believe that something like this can happen in the world without a bigger outcry about it. . . .

Just want to write to my Mom and tell her that I'm witnessing this chronic, insidious genocide and I'm really scared, and questioning my fundamental belief in the goodness of human nature. . . .

When I come back from Palestine, I probably will have nightmares and constantly feel guilty for not being here, but I can channel that into more work. Coming here is one of the better things I've ever done. . . .

I love you and Dad. . . .

Rachel

On March 16, 2003, the IDF was engaged in a large-scale operation to demolish Palestinian homes where Rachel lived in Rafah. In protest, Rachel stood in the area where the IDF was bulldozing. According to an eyewitness account, "She was raising her hands and yelling at the bulldozer driver to stop. The bulldozer driver paid no attention. . . . He buried Rachel with dirt, which ended up, obviously, knocking her down. Then he ran over her, and then reversed and ran over her again." Rachel was severally injured and taken by a Red Crescent (Arab version of the Red Cross) ambulance to the Palestinian Al-Najjar hospital, arriving at the emergency room at 5:05 p.m., still alive but near death. At 5:20 p.m. she was declared dead.

Rachel had sent an email on February 28 which said, "I think I could see a Palestinian state or a democratic Israeli-Palestinian state within my lifetime." Rachel's lifetime was too short; she was killed at age 23. As an 11-year-old she gave a speech to her fifth grade class in which she stated, "I am here for other children, I am here because I care." She, unfortunately, was not here very long.

The United Nations said during this operation in Rafah, the IDF demolished 582 homes and damaged 721 others, with 5,305 people made homeless.

The Israelis said her death was an accident. No soldier spent a day in jail.

I researched the March 2003 mainstream media coverage of this violent death of an American girl on foreign soil. We had 24-hour cable news then, however, there was an eerie silence. To the best of my review, CNN had nothing about it on its live news segments—it placed one *online* story instead. The *New York Times* did provide a detailed account on March 17, 2003, under the title "Israeli Army Bulldozer Kills American Protesting in Gaza." Do you ever recall an interview on one of the main networks or CNN with Rachel's parents or siblings to ask them about the ordeal they went through? I could not find one. Had a 23-year-old American been killed so violently in any other country (especially if it had been an Arab or Muslim country), Rachel Corrie would have become a household name (Fig. 9-12).

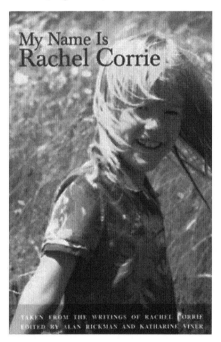

**Figure 9-12:** *My Name Is Rachel Corrie* is a theatrical production based on the diaries and email excerpts, some of which I shared above. It was jointly edited by journalist Katharine Viner and actor Alan Rickman, who also directed it. It opened at the Royal Court Theatre, London, in April 2005 and won a number of awards. It was scheduled to open in New York on March 22, 2006, but following the intervention of local Jewish religious and community leaders, it was suddenly "postponed indefinitely"— meaning canceled. The play's director (Rickman) accurately called it "censorship." In America, freedom of speech is untouchable; in this chapter I have shown that there is an exception to this rule: anything that vilifies the Israelis or paints Arabs and Muslims in a positive light.

In May 2020, a police officer in Minneapolis, Minnesota, brutally held his knee on the neck of a 46-year-old African American man, George Floyd, for almost nine minutes, resulting in his death. The media did its job and widely reported the incident. As a result there were protests in cities across the US. The mainstream media's wide censorship and silence over Rachel's no less brutal killing deprived her of the conversations about her life and what she stood for, and the American people were deprived of their right to protest her death.

What effect has the decades-old practice of the combined efforts of the mainstream media and Hollywood of covering up for Israel while vilifying Arabs and Muslims had on the American public perception? According to Sam Goldman, the executive director at the Loeb Institute for Religious Freedom at George Washington University, "Surveys conducted between 1947 and 1949 showed that nearly three times as many Americans sympathized with Jews over Arabs in the conflict in the former Mandatory Palestine." In the 2020 Gallup poll asking, "In the Middle East situation, are your sympathies more with the Israelis or more with the Palestinians?", 60% of Americans sympathize with Israelis, while 23% with the Palestinians. When it comes to polarizing issues, Americans are typically divided half and half, but not on this one.

## Déjà Vu

I started this book with the movie *Back to the Future*, so let me take you back a few centuries earlier to the sixteenth century. Pope Carafa—Paul IV—issued a papal bull, *Cum nimis absurdum* on July 17, 1555, to create a Jewish ghetto in Rome (in the Rione Sant'Angelo area):

> Jews are to own no real estate . . . Jews are to live in a distinct quarter, cut off from the rest of the city . . . This quarter is to have only one entrance, to be locked at sundown . . .

Christians of all ages were encouraged to treat the Jews as second-class citizens. For a Jew to defy a Christian in any way was to invite severe punishment.

Now let's look at the Palestinians living under Israeli occupation in the twentieth and the twenty-first centuries. They are restricted to live in special quarters. Their daily exits and entrances are heavily controlled. They are essentially cut off from the rest of the world. They are treated as second-class citizens by the Jewish settlers in the West Bank, and for them to defy the settlers brings severe punishment. Gaza is the world's biggest ghetto, the world's largest open-air prison.

This is not déjà vu for the Palestinians; they had never been exposed to such treatment in the 2,000 years of written history. It is for the Jews, who have been exposed to such dehumanizing treatment. The abused became the abusers, the jailed became the jailers.

# An Observation: The Most Violent & the Most Tolerant Religion: A Study

The three preceding chapters reviewed each of the three Abrahamic religions' invasion of the city that is holy to each of them, Jerusalem. Chapter 7: Deus Vult looked at the Christian invasion (First Crusade), Chapter 8: Clash of the Titans looked at the Muslim invasions and subsequent Crusades, and Chapter 9: Birth of a Nation looked at the Jewish invasions of Jerusalem.

The actions of each of the three invaders of the same city lend themselves to a unique experiment! It is a study to evaluate religious-based violence and how each treated the local population of Jerusalem outside of their own religious communities.

In science we call this an observational study.

## Methods

A retrospective review of a 1,694-year period extending from AD 326 to AD 2020 (when this book was written). Emperor Constantine took Jerusalem in 326 and the city was under Christian rule until 614, when the Persians invaded and briefly ruled until Emperor Heraclius retook the city in 630. It briefly remained under Christian control until 638 when the Muslim Caliph Umar conquered the city. Muslims then ruled until 1099 when the Christian Crusaders invaded. It remained under Christian control until Saladin retook the city in 1187. It stayed in Muslim hands (except for a short period of time from 1229–1244 when the Crusaders had control) all the way until the British invaded the city in 1917. Until 1948 it was controlled by Christians, at which point the State of Israel was created. It remains under Jewish control to the present time.

Available original sources were reviewed to document the events that took place during the invasions of Jerusalem with particular focus on the killing of civilians in the city.

## Results

Over the 1,694-year study period, violence committed in the name of all three religions was observed. Muslims had control of Jerusalem significantly longer than both Christians and Jews combined: 1,176 years (70 percent). Christianity held the city for 430 years (26 percent). Judaism held the city 72 years (4 percent).

Acts of terror and massacres in Jerusalem were committed significantly more by Christian invaders when compared to both Muslim and Jewish ones combined. Historical chronicles have documented the killing of thousands of Muslim civilians by Christian invaders, and thousands of Christian civilians by Jewish invaders. There has been no documented killings of thousands of Christians or Jewish civilians by Muslim invaders of Jerusalem.

## Discussion

Although it is commonly perceived by the popular culture in the West, and by extension in the global popular culture, that Islam has been the most violent of the three Abrahamic faiths; pure objective facts do not support this theory.

# Three Lions

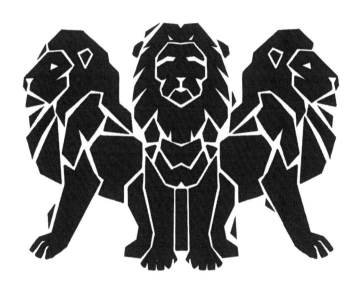

# Chapter 10
# Dracula: A Lion from Transylvania

I had just finished giving my lectures at a neurosurgery conference in the Romanian capital of Bucharest and decided to take two extra days before returning to the US. There is something I had wanted to do for a very long time, to drive to a small town by the name of Sighişoara in the middle of Romania. I drove through some of the most beautiful landscapes I had ever seen—the Carpathian Mountains of Transylvania (Fig. 10-1).

**Figure 10-1:** Map representing the fifteenth-century territories we define as Romania today. The three main regions were Transylvania, Wallachia, and Moldavia. The Ottoman territories to the south and southwest are now the countries of Bulgaria and Serbia.

The region of Transylvania was part of the Hungarian Empire (eleventh to sixteenth centuries) and subsequently a principality

*Saleem I. Abdulrauf*

within the Ottoman Empire (sixteenth and seventeenth centuries). Here I found the medieval walled city I was looking for (one of the very few medieval towns in Eastern Europe that is still inhabited). I was specifically looking for a three-story stone house located in the old part of town (Figs. 10-2 and 10-3).

**Figures 10-2 and 10-3:** I found the three-story house I was looking for (bottom) next to a clock tower (left) on a hill in the old town.

The sign on the wall of the house is in Romanian and reads: "In this house lived during 1431–1435 the ruler of Romania [Wallachia] Vlad Dracul, the son of Mircea cel Bătrân."

I was looking for this house to understand the deeply rooted history and myths behind the Muslim Ottoman Empire's relationship with Christian Europe (which we began discussing in Chapter 2). In this house lived Vlad II Dracul. The title *Dracul* comes from his membership in the society known as the Order of the Dragon, which was an extremist Christian militant fraternity founded by the king of Hungary, Sigismund von Luxembourg, who also became the Holy Roman emperor in the mid-fifteenth century. Sigismund's aim in creating the order was to reignite the zeal for the Crusades

234

by tapping into the deeply held feelings among the nobility of Europe that over-taking Jerusalem and defeating Islam was still attainable. After the Crusades (discussed in Chapters 7 and 8), Palestine and Jerusalem remained under Muslim control from the thirteenth century to the time of Sigismund's reign as Holy Roman emperor in the 1430s (Fig. 10-4).

**Figure 10-4:** The patch of the Order of the Dragon.

Dracul would have two sons born in this house, Vlad III and Radu. Vlad III was born in November or December 1431. We do not know who his mother was, as Dracul had a wife (Princess Cneajna) but also had a number of mistresses. After the boys got older, their father became the ruler of Wallachia (the region just south of Transylvania). As we saw in Chapter 2, many of these regions in the Balkans (all the way up to Hungary) were under Ottoman rule. It was a vassalage system much like what we see in the "Middle East" today. The ruler pays homage to the superpower.

## The Devout Crusader

It has been a custom now for over a hundred years that the sons of the aristocracy in the "Middle East" and the larger Muslim world are educated in top institutions in the US and England. Many of those educated in prestigious institutions like Harvard, Oxford, and Cambridge go on to be become dictators, ministers, and diplomats in their respective countries. This is a system by which Western powers have significant influence in "indoctrinating" future leaders of nations. This system was not invented by the West, however. The Ottoman Empire, which was the superpower of its time, created the original model of educating the sons of the European aristocracy. The sons of rulers, especially from the Balkan region, were recruited. They grew up living with select Turkish noble families in Anatolia (current-day Turkey) and were educated together in the same class-rooms as the sons of the ruling Ottoman royal family. Some of these European boys stayed on and became part of the ruling classes of the Ottoman Empire—they became part of the Turkish aristocracy. The most elite Ottoman infantry military unit was made up of Janissaries

(Turkish word meaning "new soldier"), who were the sons of European aristocrats educated and trained in Anatolia.

Dracul accepted his role as a vassal prince for the Ottomans in Wallachia. In 1442, the two boys, Vlad III (11) and Radu (7), were sent to Anatolia as part of the "boarding school" arrangement described above. Vlad III would study together with another young boy named Mehmed, an Ottoman prince and future sultan. (Mehmed was only a few months younger than Vlad III.) This is the same Mehmed we met in Chapter 8 (Fig. 8-9) who would go on to be the young sultan who conquered Constantinople in AD 1453.

In the years Vlad III and Radu spent in Anatolia, the relationship between the two deteriorated. While Vlad III enjoyed training in Turkish military skills and strategy (the most advanced in the world at the time), he was a devout Christian and hated Turkish culture. It is interesting to note that over the past few decades there have been Muslim students who went to school in the West and became more radical in their views as a result; similarly, Vlad III became more radical in his Christianity. Radu, on the other hand, enjoyed all aspects of his life in the Ottoman Empire, and as compared to Vlad III, was very handsome. He is known in European Chronicles as Radu the Handsome and supposedly enjoyed the social life in Anatolia quite a bit! These two brothers' polar opposite experiences while studying abroad is very similar to what we see from "Middle East" students studying in the US in the present day. Some are akin to Radu and excel in the social life far more than the academic life, but a few follow in Vlad III's path to become radicalized. A third segment, which perhaps is the majority, have a balanced experience and go back to their home countries and contribute positively.

Back home, Dracul's archenemy, the Hungarian governor of Transylvania, John Hunyadi, invaded Wallachia in November 1447. Dracul was captured and killed. His oldest son, Mircea (the older brother of the two boys), was buried alive in Târgoviște. Dracul is believed to be buried in the chapel of the Dealu Monastery near Târgoviște.

Vlad III, the main subject of this chapter, would later be known in Romanian history as *Vlad Țepeș* (or "Vlad the Impaler") and as Dracula (by adding the suffix *a* after Dracul, it means the "son of," meaning "the son of Dracul"). He himself signed his name as

"Dragulya" or "Drakulya" in the late 1470s, and I will refer to him by the name of Dracula for the remainder of the chapter (Fig. 10-5).

**Figure 10-5:** Fifteenth-century portrait of Vlad III, which hangs in the Portrait Galerie, Schloss Ambras, Innsbruck, Austria.

[Vlad (Dracula)] was not very tall, but very stocky and strong, with a cold and terrible appearance, a strong and aquiline nose, swollen nostrils, a thin and reddish face in which the very long eyelashes framed large wide-open green eyes; the bushy black eyebrows made them appear threatening. His face and chin were shaven, but for a moustache. The swollen temples increased the bulk of his head. A bull's neck connected [with] his head from which black curly locks hung on his wide-shouldered person.

—Niccolò Modrussa's description of Vlad the Impaler

Dracula was the heir apparent to claim his father's throne in Wallachia. The Ottomans, who were Dracul's patron, sent an army that defeated Hunyadi's forces. They installed the 17-year-old Dracula as the ruler of Wallachia in 1448. His official title was *voivode*, which is a Slavic term meaning military commander or governor. This only lasted a few months, since after the departure of the Ottoman forces, Dracula was unable to keep his throne against the much stronger Hungarian military. He fled to safety to the Ottoman Empire and lived in the city of Edirne (the Ottoman capital prior to the capture of Constantinople).

The next few years (the exile years) of Dracula's life we know very little about; he spent time both in the Ottoman Empire as well as Moldavia where his uncle was the ruler. It is my impression that these were formative years that made him the ultra-extremist Christian he would go on to become. While in exile he would have received the news in May 1453 that his childhood classmate, Mehmed, had conquered Constantinople, thereby closing the door on the Crusades that had been a core mission of Europe for over 350 years. Constantinople had been pivotal both from a geographic and re-supply standpoint for the Crusaders on their way to Palestine from Europe. This news must have been very difficult for the ultra-extremist Christian that Dracula had become.

By the summer of 1456 Dracula was finally able to gain military support from his allies and retook Wallachia. His actions as he took reign reflect his deep beliefs and his interpretations of Christianity. He was opposed to the boyars (the nobles) who he believed were corrupt and un-Christian. He invited some 200 boyars with their wives and children for a feast to his palace in Târgoviște on Easter Day, 1457. After the feast, he had his guards lock all doors of the palace. He had all older people impaled, and all younger ones taken as his servants, or more like slaves, who were taken to an old castle, the Poenari Castle, and forced to reconstruct it for him (Fig. 10-6). By choosing this mountaintop castle, Dracula made it obvious that he had already decided to take on the Ottomans. It would make a formidable hiding place.

Impaling is a combined torture and killing method. It involves a large wooden stake inserted through the anus and exited through the neck, mouth, or shoulders. The stake is then mounted in the ground vertically. For those whom Dracula wanted to prolong the suffering, the stake used was not sharp but rather rounded and blunt, thus avoiding injury to major blood vessels inside the abdomen and chest.

In Dracula's extreme interpretations of Christianity, he believed that women who do not remain virgins before marriage must be punished. He had them impaled with the stake going through the vagina. During my research for this book, I found it to be a pattern that women are often in the crosshairs of religious extremists. The Wahhabis, the Crusaders, ISIS, and White supremacists in the US and Europe all have peddled in this philosophy.

Moreover, Dracula's killing of other Christians is in keeping with religious extremist philosophies across religions. The Wahhabis, Al-Qaeda, and ISIS have killed more Muslims than that of any other religion. They do not consider these Muslims as "true" Muslims. The same was true for Dracula: he did not consider the Christians he was killing as "true" Christians.

**Figure 10-6:** Aerial view of the ruins of Poenari Castle, perched like an eagle's nest standing high on a cliff overlooking the Argeș River, at the foothills of the Carpathian Mountains. I found out that is not an easy place to get to: you have to climb 1,462 concrete steps!

## Forest of the Impaled

Pope Pius II admired Dracula for his devout Christianity. Dracula would get the news that he had prepared for all his adult life. Pius II announced a new Crusade in September of 1459. This was not the same Europe we witnessed at the height of the Crusading fervor seen in the twelfth and thirteenth centuries. There were no prominent nobility in Europe lining up to heed Pius II's call, except for Dracula, who committed to the pope to take the lead. Dracula also had the full support of Hungarian King Matthias Corvinus.

Once Mehmed heard the news, he attempted diplomacy with his childhood classmate, Dracula, by sending senior diplomats to speak with him. Dracula would use this opportunity to send a resounding message. He knew that asking the diplomats to remove their turbans was not appropriate for them due to their religious customs. So when they arrived at his court, he told them to remove their turbans to show him respect, and as expected, they declined. Dracula ordered his guards to hold them down and kill them by hammering nails through their turbans into their skulls.

Next, Dracula invaded Ottoman lands to the south (in present-day Bulgaria). To explain what Dracula did, I will share his own words in a letter he sent to King Corvinus in 1462: "We killed 23,884 Turks without counting those whom we burned in homes," adding that he had done so "for the preservation of Christianity and the strengthening of the Catholic faith." In the 2,000-year journey of this book, specifically regarding the relationship between Christianity and Islam, this was the largest single act of terrorism. As per Dracula himself, these nearly 24,000 people who were impaled or burned alive were not soldiers but civilians (villagers), and he did it for religious reasons. The acts of Osama bin Laden and ISIS pale in comparison to the acts of religious-based terrorism committed by the ruler of Wallachia in collaboration with the pope and the king of Hungary.

Dracula's actions were celebrated throughout Western Europe and he was hailed a hero by Pope Pius II.

Once the above news reached Mehmed, he decided that this Crusade must be stopped, and to do so, Dracula must be removed. He planned to replace Dracula with Radu the Handsome.

Mehmed arrived in Wallachia and pursued Dracula all the way to the capital Târgoviște. The sultan found the city deserted, but he witnessed yet another one of Dracula's cruel acts—the "forest of the impaled" (term used by European chronicles for the sight that Mehmed witnessed). The city had been turned into a graveyard composed of concentric circles of some 20,000 impaled Ottoman prisoners. The Greek historian Laonikos Chalkokondyles described the scene:

> The sultan's army entered into the area of the impalements, which was seventeen stades long and seven stades wide [approximately 1.95 miles long and 0.8 miles wide]. There were large stakes there on which, as it was said, about twenty

thousand men, women, and children had been spitted, quite a sight for the Turks and the sultan himself . . . There were infants too affixed to their mothers on the stakes, and birds had made their nests in their entrails.

Dracula had fled to the Poenari Castle, and the Ottoman army followed him there. He knew the castle better than the advancing Ottoman troops and was able to escape through a back exit. He fled to Hungary to his patron, King Matthias Corvinus.

Mehmed made Radu the Handsome the governor of Wallachia and returned to Constantinople.

King Mathias Corvinus, a shrewd politician, seeing the situation was no longer viable for continuing the Crusade, decided to imprison Dracula by placing him under house arrest. During this time Dracula married the king's cousin and they had two sons. When Radu the Handsome, after ruling Wallachia for 11 years, suddenly died at age 40 in 1475, Dracula decided to regain his kingdom. King Corvinus supported Dracula in his military takeover of Wallachia in 1476. Mehmed was not going to accept that, so he sent a special force into Wallachia that killed Dracula in January 1477. Dracula was beheaded and his head was sent to Constantinople and placed on a stake for all to see. It is said that monks buried his headless body at the altar in the Snagov Monastery (located on a tiny island in a lake just outside Bucharest). Dracula had been very generous to monasteries and churches throughout his life.

## Dracula Lives!

The region immediately south of Romania that was politically and militarily involved in all the events discussed in this chapter is collectively called the Balkans. It is a triangular area in southeastern Europe which for hundreds of years (going back to the fourteenth century) was part of the Ottoman Empire. It was not until the nineteenth century that the countries that we currently associate with it (e.g., Serbia, Croatia, Bosnia and Herzegovina) started to form. The term *Balkan* is a politically charged one, very similar to the term "Middle East." *Balkanization* refers to the specific process by which this region was divided up along ethnic lines into smaller countries starting in the nineteenth century. Therefore, the term is considered pejorative and for the most part has been abandoned. However, the term "Middle East," which is the best example of externally designed "Balkanization," is widely used (Fig. 10-7)!

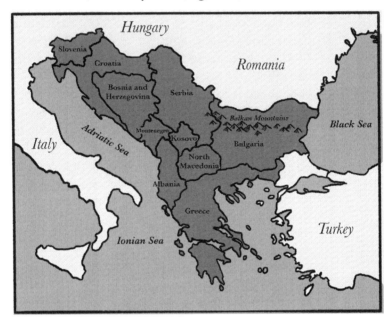

**Figure 10-7:** Southeast Europe/the Balkan Peninsula: This triangular region between the Adriatic and Aegean Seas was part of the Ottoman Empire for some 500 years until the 1800s when the empire started to weaken. The countries that are considered geopolitically "Balkan" are shaded in dark gray. For most of the twentieth century up to the 1980s, Bosnia and Herzegovina, Croatia, Kosovo, North Macedonia, Montenegro, Serbia, and Slovenia were one single country: Yugoslavia.

The word *Balkan* comes from the Balkan mountain range which extends from Bulgaria to Serbia. The origin of the term *Balkan* is not so clear; it may have come from the Persian term *balakhana* meaning "big high house" (the Persians were in the peninsula in the first millennium during the Greco–Persian wars) or from Turkish in which *balkan* means "chain of wooded mountains."

We have reviewed the extremist religious movements within the two branches of Christendom, the Crusades within Catholicism (Chapters 7 and 8) and Christian Zionism within Protestantism

(Chapter 6). The third branch is Orthodox Christianity, and extremism in this branch is the subject of this chapter. Just like Romania, all countries in the Balkan Peninsula are majority Orthodox Christian (with the exception of Croatia, which is majority Catholic, and Bosnia and Herzegovina, Albania, and Kosovo, which are majority Muslim). The legend of historical Dracula is well known in this region, and the specter of his ethnically based Christian extremism reared its ugly head once again in the twentieth century.

In the early 1990s, three Serb men with extremist Christian Orthodox ideations similar to those of Dracula—Slobodan Milošević, the president of Serbia, Radovan Karadžić, a psychiatrist, and Ratko Mladić, a military commander—would plan another genocide in the Balkans.

Just like ISIS recruiting extremists from Muslim countries, the three masterminds recruited militant extremist Orthodox Christians from Russia, Bulgaria, and Greece. Moreover, Milošević created the Scorpions, a paramilitary Orthodox Christian extremist group, remarkably similar to the Order of the Dragon that Dracula's father was a member of.

On July 11, 1995, the Serb extremists entered a small Bosnian town located in Eastern Bosnia by the name of Srebrenica. They separated the women and girls from the men and boys, and in the largest act of terrorism on European soil since WWII, over the next few days massacred 7,000–8,000 Bosnian Muslim men and their young boys (Fig. 10-8). Reminiscent of

**Figure 10-8:** Coffins containing the recovered remains of victims of the Srebrenica massacre in Bosnia and Herzegovina, July 2008.

Dracula's actions, many were tortured before being killed. The ordeal for the women and young girls was no better. Going back to the theme we have seen throughout this book, religious-based terrorists have a fixation with women. One European Union study estimated that in 1992 alone, 20,000 Muslim women and girls were raped by Serbs. A UN commission of experts concluded that a "systematic rape policy" was being implemented by the Serbs. Serb terrorists set up "rape camps" where women and girls as young as 12 years of age were repeatedly raped and only released when pregnant. The pregnancy was a critical element in the overall ethnic cleansing policy, as it was aimed at impregnating Muslim women with Serb Orthodox Christian progeny.

The United Nations Security Council set up an international tribunal for the prosecution of those responsible for violating international humanitarian law committed in this conflict—the International Criminal Tribunal for the former Yugoslavia (ICTY). Milošević was charged with genocide by the ICTY but he died in 2006 before the trial was concluded. Karadžić was found guilty of genocide by the ICTY and sentenced to life in prison in 2016. Similarly, Mladić, who was dubbed the "Butcher of Bosnia," was found guilty by the ICTY for crimes against humanity and was sentenced to life in prison in 2017.

All the hatred toward Muslims in this conflict was connected to the earlier story of Dracula. For example, during the ICTY trial it came out that Mladić routinely invoked the "Ottoman Empire" and referred to Bosnian Muslims as "Turks." He said in a TV interview during his incursion into Bosnia, "Let our Serbs see what we have done to them [Muslims], how we took care of the Turks . . ." In Serbia there continued to be significant support for the three masterminds and their actions before, during, and after the ICTY convictions, similar to the moral support for Al-Qaeda seen in a number of Muslim countries. Milorad Dodik, the president of the autonomous Serb region, said that regardless of the international tribunal's verdict, Mladić "remains a legend of the Serb nation" (Fig. 10-9).

The Serb acts of terrorism against the Muslim population of the Balkans confirms that the hatred of hundreds of years ago is still alive and well in Europe today. When Turkey applied to become a member of the European Union, who in Europe was opposed to it? Europe's ultra-right-wing religious leaders. For example, when Pope Benedict XVI (Ratzinger) was a cardinal in 2004, he expressed his disapproval of the candidacy of Turkey by saying that due to its Muslim Ottoman history, it was "in permanent contrast to Europe."

**Figure 10-9:** Graffiti of Ratko Mladić (the "Butcher of Bosnia")
on a wall in Belgrade, Serbia (photo taken December 2, 2017).
Graffiti appeared all over, especially in downtown Belgrade, in
support of Mladić the week after his ICTY trial for genocide and
sentencing of life in prison. Mladić is revered as a hero by some in
the media as well as among young Orthodox White Serbs.

The young Sultan Mehmed's occupation of Constantinople
(now Istanbul) over 500 years ago remains a deeply sensitive issue
for many traditionalists within Christendom to this date. The most
iconic historical site in the city is the Hagia Sophia (from Greek
meaning "Holy Wisdom"), with its grand basilica commissioned by
Roman Emperor Justinian I in AD 532 (Figs. 10-10 and 10-11).
The Hagia Sophia would remain the seat of the Christian (Eastern)
Orthodox Church for 667 years until the Catholic Church's Fourth
Crusade sacked Constantinople on its way to Palestine in 1204 and
desecrated the church. It then served as a Roman Catholic cathedral for 57 years before it was converted back to become the seat
of the Eastern Orthodox Church when the Byzantine Empire
returned to power in 1261. Once Mehmet II invaded the city in
1453, he converted it into a mosque, and it remained so for 481 years,
at which time the Turkish government turned it into a museum in
1934. In July 2020, the Turkish government returned its status back
to a mosque but assured that Christian emblems inside the structure would not be removed, and it would continue to be open for all
faiths to visit. The Christian Orthodox Church in Russia (home to

the largest Orthodox community in the world) expressed its regret over the Turkish decision. In Greece, home of the historic vision of Christian Orthodoxy, the minister of culture was not so subtle, calling the move "an open provocation to the entire civilized world." The Hagia Sophia is an example that the emotions that ran deep during Dracula's era still run deep today. I would be remiss not to point out the hypocrisy of many politicians, religious leaders, and major news outlets in Europe regarding the conversion of the Hagia Sophia, when there has been complete silence over the conversion of hundreds of mosques into churches in Spain and Greece as well as the destruction of historical mosques by the Chinese government as part of its current policy interning Muslims in concentration camps.

**Figure 10-10:** The Hagia Sophia (exterior view) under the moonlight. A grand structure that has stood for close to 1,500 years. It has served as the seat of the Eastern Orthodox Church, a Catholic cathedral, a museum, and a mosque.

**Figure 10-11:** Interior view of the majestic dome of the Hagia Sophia. Christian emblems and Islamic calligraphy adorn the walls and ceiling.

## Hollywood: The Defender of the Faith

Bram Stoker was an Irish author who wrote the novel *Dracula* in 1897. Stoker was not versed in the history of Vlad III, and he used bits of information about Romanian history to pen his novel.

His novel would lead to multitudes of films about Vlad the Impaler—Dracula. The Hollywood directors and producers, however, would have known the story of Dracula when producing their multi-million-dollar movies. I reviewed all the major movies made about Dracula for this chapter, and the single commonality is that they removed the core motivation behind Dracula's actions—Christian extremism—from the storylines. In most of these horror movies, Dracula is a violent, blood-sucking character who is just a flawed individual, or in some versions a misunderstood gothic figure. That is exactly what the renowned Francis Ford Coppola did in 1992, when he both produced and directed *Bram Stoker's Dracula* (Columbia Pictures) (Fig. 10-12).

**Figure 10-12:** Image from Francis Ford Coppola's 1992 film *Bram Stoker's Dracula*. Shown on the left is Mina Harker (played by Winona Ryder) and on the right is Dracula (played by Gary Oldman), who, rather than a cruel terrorist, is depicted as a young, handsome, and playfully flirtatious figure.

As a physician and a neuroscientist, I am aware that children as young as three years of age can be taught to discriminate. Negative imagery of Arabs and Muslims, in a stealth fashion, has been peddled by Hollywood, not just to adults but also to children. Conversely, it has sanitized its depiction of Western White Christian extremist characters. Dracula has been sanitized by the movie and TV industry. For example, *Count Duckula* is a British animated comedy horror television series created by British studio Cosgrove Hall Films, and has been shown in countries around the world. You may recall from Chapter 8, Francis Ford Coppola displayed an "Arab" in a children's movie (*The Black Stallion*) as a man who assaults both the beloved horse and the American child. The "Arab" in that movie was a totally fictional character and not based on any historical figure. In *Dracula*, Coppola takes a real historical figure, arguably one of the biggest Christian terrorists in history who massacred thousands of Muslim civilians, and projects him as a tragic misunderstood hero!

This brings me to a core question I sought to understand and delve into in writing this book. When a White Christian extremist male belonging to the KKK or other similar White supremacy groups commits a mass murder, the mainstream media is deeply reluctant to call him a "terrorist." Similarly, Hollywood's narrative about these characters has been one of tragic individuals, rather than vicious villains. The question is why?

Invariably the discussion in the mainstream media following a terrorist attack by a White Christian male focuses on the mental stability of the individual, the stresses he was facing, and potential childhood trauma. As the reader, I wish to engage you in the following question: Do you remember questions in the mainstream media about Osama bin Laden or ISIS terrorist leaders' life stresses, mental stability, or childhood trauma they may have potentially been exposed to?

In the 2019 highly acclaimed Warner Bros. movie, *Joker*, the protagonist (played by Joaquin Phoenix) was a stand-up comedian who was abused as a child, disenfranchised and impoverished, and ultimately turned to violence and murder. The *New York Times* columnist Dan Brooks used the term "moral ambiguity" when reviewing the portrayal of the main character as a hero who took revenge using deadly violence against innocent civilians (terrorism) in his reaction to a world that had been unjust to him. This narrative can and is only used by Hollywood when rationalizing acts of terror by White Christian males.

What has been the impact of such biased narratives by the mainstream media and Hollywood of protecting White Christian terrorists in the popular culture and society at large? Let me share some specific examples.

## A Trip to Burger King!

On June 17, 2015, White supremacist Dylann Roof walked into the Emanuel African Methodist Episcopal Church in South Carolina and used a semi-automatic handgun to kill nine African Americans. All victims were shot multiple times, with the eldest, Susie Jackson, an 87-year-old grandmother, struck at least 10 times.

Dylann Roof said while killing people in the church that day, "You blacks…raping white women every day" (per a journal entry after his arrest). This is once again the common thread that I have mentioned about religious extremist terrorists throughout this book: there is a deep link to misogyny under the guise of protecting female chastity.

Roof was arrested the next morning in Shelby, North Carolina. After the arrest he told the officers he was hungry, so they took him to Burger King before taking him taking to the police station! Imagine if this had been a non-White, non-Christian, "Brown" terrorist, he would have been fortunate if he had not been killed during the arrest, let alone getting a trip to Burger King.

Immediately it became important to check for other factors that would have led Roof to commit this massacre, as being a White Christian extremist was not in and of itself enough to be considered the reason! The official psychiatric evaluation by the court revealed that Roof suffered from no psychiatric illness. I would like to add that he had no childhood trauma, drug abuse issues, or any other of the common tropes peddled in the mainstream media and by Hollywood to explain away how an innocent White Christian extremist would commit such heinous acts.

The Council of Conservative Citizens (a White nationalist group) issued a statement saying that Dylann Roof had "legitimate grievances" against Black people. This was akin to a statement made

by President Donald Trump in August 2017 about White supremacists gathered in Charlottesville, Virginia, when he said there were
"very fine people on both sides." These statements could not be made
in the American culture regarding any religious terrorists, except in
the defense of White Christian extremists. Such vile narratives can
be peddled openly in American popular culture due to the normalization by the mainstream media and Hollywood of the concept that
a White Christian extremist mass murderer can never be equated
with "Brown" non-Christian terrorists.

Let me share with you an example regarding the ubiquity of this
concept. In August 2019 there was yet another act of terrorism by a
White Christian extremist, Patrick Crusius, who shot and killed 23
people and injured 23 others in El Paso, Texas. On CNN the day
afterward, the highly respected counter-terrorism expert Phil Mudd,
despite the fact the shooter had a hatred-filled manifesto, posited,
"Did he break up with his girlfriend yesterday?" I can assure you such
a question has never been raised about an Al-Qaeda or ISIS terrorist
who just committed a massacre.

While the default conclusion when a "Brown" Muslim male
commits an act of terrorism is that he is inherently evil, the default
conclusion following an act of terrorism by a White Christian is that
he is not inherently evil, there must have been something else at
play—childhood trauma, had too much to drink, his girlfriend broke
up with him, etc. This glaring dichotomy is a result of decades of
media and Hollywood impact on the popular culture. In my research
of the historical Dracula, I came across a Romanian historian who
said the "only" explanation of Dracula's cruel acts is that he "must"
have been abused by the Ottomans when he was a child living in
Anatolia. In other words, a White Christian male cannot possibly be
evil even if he commits acts of terrorism, and if he does, it must be
someone else's fault!

## The Populist Leaders of the Twenty-First Century

Let me take you back to current-day Romania, where we started
this chapter looking for the house where Dracula was born. I was
very interested to know what Romanian people thought of Dracula.
I must admit, I was surprised by the answers I heard. The majority

of the people I spoke to consider Dracula a national hero. This was the impression I was getting across generations, not only from the older generation but also university students. They are proud of the historic Dracula but not of the Hollywood one in which he is often portrayed as a vampire.

The Romanians have very deliberately separated the two Draculas. Tourists coming to Romania looking for artifacts of the real Dracula end up going to Bran Castle (known as Dracula's Castle), which is located some 16 miles southwest of Brasov. While this castle has historical significance as the residence for the Romanian royal family in the early part of the twentieth century, based on the research I did for this chapter, I did not see any evidence that Dracula ever even entered it. The location was in an inhospitable area, since it was dominated by Transylvanian Saxons and not Wallachians, and Dracula was too smart to use such an exposed location.

The other Dracula, the historical Dracula's image is well preserved, and exists right in the city of Bucharest, where the tourists fly into to head to Bran Castle!

In the old city area of Bucharest, in front of the Church of St. Anthony and the Old Court, there is a statue in tribute to Dracula (Fig. 10-13).

**Figure 10-13:** Statue of Vlad Țepeș at the Curtea Veche (Old Princely Court) which was the palace built during the reign of Dracula and was the place from which he ruled. The associated church is the Church of Saint Anthony, the oldest church in the city of Bucharest, Romania.

As I drove into picturesque small towns in Transylvania, I found memorabilia in small shops that had Dracula's name, image, or insignia. When I investigated this more, I found out that Dracula has been celebrated in Romanian poetry and art for over a hundred years now. As part of giving lectures in Europe over the past 10 years (within my field of neurosurgery), I have been to Romania a number of times and have developed some close friendships. The Romanian people are indeed impressive; despite having struggled under decades of Communist rule by the Soviet Union and achieving freedom only recently (1989), they have persevered. Romania is one of the most economically challenged nations within the EU, but its people have a tremendous spirit to develop their nation. I was puzzled as to why these peace-loving, hard-working people would so admire Dracula. To answer this question, we need to delve into a larger phenomenon seen around the world in the early part of the twenty-first century.

*Populism* is a vague term, in use since the nineteenth century, and refers to engagement of the population in political decision-making. It has come to stand for the idea of "common people" taking a stand against the "elite." From the context of this book, I am referring to a very specific type of populism seen in the early part of the twenty-first century—the populist leaders that emerged in otherwise democratic nations. (Dictators in traditional autocratic societies, like most of the Arab countries, are not per this narrow definition "populist" leaders because the people did not choose/elect them.) These democratically elected leaders, under the claim of representing the "common people," identify specific ethnic or religious groups as the "enemy." I would like to give five examples: Donald Trump in the US (elected president in 2016), Jair Bolsonaro in Brazil (elected president in 2018), Viktor Orbán in Hungary (elected prime minister in 2010), Benjamin Netanyahu in Israel (elected prime minister in 1996), and Narendra Modi in India (elected prime minister in 2014).

For Donald Trump, the enemy was Mexicans, Muslims, and people of African descent. He labeled African countries as "shitholes" and Scandinavian ones as "beautiful."

For Jair Bolsonaro, the enemy was people of African descent and the indigenous people of South America, about whom he said, "The North American cavalry were the competent ones because they decimated their indigenous people in the past and today, they don't have this problem [American Indians] in their country." In keeping with the common link identified in this book about religious extremists' hate for women, Bolsonaro said "I had four sons, but then I had a moment of weakness, and the fifth was a girl."

Viktor Orbán of Hungary, a country where Dracula lived for some 10 years, would endorse Dracula's call for a Crusading battle by defining himself as the commander who will defend "Christian Europe" against "Muslim invaders." He is referring to Muslim immigrants—who became immigrants as a result, I may add, of the Western Christian power play inside the "Middle East," as is well described in this book. Another common theme we have witnessed in every Crusade is the targeting of Jews in the march to Palestine. The same is true now during Orbán's "crusade." Some Jews have been told to "go back to Israel." Hungary had an estimated 800,000 Jews in 1941, and today fewer than a 100,000.

For Benjamin Netanyahu of Israel, his enemies have been the Palestinians and the Arabs. It is this stand that has allowed Netanyahu to win election after election, making him the longest-serving prime minister in Israeli history.

For Narendra Modi, the enemy is the minority Muslim population (14.2 percent) of India. In 1996, Ashis Nandy, a prominent Hindu Indian psychologist, interviewed Modi for several hours and concluded, "Modi was a fascist in every sense . . . I don't mean this as a term of abuse. It's a diagnostic category." Events leading to the killings of hundreds of Muslim civilians have occurred in every town Modi has governed, all the way up to and including his rule as prime minister of India. He was actually barred from entering the US prior to becoming prime minister because he was part of an extremist organization in India, and based on US regulations, his role in advancing "severe violations of religious freedom" led to the decision.

Although the media labels the above five leaders as "populists," the traditional definition of populism means standing up against the "elite"; for these five, the enemy is not the elite but rather minorities!

The public platform all these right-wing leaders stand for is the preservation of the historical privilege of the majority (e.g., Christian Whites in America, Hindus in India). To achieve this, they treat the "other" as the villain. It was through a wink and nod to their constituencies that they claimed that success, or the preservation of privilege, could only be achieved through good old xenophobia. So, the term "populist" is nothing but a sanitized term to describe them and clearly does not apply. The irony is, their supporters despise political correctness, but rather than calling these five men with the correct defining term "xenophobic leaders," they prefer the politically correct term of "populist leaders."

It is a common belief that each extreme-right or -left "populist" dictator comes into power from within the country organically. I question that train of thought. There is external help, propagation, and inspiration. Benito Mussolini came into power in Italy in 1922 with a fascist platform. This founder of fascism would go on to inspire Adolf Hitler (Germany), Francisco Franco (Spain), and António de Oliveira Salazar (Portugal). Similarly, Donald Trump has inspired leaders outside the US. Steve Bannon, who served as the chief executive of Donald Trump's presidential campaign in 2016, has traveled throughout Europe to inspire extreme-right populist movements. Bernard-Henri Lévy, the renowned French philosopher and author, said in a comment directed at Bannon, "I think you do a very dirty job in Europe."

That brings me back to Dracula. How does his story connect to this right-wing so-called populist movement of the twenty-first century? I believe, and not based on any scientific survey, that if Dracula were to come back from the dead today, he would be elected president of Romania by an overwhelming majority. I got to speak to some of my friends in Romania while writing this chapter and I found them to be defensive, and by that, I mean they were defending Dracula's violent actions. One physician told me, "He was doing it for our people."

The story of Dracula's Romania for me is a microcosm of the right-wing "populist" movement of the early twenty-first century. Although we think of Dracula as a Transylvanian, and yes, he was born there, he was a Wallachian through and through. He saw the Saxons (people of Germanic descent) of Transylvania as outsiders. He saw the Hungarians, who were Catholic (Wallachians and Romanians are mostly Christian Orthodox), as outsiders. Of course, the Ottoman Muslims were seen as the greatest enemy. This idea of "outsiders/foreigners" is most intriguing to me. The Saxons of Transylvania had been there for hundreds of years. The indigenous peoples of the Americas, by definition, have been there far longer than the ancestors of Donald Trump and Jair Bolsonaro arrived by boat to those lands. Muslims have been in India for over 1,000 years!

I believe what happened in the Balkans in the late twentieth century, the massacre of Muslims by the Serbs, was a spark that helped propel the right-wing movements seen in Europe in the early twenty-first century. An incident involving the Serb "populist" commander Mladić (the "Butcher of Bosnia"), provides an insight that helps to connect all of this. The UN had a Dutch battalion ostensibly to protect Muslim civilians from Serb acts of terrorism, and they were in regular contact with Mladić. One day, Mladić saw a dark-skinned Dutch battalion officer, which prompted him to tell a White Dutch officer (a witness in the above-mentioned ICTY trial), "Multi-ethnic societies were a problem for the Netherlands and that in ten years' time he [Mladić] would be in the Netherlands, with his soldiers to protect the Dutch from Muslims and other races." Mladić's prophecy actually came true, although it was not him personally; within 10 years those forces to protect people from "other races" were established in the form of the "populist" leaders of the early twenty-first century. Hollywood was right once: Dracula lives!

Mladić pointed out the need for the use of the military to achieve his goals. Donald Trump routinely touts the heritage of the Confederate army that fought the US Army during the American Civil War with the aim to preserve slavery. Jair Bolsonaro speaks nostalgically of the Brazilian right-wing military dictatorships which ruled with brutality before Brazil became a democracy. Narendra Modi has used the Indian police force in every incident under his watch that led to the massacre of Muslim civilians.

Dracula also achieved his goals using the military. His role as part of the military history of Romania is acknowledged and revered by some to this day. I visited the National Military Museum of Romania in Bucharest, and a sculpture of Dracula stands at the entrance in tribute to him (Figs. 10-14 and 10-15).

**Figures 10-14 and 10-15:** Statue of Dracula at the National Military Museum of Romania in Bucharest (left). On the wall of the museum is a plate (below) which reads: "Vlad Țepeș (1431–1476). The ruler of the Romanian country in [three periods] 1448, 1456–1462, and 1476."

# Chapter 11
# Omar al-Mukhtar:
# A Lion from the Desert

We discussed back in Chapter 2 that by the late nineteenth century, the Ottoman Empire was pejoratively labeled the "The Sick Man of Europe." The British and French took advantage of that weakness during WWI and created the "Middle East" which they shared between them. That was the result of the WWI eastern front campaign—the battles for the Arabian Peninsula and the Levant. The weakness of the Ottoman Empire, specifically its inability to protect its borders, actually started in the 1800s and was most pronounced at its periphery, particularly in North Africa. The French capitalized on this frailty and invaded and occupied the Ottoman regency of Algiers (current-day Algeria) in 1830. Ben Kiernan, in his book *Blood and Soil: A World History of Genocide and Extermination from Sparta to Darfur*, wrote that within three decades of the French conquest war, mass killings, famine, and disease reduced the original Algerian population of 3 million by a figure ranging from 500,000 to 1,000,000.

For the first time since the twelfth-century Crusades, Arabs and Muslims were confronting the phenomenon of a brutal foreign occupation. I am sure it is not lost on readers that the Crusades were mainly French, and the next brutal occupation of an Arab Muslim land some 600 years later would also occur at the hands of the French. The only playbook the North Africans had of successfully dealing with violent foreign occupation was the memory in their history books of Saladin.

Among the Algerians would emerge a 24-year-old man by the name of Abdelkader ibn Muhieddine (later referred to as Abdelkader El Djezairi) who, like Saladin, grew up memorizing the Qur'an and was an avid horseman. He would become the leader of the Algerian resistance movement. He was able to garner the support of the local tribes and create a 2,000-man army. While this force was no comparison to the massive French military operation in Algeria, he was able to win a number of tactical battles. Abdelkader became highly respected by his people. His statement, "Don't ask about a man's genealogy, ask about his character," reminded them of a nostalgic time from long ago when the Muslims were ruled by the original caliphs in the seventh century. They honored him by bestowing upon him the title of emir (meaning "prince" or "commander" during wartime) (Fig. 11-1).

**Figure 11-1:** Abdelkader El Djezairi. The warrior who would go on to become the beacon for the concept of humanitarianism. When he died in 1883, the *New York Times* eulogized him as "one of the few great men of the century. The nobility of his character won him the admiration of the world." Nineteenth-century drawing (unknown artist).

Behind the scenes, accounts emerged of how kind Abdelkader was toward the French prisoners of war (POWs), which he based on Qur'anic principles. At a time when there were no conventions on the treatment of prisoners, he turned to the Qur'an: he forbade torture, he made sure the prisoners were given the same food as his own soldiers, and he allowed religious freedom of the Christian prisoners. At times, the number of POWs was so large that he could not provide hospitable treatment, so he released them, knowing that they could return to the battlefield. Through these released French soldiers, the stories of Abdelkader's honor code made it back to the French public. For French generals however, Abdelkader's successes on the battlefield were met with a scorched-earth policy. Ultimately, the generals prevailed; Abdelkader surrendered in December 1847 after almost two decades of fighting the French occupation. They reached an agreement that Abdelkader would go into exile in Alexandria, Egypt. However, the French reneged on the agreement and sent Abdelkader and his family to be imprisoned in France. During his imprisonment, there was significant outcry by the French public to release him. A number of high-profile figures intervened and ultimately, after five years of imprisonment, he was released in 1852 with the promise that he would never return to Algeria. During these five years, and due to poor conditions in the jail, his wife and two children died. The French failed to reciprocate Abdelkader's honor code for the civil treatment of prisoners.

A few years later, just east of Algeria, a boy was born in 1858 to a poor family in the town of Zanzur in the Ottoman Empire's coastal plains along the Mediterranean. His family named him Omar. The boy was orphaned at a young age and lived in poverty. He grew up much like Saladin and Abdelkader, studying the Qur'an and learning to ride Arabian horses.

Meanwhile, Italy, a country neighboring France to the east, witnessed the colonial successes of France in the late nineteenth century in Algeria. It set its sights on the Muslim lands neighboring Algeria to the east: Libya—which is where Omar was born and raised.

## The Reconquista

Italy invaded Libya in 1911. The mild-mannered Omar, now 53 years of age, who had been an elementary school teacher most of his life, would take on a role similar to Abdelkader. He unified the desert tribes to create a resistance force—a very efficient small army. Omar knew the desert terrain far better than the occupying Italian forces. He was able to cause significant damage to their supply lines and became enemy number one for the Italian generals. His treatment of Italian POWs was also exemplary. In a well-noted account, after winning a battle, some of his soldiers pushed for the execution of the Italian POWs as the Italians had done to Arab POWs; Omar forbade it by saying, "They [the Italians] are not our teachers." He, like Abdelkader and Saladin before him, made the Qur'anic principles the cornerstone of his policies (Fig. 11-2).

**Figure 11-2:** Omar al-Mukhtar Mohammad bin Farhat al-Manifi. Known in Arab culture and poetry as the "Lion of the Desert."

I would like to take you back to Chapter 2, where we discussed the events in the "Middle East" during WWI, when Britain and France betrayed the Arabs. Italy was an ally of Britain and France while Omar was fighting the Italian occupation.

The Italian occupation of Libya was no less brutal than the French occupation of Algeria. They placed a good portion of Libyans of the northeastern region (Al-Jabal al-Akhdar) bordering Egypt in concentration camps. Thousands of Libyan families (an estimated 80,000) died in those concentration camps. In 1922 Benito Mussolini, the leader of the National Fascist Party, became the prime minister of Italy (Fig. 11-3). The Fascist labeled the occupation the Libyan Reconquista—a rebirth of the Roman Empire in Africa. One of Mussolini's first major actions was to institute a scorched-earth policy in Libya, aiming to bring down Omar al-Mukhtar.

**Figure 11-3:** Benito Mussolini (1883–1945). Italy's prime minister from 1922 to 1943. Considered the founder of the twentieth-century Fascist movement in Europe. He served as an inspirational figure for Adolf Hitler.

After some 20 years of fighting the Italian occupation of Libya, Omar, at age 73, was injured in battle and captured by the Italians on September 11, 1931 (Fig. 11-4).

**Figure 11-4:** Italian commanders posing next to the 73-year-old Omar, who was brought to the city of Benghazi in chains after he was captured in 1931.

The Italian army immediately began a trial for the desert warrior. At the trial, Omar remained as he had been all his life: brave, valiant, and honorable. I would like to share the following direct answers Omar gave at the trial:

> I took part in all battles. If sometimes I was not there, the operation was likewise carried out under my orders. . . .

It is useless for you to ask me single facts. Whatever has been committed against Italy and the Italians for the past ten years was willed and permitted by me, whenever I did not personally take part in the acts themselves.

Once he was handed down the execution sentence, he said the following words from the Qur'an:

From God we have come and to God we must return.

After a one-day trial that was merely for show, the lion of the desert was executed in front of his people at the prison camp in Suluq, 55 kilometers (34 miles) south of Benghazi, on September 16, 1931.

When I learned during my research for this chapter what Omar al-Mukhtar said about the Arab's struggle against European occupation—"We don't surrender, we win or we die"—it brought back a nostalgic childhood memory of learning what Patrick Henry said in 1775 regarding America's struggle against European occupation: "Give me liberty, or give me death."

Contrary to what I have been saying throughout this book about Hollywood's deliberate vilification of Arabs and Islam, there was a movie released in 1981, *Lion of the Desert* (Falcon International Productions), that fairly represented the life and struggle of Omar al-Mukhtar. What was the difference? The movie director and producer, Moustapha Akkad, was a man of Arab heritage. After this movie, to the best of my knowledge, he would be the first and last Hollywood movie director of Arab and Muslim background (Fig. 11-5).

The story of the film director Moustapha Akkad befits the larger narrative of this book. In Chapter 1, we discussed how Europeans sent their kids to study in the Muslim Empire during its golden age at the turn of the first millennium. In later chapters we witnessed how people from the "Middle East" sent their kids to school in the US and Europe at the turn of the second millennium. Moustapha Akkad was one of those kids. He was born into an Arab Muslim family in Aleppo, Syria, in 1930. After finishing high school, his family sent him to university in the US. He received an undergraduate degree in film direction and production from the University of California, Los Angeles (UCLA) and a master's degree from the University of Southern California (USC). Before the movie *Lion of the Desert*, he was best known for producing the original film series *Halloween* and the movie *The Message*. Akkad, whom I am sure was fully aware of the decades-old practice of Hollywood vilifying Arabs, saw himself as someone who could change that Hollywood narrative. He said in an interview in 1976, "I felt that it was my obligation, my duty to tell the truth about Islam." His next project after the *Lion of the Desert* movie was going to be a film about Saladin featuring the acclaimed actor Sean Connery. Akkad said, "Saladin exactly portrays Islam. Right now, Islam is portrayed as a terrorist religion. Because a few terrorists are Muslims, the whole religion has that image. If there ever was a religious war full of terror, it was the Crusades. But you can't blame Christianity because a few adventurers did this. That's my message." He might as well have written the foreword to this book.

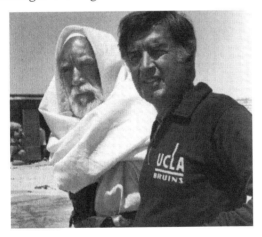

**Figure 11-5:** Photograph from the set of the movie *Lion of the Desert*. Actor Anthony Quinn, who played the role of Omar al-Mukhtar (left), and movie director and producer Moustapha Akkad (right).

Moustapha Akkad and his 34-year-old daughter Rima were together on trip to Amman, Jordan, in November 2005. They were in the lobby of the Grand Hyatt hotel when a group of Islamist terrorists bombed the hotel. Rima died instantly and Akkad died in the hospital two days later. This proves yet another major point made in this book: the biggest single victim of Islamist terrorists has been Arabs and Muslims. By killing Akkad, the terrorists eliminated a giant who was trying to preserve the legacy of Islam in the world.

## "The Compassionate Warrior"

Are you wondering what happened to Abdelkader after he was released from prison in France? Well, he went and lived for a short time in Bursa (current-day Turkey), but ultimately settled in Damascus. There he dedicated his time to philosophy, theology, and writing. During this time, he would write his book *Arabian Horse*. In July 1860, while he was in Damascus, a conflict arose between two local communities, the Druze (a small monotheistic religious sect that incorporates doctrines from multiple faiths) and the Maronites (an Eastern Catholic denomination). Once Abdelkader observed that the extremist element within the Druze was killing the outnumbered Christians, he came to the aid of the Christians. In one specific account, he sheltered a large number of Christians including the Sisters of Mercy in his home. When militant Druze came to his house, he said to them, "I will not hand over a single Christian, they are my brothers." The account of Abdelkader saving the Christians in Damascus reverberated throughout Europe. He was subsequently honored by the French, Greek, and Ottoman governments as well as the Vatican. US President Abraham Lincoln, having heard the stories of Abdelkader's valiance, sent him a gift of a pair of fancy inlaid Colt pistols (Fig. 11-6).

**Figure 11-6:** President Lincoln honored Abdelkader as a great humanitarian for saving thousands of Christian lives in Syria in 1860. The two Colt pistols, with the inscription "From the President of the United States, to his Excellency, Lord Abdelkader," are on display in the Algiers Museum.

In 1864, when the first Geneva Convention was signed, Abdelkader was considered to be one of the figures who inspired this historic humanitarian act. Also, since I grew up in America's Midwest, I would be remiss if I were not to mention that there is a small town in northeast Iowa that is named Elkader. In 1846, the town's first settler, Timothy Davis, was so taken by Abdelkader's valiant resistance to the brutal French occupation that he named the town after him! The town of Elkader has hosted the international forum of the

Abdelkader Education Project, an organization devoted to tolerance and understanding between the United States and Islam.

## The Formation of the "Middle East"

For the British, French, and Italian Allies at the end of WWI, the stories of honor, bravery, and chivalry of the Sharif of Mecca (Chapter 2), Abdelkader of Algeria, and Omar al-Mukhtar of Libya were an existential threat to their strategic idea of creating their own "Middle East." These three men categorically stood against the Western occupation of Arab peoples and lands. There was nothing about the mental makeup of these three men that would convert them into vassal-puppet leaders serving the interests of Western powers. Abdelkader died in exile by the French in Damascus in 1883. Sharif Hussein was exiled by the British to Cyprus where he lived until age 79 when he had a stroke, and was moved to Amman, Jordan, where he died in 1931. The same year, Omar al-Mukhtar was executed by the Italians.

As discussed in Chapter 3, the mastermind behind the creation of the region we know today as the "Middle East" was Winston Churchill. His prototype vassal leader for this region was inherently different from those three men. Abdulaziz ibn Saud fit the bill perfectly. He despised Arabism (Arab nationalism), did not believe that Palestine should retain its Arab governance, and believed that large swaths of Arab lands in the Levant and North Africa ought to be under European occupation. For him, what was important was himself, his family, and his tribe. That formula was music to the ears of the European strategists, and all Arab dictators since then have been chosen for their adherence to those principles. For Arab vassal leaders, the memory, aspirations, and dreams of the Sharif, Abdelkader, and Omar had to be erased to prevent any ideations of liberty and freedom. In my conversations with people across the "Middle East" in my research for this book, I was truly surprised how little people knew about these three doyens of Arab heritage and Islamic benevolence. In Libya, the brutal dictator Muammar Gaddafi ruled his people with an iron fist from 1969 to 2011. He demolished the areas in Benghazi and Suluq where people would visit in remembrance of Omar. In the anti-Gaddafi rebellion, as part of the Arab Spring

*Saleem I. Abdulrauf*

uprising against dictators in Arab countries, Libyans held banners with Omar al-Mukhtar's name and images. This is the nightmare scenario for vassal Arab dictators—the legacies of men like Saladin, Abdelkader, the Sharif of Mecca, and Omar al-Mukhtar haunt them.

## Bravery vs. Terrorism

While Dracula was fighting Ottoman occupation and Omar was fighting Fascist occupation, their behavior toward the civilian population was diametrically opposed. This concept cuts deep into the ethos of this book. The Crusaders, Dracula, and the extremist Serbs rationalized the killings of thousands of Muslim civilians based on their supposed interpretations of their faith. Saladin, Abdelkader, and Omar al-Mukhtar all avoided killing Christian civilians who were occupying their ancestral lands based on the interpretations of their faith. The extremist Wahhabis, Al-Qaeda, and ISIS used the Crusaders, Dracula, and the Serbs as their standard rather than the commanders of the faith they profess to belong to: men like Saladin, Abdelkader, and Omar.

# Chapter 12
# Ulysses S. Grant:
# A Lion from the Midwest

You may recall in Chapter 2, the Spanish monarchs Queen Isabella and King Ferdinand issued the Alhambra Decree in March 1492 to expel the Jews, who were then welcomed by the Muslim Ottoman Empire to live free from religious persecution. Just a few months later, the two monarchs funded an Italian sailor by the name of Christopher Columbus to find a western sea route to the East Indies islands. Columbus, using three ships, set sail in August 1492 and arrived in the Americas (the Bahamas) on October 12 (which is the day celebrated in Spain and the US as "Columbus Day"). He also visited the islands of Cuba, Haiti, and the island he called Hispaniola (now known as the Dominican Republic). The language used for official purposes on the trip was Arabic, as documented in the account provided by the historian Sam Haselby: "Columbus's interpreter, a Spanish Jew, spoke to the Taíno of Hispaniola, he did so in Arabic."

Columbus returned to Spain and news of his discoveries spread throughout Europe. He would make three more voyages to the Americas, during which he explored the northern coast of South America, the eastern coast of Central America, and the islands of Trinidad, Puerto Rico, and the Lesser Antilles. While Columbus was very religious and believed his accomplishments were the result of a fulfillment of a biblical prophecy, he was also very brutal to the indigenous populations of the lands he entered—similar to the Crusaders in Palestine. Pope Alexander VI issued the papal bull *Inter caetera* in May 1493, granting the new lands to the Kingdom of Spain, in exchange for the evangelization of the indigenous populations. That is why Columbus's voyages were subsequently accompanied by priests and Benedictine monks. The Harvard historian and author of a multi-volume biography on Columbus, Samuel Eliot Morison, wrote, "The cruel policy initiated by Columbus and pursued by his successors resulted in complete genocide." It is my observation that there has been an attempt by a number of authors and historians, through omissions and revisions, to provide a more sterile narrative of Christopher Columbus (Fig 12-1).

**Figure 12-1:** The tomb of Christopher Columbus in the Christianized Almohad mosque in Seville, Spain. The building of the mosque was commissioned by the caliph Abu Yaqub Yusuf and was completed in 1198. Once Seville was conquered by Ferdinand III, it was turned into a cathedral (Seville Cathedral). As I walked through this cathedral, I was able to find areas that still have the Arabic Qur'anic writings dating back to the original mosque. While it may appear ironic for the discoverer of "America" to be entombed in what was a mosque, it is also befitting. Columbus used the calculations of the Arab astronomer Al-Farghani and the geographer Al-Idrisi to chart his course. Columbus's vocabulary was rich in Arabized words, and the title he used in his most important documents and letters was Almirante (stemming from the Arabic word *al emir* meaning "prince" or "commander"). His official title bestowed upon him by Queen Isabella was Almirante del Mar Oceano ("Commander of the Ocean Sea"). The Spain that Columbus embarked from, which ultimately led to the West's discovery of America, was heavily influenced by Muslim culture, civilization, and science.

Following Columbus, a number of other European explorers from England, France, Spain, and Portugal set sail to the Americas. While the Spanish and French set up outposts, the first major colony in what is today the United States was driven by religious persecution in England. They were Protestants who called themselves "Puritan," to purify themselves from all Catholic practices that they believed were still influencing the Church of England. They settled in 1607 in what is now is Jamestown, Virginia. A total of 13 colonies developed along the Atlantic Coast from 1607 to 1776. These colonies and surrounding territories were under the control of the British Crown. As is true for all people living under occupation throughout history—as did the Jews against Roman occupation, as did Omar al-Mukhtar against European colonial occupation of North Africa, as did the Palestinians against Zionist occupation—so did the Americans against their British occupiers: they rebelled.

## The American Experiment

For the third time in human history, a group of men with visionary thinking far ahead of their time would come together and create a concept that would forever change human civilization. The first group included Socrates, Plato, and Aristotle from Athens, Greece, during the fourth and fifth centuries BC, whose visionary thinking would transform the world to come. The second group of men included Abu Bakr, Umar, Uthman, and Ali in Hejaz along the Red Sea in the seventh century who planted a seed for a new civilization, the Islamic civilization (Chapter 1), that would transform scientific thought for centuries to come and become the progenitor of the Renaissance in Europe. The third group, including George Washington, Thomas Jefferson, John Adams, and Alexander Hamilton, would also forever change human civilization. They confronted the question of their time, that no man must kneel to a king, and based on that, they would go on to create "a government of the people, by the people, for the people."

In the largest and most iconic example of a people rebelling against an occupying force in modern history, the American War of Independence, also known as the American Revolutionary War, against the British set the stage for the formation of a new country, the United States of America.

Religion played a key role during the American rebellion. The president of a college which is now Princeton University, John Witherspoon, wrote sermons linking the American Revolution to the teachings of the Bible. Protestant ministers preached revolutionary themes in their sermons.

The greatest experiment in modern history worked; the most successful country in the world was created because it rebelled against the concept of populist dictators and kings. This sent a warning shot across the bow of all dictators and kings worldwide; their people now knew that freedom from oppression was possible.

The American experiment did however have a dark stain: the stain of slavery. Slavery was an integral part of the 13 British colonies from the beginning. Just 12 years after the first colony in Jamestown was established, a ship carrying 20 to 30 enslaved people arrived in August 1619. While I have criticized the mainstream media of flagrant bias against Arabs and Muslims throughout this book, I do wish to commend the *New York Times* for its 2019 publication of the 1619 Project, which marked the 400th anniversary of the arrival of the first enslaved African people in Virginia with the goal of re-examining the legacy of slavery in the United States. Jake Silverstein, the magazine's editor-in-chief, said about the arrival of enslaved people in Virginia in 1619, "Their arrival inaugurated a barbaric system of chattel slavery that would last for the next 250 years. This is sometimes referred to as the country's original sin, but it is more than that: It is the country's very origin." Project creator Nikole Hannah-Jones was awarded the 2020 Pulitzer Prize for Commentary for the 1619 Project.

## A Lion Is Born

Let's fast forward from America's birth in 1776 to a small town in the Midwestern State of Ohio in the year 1822, when a boy was born, the first child of Hannah and Jesse Grant. They named him Ulysses. The Grants, though they lived in a country that allowed slavery, were deeply opposed to it, and instilled these values in Ulysses. As a boy, Ulysses loved horses and became an expert horseman at a young age.

In writing this book it appears to me that those who grew up loving horses are destined to do great things.

Grant would not and was not forced by his parents to attend the Methodist Church they belonged to. For the rest of his life, he prayed privately without being attached to any one specific faith. He took on his mother's values of piety and respectable manners. His grandfather had fought in the Revolutionary War against the British occupation, so following in his footsteps, Ulysses attended the United States Military Academy at West Point, which had been established in 1801 by one of America's Founding Fathers, Thomas Jefferson (Fig. 12-2). His first assignment out of school would take him to America's largest military base in the west—Jefferson Barracks near St. Louis, Missouri. I nostalgically recall performing one of my clinical rotations at Jefferson Barracks as a medical student.

In Missouri, Ulysses visited his close friend from West Point, Frederick Dent, and there he met Dent's sister Julia, and they were shortly engaged. The wedding took place in Julia's parents' home in St. Louis. Julia's father was an enslaver, and because of that, Ulysses's parents did not attend the wedding.

**Figure 12-2:** Commanding General Ulysses S. Grant, June 1864.

## An American Warrior

Grant was then called to fight in the Mexican–American War. There his bravery became the talk among the soldiers, especially the incident at the Battle of Monterrey where he volunteered to carry dispatch past Mexican snipers by hanging off the side of his horse, keeping the animal between him and the enemy. While Grant did what any good soldier does, carry out orders, he would later opine in his memoirs that the Mexican–American war was morally unjust. He felt that the territorial gains were designed to expand slavery, saying, "I was bitterly opposed to the measure . . . and to this day, regard the war which resulted as one of the most unjust ever waged by a stronger against a weaker nation."

The long separation from his wife Julia and his children ultimately got to him; he resigned from the army in July 1854 and returned to St. Louis. He had not been trained in any other occupation, and for the next seven years, the family lived in poverty. While financially struggling, his father-in-law gave him an enslaved 35-year-old man by the name of William Jones to work for him. Ulysses, despite the desperate need for someone to work for him and the fact that he could have sold Jones for a considerable sum of money, freed him.

In 1860 Americans voted to elect a man also from the Midwest, Abraham Lincoln, as the 16th president of the country (Fig. 12-3). This would go on to become the most consequential presidency in the history of the young country. Lincoln wanted to ban slavery. Seven Southern states (of the total 34 states making up the US at that time), for whom slavery was core to their cotton farming, were outraged by his election and decided to secede from the US to form their own "Confederacy." Just a few months after Lincoln's inauguration, in April 1861, the Confederate forces attacked Fort Sumter in South Carolina. This would start the bloodiest war in America's history.

**Figure 12-3:** President Abraham Lincoln. Picture taken on November 8, 1863.

For Grant, now age 39, this was perhaps the first time he had found a cause worth fighting for. He was immediately called back into the army, and within a few months he was promoted to command the District of Southeastern Missouri for the US Army (known as the Union army). The Civil War was being fought in two theaters, the eastern and the western. Grant as commander had successive wins in the western theater while the generals in the eastern theater were struggling against the Confederate army. Grant would not negotiate with the Confederate generals, which won him the reputation of "Unconditional Surrender Grant." Grant's wins, strategies, and stories of his courage reached President Lincoln back in Washington.

During the western campaign in Vicksburg, Mississippi, Grant made a decision that, to me, seemed very uncharacteristic of him. In December 1862, he issued General Order No. 11, which expelled Jews from Grant's military district, which included areas of Tennessee, Mississippi, and Kentucky. His rationale for this extreme order was to reduce corruption in the army, and specifically stop the illicit trade of cotton from the enemy (Confederate states), which Grant thought was being run "mostly by Jews and other unprincipled traders." Grant was heavily criticized by some members of the Congress and media. President Lincoln countermanded the General Order within two weeks of its issue on January 4, 1863. The *New York Times* wrote a strongly worded editorial on January 18, 1863, and I share excerpts of which below (original capitalizations):

> . . . GRANT has not been dismissed from the service on account of his unrighteous act. . . . Gen. GRANT may have been harassed by hangers-on of his army, who were swindlers and extortionists. It was desirable that he should be rid of such. But will he say that all the swindlers that beset him are Jews? . . . If we take a merely selfish view of GRANT's treatment of the Jews, it will appear in the highest degree impolitic. Persons "of this class" [Jews] have come to hold high positions in the leading Governments of Europe, whose good opinions we cannot afford to despise. M. FOULD, of LOUIS NAPOLEON's Cabinet, is a Jew, and his voice might, in the possibilities of things, go far to decide the fate

of the American Union. The ROTHSCHILDS wield a power in the financial world that is well nigh omnipotent to raise or destroy the credit of any nation. We may find it better to have their friendship than enmity . . . The immediate and peremptory abrogation of GRANT's order by the President saved the Government from a blot, and redeemed us from the disgrace of a military assault upon a people whose equal rights and immunities are as sacred under the Constitution as those of any other sect, class or race.

Ironically, it was this campaign, the Vicksburg campaign, that ultimately brought the Confederate army to its knees on the western front. Lincoln promoted Grant to the rank of major general and by March of 1964 to the rank of lieutenant general, giving him command over all US armies (a rank only held by George Washington before him). At this point Grant would take on the Confederate army in the east, which was commanded by the legendary Confederate General Robert E. Lee. After about 12 months of battles with tremendous casualties on both sides, Robert E. Lee surrendered to Grant on April 9, 1865. Grant respected Lee and called him "a foe who had fought so long and valiantly." In a classic act of humility, Grant stopped his troops from celebrating, noting, "War is over; the rebels are our countrymen again."

The Civil War left 618,222 men dead. Recent work by the historian J. David Hacker from Binghamton University in New York, using census data, suggests the casualties may have been much higher. "The data suggested that 650,000 to 850,000 men died as a result of the war," said Hacker. It remains the deadliest military conflict in America's history.

A few days after the major victory, on the evening of April 14, 1865, Lincoln was attending a play at the Ford's Theatre in Washington, DC, when a former Confederate spy shot him in the back of the head. The president remained in a coma for about nine hours and was pronounced dead at 7:22 a.m. on April 15. At Lincoln's funeral, Grant, while standing alone, is said to have wept openly. He later described Lincoln as "the greatest man I have ever known."

Abraham Lincoln, who had defined the US as a nation "conceived in liberty, and dedicated to the proposition that all men are created equal," would in his death abolish slavery and free four million enslaved people. I would like to note that while slavery was abolished, its legacy continues to haunt Americans of African descent to this day.

Grant would go on to become president of the United States in 1869, and throughout his presidency he remained true to his principles and his moral code. He fought for increased rights for the newly freed enslaved people in the nation. Grant, a heavy cigar smoker, developed throat cancer and died as a result at age 63 in July 1885.

## Three Lions: An Epilogue

At the end of this section of the book about three lions, I would like to state that Vlad/Dracula was a lion who fought using terror based on religious extremist ideations, Omar al-Mukhtar was a lion who fought to protect the honor of his people facing terror, and Ulysses S. Grant was a lion who fought to protect the honor of others, the honor of enslaved Black Americans.

You may be wondering what the story of an American warrior, Ulysses S. Grant, has to do with a book centered on the historical interactions of the three Abrahamic religions. The answer is, quite a bit. The single largest religion in the western part of Africa from which Africans were kidnapped for slavery was Islam. American historians have estimated that 30 percent of the enslaved Africans brought to the US were Muslim; however, I believe it was much higher. They were forced to convert to Christianity. The next chapter will provide a more detailed answer to the question.

# Three Outsiders

# Chapter 13
# "Am I Not a Man and a Brother?"

**O**mar, an enslaved man who escaped from his cruel enslaver in Charleston, South Carolina, was captured and jailed in Fayetteville, North Carolina. Using ashes of coal, he wrote in Arabic on the wall of his cell about his family back in Africa and the cruelty he faced as an enslaved man. His captors, though unable to read Arabic, were intrigued by the beautiful calligraphy of his writing. A local man, James Owen (the governor's brother), purchased him and he was enslaved by Owen and his family for the rest of his life. Owen was kind to Omar and allowed him to write, and Omar became known as an author. (A Southern diplomat, William Hodgson, who had served as a US counsel in Africa upon hearing about this wrote, "Let not the humanizing influence of the Koran, upon the fetishes, greegrees, and the human sacrifices of pagan, homicidal Africa be depreciated." The xenophobic comments of the diplomat reflected his lack of knowledge about the Islamic culture and civilization that existed in Africa.)

Omar was born to a wealthy family and was highly educated in West Africa before he was captured by Western enslavers in 1807. He wrote in his memoirs:

> My birthplace is Fut Tur [in modern-day Senegal] . . . I sought knowledge [and] continued seeking knowledge for 25 years. . . . [Then there] came to our country a big army. It killed many people. It took me and walked me to the big Sea, and sold me into the hand of a Christian man who bought me and walked me to the big Ship in the big Sea.
>
> We sailed in the big Sea for a month and a half until we came to a place called Charleston . . . And in a Christian language,

they sold me. A weak, small, evil man called Johnson, an infidel who did not fear Allah [God] at all, bought me.

The Library of Congress in 2019 acquired his memoirs, *The Life of Omar ibn Said*. Mary-Jane Deeb, chief of the library's African and Middle Eastern division, noted that he started his biography with a Qur'anic verse that states: "In Islam, everything belongs to God. No one really is an owner" to send a message that though he is labeled a "slave," no one owns him but God. He was providing a "fundamental criticism of the right to own another human being," said Deeb.

His enslavers indicated that Omar converted to Christianity, but his writings, which were in Arabic (which he knew they could not read), were heavily based on Qur'anic verses. Regardless, they changed his name to Moreau. Omar died at age 94 as an enslaved man (Fig. 13-1).

**Figure 13-1:** Omar ibn Said, an enslaved man who got to write his story.

We know Omar's story only because of a coincidence: he wrote on the walls of his jail cell which led to a relatively more tolerant enslaver who allowed him to write his story. What about the hundreds of thousands of other enslaved people who never got to tell their stories? Those like Omar, who spoke Arabic and were highly educated, but who were never allowed to write about the families they left behind in Africa? The point I am trying to make in this chapter is that not only were enslaved Africans forced to convert to Christianity, they were stripped of their family names, given Christianized names, and prohibited to write; thus, all historical links to their past were erased—a form of ethnic cleansing. The only reason we know Omar's real name is because of the freedom he was given to write, since his given name by his enslavers was Moreau. There are millions of African Americans today who are descended from honorable families like that of Omar's, but they have had stripped from them the rights and privilege of knowing their heritage. I heard an interview with Dr. Martin Luther King Jr. (recorded in 1967) in which he talked about the irony of asking the Black man to lift himself up from his bootstraps (an American saying), but he was left "bootless" as a result of the oppression. I think it may be even deeper than that—he was left faceless, identity-less, and heritage-less.

That brings me to one of the key issues that dismayed me as I was conducting research for this chapter: the insistence of early American historians to underestimate the numbers of enslaved Africans brought to America who were Muslim before the forced conversions. Clearly there were political pressures to do so. The Protestants, who were the overwhelming majority in the American colonies, came from a Europe that was deeply anti-Islamic. Also, the enslavers were opposed to anything organized that the enslaved people could rally around, and Islam would have been such a cause. Those who were kidnapped as a family were intentionally sold to separate enslavers. By separating families and stripping away their religion and identity, they became dehumanized property. I do not know of a bigger indoctrination campaign in history. If you look at the American society, especially in the South, some of the most religious communities, as evidenced by church gatherings every Sunday, are African American, many of whom are descendants of families like that of Omar, descendants of generations of respectable Muslim families from West Africa.

The mainstream media and Hollywood, in keeping with their motives as witnessed throughout this book, were and are fully on board in censoring the story of enslaved Muslims. Perhaps the first major media exposure of the American people and the world at large to the journey of enslaved people from Africa to America came from

Saleem I. Abdulrauf

Alex Haley's 1976 book, *Roots: The Saga of an American Family*, and the subsequent 1977 ABC TV series called *Roots*. The book and the series were based on a partially fictionalized (it was purportedly Alex Haley's family story) account of a young boy from the Mandinka people who was brutally kidnapped and sold into slavery in the US. The Mandinka are a very proud Muslim people with a rich history. Although the book acknowledges that the teenage protagonist, Kunta Kinte, was a Muslim, that part of the story is essentially missing from the narrative of the book and the series.

I come from an American academic background, but I do not excuse the complicity of academic institutions in the US in many of the issues raised in this book, particularly on the topic of omitting and revising the history of Muslims who were enslaved. America's earliest and now some of its most respected institutions of higher learning in the Northeast had a significant "Christian Puritan" bent or influence since their inception. That inclination easily fits the narrative of undermining the role of Islam during the formation of the country. While these institutions teach courses and their professors have written books on the history of early American religions, Islam has essentially been omitted. This is especially ironic considering Islam existed in the Americas before the Protestant movement was even established in Europe. "The religion [Islam] itself likely arrived in America in 1492, more than 20 years before Martin Luther nailed his theses to the door, igniting the Protestant reformation," said Sam Haselby, the author of the book *The Origins of American Religious Nationalism.*

## What Was the Religious Background of Enslaved Africans?

So, what are the facts? What percentage of enslaved Africans brought to America were from Muslim families? This is not an easy question to answer, and to the best I can ascertain, there were no records kept on the religious backgrounds of the enslaved Africans on the ships nor once they set foot on American soil. The most comprehensive data available comes from the Trans-Atlantic Slave Trade Database—an extensive effort conducted under the direction of historian David Eltis of Emory University detailing information on 35,000 trans-Atlantic slave trading voyages that occurred between 1520 and 1866. It also provides detailed personal information (including African names) of over 90,000 Africans brought by slave ships in the nineteenth century.

Historians have extrapolated the percentage of enslaved people who were of Muslim background, and the estimates have ranged from 20 to 30 percent. What these extrapolations were based on is not easy to figure out.

Islam arrived in West Africa as early as the eighth century, and by the eleventh century it had a stable presence which still endures. By the time the American slave trade was active in West Africa, Islam was well entrenched in those communities, communities that exist to this date. The historian Philip D. Curtin identified six zones in West Africa, and later historians added Angola as the seventh, that account for the overwhelming majority of captives who became enslaved (Fig. 13-2).

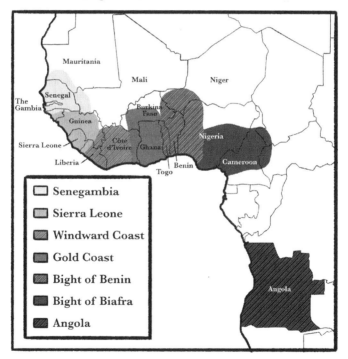

**Figure 13-2:** Map of West Africa showing current-day countries. Superimposed are the seven regions that have been identified by US historians as the main areas from which Africans were captured for the slave trade.

Based on the principle that but for massive migrations (which did not happen in this region of the world), the religious demographic of regions remains relatively stable across generations. Below I list the percentage of Muslims in the seven zones (now represented by 16 countries) from which the overwhelming majority of enslaved people were captured. I have based the table below on CIA information (2019–2020).

| Country | Percentage of Muslims | Total Population | Muslim Population |
|---|---|---|---|
| Mauritania | 100.0 | 3,840,429 | 3,840,429 |
| Niger | 99.3 | 19,866,231 | 19,470,893 |
| Senegal | 95.9 | 15,020,945 | 14,420,107 |
| Gambia | 95.7 | 2,092,731 | 2,009,021 |
| Mali | 94.8 | 18,429,893 | 17,508,394 |
| Guinea | 89.1 | 11,855,411 | 10,551,316 |
| Sierra Leone | 78.6 | 6,312,212 | 4,986,642 |
| Burkina Faso | 61.5 | 19,742,715 | 12,043,056 |
| Nigeria | 51.6 | 203,452,505 | 105,795,303 |
| Côte d'Ivoire | 42.9 | 26,260,582 | 11,292,050 |
| Benin | 27.7 | 11,340,504 | 3,175,341 |
| Cameron | 20.9 | 25,640,965 | 5,384,602 |
| Ghana | 18.0 | 28,102,471 | 5,058,445 |
| Togo | 20.0 | 8,176,449 | 1,635,289 |
| Liberia | 12.2 | 4,809,768 | 961,954 |
| Angola | 2.5 | 30,355,880 | 758,897 |

Before I share the conclusions drawn from the data shown in the table, I would like to state the following: 1) Islam has been well entrenched in West Africa since the eleventh century, well before the trans-atlantic slave trade (sixteenth to nineteenth centuries), 2) There has been a peculiar paucity of research among American historians looking at the religious background of enslaved people, and the information that I have been able to find regarding the percentage of the enslaved people who were Muslim appears to be based on qualitative rather than quantitative data, and 3) There have been no unusual major population shifts in the respective areas of West Africa in the time period under review.

Based on the population data provided in the above table, the Muslim population of the combined 16 countries comprises 53 percent of the population. Based on the assumptions I have made above, I have drawn the following conclusion: the majority of African Americans in the US today, or at least one in every two, descended from a Muslim family.

I am a scientist and a surgeon, not a historian. For me to delve into historical data may appear as a "clash of civilizations" for historians! Yet, I wholeheartedly believe, and I have always emphasized in my lectures, the importance of the concept of "looking outside the box" to further evolve our knowledge and understanding.

## What Was the Appeal of Islam for Africans?

For this book I interviewed people from many regions of the world of many different religions. I have been asked, "What is the allure of Islam to the people of Africa?" It is a good question as six of the above seven slave trade regions of West Africa (all but Angola) were physically much closer to Europe than to Mecca and Medina in the Arabian Peninsula. These regions had seen far more incursions by European than Muslim armies, and therefore had far more Christian missionary activity than Islamic.

There is a fundamental issue at play. As this is not a politically correct book, it allows me to discuss it openly. While Jesus, the son of Mary, was a deeply magnanimous and altruistic figure, Christianity a thousand years after his death had developed into a movement with deep racial biases as the result of the Crusades (Chapters 7 and 8). That was on the Catholic side. The Protestants emerged from a uniformly White ethnic region (Germany), and later gave rise to the evangelical movement in the US, which likewise had a clearcut racial bent (Chapter 6). While forcing Africans to convert to Christianity, their enslavers did not see fit to worship in the same church as the people they enslaved. Therefore, to this date, there are separate White and Black churches throughout the US.

The people of the "Middle East" were and are no better. Prejudice exists throughout those societies. However, they have a limitation that they cannot cross: the Qur'an.

> And of His signs is the creation of the heavens and the earth and the diversity of your languages and your colors. Indeed in that surely are signs for those of knowledge. (Qur'an 30:22)

The Qur'an categorically states that diversity of colors is God's work, so to be prejudiced is akin to transgressing God Himself. For Africans, who have been victims of prejudice for centuries, the Qur'an stood on their side against those who sought to harm them. The prejudiced Muslims were not able to do what their Christian counterparts were able to do; there are no separate mosques for Blacks and Whites. The Qur'an and the mosque became the great equalizers.

Malcolm X (Malik El-Shabazz), the American civil rights activist who, once he embraced traditional Islam, went to Hejaz to perform the Hajj pilgrimage in 1964 (Fig. 13-3). In a letter to his family he wrote:

> During the past eleven days here in the Muslim world, I have eaten from the same plate, drunk from the same glass, and slept on the same rug—while praying to the same God—with fellow Muslims, whose eyes were the bluest of blue, whose hair was the blondest of blond, and whose skin was the whitest of white. And in the words and in the deeds of the "white" Muslims, I felt the same sincerity that I felt among the black African Muslims of Nigeria, Sudan, and Ghana.

**Figure 13-3:** Malcolm X (1925–1965). His visit to Mecca would forever change his view of religion and race. He stated, "There were tens of thousands of pilgrims, from all over the world. They were of all colors, from blue-eyed blondes to black-skinned Africans. But we were all participating in the same ritual, displaying a spirit of unity and brotherhood that my experiences in America had led me to believe never could exist between the white and non-white."

Because the Qur'anic verses and the sayings of the Prophet Muhammad preached equality, the Muslim Empire from the seventh century on would witness a number of leaders of African origin, something that is totally unique to Islam when compared to other major religions of the world.

Just as the early Christian converts were targeted and abused by the local Roman and Jewish authorities, the early Muslim converts became targets of the powerful pagan authorities of Mecca. Bilal was enslaved in his thirties when he heard Muhammad's message and decided to give up idol worship and become a Muslim. His cruel enslaver had him bound and tied spread-eagle at a stake and then whipped mercilessly under the desert sun. Bilal refused to renounce his religion. As soon as Muhammad, who came from the prominent Hashemite clan, heard of the incident, he used all his connections to have Bilal set free from his enslavement. The merciless beating of enslaved people would rear its ugly head once again some 1,000 years later (Fig. 13-4).

*Saleem I. Abdulrauf*

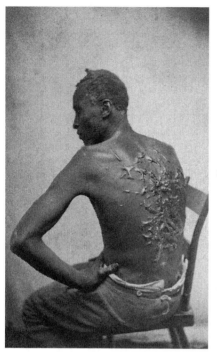

**Figure 13-4:** "Gordon" (surname of the enslaver) was an enslaved man who escaped from his cruel enslaver in Louisiana in March 1863 and found safety once he reached the Union army camp near Baton Rouge. In order to mask his scent from his enslaver's bloodhounds, "Gordon" rubbed onions on his body until reaching safety. This picture was published in March 1863 in *Harper's Weekly* (the most widely read journal during America's Civil War). We do not know who "Gordon" truly was, his family, or religious background; we only know him by his cruel enslaver's name. Looking at him sitting on the chair, I cannot but notice a certain level of dignity in a man who had endured so much.

Bilal had a deep, melodious, resonant voice, so when it came time to select the first person in Islam's history to deliver the call to prayer known as Al-Adhan (or Al-Azaan), it was Bilal that the Prophet selected. Bilal's role would go on to become an honorable one within Islam, and the person reciting the call to prayer would go on to be called the muezzin (muʾaḏḏin), who projects his voice from the tallest part of the mosque built for this purpose, the minaret. This happens at every mosque in the world five times a day, and it is done in the tradition of Bilal.

About 100 years after Bilal's story, yet another young African Muslim, Tariq, would challenge fate as he looked across the nine-mile ocean strait separating Africa from Europe with a plan in mind. As Islam expanded out of the Arabian Peninsula in the seventh century, one of the places it found a welcoming home was in the hearts of the indigenous pre-Arab people of North Africa, known as the Berbers (or Amazighs). Tariq ibn Ziyad was one such Berber who is said to have been freed from slavery (Fig. 13-5).

**Figure 13-5:** An engraving of Tariq ibn Ziyad gazing from Africa across the sea strait toward Hispania (Iberian Peninsula).

Tariq was gazing across the strait at the Visigothic Kingdom on the Iberian Peninsula (current-day Spain and Portugal combined) which had targeted and enslaved Jews in the late seventh century. By 710 Roderic was the Visigothic king (Fig. 13-6). Count Julian, the Visigothic governor of Ceuta (a Spanish territory in Northern Africa), based on tradition, sent his young daughter Florinda to the king's court in Toledo (southwest of Madrid) for education. Roderic raped Florinda, and once Julian found out, he wanted to exact revenge. Julian had good relations

**Figure 13-6:** Roderic, the king of the Visigothic Kingdom (portrait/engraving).

with the Muslim Umayyad Empire, his neighbors at the northern tip of Africa (current-day Morocco). Julian approached the Umayyad governor of Africa (Musa ibn Nusayr) and asked that the Umayyads invade Spain to bring down the cruel king. There is perhaps nothing more that would get the blood of the chivalrous Arab culture of the time boiling than a cruel man dishonoring a young woman, a princess. Umayyad Governor Ibn Nusayr sent a reconnaissance mission to the Spanish coast that was coordinated by Julian. Subsequently, once Ibn Nusayr got the green light from the caliph in Damascus, he tasked the job of invading Spain to the young African commander, Tariq.

Since the assault on Florinda by Roderic played a critical role in the inception of the events leading to the attack on Spain, later Christian ballads would make her into a seductress, while Muslim ones would uphold the original story of an innocent girl being raped by a viscous king. Florinda is known in Spanish popular culture as La Cava (meaning scarlet woman). Based on the anti-Muslim narrative in Western thought and popular culture, Florinda's legacy has become one of a "bad" girl who seduced the innocent king, rather than the true story of Roderic raping a teenager. A musical about the life of Florinda (opened in London in June 2000), instead of it being named for her, was named *La Cava*, and the story stuck to the Western narrative that it was Florinda's fault that she became pregnant by Roderic!

In all fairness, it is important to note that by the early eighth century when Roderic raped Florinda, there had been a centuries-old culture of chivalry in the Arabian Peninsula but not so in Europe. We discussed the concept of a "knight" centered around the Arabian horse in Chapter 8; combined with that we see evidence of poetry centered around the concept of courtly love in the Arabian Peninsula in the first millennium. By the ninth century, wandering Arab poet-singers were seen in Spain and influenced local culture. Subsequently, the idea of singing to a loved one emerged in Europe for the first time: the concept of a love song was born. The renowned author Michael Hamilton Morgan would say about the influence of Arab love poems and songs on European culture, "With it will come a new awareness of the value of women and the concept of chivalry and honor will begin to lay the seeds for a more humane and enlightened European society."

I am sure the irony is not lost on you. The people who taught Europeans the concept of chivalry now live in countries in which women are second-class citizens, such as Saudi Arabia and Iran.

Tariq crossed the strait on ships provided by Julian with an army of 7,000 African Berbers and 300 Arab soldiers. On April 26, 711, Tariq disembarked at the foothills of a large mountain at the southern tip of the Iberian Peninsula. In Arabic a mountain is called *jabal*, so the area was named Jabal Tariq, which became Gibraltar!

What would follow has etched Tariq's bravery in the psyche of kids in Africa and beyond for centuries. Tariq knew he was going to be outnumbered by Roderic's forces multifold, so he ordered the ships they in arrived in burned, and then told his men, "Oh my warriors, the enemy is before you, and the sea is behind you, you have now left only your courage" (rough translation). Tariq's words about courage and bravery that day holds a place in the consciousness of Muslims just as the words of US President Abraham Lincoln at Gettysburg in 1863—"The brave men, living and dead, who struggled here, have consecrated it, far above our poor power to add or detract. The world will little note, nor long remember what we say here, but it can never forget what they did here"—does for Americans.

Courage they did show. After capturing territories in southern Spain, they met Roderic at the head of an army of 33,000 men. Tariq defeated Roderic decisively at the Battle of Guadalete on July 19, 711. Roderic was killed in the battle. Guadalete would become the third-most transformative battle in the history of "East" vs "West." The first was Khalid ibn al-Walid's defeat of the larger Roman army in the Battle of Yarmouk on August 20, 636. The second was Saladin's defeat of the Crusaders at the Battle of Hattin on July 4, 1187. Due to religious and political factors, these three epic battles have been omitted from history books and popular culture in the West (Figs. 13-7 and 13-8).

**Figure 13-7:** Artist depiction of the eighth-century Visigothic Iberian Peninsula. Shown: Ceuta (Julian's governorship at the tip of North Africa), Gibraltar, and the location of the battle of Guadalete. In the center is a depiction of a Visigothic coin. Artist depiction of Roderic in the upper left and Tariq in the upper right.

**Figure 13-8:** The Spanish painter Martinez Cubells (1845–1914) depicts the retreat of the Visigothic army at the Battle of Guadalete.

Following Guadalete, Tariq traveled north to the Visogothic capital of Toledo and captured it. This would start a 781-year Islamic rule in Spain (711–1492 AD). By the tenth century, Spain under Muslim rule was the most advanced country in Europe from cultural, artistic, and scientific standpoints. The presence of the Islamic civilization and the ongoing transfer of its scientific and cultural knowledge to the rest of Europe would go on to become key for the development of the Renaissance. The Jews of Spain welcomed Muslim rule, because they were not persecuted by the Muslims as they had been by the Visigoths. They were persecuted once again after the Muslims left and Queen Isabella and King Ferdinand took power.

The channel of water that Tariq, as a young commander, was staring at in the beginning of this section is now named for him, the Strait of Gibraltar.

Let's fast forward a few hundred years to the year 1280 in West Africa, when another man is born, this time not into slavery, but into royalty: a prince by the name of Musa (Arabic for Moses). He was the son of the king of the Mali Empire. Everything we know about him comes from the writings of Ibn Khaldun, the great Arab historian that President Ronald Reagan had referred to in Chapter 1. When Musa became king, he was referred to as Mansa Musa. (*Mansa* in the Mandinka language—that is the tribe that Kunta Kinte of the book *Roots* came from—means "king" or "emperor.") During Musa's reign, Mali became the biggest producer of gold in the world, accounting for half of the world's gold according to the British Museum. Musa is considered by a number of economics authorities to have been the richest man in human history.

Under Musa's reign, the Muslim Mali Empire extended into six of the seven regions described above as the key areas from which Africans were captured to be sold into slavery in America (Fig. 13-9).

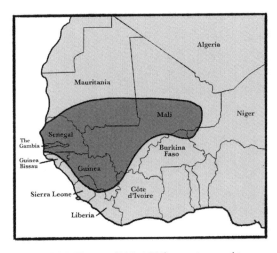

**Figure 13-9:** Mali Empire (800–1550) superimposed in gray over current-day countries, all of which were part of the six slave capture zones as defined by the historian Philip D. Curtin.

When Musa made the Hajj pilgrimage to Mecca, he financed the trip for 60,000 people to make the pilgrimage with him. They were essentially like a city moving through the Sahara Desert to Egypt on their way to Hejaz. Musa, who was known for his generosity, handed out gold to the poor he met along his route. This would cause an international incident like no other. During his three-month journey through Egypt, he gave so much gold to the poor that it led to the price of gold plummeting for 10 years, with significant negative impact on the economy! US-based technology company SmartAsset. com estimates that Musa's gifting of gold to the poor throughout his pilgrimage led to about $1.5 billion of economic losses across the "Middle East" region as a result of the depreciation of the price of gold.

While in Hejaz, Musa hired highly respected scholars, including some who were descendants of the Prophet Muhammad, and brought them back to Mali to initiate the largest intellectual and educational initiative in the history of West Africa. Musa was a patron of literature. He built schools, libraries, and mosques. Timbuktu became a major intellectual center. Scholars, including engineers, poets, philosophers, and physicians, came to debate, exchange ideas, teach, conduct research, and publish. The *New York Times* reporter Ben Macintyre said, "Timbuktu was a beacon of intellectual enlightenment, and probably the most bibliophilic city on earth." Author Joshua Hammer called Timbuktu an "incubator for the richness of Islam." The University of Sankoré in Timbuktu had one of the largest libraries and collections of books in the world. It housed an astounding 25,000 students, making it the largest university system in history until the inception of the large US university campuses in the twentieth century. Omar ibn Said, mentioned above, and countless other enslaved people brought to America came from this intellectual culture of West Africa (Figs. 13-10a and 13-10b).

**Figures 13-10a and 13-10b:** The Djinguereber Mosque built by Mansa Musa in Timbuktu in the fourteenth century. The structure was constructed using beaten earth reinforced with wood, which often sticks out in beams from the exterior surfaces—an ingenious way to build a large structure in a region that lacks stones. It became a UNESCO World Heritage Site in 1988.

The British historian Hugh Trevor-Roper would say "There is only the history of Europeans in Africa. The rest is darkness." This xenophobic statement explains the colonization of Africa which was one of the main factors leading to the destruction of the intellectual civilization that Musa had built and explains the mentality that led to the slave trade.

The most recent instance of outsiders attacking what remained of Timbuktu's intellectual heritage came in the twenty-first century by the terrorist group Al-Qaeda (from its Africa branch known as "Al-Qaeda in the Islamic Maghreb"). Al-Qaeda is a deep adherent to the Wahhabi philosophy (Chapter 3), and all of the books in the libraries of Timbuktu are problematic to these extremists because they do not know what is written in them, and therefore they must be destroyed. In the book *The Bad-Ass Librarians of Timbuktu*, Joshua Hammer provides an intriguing account of how a young, mild-mannered archivist, Abdel Kader Haidara, organized a heroic heist to sneak all 350,000 manuscripts from Timbuktu's ancient libraries to safety from the Al-Qaeda terrorists who were aiming to destroy them.

Bilal, the enslaved man who became one of Islam's most respected figures; Tariq, the freed man who would become the general who accomplished a transformational military feat by conquering Spain; and Musa, the prince who became the pious king who developed one of Islam's great intellectual civilizations—all examples that are unique to Islam. No other major religion in human history has had such consequential African figures that played key roles in the evolution of its history and civilization.

## Where Did Blues Music Originate?

The Islamic call to prayer (Al-Adhan), with its roots in Bilal's melodic voice in the seventh century, has become standard in Muslim cultures ever since. The enslaved people captured from West Africa had nothing with them when they were brought on ships to America except the memories of the sights and the sounds of their homes.

Blues originated in America's South in the 1870s on cotton plantations by enslaved people who sang melancholic ballads about the torment they suffered and the sadness of being away from home. The frame of reference for these ballads could only have been the memories of melodic voices from back home, since they had no exposure to any Western music. The most common musically sounding voices they would have been exposed to back home (in West Africa) would have been the call to prayers five times a day and the melodic recitations of the Qur'an.

Did the blues, a quintessentially American genre which gave birth to jazz, have Islamic roots?

The award-winning historian and scholar at New York's Schomburg Center for Research in Black Culture, Sylviane Diouf, has said enslaved Muslims who sang in a melancholic fashion "would sing in the same manner, time and again, on the plantations of the

South, and their lonesome 'song' probably became one ancestor of the blues." To demonstrate her point, at lectures she plays the Al-Adhan and "Levee Camp Holler" (a classic early blues song from enslaved people of the Civil War era), showcasing the similarities between the two.

Gerhard Kubik, professor of ethnomusicology at the University of Mainz in Germany, has traveled and lived in Africa to research the connections of Africa and blues music. He wrote the most comprehensive textbook on this topic, *Africa and the Blues*. He believes in the Arab Muslim impact on the origins of the blues.

If blues music originated from an Arabic background, that ought not be surprising. As discussed widely in this book, the Arab culture's introductions to Spain and consequently to Europe following Tariq's invasion were not limited to science, math, medicine, and engineering, but also in the arts, music, and poetry. Flamenco, the folkloric music tradition of southern Spain, is rooted in Arab influences. The Renaissance music that heavily used lutes is rooted in the instrument Arabs brought to Spain, the oud (from which the lute originated and was named). The guitar, the core instrument of the quintessentially American genre of music, rock and roll, came from its progenitor the *qitharah*, introduced by the Arabs to Spain. The word *qitharah* was adapted as *guitarra* in Spain, *gitarre* in Germany, *guitare* in France, and finally *guitar* in Britain and the US.

While Arab contributions to European science and literature via Spain is well known, not as well known are the Arab contributions to the European Renaissance via Italy. The Arabs ruled Sicily as the Emirate of Sicily for 260 years (831–1091). Under Arab Muslim rule, the capital, Palermo, became one of Europe's most cosmopolitan cities and reached its economic and cultural zenith in its recorded history. The historian Henry George Farmer has studied the Arab musical contributions to Europe. The notes in the scale used to teach Western music, "Do Re Mi Fa So La Ti," is well known to be Italian, dating back to the eleventh century. That century happened to be when Arabs ruled Sicily. Farmer provides the following evidence to support the Arab origin of the classic scale:

| Arabic Alphabet | Mi | Fa | Sad | Ia | Sin | Dal | Ra |
|---|---|---|---|---|---|---|---|
| solfège syllable | Mi | Fa | Sol | La | Si | Do | Re |

You will note that the syllables that represent the different notes on a scale that are used to teach Western music (bottom row) are rooted in the sounds of Arabic letters.

When I spoke to some of my Italian friends about this, they were not going to have it—they told me those notations were as Italian as pasta!

Finally, one of my favorite musicians of all time, Bob Dylan, in his famous song "Mr. Tambourine Man," is referring to a popular instrument from the Arab culture of Palestine that the Crusaders brought back to Europe. Dylan was awarded the Nobel Prize in 2016 "for having created new poetic expressions within the great American song tradition." Those poetic expressions and the great American song tradition have many roots, some of which are yet to be acknowledged.

## Why Did Thomas Jefferson Own a Qur'an?

There have been but a few men in modern human history who have had an impact as that of Thomas Jefferson. Truly a Renaissance man, he authored America's Declaration of Independence, and in doing so penned the most profound words of the second millennium: "Governments are instituted among Men, deriving their just powers from the consent of the governed, --That whenever any Form of Government becomes destructive of these ends, it is the Right of the People to alter or to abolish it, and to institute new Government." His words will go on to challenge kings and dictators for eternity.

Some 10 years before writing the document that would challenge the English king and set the course for establishing a new nation, Thomas Jefferson purchased a Qur'an—why?

Not only did Thomas Jefferson own a Qur'an, but his interest in it may have been deeper than we think. Jefferson bought the Qur'an in 1765 as a law student at William and Mary College in

Williamsburg, when he was a political activist against the British occupation of America. The most logical reason that has been suggested for purchasing the Qur'an is that he wanted to be educated in Islamic law in his effort to confront the policies of the British occupation. Five years after he bought the Qur'an, in February 1770, the most unfortunate event occurred, one that he wrote about to his good friend John Page: "My late loss may perhaps have reached you by this time, I mean the loss of my mother's house by fire, and in it, of every paper I had in the world, and almost every book." The fire at his mother's house destroyed all his most prized possessions—his papers and books. He valued them more than any wealth he could have had. So where did his personally initialized Qur'an at the Library of Congress come from? Either the Qur'an miraculously survived the fire, or Jefferson bought another copy, thus reflecting a deep interest.

I would like to share a very specific example about Jefferson's use of Islamic law principles. Two years after purchasing the Qur'an, as a lawyer, Jefferson would deal with a case in which Kitty Eustace, the ex-wife of Dr. James Blair, was suing him for alimony payments following their divorce. In Anglican Protestant thinking at that time, that was not possible. So where did Jefferson look to find support for women's rights? The answer is Islamic law, of which Jefferson stated, "Among the Turks [a name given to describe Muslims at the time] is a kind of marriage called Kabin [monies paid to the wife upon divorce] where parties agree to the fixt time of separation, securing to the woman a sum of money on dismission."

Years after purchasing the Qur'an, Thomas Jefferson penned the Declaration of Independence, including the most profound 37 words every American holds dear: "We hold these truths to be self-evident, that all men are created equal, that they are endowed by their Creator with certain unalienable Rights, that among these are Life, Liberty and the pursuit of Happiness."

Jefferson would have read within verses in his Qur'an declarations about equality among men regardless of their skin color in affirming that all humans come from the same origin: "O people, we created you from the same male and female" (49:13), and about the sanctity of human life: "Whosoever kills a human being, it is as though he had killed all mankind" (5:31).

Whether Thomas Jefferson was influenced by Qur'anic verses that spoke about equality, sanctity of life, liberty, and happiness when penning the Declaration of Independence, we do not know. But Jefferson did not stop there; he continued throughout his life to study Arabic and Islamic cultures (Fig. 13-11).

**Figure 13-11:** Thomas Jefferson's personal two-volume copy of the 1734 English translation of the Qur'an from Arabic by British lawyer George Sale. (The authenticity of George Sale's translation, to the best of my knowledge, has never been fully confirmed by Muslim scholars.) Jefferson's Qur'an is now in the collections of the Library of Congress.

To develop a comprehensive understanding and to find original sources as to why Thomas Jefferson owned a Qur'an, I tapped into the authoritative textbook on this topic, *Thomas Jefferson's Qur'an* by the historian Denise A. Spellberg.

All Founding Fathers of the US were Protestants, which was the religion of the overwhelming majority of the initial 13 colonies. When forming the foundation for the new nation however, Thomas Jefferson and other Founding Fathers debated whether this nation should be a religiously plural society that would include Muslims, Catholics, and Jews, or an exclusively Protestant one.

While Jefferson was an Anglican Christian, he framed the argument from a larger perspective and wanted the new nation to be different from the Christian-based European powers. He argued, "Who are reputed to be good Christians? Go to Rome, they are papists. Go to Geneva, they are Calvinists. Go to the north of Germany, they are Lutherans. Come to London, they are none of these. Orthodoxy is a mode." He opposed the establishment of a state religion in his own state of Virginia. He would later say, "Is uniformity attainable? Millions of innocent men, women, and children, since the introduction of Christianity, have been burnt, tortured, fined, imprisoned; yet we have not advanced one inch towards uniformity."

That was from a larger perspective, but now I wish to raise a truly peculiar question. Within this conversation among the Founding Fathers, why would they even discuss Muslims? We are told by politicians, mainstream media, and therefore the popular culture that Muslims are totally new immigrants to America. What did the Founding Fathers know that we, as a result of historical revisions and omissions, do not know?

If we look into the taxable property of George Washington, the general who defeated the British and went on to become the first US president, we see two names that shed light on the answer to the above question: two enslaved women, a mother and daughter from West Africa, "Fatimer" and "Little Fatimer." Fatima is a common name in Muslim communities since it was the name of one of Prophet Muhammad's daughters. It is conceivable that America's Founding Fathers were fully aware that a large portion, if not the overwhelming majority as I have suggested in this chapter, of those who were captured in West Africa and enslaved in America were Muslim. That would fit very well with the observation made by historian Michael A. Gomez that the number of Muslims brought to North America was in the "tens of thousands" and historian Denise A. Spellberg who wrote that it was "certainly greater than the resident Jews and possibly even the Catholics." If Muslims were the second-largest religious group after Protestants at that time, why are they not so now? Enslaved Muslims were not only prohibited from practicing their religion, they underwent forced proselytization and conversion, something that Jews and Catholics were not subjected to since they were not enslaved.

I also believe that based on Jefferson's global exposure, he had more of a world view than most American politicians that would follow him over the next centuries. Thomas Jefferson was sent to France as an American minister to negotiate treaties with European countries and lived in Paris for five years (August 1784 to September 1789). Historians Lucia Stanton and Douglas Wilson wrote that these years were "arguably the most memorable of his life. Paris— with its music, its architecture, its savants and salons, its learning and enlightenment, not to mention its elegant social life . . . had worked its enchantments on this rigidly self-controlled Virginia gentleman, and had stimulated him to say and do and write remarkable things." While in France he would witness the impact of what he and the other American Founding Fathers had done by fighting for rights and equality for all citizens against an authoritarian regime. The inspired French people would rebel against their dictator, the French king. Jefferson would witness the pivotal event of the French Revolution on July 14, 1789: the storming of France's notorious prison for political activists, the Bastille, by the French people. According to Jefferson, he saw their violent struggle to obtain freedom "with my own eyes in order to be satisfied of their objects, and declare to you that I saw so plainly the legitimacy of them."

Jefferson knew the world and knew that Islam was a major player in it. He was an enslaver (enslaving over 600 West Africans) and would have known that many of the enslaved Africans came from Muslim families. His visionary outlook as codified in the Declaration of Independence was that this new nation be a pluralistic one, and only in doing so could the nation prosper and benefit from other cultures.

I would be remiss not to bring up the moral ambiguity Thomas Jefferson was living in; on one hand, the Declaration of Independence stated that all men are created equal, on the other hand, he was an enslaver (Fig. 13-12). In his own words he reflects on this:

**Figure 13-12:** Portrait of the third president of the United States, Thomas Jefferson, at the Portrait Gallery of the Second Bank of the United States, in Philadelphia, Pennsylvania.

We might as well require a man to wear still the coat which fitted him when a boy as a civilized society to remain ever under the regimen of their barbarous ancestors.

## The Cleansing of History

Slavery is not unique to America; it existed for centuries in Africa, the Middle East, and Europe. This book examines the military and cultural interactions and conflicts among the three Abrahamic religions that have led to the geopolitical realities of today. The large-scale kidnapping of Muslims from West Africa to be sold into slavery in America is one of those ugly historic realities. My research did not disclose large-scale enslavement of Christians by either Jews or Muslims, nor a large-scale enslavement of Jews by Christians or Muslims in the 2,000-year period examined in this book.

Moreover, American slavery is unique in one very fundamental aspect. It involved the mass forced assimilation-indoctrination-conversion of those enslaved to the religion of their enslavers, a process by which the enslaved were cleansed of all connections to the families they left behind, even their very name. Another aspect that I observed in my research that has been erased or avoided by American historians is the treatment of enslaved women. Women coming from dignified Muslim families were treated as sex slaves by the White Christian plantation owners. As uncomfortable as this topic might be for historians to write about, it is part of the history suffered by the enslaved women and therefore it deserves critical review and documentation. I also want to share a finding in writing this chapter that will be seared in my memory forever—the children. In every ship that sailed, the logs of which are available for review, I noticed children listed on board. These children were forcibly separated from their mothers, and many did not survive the cruelty and the miserable accommodations and died en route.

It is estimated that 12 million people were brought on ships via the Atlantic from West Africa to be sold into slavery. Besides the cruelty of slavery itself, what has been missing from history books and from the consciousness of the public is all the captured Africans who died on the journey to America. Historian Patrick Manning estimates that about 1.5 million Africans died on board these ships (Fig. 13-13).

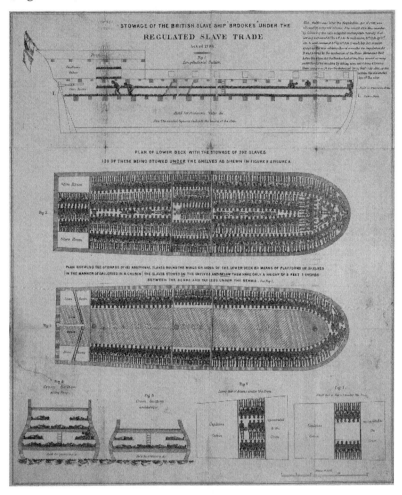

**Figure 13-13:** Stowage plan of a British slave ship from 1788.

But it gets worse. During the violent process of kidnapping the victims and transporting them to concentration camps on the West African coast to await shipment, millions lost their lives (estimates go as high as tens of millions). It is impossible to know the exact number. Historian Sylvester A. Johnson has stated that the trans-Atlantic slave trade "culminated in the deaths of between 50 and 100 million

Africans." In this book I have heavily explored Hollywood and the mainstream media in their pivotal roles in developing the concepts that exist in our popular culture. Hollywood has produced many blockbuster movies covering genocides, especially those committed against Europeans in Europe, movies that we all love and support. I tried to recall which movie or movies Hollywood has made about this genocide of West Africans, especially given the fact that America was directly involved, but I could not remember any.

Hollywood and the mainstream media's influence on popular culture is directly linked to our historical memory. Most of us become aware of major crimes against humanity/genocides through our history books, the media, and Hollywood movies, and not through independent research. As a result, we do not associate the slave trade with genocide since it has not been depicted as such. The Merriam-Webster Dictionary defines genocide as "the deliberate and systematic destruction of a racial, political, or cultural group." The trans-Atlantic slave trade fits that definition completely. If you conduct a search of the largest scale genocides in human history, as I have, you will not find the above genocide even listed in any of the major historical listings of genocides.

In writing this book, I have often wondered what is worse, to be a victim of a genocide or to be enslaved and forcibly indoctrinated, where all of your history has been erased, where your children and grandchildren would never know their family background, religion, or heritage, as has been done to the millions of African Americans in America today.

Four hundred years after that infamous day in August 1619 when the ship carrying enslaved Africans docked in Jamestown, Virginia, slavery has long since been abolished, but its legacy is alive and well. More than 1,500 Confederate monuments recognizing men who fought to preserve slavery adorn cities around the country when this book was completed in 2020. Four hundred years later, African Americans are not enslaved like Omar ibn Said, but still feel a knee on their necks making it difficult to breathe.

# Chapter 14
# The Iran Dilemma

**A**n issue we still need to discuss in this book is, what is the Sunni–Shia divide in Islam? Why is there so much conflict related to Iran?

In this last section of the book, let me take you back to where we started in Section 1, in the 1920s at a time when the Christian evangelical Zionists in the British government had established the vassalage program to create the "Middle East." As part of this program, the puppet leader in Iran under British control was the shah. By having Abdulaziz ibn Saud as their vassal in the Sunni Arabian Peninsula and the shah as their vassal in Shia Iran, Churchill and his colleagues assured British hegemony and prevented any rebellion against their Zionist agenda in the region. While in the Arabian Kingdom the British and their vassal kings had complete control, in Iran, the shah had to contend with an existing system of a parliament and a prime minister. In 1951, a man with tremendous popularity among the Iranian people, Mohammad Mosaddegh, became prime minister (Fig. 14-1).

Mosaddegh's popularity among the masses was due to his life-long mission of establishing democracy and getting rid of foreign influence in Iran. These two aspirations were nothing but fighting words for the Western evangelical Zionist vision of Churchill and his colleagues.

**Figure 14-1:** Mohammad Mosaddegh, Iran's prime minister from 1951 to 1953. His dream to establish meritocracy and democracy in Iran would spell his end.

In the 1950s, the average Iranian was economically struggling, while the monies made from the oil on their land were going to Britain's coffers—The Anglo-Persian Oil Company (APOC) was in charge. Only a few months into his job as prime minister, Mosaddegh, to help the struggling Iranian people, nationalized the APOC, which he had the right to do under international law.

We met the young Churchill in the 1920s after WWI in Chapter 3 as the architect of the new "Middle East," a model based on installing vassal kings. The older Churchill in the 1950s after WWII was not going to allow the challenge to his control over the "Middle East" by the new prime minister in Iran, Mosaddegh. Democracy in the "Middle East" would upend the whole vassal system, the cornerstone of the Lloyd–Balfour–Churchill Christian evangelical Zionist hegemonic plan for the region.

Churchill decided that the Iranian prime minister must be stopped immediately. Churchill, the shrewd man that he was, fully recognized that the baton of his "Middle East" vision was being passed to the US in the 1950s, and to overthrow the democracy-seeking government in Iran, the US needed to participate to prove its allegiance to the cause. He accomplished that. A combined operation by the CIA and MI5 orchestrated a coup, arrested Mosaddegh, and established the iron rule of the shah in Iran. Every Iranian from that day forward knows that their biggest chance of freedom was taken away by a sinister act by Britain and the US combined. Mosaddegh was kept under house arrest until he died in 1967. The Iranian regime, now a US vassal, knew the heroic status Mosaddegh had held in the Iranian psyche, so to avoid crowds they denied him a funeral and he was buried in the living room of his house. The CIA on August 19, 2013, for the first time admitted to its role in the 1953 coup against Iran's elected prime minister and champion of democracy, Mohammad Mosaddegh.

## King Cyrus 2.0

With democracy crushed, the shah (Persian term for "emperor" or "king") had proclaimed himself *shahenshah* (an ancient pre-Islamic Persian term meaning "king of kings") would rule with an iron fist for decades to come (Fig. 14-2).

**Figure 14-2:** A 1973 official portrait of the shah, Mohammad Reza Pahlavi, who proclaimed himself emperor, with self-awarded medals on display. The Al-Saud family in the Arab world and the Pahlavi family in Persia (Iran) became the two pillars of the US vassalage program's heavy-handed rule to sustain the Christian Zionist mission of the "Middle East" as originally envisioned by Lloyd, Balfour, and Churchill.

Persian King Cyrus (Cyrus the Great), whom we met in Chapter 6, established the first Persian empire in 529 BC—the Achaemenid Empire. The shah, in October 1971, decided to celebrate the 2,500th birthday of the empire by throwing a party the likes of which had never been seen before nor since.

Before I give a few details about the party, I think it is important to note that the average Iranian was living in dire economic conditions in 1971.

The party would take place at Persepolis, the ancient capital city of the Achaemenid Empire, where Darius and Xerxes, also mentioned in Chapter 6, held court.

For the 600 guests, including emperors, kings, presidents, dictators, sheikhs, and prime ministers from around the world, 50 tents were built right next to the ruins by the renowned Paris interior design house Maison Jansen. They all had marble bathrooms and the finest French linens. The floors were covered by priceless Persian carpets. Fifty thousand singing birds were imported from Europe, all of whom died a few days later due to the hot temperatures.

Catering was provided by the world's culinary giant, Maxim's de Paris. Maxim's shipped 2,500 bottles of champagne, 1,000 bottles of Bordeaux, and 1,000 bottles of Burgundy, all packed in 410 crates to a cellar built especially for this purpose in Persepolis. The champagne was from 1911 and the vintage cognac from 1860. The wine

Saleem I. Abdulrauf

was no less extravagant; a senior waiter at the event said, "We served
one of the world's most superb red wines, a magnum Château Lafite
Rothschild, vintage 1945." Makeup giant Elizabeth Arden created a
new line called Farah, named after the shah's wife, which was given
away to all the guests. Baccarat made the crystal and Porthault provided the linen. According to successive editions of *The Guinness Book
of World Records*, this was the most lavish banquet in modern history.
The cost of the party is estimated at $200 million (when adjusted
for inflation, $1.2 billion by today's standards).

The Iranian people were not allowed anywhere close to the ceremony, but university students devoid of basic freedoms, economically strained middle-class people, and peasants who had a hard time
putting food on the table were all watching the opulent ceremony
on TV. Also watching was another group, the clerics, including an
exiled revolutionary religious old man by the name of Khomeini who
would call the shah's ceremony at Persepolis the "devil's festival."

While Persepolis had served as the capital of the greatest empire
of its time, it was burned to the ground by Alexander the Great in
330 BC—perhaps an omen of the storm that awaited the shah.

## Family Rule vs. Elected Leader

Throughout this book, when I spoke of Muslims, I was talking about
traditional Islam, also known as Sunni Islam. Iran is a majority Shia
Islam country. What is the Sunni–Shia divide about?

There is no mention of the Sunni–Shia division in the Qur'an
nor in the Hadith (cumulative literature of the sayings of the Prophet
Muhammad). It is a political division that had nothing to do with
the core religion.

After the Prophet died on June 8, 632, a group of men representing the various clans (electoral council) selected the Prophet's closest
companion, Abu Bakr, to become the first caliph—a steward with
both political and religious authority to steer the larger Islamic community. There were some who were campaigning for the Prophet's
cousin Ali to become the caliph, but, due to Ali's honorable character, he accepted the decision of the electors and fully pledged allegiance to Abu Bakr and to the next two caliphs, Umar and Uthman,
and would go on to become the fourth caliph in 656 at age 55.

The most significant crisis faced by the budding Islamic Empire was when the power-hungry governor of the empire in Syria, Muawiyah, challenged the newly elected Caliph Ali for the caliphate. This would lead to the first civil war in Islam between the two camps. Ali was assassinated by an extremist in the city of Kufa (current-day Iraq) in January 661. Muawiyah immediately proclaimed himself as the caliph.

The word *shia* in Arabic means "party," and specifically refers to Ali's supporters in his struggle against Muawiyah. This designation had no religious element at that point; it stood purely for political-military differences. During the lifetime of the Prophet Muhammad, Ali married the Prophet's daughter Fatima, and they had two sons, Al-Hasan and Al-Husayn. The Prophet loved the two grandsons dearly. After the death of Ali, these two men were the only male descendants of the Prophet. Ali's supporters during his struggle against Muawiyah, the Shia, demanded that the only credible caliph would have to be one of Ali's two sons.

When Muawiyah died in 680, he had already appointed his son, Yazid, to become the next caliph. Al-Hasan had died recently, but the younger of the two brothers, Al-Husayn, refused to pledge allegiance to Yazid. The people of Kufa, the strong supporters of his father Ali, requested that Al-Husayn come to Iraq and stand up to the rule of Yazid. Al-Husayn heeded the call and traveled with his family and a small force of close supporters from Hejaz to Iraq. Yazid's spies tracked Al-Husayn for ten days and intercepted him before he could reach Kufa at an area called Karbala. In the ensuing battle, on October 10, 680, multiple members of Al-Husayn's family were killed, including his infant son and his young nephew (the son of his brother, Al-Hasan), both great-grandchildren of the Prophet Muhammad. Al-Husayn was beheaded, and his head was sent to Yazid in Damascus. The Kufans failed to come out to defend Al-Husayn.

The massacre at Karbala occurred 48 years after the death of the Prophet. During those years, despite the war between Ali and Muawiyah, the Islamic religion was undivided. Karbala would create a fissure—the martyrdom of Al-Husayn was the historical lightning rod that led to the inception of the Shia religious ideology. The Kufans, who had requested Al-Husayn to come to Iraq, had failed to protect him when he needed them. Among them would emerge a group who would be called "the penitents." These Kufans delved into exploring repentance and even punishment for their cowardice in not fighting to defend Al-Husayn. The Shia ritual of Ashura, self-flagellation, emerged as a repentance for their failure to appear at Karbala. This penitent ideology which emerged in Kufa, Iraq, marked the inception of the Shia religious separation from traditional Sunni Islam. Ali's "party" (*shia* in Arabic) only took on religious significance after Karbala; prior to that it was purely a political stance against the first corrupt dynastic regime in the history of Islam: Muawiyah and his son Yazid. While it is perceived that Shiism is a Persian Iranian phenomenon, it is important to note that its origins come from the Arabs in the Arab Iraqi city of Kufa.

The word *sunni* refers to the traditions of the Prophet Muhammad and his closest companions. While Sunnis see the events at Karbala as tragic and barbarous acts committed against the family members of the Prophet, the Shia see them as an integral part of the religion itself. The Shia would go on to believe that leadership and succession in Islam must be based on the bloodline of Ali and Fatima, while the Sunnis believe that succession should be divorced from the bloodline and should instead be based on electoral counsel selections.

There is no evidence to show that Ali, at any point in his life, believed that there would be a religious movement in Islam that advocated for his bloodline, one that would create a schism in the religion. Based on his honorable and valiant character, I believe he would have opposed any such thinking.

From a larger perspective, the Shia belief set would make it closer to Christianity than Islam from a theological conceptual standpoint. In traditional Islam, every human is born free of sin, while Christian doctrine is based on the premise that everyone is born sinful. The Shia belief that they have sinned for failing to defend Al-Husayn and need to repent for that sin is more akin to Christian theology than that of traditional Islam. There are parallels to Jesus on the cross and Al-Husayn at Karbala according to some Shia scholars. Moreover, in Shiism the 12 descendants of Ali, known as imams, are akin to saints in Christianity, while the concept of sainthood does not exist in Sunni Islam.

In Sunnism, religious scholars are known by the Arabic word *ulama*. In Shiism, they are known by the Persian word *mullah*.

The prevailing view in much of the Muslim world is that Iran has been a Shia country since the inception of Islam in the seventh century, but this is incorrect. It was actually a predominantly Sunni country until the beginning of the sixteenth century. The Safavid Empire takeover of Iran in 1501 transformed the country forever. The Safavid Shia religious zealotry in Iran was akin to the Wahhabi religious zealotry in the Arabian Peninsula (Chapter 3). The Safavids enacted a forced conversion policy to Shiism, and Sunni scholars (ulama) were forced to either leave or be killed.

As a disclosure, I come from a traditional Sunni ancestry, and in my review above, I made sure to purely base it on historical accounts to avoid any bias.

I would be remiss not to mention the irony of the contradiction. In Saudi Arabia, the mantle-holder of Sunni Islam, the succession in monarchy is nepotistic and purely based on bloodline. In Iran, the mantle-holder of Shia Islam, there has been more of a tradition of voting for the parliament, as well as an attempt, albeit failed, at a full democracy by Mohammad Mosaddegh in the 1950s.

## The Three Storms of 1979

The opulent "party of the century" thrown by the shah in October 1971 helped solidify the view among the Iranian public that he was the enemy, an agent of Western colonial power. As opposition grew, the shah would use his secret police unit known as the SAVAK (Sāzemān-e Ettelā'āt va Amniyat-e Keshvar) to censor the media and hunt down dissidents. The SAVAK had close ties to the CIA and had thousands of agents who were known for committing torture and targeted killings. The SAVAK is the classic secret police unit, the likes of which exist with various names in every Arab dictatorship. Western leaders have known, since the inception of the "Middle East" in the early part of the twentieth century, that for them to guarantee the survival of their vassal dictators, they must allow them to use whatever means necessary to control their population.

By the mid-1970s, the shah was getting older, and all segments of the population, including the middle class, peasants, university students, and the clergy, decided that they could take no more.

While initially the movement against the shah was a secular freedom-seeking movement, the return of an old man from exile would change all that.

It is well known that Osama bin Laden, the founder of the Al-Qaeda terrorist organization, had rebelled against the Al-Saud family in the 1980s for allowing US military bases in the Arabian Peninsula. What is not widely known is that a couple decades earlier in Iran, another religious rebel by the name of Khomeini openly criticized the shah for having senior US military advisors help chart the strategy of the country in 1964. The core element, as shown in both examples, behind "Middle East" extremism stemmed from strong anti-colonial beliefs within both the public and religious communities living within these Western-controlled vassal regimes (Fig. 14-3).

**Figure 14-3:** Ruhollah Musavi Khomeini in a picture taken in 1938. The story of Khomeini is intertwined with the story of twentieth-century Iran. He was born in 1902 and studied at the preeminent Shia theological higher education center in the city of Qom, Iran. In the 1960s he became a respected and highly published religious scholar among the Iranian population.

The statements made by Khomeini in the 1960s criticizing the shah resulted in him having to leave the country to live in exile. He lived in Turkey, Iraq, and ultimately France. The shah left Iran for medical treatment in January 1979, and within two weeks, the then 77-year-old Khomeini returned to Iran. He would transform the centuries-old standard of Shia clergy refraining from political leadership to becoming the leaders of the Iranian regime. The anger of university students toward the shah and the US for the coup against the secular democracy attempt by Mosaddegh in the 1950s and for living under brutality for decades was turned toward the US Embassy in the capital of Tehran. The students stormed the embassy on November 4, 1979, and took 52 American diplomats and citizens hostage for 444 days.

The end result of Khomeini's return and the student revolt was the creation of the first Shia theocracy rule in history. The students and the middle class were not organized enough; the clergy were able to take charge. The head of state, or the supreme leader, in 1979 post-revolution Iran would be from the clergy, specifically someone who had attained high recognition in religious scholarship.

Did the Iranian people get what they bargained for? The answer is, unfortunately, no. The new regime in Iran was even more brutal than the shah's regime. Thousands of political prisoners were executed in the years that followed the establishment of the Shia theocracy. The Iranian people were victims of both the shah and the Shia clergy reign that followed.

Iran was not the only country in the "Middle East" that was jolted in 1979. Let me take you across the sand to the Kingdom of Saudi Arabia in the Arabian Peninsula. You will recall from Chapter 3 that King Faisal and his wife, Queen Effat, had advanced women's education despite the Wahhabi opposition. Although Faisal was assassinated in 1975, the progress continued. Women entered the workforce and female TV announcers were common. Just as there was a gathering storm in Iran, there was one in Saudi Arabia: the ire of the fundamentalist Sunni Wahhabis.

The Saudi royal family derives respect and credibility in the "Middle East" and the wider Muslim world by claiming that it is the custodian of the two holy mosques in Mecca and Medina. A group of Wahhabi zealots decided that to bring down the Al-Saud family, they must do something that had not been done in 1,400 years: violently seize the Grand Mosque in Mecca. Their purpose was to replicate what had happened in Iran in the preceding months, overthrow the ruling royal family. The group was led by a charismatic, soft-spoken 43-year-old man named Juhayman, who had come from a family that was part of the militant Wahhabi movement known as Ikhwan (discussed in Chapter 3), and he had also served in the Saudi Arabian National Guard for 20 years (Fig. 14-4).

Three weeks after the Iranian students stormed the US Embassy in Tehran, Juhayman, leading some 400 militants, stormed the Grand Mosque on November 20, 1979, at 5:25 a.m. Thousands of pilgrims were inside, since this was the time of the first prayer of the day, the Fajr prayer. I listened to the original tapes from inside the Grand Mosque on that day; Juhayman used the loudspeaker system to speak to his men who were spread throughout the mosque. "Go up to the Minarets [7 Minarets] and put snipers in place. Close all gates [51 grand gates of the Mosque]," ordered Juhayman. Most of

**Figure 14-4:** Juhayman al-Otaybi, the mastermind behind the takeover of the Grand Mosque in Mecca in 1979. He believed the Saudi royal family did not have legitimacy to rule.

the pilgrims were allowed to escape; the extremists were not targeting them. The soldiers in Mecca were no match and the siege continued for days. With each passing moment, the Saudi royal family's credibility and reputation were on the line. The royal family found itself in a very difficult bind in making the next decision. The Prophet Muhammad had categorically forbidden violence inside the Grand Mosque. Not only would the royal family have to bring significant weaponry and violence inside the mosque to deal with the insurrection, but they knew they needed external Western help. The idea of having non-Muslim soldiers entering the holiest site in Islam was unthinkable by the millions of Muslims around the world, let alone the fundamentalist Wahhabis of Saudi Arabia. They needed the support of the kingdom's most respected Wahhabi cleric among the most stringent Wahhabis. His name was Abdul Aziz bin Baz. This, for Bin Baz and the Wahhabi extremist element within the royal family, was the golden opportunity they had been waiting for all their lives. The ruling portion of the royal family, which up to that point had been carrying out the progressive work of King Faisal (assassinated just four years earlier), was now on its knees seeking the support of the chief Wahhabi cleric, Bin Baz. They had not listened to him in the past about his views on decreasing the role of women in public life and eliminating entertainment activities in the kingdom. Bin Baz drove a tough bargain; the man who believed that the earth was flat and the sun orbits the earth got his way, which would change life in the Arabian Peninsula for decades to come.

What the royal family did not tell Bin Baz and his extremist Wahhabi brethren was that the US was assisting them in handling the crisis in Mecca. American pilots were flying reconnaissance helicopter missions on top of the Grand Mosque to gather intelligence about the occupying force. Mark Hambley, the political-military officer at the US Embassy in Jeddah, went to Mecca to speak directly with officials. The aircraft carrier USS *Kitty Hawk* was placed on alert in the Arabian Sea for any actions necessary to protect the Saudi royal family. This crisis was taking place in the middle of the Iran hostage crisis, so bringing American troops to Mecca seemed politically problematic. Fahad, the effective leader of Saudi Arabia at the time, contacted the French president to help with the standoff in Mecca.

Once Bin Baz gave his approval, the commandos belonging to the French tactical unit Groupe d'Intervention de la Gendarmerie Nationale (GIGN) arrived at the military base in Taif (a city 40 miles or 64 kilometers from Mecca). There the French commandos observed that the Saudi forces were demoralized and did not want to fight anymore—they had seen a number of their comrades get killed in the fight. A top-secret report sent back to France revealed that the Saudi forces had incurred hundreds of deaths at the hands of the rebels in just the first few days of the conflict (Fig. 14-5).

The French team had detailed maps of the Grand Mosque and was armed with the intelligence that the rebels were holed up in the basement level; they came up

**Figure 14-5:** Christian Prouteau, commander of the GIGN (Groupe d'intervention de la Gendarmerie nationale). He initially refused for his force to go into Mecca, Islam's holiest site. He agreed once the French government told him by saving the Al-Saud monarchy they would be protecting the Western world.

with the plan of using liquid gas to push the rebels out of the underground. On December 3, 1979, an unmarked French plane delivered 300 kilos (660 pounds) of concentrated liquid tear gas to the military base in Taif. The Grand Mosque was subsequently stormed. A large number of the rebels were killed and Juhayman and 62 of his men were arrested.

In the single largest show of beheadings in modern human history, Juhayman and the other 62 men were publicly beheaded on January 9, 1980, in eight cities across Saudi Arabia to send a loud message to the populace: if you dare stand up against us, this will be your fate.

I was intrigued by what the commander of the French tactical force GIGN, Christian Prouteau, said many years later. He said he was told by French President Valéry Giscard d'Estaing and the minister of foreign affairs François-Poncet that the French armed intervention in the Holy Mosque would save the "fate of the Western world." So, let me pose this question: why would the top leadership of the French government believe that intervening in the Grand Mosque and protecting the Al-Saud family was so critical to the "fate of the Western world"? I will answer this question in the conclusion of this book.

The man who emerged as the new king of Saudi Arabia following the crisis in Mecca was Fahad. He was arguably the most corrupt king Saudi Arabia has ever had. He was neither religious, like many of the zealot Wahhabis within the royal family, nor was he egalitarian, like Faisal before him. His only priority was himself and his clan within the Saudi royal family. His fear that there were elements within the Saudi population that could overthrow his regime led him to enact massive social change in the nation; he rolled back all the freedoms and rights for women that Faisal and Effat had fought so hard to establish. The second action, a very selfish and shrewd one, would forever change the "Middle East" and the world at large. He recognized there were militant extremist Wahhabis in the country, so instead of engaging them to reverse the radicalization, he decided to export them and get this problem out of his hands. The Saudi royal family was shaken up that the Wahhabis, who had been their brethren since the inception of the country had targeted them directly, since the Mecca takeover was part of a plan to bring down the Saudi ruling family. Fahad and his inner circle were sending a message to the extremists: we are not the enemy, the "West" is!

While the confrontation in the Grand Mosque in Mecca was going on, there was a 22-year-old university student in the nearby port city of Jeddah who was watching and observing closely; his name was Osama bin Laden. It was the Fahad plan of exporting extremists that led to the newly Juhayman-inspired Wahhabi extremists to end up as jihadis in Afghanistan. It is there that Al-Qaeda was formed and the plans for the September 11, 2001, terrorist attacks targeting the US were made.

In the confrontation between Juhayman and Fahad in 1979, although Juhayman was beheaded, he was the winner. He achieved his goals; he transformed the Saudi kingdom and life within it, and he set forth a new generation of Wahhabi extremists who were tacitly supported by the Saudi royal family, and who therefore turned their sights on all non-Wahhabi Muslims and the West. By supporting the extremist Wahhabi element within the kingdom (limiting women's rights and shutting down all entertainment) and outside it (building Wahhabi mosques and centers), the royal family was sending the message to them that they are visionary partners so long as they do not target the royal family.

The Sunni Al-Sauds and the Shia Pahlavis (the shah's family) were close allies and friends. Throughout the twentieth century there was no animosity between the two sects of Islam. Once the shah fell, the tone of the Saudi royal family changed. Their concern was that what happened in Iran could happen in Saudi Arabia, the overthrow of the regime. So once again they had to make an external entity the boogeyman that they could rally their people against; the enemy now became the Shia! The mullahs in revolutionary Iran, likewise, were ready to export their revolution throughout the region. They proclaimed themselves as the visionaries for the future of the "Middle East," which would set them in a direct clash with the US-backed Sunni powers in the region.

The author Kim Ghattas, in her book *Black Wave*, gives a vivid account of both the 1979 Iranian revolution and the siege of the Grand Mosque in Mecca.

There was one more gathering storm far from the Arabian deserts but yet so close. Within a year of the above events, in January

1980, a new US president entered the White House, Ronald Reagan. That month some 2,500 evangelical leaders gathered for five days in Washington, DC. The leaders were from the National Association of Evangelicals and the National Religious Broadcasters, representing at that time 40 to 50 million born-again Christian Americans. "The sleeping giant that has lain prostrate across America is beginning to wake itself," said Reverend D. James Kennedy at the conference.

We saw throughout the journey of this book the pivotal role that evangelical Christian Zionists have played in all the secret deals that led to the formation of the "Middle East." The 1980s would take that movement out of the shadows and bring it to the surface. Evangelical Christian Zionists do not believe in the separation of church and state when it comes to decisions, especially regarding Israel. Starting from the 1980s, which they labeled "the decade of the evangelicals," they would use their mammoth political and financial power to impact all decisions stemming from the White House concerning the "Middle East."

The three extremist movements—Shiism in Iran, Wahhabism in Saudi Arabia, and evangelicalism in the US—were inherently intertwined. While the decades-old Saudi support for Israel had been welcomed by the evangelical Christian Zionist powers in the US, the new post-revolution Iran was an entity never before seen in the "Middle East." It was an entity that was not under their control and did not fit into nor adhere to the Zionist "Middle East" envisioned by Churchill. It did not fit the secret evangelical Christian Zionist script that was set 100 years ago.

# Chapter 15
# A Plan to Demolish the Taj Mahal!

When I spoke to people as part of my research for this book, I asked them what came to mind when they thought of India, and consistently three things came up: the Taj Mahal, Gandhi, and Bollywood. There was one key element missing that defines all three of these in India today.

You may wonder, why include India in this book? This book deals with fundamentalism within Judaism, Christianity, and Islam and its impact on the current world. Hinduism is a polytheistic belief with no connection to the monotheistic Abrahamic religions. However, I intend to demonstrate to you that India is also a microcosm for all of the key issues discussed in this book.

Mahatma Gandhi was a man who utilized nonviolent resistance against British occupation, which led to India attaining its independence in 1947, and in the process he inspired movements for freedom and civil rights around the world. On January 30, 1948, while preparing to conduct a multifaith prayer meeting in Delhi, a 38-year-old Hindu man, Nathuram Vinayak Godse, approached Gandhi and, in the traditional style of showing respect to an elder, Godse bent and touched Gandhi's feet with his hands. As he stood up, he pulled out a gun and shot the frail 78-year-old icon three times in the abdomen and chest (Fig. 15-1).

Why would Godse kill a Hindu figure idolized all over the world as a symbol

**Figure 15-1:** India's first prime minister, Jawaharlal Nehru, announced to the world the news that Gandhi had been assassinated and said, "light has gone out of our lives."

of freedom? Godse was member of a Hindu terrorist organization, Rashtriya Swayamsevak Sangh (RSS), which was established in the mid-twentieth century based on Fascist and Nazi ideologies in Europe. M. S. Golwalkar, the RSS leader in the 1940s, admired Adolf Hitler and Benito Mussolini and was specifically inspired by the ideology of racial purity. The RSS, from its inception to this day, sees the Muslim population of the Indian subcontinent as its core enemy, but it has also targeted India's Christian population. Golwalkar declared, "In this land Hindus have been the owners . . . Muslims and Christians the dacoits [band of armed robbers]." Golwalkar was not speaking of literal owners of lands and literal robbers, but he was speaking of his deep belief that only Hindus belong in India, a concept of "blood and soil," and the mere presence of Christians and Muslims on that soil makes them fair targets.

## Blood and Soil

The RSS was enraged when, at the end of the British occupation, India was partitioned to give land to the Muslims in the northwest of the subcontinent—Pakistan (Fig. 15-2). The support of the partition plan by India's two Hindu founding fathers, Mahatma Gandhi and Jawaharlal Nehru, made them a target of the RSS. Gandhi and Nehru's vision for the newly independent India was to be a pluralistic, multicultural democracy that enjoyed a harmonious relationship between Muslims and Hindus (Fig. 15-3). For the RSS, those were fighting words. At its independence, India selected a flag that incorporated three colors reflecting inclusivity (saffron for Hindus, green for Muslims, and white for other religious communities). The RSS vehemently opposed this flag, stating in its official publication in 1947, "The word three is in itself an evil." It insisted the flag of India could only have one color—saffron.

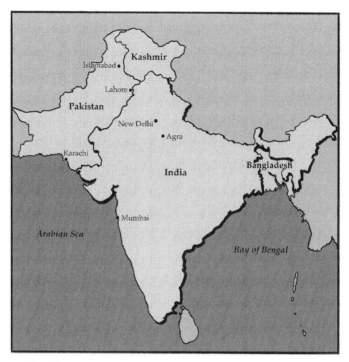

**Figure 15-2:** The 1947 partition of the Indian subcontinent led to the creation of India and Pakistan. Bangladesh was initially named "East Pakistan" until it ceded as an independent nation in 1971. The majority Muslim region of Kashmir became a flashpoint for India and Pakistan, and they have fought a number of wars over it ever since. The term *Indian subcontinent* as used in this chapter refers to the combined peninsular area that includes India, Pakistan, Bangladesh, and Kashmir.

**Figure 15-3:** The camaraderie and mutual respect that Gandhi (right) and Mohammed Ali Jinnah (left)—the founder of Pakistan showed each other in the 1940s would go on to enrage militant Hindu nationalists.

Some two years after the assassination of Gandhi, in September 1950, a boy was born to a family in the western coastal region of Gujrat, India; they named him Narendra. Since childhood he became mesmerized by the RSS, and just like Godse, he joined the organization as a young boy. In 2014 Narendra Modi became the prime minister of India. He got to that post by heading the Bharatiya Janata Party (BJP), which is nothing but the political wing of the RSS.

For Modi, the RSS, and the BJP, the enemy was not just the Muslims. They viewed the emergence of highly educated and career-oriented women in India as anathema to their views of women. They resented the elevation of the rights of the lower-caste Hindus, which went against their view of these people as inferior human beings. While Islamic extremist groups capture the imagination and coverage of the media in Western countries, it is important to note the RSS is not some obscure organization; it has more than 500 branches in 39 countries.

In August 2017, White supremacists held a rally in Charlottesville, Virginia, holding signs that said "Jews will not replace us." Their rallying cry was "blood and soil"—which comes from the Nazi German "Blut und Boden," expressing the ideal of a "racially" defined national body ("blood") united within a land ("soil"). Similarly, the RSS, Godse, and Modi in India pushed for the concept that India was not a multicultural, multiethnic nation, and therefore, the Muslim and Christian minorities must "subscribe to Hindu primacy."

Modi, unlike the many other religious extremist "populist" leaders discussed in this book, does not boast about his hatred toward Muslims—he is careful with his words publicly—but is instead rather insidious. Deaths of Indian Muslim civilians have occurred everywhere he governed throughout his career up to and including his role as prime minister. As the chief minister of the state of Gujarat in 2002, he encouraged sectarian riots between Hindus and Muslims that resulted in the death of more than 1,000 citizens (overwhelmingly Muslims). Dexter Filkins of the *New Yorker* wrote that according to eyewitnesses, "Rioters cut open the bellies of [Muslim] pregnant women and killed their babies; others gang-raped women and girls. In at least one instance, a Muslim boy was forced to drink kerosene and swallow a lighted match. Ehsan Jafri, an elderly Congress Party politician [a political party opposed to the RSS], was paraded naked and then dismembered and burned." A heroic Hindu police officer, Rahul Sharma, saved hundreds of Muslim school children by spoiling the plot of Hindu terrorists who were planning to massacre them. The massacre of Muslims in Gujrat was orchestrated by the RSS with Modi as the minister of the state. Furthermore, Modi held the Indian soldiers in their barracks while the mass killings were occurring to prevent them from stopping the massacre. Sharma, the heroic officer, was demoted from his position. A citizen-led inquiry that included former Supreme Court justices and a former senior police official concluded, "These instructions [mass killings of Muslims] were blatantly disseminated by the government [Modi's government], and in most cases, barring a few sterling exceptions, methodically carried out by the police and Indian Administrative Service." Though Modi was subsequently cleared for his actions by a court of majority Hindu judges, he was barred from entering the United States.

Modi's modus operandi—which he learned from his Gujrat governorship—was the concept of "pogroms." This is when the police join one side of a mob to participate in the violence being committed against the other side. The term comes from Tsarist Russia where pogroms were used against Jews. In February 2020, RSS mobs targeted Muslim homes in the capital city of Delhi. Ashutosh Varshney, a Brown University professor and author of the book *Ethnic Conflict and Civic Life: Hindus and Muslims in India*, said "A mosque, a Muslim shrine, and Muslim homes and shops were attacked. The police did not respond to calls for help. Logs suggest a high volume of those calls came from predominantly Muslim parts of northeast Delhi. But the police failed to show up. Hindu mobs then attacked with abandon." He added, "There are videos, in particular one which shows young Muslim men being hit by a Hindu mob. And the cops are asking the fallen and beaten Muslim men to sing the national anthem—as they're being hit." The person in charge of the police in Delhi at the time was Modi's right-hand man, Amit Shah.

Regarding the Modi era in India, Aditya Mukherjee, a respected Hindu Indian historian, told the *New York Times* that India's first prime minister, Jawaharlal Nehru, had said, "If fascism ever came to India it would come in the form of majoritarian Hindu communalism." The historian opined, "That is exactly what is happening." He would go on to add about Modi and his allies "In plain language, they are what we now call communal fascists."

In Modi's India, Godse, the terrorist who assassinated Gandhi, reemerged as a venerated national hero. More than a dozen statues of Godse have been erected and a number of Hindu temples across the country are being converted into Godse temples. The governor of the state Uttar Pradesh has proposed to change the name of the city of Meerut to "Godse City"!

Ramachandra Guha, a preeminent biographer of Gandhi, said about the newly emerging admiration for Godse in Modi's India among a large segment of the population: "It is foul, despicable, but it is real and widespread."

All recent populist extremist nationalist movements around the world lionize their respective leaders as alpha males. Allow me to comment on this issue as related to the two revered extremist Hindu nationalist heroes, Modi and Godse, as they share certain characteristics. Before Nathuram Godse's birth, his parents had three boys and a daughter; all three boys died in infancy. Fearing a curse targeting male children, Godse was raised as a girl for the first few years of his life. His name Nathuram means the pierced one (as he had both nose piercing and earrings). Modi entered into an arranged marriage with a 16-year-old teenager by the name of Jashodaben in 1968. He soon deserted her. He did not publicly acknowledge that he was married and left blank the marital status question in forms in several election cycles. Ultimately, a Modi biography distributed by the BJP stated that the marriage had never been consummated. Jashodaben, now 62 years old, lives a very modest life as a retired teacher. The fact that Modi never divorced her prevented her from seeking her own family life, which reflects the attitude Modi has toward women.

## The Mughals

The xenophobic concept of "blood and soil" is based on labeling another ethnic or religious group as "outsiders." They perceive the outsiders as "new" or immigrant arrivals to the land. In the case of American White supremacists, outsiders are Jews, Black people, and other minorities; in the case of Hindu nationalism, outsiders are the

Christians and Muslims. Therefore, it is important to address the question: when did Christians and Muslims arrive in the land we call India?

According to the beliefs of the Christian community of India, the Apostle Thomas (one of the 12 Apostles of Jesus in the New Testament) traveled to the Malabar Coast (in the Kerala region of India) in AD 52 and established Christianity in the Indian subcontinent. There is clear-cut evidence that Christian communities were well established in the Malabar Coast by the sixth century.

The first mosque was built in Gujarat (the state mentioned above where Muslims were massacred) over a thousand years ago (between 610 and 623). Let me take you back to Chapter 1 to the seventh century, during which the emerging Muslim Empire was involved in economic and scientific expansion. The concept of "India" we have today as one large, centrally governed nation is a relatively new one. It was not until the middle of the second millennium that the Muslim Delhi Sultanate and Mughal Empire created this concept. From the sixth century up to the point the Muslims created a large centralized federal system, the Indian subcontinent was made up of warring Hindu kingdoms.

Starting in the seventh century, Muslim caliphs began making diplomatic and commercial connections with kingdoms and empires across Asia all the way to China. Arab ships sailing in the Arabian Sea along India's western border carried goods to and from Asian countries. The Hindu king Dahir Sen of Sindh (a region in current-day Pakistan) engaged in pirating Arab ships. One specific raid forced the caliph to react. A ship carrying gifts from the king of Serendib (modern Sri Lanka) to Caliph Al-Walid was attacked by King Dahir. They kidnapped Muslim women on board and stole all the cargo. A young Hejaz-born commander, Mohammad ibn Qasim al-Thaqafi, was dispatched with a 6,000-man army to deal with Dahir. When Ibn Qasim arrived in Sindh, it became apparent that Dahir was not popular among the Hindus of the region, and many joined his army to fight Dahir. Ibn Qasim defeated Dahir at the battle of Ar-rur (also known as Rohri) at which Dahir was killed and Ibn Qasim freed the Muslim women. Sindh became part of the Islamic Empire.

During the tenth century, as we saw in Chapter 2 (Fig 2-4), the Turkestan people of Central Asia started to expand and conquer other territories within Asia. One such nomadic Turkic cavalry army entered the Northern Indian subcontinent and established the Muslim Delhi Sultanate in 1206, which at its peak in the fourteenth century ruled most of the Indian subcontinent. It is this sultanate (a country governed by a Muslim sultan, meaning "king" or "prince" in Arabic) that transformed the Indian subcontinent into a "global cosmopolitan culture." The Delhi Sultanate developed a common language (using a combination of Sanskrit, Persian, and Arabic) for the peoples of the subcontinent: the Hindustani language (also known as Hindi–Urdu). It is considered the third-most common language (after English and Mandarin) spoken in the world today. It is the language of the Bollywood movies and the rich Indian poetry and song culture. The sultanate also introduced the subcontinent to emerging technologies from the Muslim world, including gears, cams, cranks, spinning wheels, and paper-making techniques, all of which would go on to evolve the Indian economy. We witnessed in Chapter 1 how the Mongol invasion of Baghdad in the thirteenth century devastated the Arab Muslim Empire and its culture. The Delhi Sultanate valiantly defended India from the Mongol invasion and in doing so prevented the destruction that could have happened had the Mongols succeeded.

The Delhi Sultanate would also witness the first major female ruler of India, the Muslim princess, Razia. Her father, Sultan Iltutmish, knew she was much smarter and far more capable than her brothers. He chose her to become his successor. What Razia would face is so similar to what I hear women in leadership positions say in the twenty-first century! The minute she became the sultana, the nobility around her were just waiting for her to make a mistake. She dressed in a man's headdress and armor for her cabinet meetings and public appearances. Despite all the challenges the male military officers and politicians threw her way, she became beloved by the masses for her fair and just rule. Sultana Razia was killed in battle in 1240 at age 35.

After three and half centuries of Delhi Sultanate rule, a new and even more powerful empire would take over the Indian subcontinent, the Mughals. They also emerged from the central Asian Turkic tribes. Although the Mughal Empire was established in 1526, it was the rule of Emperor Akbar from 1556 to 1605 that set the cultural and social character of the empire. Akbar made sure that the rights of Hindus in the Muslim Empire were respected. His wife, who is popularly known as Jodha, was a Hindu princess from Amber who was allowed to openly practice her religion in the Mughal Muslim palaces. Her Mughal name was Mariam-uz-Zamani. (*Mariam* is the Arabic name for "Mary"; with the addition *uz-Zamani*, it means "Mary of our Time," reflecting the respect she had within the Mughal dynasty.) Hindus and Sikhs held major political and military leadership positions throughout the span of the empire.

The Mughal Empire's open economic policies that allowed farmers to enter larger markets, combined with the introduction of technologies to the subcontinent, led to its emergence as a major world economic power. It reached its peak during the reign of Aurangzeb, who reigned from 1658 to 1707 (arrow in Fig. 15-4). The Mughal Empire had the world's largest GDP in the seventeenth century, producing about a quarter of the world's economic and industrial output (Fig. 15-4).

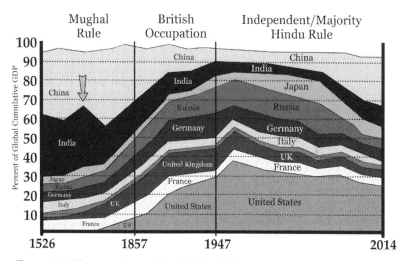

**Figure 15-4:** Percent of cumulative GDP of India compared to other major world powers. Three phases of India are shown: Mughal Rule (1526–1857), under British occupation (1858–1947), and India following independence under majority Hindu rule (1947–2014). The Mughals inherited a very vibrant economy from the Muslim Delhi Sultanate and built upon it. The peak of India as the largest economic power in the world occurred during the Mughal rule. Neither the British occupation nor the current Hindu rule has been able to replicate such economic vigor. Adapted from the work of British Economist Angus Maddison, Maddison Project (2013), and Stratfor (2018).

One of the theories routinely peddled in Hindu nationalist circles is that the Mughals had systematically forced Hindus to convert to Islam. I am sure there may have been anecdotal cases, but there is no evidence that any such systematic conversions ever occurred. It is well established that proselytizing campaigns around the world yield quantifiable results. For example, according to a Pew Research Center survey in 2014, 79 percent of Black Americans are Christians, despite the fact that none of their ancestors who were brought as slaves to America came from a Christian background. Similarly, the overwhelming indigenous populations of Latin America are Christian today, when none were before the forced conversion campaigns by the Spanish and Portuguese invaders. Based on the Indian government's own census in 2001, Muslims constitute 14.2 percent of the population. Throughout the over 600-year Muslim rule over the Indian subcontinent, Muslims consistently have been a minority; both logic and math go against the theory of a mass systematic conversion campaign by the Mughals. This fits the pattern of Muslim Empires throughout history; for example, in the over 700-year rule of Spain (711–1492), there was no policy of forced conversions. Muslims represent 4.4 percent of Spain's population today.

In answering the question posed earlier in this chapter regarding the term "outsiders," it can be definitively stated that Christians and Muslims have been part of the fiber and civilization of the Indian subcontinent for over 1,000 years. If they are labeled as outsiders, that means most people in most countries in the world today are also outsiders!

The title of this chapter, "A Plan to Demolish the Taj Mahal!" is not meant literally; however, it does metaphorically represent the culture fostered by Modi and the RSS in India today. The Hindu nationalist government has revised history books taught to school children to omit and revise the history of the past 1,000 years of pivotal Islamic contributions to the Indian civilization as summarized above. The Taj Mahal, a UNESCO World Heritage Site and the single biggest attraction for foreign tourists to India with some 6 million annual visitors, was removed in 2017 from the tourism booklet of Uttar Pradesh, the state in which the Taj Mahal is located. The chief minister of Uttar Pradesh, a fellow Modi Hindu nationalist, Yogi Adityanath, said it "did not reflect Indian culture" (Fig. 15-5).

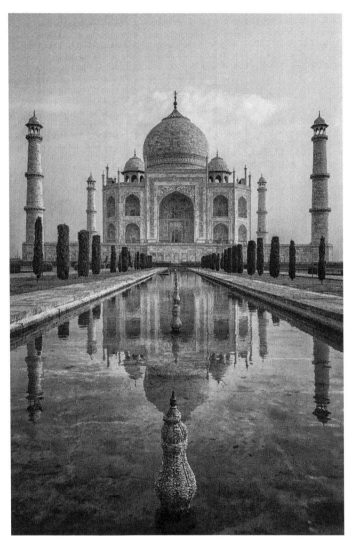

**Figure 15-5:** The Mughals were patrons of the arts, poetry, and architecture. The Taj Mahal in the city of Agra, labeled as one of the seven wonders of the world, demonstrates the preeminence of Mughal contributions to Indian culture and history. It was commissioned by Emperor Shah Jahan in 1631 as a symbol of love in memory of his wife Mumtaz. She had died that year while giving birth to their fourteenth child. The Indian poet Rabindranath Tagore would reflect, the Taj is "the teardrop on the cheek of time."

# Eve and Sati

The view within the global popular culture that women in Islamic cultures are the most poorly treated around the world is a relatively recent generalization, one that has been propagated over the last 100 years. Prior to that, as we saw in Chapter 3, in sixteenth-century France, the notable publication *Promptuarium Iconum Insigniorum* selected the Prophet Muhammad's wife Khadija as an iconic example of women's leadership within societies. We saw in Chapter 13 how one of America's iconic Founding Fathers, Thomas Jefferson, as a young lawyer in his research for sources on women's rights, investigated Islamic law. The past 100 years of labeling Muslims as the most anti-women's rights religious group does interestingly coincide with the campaign by Hollywood, mainstream media, and the political establishment to vilify Arabs and Muslims for deep-seated geopolitical reasons outlined in this book. They were clearly helped by the Wahhabi takeover—which they made possible—of the Arabian Peninsula in the early twentieth century, a group that is deeply misogynistic toward women and their rights.

On September 4, 1987, in a village 100 miles southwest of Delhi, a large group gathered to witness the funeral pyre of a 24-year-old Hindu man, Maal Singh, who died from a gastrointestinal infection the day before. As the pyre burned, Singh's 18-year-old widow, Roop Kanwar, was burned alive. This pagan ritual of the widowed wife volitionally burning herself in the funeral pyre of her husband is known as *sati*. It was originally rooted in the upper castes of Hinduism, but throughout history, it was adapted by the lower castes as well (Fig. 15-6).

**Figure 15-6:** A picture of the 17-year-old Roop Kanwar on her wedding night. Her sati occurred eight months later.

The Muslim Mughal rulers of India were categorically opposed to this practice. Akbar is said to have spoken out against it, but I could not find historical documents of him banning it. The last of the powerful Mughal emperors, Aurangzeb, issued an official order: "In all lands under Mughal control, never again should the officials allow a woman to be burnt." The British during their occupation of India initially tolerated it, but like the Mughals before them, banned it in 1829. The practice continues to be banned in modern India, but scattered satis still take place.

In my review of the history of sati, there are mentions of "honor" and "love" as a rationale for the widowed woman to commit suicide. If it was truly an act of "love," the reverse would be practiced as well. However, a man burning himself in his wife's funeral pyre has never been documented in Indian history. What is not mentioned in these historical records is the fact that the practice of sati is rooted in the subservient role of the woman to her husband, and with his death, there is no function left for her. The term *sati* is interpreted as "good and devoted wife."

Regardless, based on Hindu tradition, such death is expected to occur voluntarily, not from coercion. Of course, the reality of what actually happens during these ceremonies is not so clear. News reports of the sati of the young Roop Kanwar indicate that she had been beaten, and eyewitnesses who were present at the immolation ceremony testified that she was bleeding and frothing at the mouth when she was placed on top of the funeral pyre. Eleven people were charged with murder, including Roop's father-in-law, but all were acquitted by a local court. It is hard to assess historically what percentage of satis were coerced by in-laws or were purely voluntary. This is especially true in the context of the Indian culture, where the woman is at the mercy of her in-laws the minute she is married off. I spoke with a number of friends in India while writing this chapter, and was surprised to learn that the practice of the newlywed wife moving into the home and under the control of her in-laws continues to be the most common model in India today!

So, what do the above cultural norms in India have to do with this book? They provide the ideal gauge for the belief sets peddled in the global popular culture. According to the Pew Research Center, there are over a billion Muslims and over a billion Hindus in the world today. They therefore have a comparable potential to interact with the rest of the globalized world. The negative stereotypes of Arabs and Muslims are in a totally different stratosphere compared to Hindus when it comes to the treatment of women. In all my travels, I have never met a Muslim family in which there were four wives, neither have I met a Hindu family in which a sati had taken place; both are exceedingly rare occurrences. Yet, the global popular culture routinely associates Islam with four marriages, while the Hindu concept of sati is essentially unknown to Western societies. Let me pose it in a different way; imagine if sati was a Muslim religious concept, what would Hollywood and the mainstream media do? I can assure you, they would have a field day and all of us would know and see more about sati than even the people living in India!

At the end of this section about women's rights, I would like to share some facts omitted from popular culture. In many cultures, a wife is seen as the property of the husband. Islam, in the seventh century, made sure that a wife retained her maiden name, and in doing so retained the full rights to her identity. A thousand years later, Lucy Stone, a pioneering American from Massachusetts, would do exactly the same in 1855; she retained her maiden name when she got married, and by doing so signaled the inception of the women's rights movement in the West.

## The Hollywoodization of Bollywood

India's rich culture of art and song led to the creation of the Hindustani language-based film industry known as Bollywood—one that is second only to Hollywood in terms of global impact and exceeds Hollywood in tickets sold annually worldwide. Just as Hollywood has peddled anti-Muslim rhetoric for over 100 years, as has been outlined throughout this book, following the election of Modi as prime minister of India in 2014, so has Bollywood. Copying Hollywood's movie storylines is no secret in Bollywood, so plagiarizing Islamophobic concepts was not a stretch. The award-winning Bollywood film director, Neeraj Ghaywan, said, "You look at the color palette, or how the production design is done, while portraying Muslims. It's mostly blacks, it's mostly dimly lit, and it's shot at low level to have a demonizing effect. But as you show the other side [Hindus], it's all flowery and bright lights and shot at an eye level." What the director is referring to is what I showed in the example of the movie *Lawrence of Arabia* in Chapter 4 (Figs. 4-2 to 4-5), where subtle changes are made in how characters appear visually to promote the subconscious vilification of Arabs and Muslims among the movie-watching audience. Bollywood is following suit (Figs. 15-7a, 15-7b, and 15-7c).

**Figure 15-7a,15-7b, and 15-7c:** In the 2019 Bollywood epic war movie, *Panipat* (named for the 1761 battle between the Hindu Maratha Empire and the Muslim Afghan Kingdom), the Afghan commander, Prince Ahmad Shāh Durrānī (15-7a) who was 39 years old at the time of the battle, was played by a 60-year-old actor depicting Durrānī using Islamophobic stereotypes (15-7b and 15-7c). Prince Durrānī was the historical founder of Afghanistan, and many Afghans refer to him as "Baba," meaning a father figure.

In this chapter I sought to illustrate how India's vilification of Muslims today is a microcosm of what has happened in the West over the past 100 years. We started this book in Chapter 1 illustrating the omissions of the Islamic contributions to Western civilization, and in this chapter I discussed how India is doing the same to the Islamic civilization which has been the bedrock of its architecture, music, poetry, arts, and language. It was the civilization that made India the global economic superpower of its age.

The two most powerful players in the world in influencing global public opinion through the genre of storytelling, Hollywood and Bollywood, are now partners in generating hate toward Muslims in the twenty-first century.

# The Ultimate
# Untold Story

# of the Past
# 100 Years

# The Biggest Untold Story
# of the Past 100 Years

In this book I sought to tell the story of a lost civilization. It was, in fact, the very first human civilization. Its people developed such advancements as the first form of writing. The numerical system used worldwide today is based on Arabic numerals, and the mathematical concepts of algebra and algorithms have ultimately led to the development of today's computer technology. All modern science is based on their development of the scientific method and the fundamentals of Western medicine were built on the foundations of this empire. The first university was built in the Islamic Empire and they were the first to establish the concept of state funding for research, emphasizing their dedication to the principles of education and intellectual thought. The humanitarian principle of philanthropy was core to its society. The Islamic Empire exported their knowledge to Europe where it became a foundation for the Renaissance and the scientific revolution that would not have been possible without it. By saying that this civilization is lost, I specifically mean the deliberate omission of this civilization and its contributions from the collective consciousness of the global popular culture by Western historians, politicians, mainstream media, and the movie industry.

The Renaissance did not happen overnight. A number of key elements had to come together for the critical mass to be reached. Spain and Italy were the two pivotal locations from which Islamic intellectual thought and science entered the European continent. Renowned Cambridge University historian and anthropologist Sir John Rankine Goody said, "In a sense the rebirth of learning in Western Europe began long before the Renaissance, and that owed a great deal to Islam and its translations." The Christian religious theocracy in Europe had banned scientific thought, and it was the introduction of the scientific method from the Islamic world that laid the foundation for experimental thinking in Europe. These new ideas were labeled *Arabicorum studiorum sensa*, which translates as the "views/studies of the Arabs." The development of mechanization was critical for the evolution of the industrial age. The Arabs in Spain introduced the concept of irrigation for agriculture using water wheels and the mechanization of corn-milling. The concept of refined architecture was introduced by building the first elegant grand structures in Europe in Cordoba, Sevilla, and the Alhambra in Granada, which laid the foundation for architectural engineering in Europe. The intricate and delicate aesthetic of the Gothic architecture in Europe stemmed from Islamic designs in Seville and Venice. While the Europeans knew how to build ships that could navigate the calm waters of the Mediterranean, it was not until the Arabs introduced their knowledge of building large ships for the high seas of the great oceans that European explorations became possible, including the discovery of America! The introduction by the Arabs of the concept of chivalry, the love song, and new musical instruments laid the foundation of the Western music culture.

The above illustrates the fact that the relationship between Muslims and Christians from the seventh to the fifteenth centuries was not just about warfare, there were positive cultural interactions that took place. Queen Elizabeth I (1558–1603) allied herself with the Muslim Empire against the Catholic powers in Europe (Chapter 2). That ought not be surprising as early Protestants believed that Islamic ideals were closer to theirs than to Catholicism, and Queen Elizabeth knew her family descended from that of the Prophet Muhammad. Inter-marriage among the various European royal families was a standard practice. The Abbasid Dynasty's ruler in Spain in the twelfth century, Abu al-Qasim bin Abbad, was a descendant of the Prophet Muhammad. Al-Qasim's daughter, Zaida, married King Alfonso VI, the Spanish king of Leon, Castile, and Galicia. Maria de Padilla, a descendant of Zaida and Alfonso, had four children in her marriage to King Peter of Castile. Two of their daughters married sons of King Edward III of England. Queen Elizabeth II, the current British queen, is a descendant of the Prophet Muhammad, 43 generations removed. This lineage has been authenticated both by Burke's Peerage, which was established in 1826 and is considered the preeminent gold standard authority on the genealogy of the British royal family, and by respected Islamic authorities.

## Electoral College

Politicians and policy experts in the mainstream media in the West have implied for decades that Islam is not compatible with democracy. Arab kings, dictators, and their paid so-called religious experts support that concept because it guarantees their survival. After the Prophet Muhammad died on June 8, 632, a group of men (electors) representing the various clans met to select the Prophet's successor—the caliph. That gathering was an electoral council. Each of the four consecutive caliphs, Abu Bakr, Umar, Uthman, and Ali were elected using this system. This form of representative democracy is called *Shura* in Arabic, a term that is mentioned in the Qur'an.

Some thousand years later, at the inception of yet another civilization, the drafters of the US Constitution met in Philadelphia, Pennsylvania, in 1787 and decided on an electoral council, known as the Electoral College, as the system to select the US president every four years. This was the first democracy since ancient Greece, the Roman Republic, and the Islamic Caliphate. The US Constitution does not mention the popular vote (one person, one vote), rather, the Electoral College determines the US president.

In addition to a representative democracy, the first caliphs of Islam in the seventh century fostered the principles of egalitarianism and meritocracy. A system of accountability for those holding public office was established. Let me share with you an anecdote about two men mentioned in this book: Umar, who served as the second caliph and was responsible for preserving the Church of the Holy Sepulchre, and Khalid, the general who defeated the Roman Empire at Yarmouk in 634 (Chapter 6). Khalid held a legendary status among the populace in the Islamic Empire, but when Umar heard that Khalid was lavishing the spoils of war onto war heroes, tribal nobles, and poets, he dismissed Khalid as the supreme commander of the armed forces. Umar was sending a message that no one was above the law. Unfortunately, the current kings and dictators in the "Middle East" base their leadership purely on nepotism. The standard for them is to lavish gifts and assign cabinet positions to their family members and inner circle.

The first caliphs respected the role of women. The Prophet's widow, Aisha, known respectfully as the "Mother of the Faithful" within Islamic culture, played a key role in the seventh century as a senior advisor to the Caliphs Abu Bakr, Umar, and Uthman. Her advice was so highly regarded that, for example, when Caliph Uthman was facing a major crisis, he requested that she consider staying in the capital (Medina) and forgoing her annual pilgrimage to Mecca, because he may need her advice as issues arose. Although she ended up going on the pilgrimage, this demonstrates her respected status. In current times, the extremist Wahhabi rule in Saudi Arabia and extremist Shia doctrine in Iran has relegated women to at best a second-class citizen role.

A core question I have struggled with for years is, why would Western countries in the twentieth century promote democracies around the world *except* in the "Middle East"? Quite the contrary, Western governments have helped Arab kings and dictators squash any and all freedom-seeking movements in the Arab world. The answer to the above question is central to understanding the Gordian knot we call the "Middle East"; I will provide the answer in this concluding chapter.

## Brothers or Enemies

Above I provided a summarized account of the historical political relationship between Christianity and Islam. I will now provide a similar summary of the political relationship between Judaism and Islam. When Caliph Umar entered the city of Jerusalem in 638 (Chapter 6), he allowed Jews to return as they had previously been evicted by the Christians.

In 711 when Tariq (Chapter 13) invaded Spain and laid siege to the city of Cordoba, the local Jewish community assisted him in capturing it. They were fully aware of the kindness of the Muslims toward Jews in Jerusalem and welcomed the Muslim rule in Spain over the oppressive Christian one.

When the first crusaders arrived in Jerusalem in 1099 (Chapter 7), not only did they massacre Muslims, but also the Jews who had fought side by side with the Muslims to defend the city. Saladin recovered the city from the crusaders in 1187 (Chapter 8). One of his first acts was to once again welcome Jews to return to Jerusalem since they had been evicted by the Christians.

Once the Christian powers defeated the Muslims in Spain, they issued the Alhambra Decree in 1492 (Chapter 2), an edict to expel Jews from Spain. The Ottoman Empire sent ships to bring Jews to live in safety on Muslim lands. For the following centuries Jews continued to be welcomed and flourished on Arab soil.

In over 2,000 years of recorded history, the only consistent force in the world protecting Jews from Christian persecution was the Muslims. The creation of a Jewish state using the hegemonic colonial powers in Palestine in the twentieth century was seen by the larger Arabic and Muslim worlds as a deep betrayal.

### The Fanatic Religious Experiment for the Ages

For 1,500 years, Christianity was based on Greek texts (the Gospels); a cataclysmic change within Christianity took place after it was translated into English. This made the Bible vulnerable to distortions. The 200-year period between 1700 and 1900 would witness tremendous activism in interpreting and editing the Bible in the US and Britain. This activist group known as the evangelicals were fixated on the concept of the end of days—Armageddon. They focused on specific translated words and phrases in the Bible and based their mission on the literal meaning rather than larger symbolic one that had been agreed upon by respected Christian scholars for over a millennium. They established a set of beliefs based on their interpretation of the Bible that they hold to this day. A group within evangelical Christianity strongly believe that Jews must be converted to Christianity, and that the Second Coming of Jesus Christ is directly tied to this conversion. They claim that for the conversions and the Second Coming to occur, Jews must be brought to Palestine; thus, the birth of the evangelical Christian Zionist ideology. There is one additional goal the evangelical Christian Zionists have yet to fulfill: the building of the Third Temple directly on top of one of Islam's most sacred sites, the Dome of the Rock.

Evangelical Christian Zionism is based on an inherently paradoxical idea—on one hand, it is a deeply anti-Semitic movement; on the other, its goal is to create a homeland for Jews in Palestine. I have labeled this contradiction the *duplicitous syndrome* in this book.

The above plan of capturing Palestine to create a Jewish homeland would have been impossible to accomplish when the Muslim Empire was a world power; however, by the turn of twentieth century, the last vestige of the Ottoman Empire was in its sunset days. During WWI, British leadership had a number of fanatic evangelical Zionists in its midst. For Prime Minister Lloyd George, Secretary of State Arthur Balfour, and Secretary of War Winston Churchill, a historical opportunity was upon them; the possibility of executing the religious interpretations of the Bible they had believed in all their lives. But they had a dilemma on their hands: they could force the Palestinians out to create a Jewish homeland in Palestine, but how could this be sustained over the decades to come, given that Palestine is surrounded by Arab peoples and lands? They came up with a shrewd and ingenious plan. For 1,000 years it was one powerful empire. In order to change this, they created the concept of the "Middle East." They divided and effectively Balkanized the Arab lands into smaller states and made each a silo that was to be ruled by a hand-selected vassal king or dictator.

This answers a question posed in the preface of this book: Why would Churchill, rather than choosing an intellectual moderate leader, select Abulaziz ibn Saud to become the king of Arabia, when in his own words he described Ibn Saud and his clan as "intolerant, well-armed, and bloodthirsty . . . very dangerous to the holy cities of Mecca and Medina"? The answer is that Ibn Saud fit exactly into the evangelical Christian Zionist plan for the region; by having weak and divided vassal Arab leaders surrounding Palestine, the Christian West would retain total control.

The "Middle East" as we know it today was created as an evangelical Christian experiment. Far-fetched interpretations of the Bible have subjected millions of Arabs to life under brutal dictators for the past 100 years.

One hundred years after George, Balfour, and Churchill set the course for the "Middle East," the evangelical Christian hold on how the "Middle East" was to be ruled remains unchanged. In 2020, the combination of US Vice President Mike Pence, Secretary of State Mike Pompeo, and President Donald Trump's son-in-law Jared Kushner are arguably even more fanatical Zionists than the original three founders a hundred years ago. I shared a quote from a Trump administration official saying that both Pence and Pompeo "have convinced themselves that they are in a biblical moment." Donald Trump's election as president in 2016 would not have been possible without the overwhelming support of the evangelical Christian community in the US. Cristina Maza of *Newsweek* explained the Trump–American evangelism connection as such: "Many evangelical Christians believe that Trump was chosen by God to usher in a new era, a part of history called the 'end times.'" Trump's son, Eric, in October 2020, said his father "saved Christianity."

A profound example of the power of evangelical Christian Zionists within the American government can be found in the US invasion of Iraq in 2003. In 2007, General Wesley Clark, who had served as the supreme allied commander for NATO (North Atlantic Treaty Organization) in Europe in the late 1990s, reflected on an encounter he had had in the fall of 2002 (months before the actual invasion of Iraq by the George W. Bush administration). A fellow general in the Pentagon told Clark that the decision had already been made to invade Iraq. Clark asked him, "Did they find any information connecting Saddam to Al-Qaeda?" The reply was "No." The general shared with Clark a document from the then secretary of defense, Donald Rumsfeld, stating that the plan was larger than just attacking Iraq; they planned to invade seven countries in five years. The seven countries were Iraq, Syria, Lebanon, Libya, Somalia, Sudan, and Iran. Ultimately, those invasions never took place because the invasion of Iraq turned out to be such a debacle.

Everyone in the George W. Bush administration knew that Saddam Hussein, a secular dictator, was not religious and had nothing to do with the September 11, 2001, terrorist attacks on the US. Both claims used to internationally justify the invasion of Iraq—that Saddam Hussein was linked to Al-Qaeda and that he had weapons of mass destruction—were completely fabricated. Who was behind the plan? The George W. Bush administration had a number of hardcore militant-minded evangelical Christian Zionists who went under the guise of "neoconservatism." These included Vice President Dick

Cheney, Secretary of Defense Donald Rumsfeld, Deputy Secretary of Defense Paul Wolfowitz, and advisors Elliott Abrams and Richard Perle. The seven countries they wanted to invade had, in their minds, veered away from the plan for total control of the "Middle East" as envisioned at the end of WWI. For President George W. Bush, the invasion of the "Middle East" was a personal calling to fulfill the mission of the Crusades that had been embarked upon in France by Pope Urban in 1095. For his cabinet members mentioned above, the invasion was a re-do of the post-WWI evangelical Christian Zionist takeover of the region in the 1920s.

That brings us to the answer to the above question as to why Western powers, while championing freedom and democracy around the world, oppose all such efforts in the "Middle East." Democracy and freedom in the "Middle East" are inherently incompatible with the evangelical Christian Zionist plan for the region. An example provided in the book (Chapter 14) was the crushing by both the US and Britain of the movement toward democracy in Iran in the 1950s. The irony is that the same politicians who tout Israel as the only "democracy" in the "Middle East" are the same who, behind the scenes, do everything in their power to prevent Democracy in the Arab world.

## The French Connection—The French Paradox

In addition to Britain and the US, there was a third conqueror of the "Middle East"; France, which was the first chronologically, starting with the Pope Urban Crusades in the eleventh and twelfth centuries (Chapter 7). France never subscribed to the evangelical Christian Zionist interpretation of the Bible; rather, it saw itself as the flag-bearer of Christian supremacy over Islam.

Among many in the militant Christian extremist movements in Europe and the US, the prevailing ideology is more of the French crusading Christian supremacy variety rather than an evangelical Zionist one. However, both extremist ideologies, the evangelical Protestant Christian Zionist and the Catholic French Christian crusading, live symbiotically and act in a complementary fashion when it comes to the real victims, the Arabs and Muslims of the "Middle East." I will share with you the real-world impact of these two ideologies on the Iraqi civilians during the US invasion by the George W. Bush administration. Blackwater (now known as Academi) was a private military company founded by a former US military man, Erik Prince, in North Carolina in 1997. It received a lucrative US government contract to operate in Iraq during the 2003 invasion. A former employee of Erik Prince is officially on record saying that Prince "views himself as a Christian crusader tasked with eliminating Muslims and the Islamic faith from the globe." Let me share an example. On September 16, 2007, a Blackwater convoy was crossing the square in the Mansour district of Baghdad when a small car with an Iraqi couple and their child did not get out of the way as quickly as they wanted, so they fired at the car, killing the whole family. A Blackwater insider provided the following official account: "Mr. Prince intentionally deployed to Iraq certain men who shared his vision of Christian supremacy, knowing and wanting these men to take every available opportunity to murder Iraqis. Many of these men used call signs based on the Knights of the Templar, the warriors who fought the Crusades."

After the Iraq war, who hired Erik Prince? It was United Arab Emirates (UAE) Crown Prince Mohammed bin Zayed Al Nahyan. This should not sound surprising nor paradoxical. Erik Prince had real-world experience killing Arab and Muslim civilians, and that is the skill set Arab kings and dictators have sought for decades. Bin Zayed asked Erik Prince to develop a force using foreign mercenaries that could be used to crush any future pro-democracy movements in the UAE. The only clear instruction for forming the mercenary force was, "hire no Muslims." This is an example of what I discussed early in this chapter: crushing democracies in the "Middle East" has always been a combined effort between Arab kings and Western powers.

When Donald Trump became president of the US in 2016, the combination of the two Christian extremist ideologies (evangelical Zionism and Christian supremacy) were raised to a level not seen in modern history. By moving the US Embassy in Israel from Tel Aviv to Jerusalem, Trump sent a strong signal to his evangelical Zionist supporters. Trump would send another signal to his Christian supremacist base; he gave a cabinet position to Betsy Devos, who happens to be Erik Prince's sister! In 2020, two days after Trump ordered the assassination of Iran's top general, Qasem Soleimani, Donald Trump Jr. posted a picture of himself holding an assault rifle bearing the Heraldic Jerusalem symbol (also known as the five-fold cross) that was worn by the French terrorists who massacred thousands of Muslim civilians in Jerusalem during the Crusades.

A perplexing issue for many Westerners is the visceral reaction of Muslims around the world toward demeaning cartoons and caricatures of the Prophet Muhammad, which predominantly stem from France, under the guise of freedom of speech. I am a strong proponent of freedom of speech; it is the principle that allowed me to write and publish this book. However, I am opposed to selective freedom of speech. Allow me to explain. I want to tell you about two intellectual European men, both genocide deniers; one was imprisoned while the other was awarded a Nobel Prize. Both the imprisonment and the presentation of the Nobel Prize occurred in Europe. Peter Handke, an Austrian author, won the Nobel Prize for literature in 2009. Handke was known as an ardent supporter of the Serb mastermind behind the genocide of Muslim civilians in Bosnia in the 1990s, Slobodan Milošević. In the same year, 2006, that Handke was eulogizing Milošević, British historian David Irving was arrested in Handke's home country of Austria and charged with "trivializing the Holocaust." He was sentenced to three years in prison, even though at his trial he stated, "The Nazis did murder millions of Jews."

The above is best exemplified by what goes on in France, which I have termed the *French paradox*. To best explain this, let me use a specific example. In October 2020, in response to yet another set of demeaning caricatures of the Prophet Muhammad in the French magazine *Charlie Hebdo* and the adorning of French government buildings with those caricatures, there was condemnation by Muslims around the world of this provocation. In response, French President Emmanuel Macron said France was being attacked for "our values, our taste for liberty, the possibility on our soil to believe freely," and "we will give up nothing." In Chapter 5, I shared an example of the heinous caricatures used by the Nazis to demonize Jews. *Charlie Hebdo* has never published such caricatures nor did those caricatures adorn French government buildings. So, what Macron is really saying about free thinking and liberty is that it applies when demonizing Muslims, but it does not apply when demonizing other groups.

As a humanitarian and a physician, I categorically denounce all acts of terrorism, regardless of the race or religion of the terrorist. The French government, on the other hand, has failed to live up to this standard. In the history of the heinous acts of terrorism committed by Muslims against French civilians (stabbings and shootings related to the *Charlie Hebdo* caricatures), and by French terrorists against Muslim civilians (in Palestine and Algeria), hundreds of innocent French civilians were killed and hundreds of thousands of innocent Muslim civilians were killed (Chapters 7 and 11). While each one of the stabbing attacks by Islamist extremists were labeled rightly as acts of terrorism, not the French government nor the ostensibly liberal/free speech French media has ever labeled the massacres of Muslims by French government–organized terror groups as acts of terrorism. France wrongly believes that by owning up to its mistakes, it would be perceived as weak. It refuses to move beyond the mindset of its colonial past. It has historically subjugated millions of Muslims and it continues to be attached to the idea of supremacy.

This brings me to a question I posed in Chapter 14. In 1979, the Saudi ruling family was in trouble when a group of religious extremists captured the Great Mosque in Mecca, demanding the overthrow of the Saudi monarchy. The leader of Saudi Arabia at the time, Crown Prince Fahad, sought the help of France. The head of the French tactical force, Groupe d'Intervention de la Gendarmerie Nationale (GIGN), Christian Prouteau, when trying to understand why he was being asked to storm Islam's holiest site, was told by the French president that this was being done to save the "fate of the Western world." The question I asked was, what does saving the Saudi monarchy have to do with the Western world's status or fate? Above I outlined how American and British leaders were deeply connected to the evangelical Christian Zionist vision, while the French were deeply attached to their historical supremacy over Muslim populations. The Al-Saud family gave cover for both. This goes back to the creation of Saudi Arabia and its leader, Abdulaziz ibn Saud, who assured his colonial handlers that he had no interest in Palestinians nor the other Arab countries being free from Western domination (Chapter 3). By the Al-Sauds having control over Islam's holy sites of Mecca and Medina, they consequently had their thumb on Muslim populations worldwide, which served the visionary interests of the colonial powers. Essentially, the three invaders of the "Middle East," France, Britain, and the US, have indirect control over Islam's holiest sites through the Al-Saud monarchy.

The predominant view and narrative are that while much of the Muslim world lives in theocracies, the Western world has evolved into secular states with separation of church and state. That may be true; however, when it comes to the "Middle East," for the US, Britain, and France, all major decisions are directly linked to religion. The separation of church and state is nothing but a ruse.

## The Deception of the Century

Christianity is the world's largest religion. Millions of Christians who read the Bible or go to church on Sundays routinely come across the words *Israel* and *Philistines*. The Bible depicts Israel as the protagonist and the Philistines as the antagonists. Most Christians transpose in their minds the *Israel* mentioned in the Bible as the current state of Israel in Palestine, and *Philistines* as the Palestinian people. I have often wondered why, since there are 195 countries in the world and Israel is a non-European non-NATO country, is it the most touted country by politicians and the mainstream media in the US, more than any other country in the world? Israel (approximately the size of the state of New Jersey) ranks 149th in the world based on its geographical size. Bhutan, North Macedonia, and Djibouti are larger, but I do not recall hearing about them very much! I believe this has to do with the religious connection to what Christians read in the Bible. Is this connection real, or is it a deception?

Jacob, the grandson of the patriarch Abraham, was also named Israel, which is where the term comes from. When Theodor Herzl, the founder of political Jewish Zionism in the nineteenth century, wrote a monograph to provide solutions to the Christian persecution of Jews in Europe, he titled it, "The Jewish State" (*Der Judenstaat* in German). He did not mention the name *Israel* for the state he envisioned. The British government, in the Balfour Declaration issued in November 1917, referred to its spoils of war (Palestine) to be given to the Jews as a "national home for the Jewish people." Nowhere in that declaration was the word *Israel* mentioned. When the heads of various militant Jewish groups met on May 14, 1948, in Tel Aviv to select a name for the Jewish state that was being created, the first option that was put on the table was Judah. That was not selected as it was felt that the borders of that ancient Jewish kingdom of Judah did not in any way correspond to that of the new country they were creating. The other names that were considered were Tzabar, Zion, and Palestine. Finally, by a vote of seven to three, the name Israel was selected. I spoke to a number of Orthodox Jews while writing about this topic, and I found it both surprising and educational that they do not consider the current State of Israel as an extension of the biblical *Israel.* To them, the "real" Israel is an end-of-days phenomenon that will occur only in connection with the appearance of the Messiah. The selection of the word *Israel* for the current Jewish state was a godsend to the evangelical Zionist community in their efforts to recruit unsuspecting Christians into believing that the end of days is upon us. It is the serendipity of history; had the name selected been Tzabar, Palestine, or Judah, most Christians would not associate the current Jewish state to biblical events, and likely, much of the violence and its support from around the world may have been avoided.

The Philistines mentioned in the Bible were ancient pagan people thought to have come from the Aegean Peninsula (Greece), who inhabited the region we know today as Israel/Palestine around 1100 BC. The coastal region of today's Israel/Palestine was termed *Philistia* by Greeks when they invaded and occupied the region from Alexander the Great to 63 BC. The Romans subsequently ruled this land for the next several centuries as the larger combined province, Syria Palaestina. The Muslim Empire took control of the region in AD 636 and it continued to be under Arab Muslim rule (with the exception of short periods of crusader rule) until the twentieth century. The Arabs living in that region were over time referred to as "Palestinians" purely based on the Romans name for the territory, Palestinia. The Philistines had ceased to exist more than a millennium before the Arabs had conquered the land.

Neither the biblical kingdom of Israel nor the Philistines have anything to do with the current Jewish state nor the Palestinians. It is an alternative reality that has been one of the greatest deceptions in modern history; one that has fooled millions of innocent Christians around the world into subconsciously associating the biblical Israel with today's Jewish country in the "Middle East" that is also named

Israel, and the antagonists known as the Philistines with the Arab Palestinians!

This alternative reality has been a tremendous recruiting tool for evangelical Zionists, especially in the US. The visceral connection Christians feel toward biblical lands took on a whole new meaning in the twentieth century. For hundreds of years prior to that, Christians were not fixated on what was happening in Palestine. Let me share with you a real-life example of the impact of the newly found Israel on the peoples of the "Middle East." For decades, especially in the 1960s, '70s, and '80s, the mainstream media and politicians in the US classified Arab countries as either radical or moderate. What was the deciding factor used for this classification? Meritocracy, egalitarianism, freedom of speech, or women's rights? The answer is, none of these. Saudi Arabia, which is sorely lacking in these qualities, was classified as moderate. The classification was based solely on one single prism: Israel. If a country was friendly toward Israel, it was moderate; if it was not, it was radical. So, hundreds of millions of people, all the way from Morocco in the west to Oman in the east, were classified based on looking through the prism of one tiny country.

## An Experiment

Allow me to perform a social experiment. Let's assume we have a society made up of three groups, Red, White, and Blue. A review reveals that acts of terrorism are committed equally by members of the three groups. For political purposes, our aim is to stigmatize the Blue group with negative stereotypes. Our plan is to manufacture prejudice and then normalize it for the people in the Red and White groups through unconscious bias to think negatively of the Blue group. Let me take you on a journey.

## The Ultimate Orchestra Conductor of How We Look at the World

Storytelling is as old as humanity itself. In early civilizations, people would sit around a campfire and tell stories. Starting in the twentieth century, Hollywood became the biggest storyteller in the world. When I was a boy, watching movies with American Indians versus cowboys, I grew up believing that American Indians were "bad" and "violent" people, and when my friends and I played Cowboys and Indians, none of us wanted to play the Indians! In Jack G. Shaheen's book, *Reel Bad Arabs: How Hollywood Vilifies a People*, he identifies 1,100 movies prior to the September 11, 2001, terrorist attacks that vilify Arabs. There are exponentially more movies vilifying Arabs and Muslims than those vilifying the KKK! The US fought in World War II against Nazi Germany and Japan, but there are more movies portraying Arabs as "evil" than there are about the Nazis or the Japanese. In actuality, there are more movies vilifying Arabs and Muslims than any other ethnic group on the planet. There is no logical method or statistical explanation to suggest that this has happened by chance! Hollywood actors have stood up for all types of humanitarian issues, but I have yet to see a single one take a stand on the deliberate vilification of Arabs and Muslims in the movie industry.

There are many examples of how Hollywood has greatly influenced real-world situations. Following the release of the 1942 animated movie *Bambi*, which depicted a mother deer being shot by a hunter in front of her baby, deer hunting dropped by half in the United States. Following the release of the 1975 movie *Jaws*, which depicted a beach terrorized by a great white shark, beach tourism in the US saw a significant decline from coast to coast. Most importantly, the 1915 movie *Birth of a Nation* inspired the reawakening of the KKK movement in the US in the twentieth century. These examples all demonstrate the impact of singular movies. We can only imagine the impact that over a thousand movies depicting Arabs and Muslims as nefarious have had on the public consciousness and world events. I believe it has been so deep to the point that it is immeasurable.

In response an interview question in 2020 about why almost all superheroes are white, Kate Ratliff, a professor who studies bias at the University of Florida, said, "Because superheroes are good . . . we associate, whether we mean to or not, white people associate white with good." She added, "Most people in the United States have a genuine desire to be fair." So, what prevents them from being fair when it comes to Arabs and Muslims? Hollywood, through its cottage industry of manufacturing prejudice against Arabs and Muslims, affects how people perceive them by manipulating how they are portrayed. I totally agree with Dr. Ratliff; most people in the US do genuinely desire to be fair, but what gets in their way is the subconscious bias created by Hollywood, which is also known as implicit bias. Our brains are trained to create associations that enable us to make short-cut decisions without us consciously thinking about them. Studies have shown that children as young as three years of age can be taught racial biases, and that is why Hollywood has introduced anti-Arab and anti-Muslim stereotypes in children's movies as well. For example, in Disney's 1992 animated movie *Aladdin*, the lyrics in the opening scene describe the Arabic land as the place "where they cut off your ear if they don't like your face," and declare, "It's barbaric, but hey, it's home!"

Ben Judah, author of *This Is London* and research fellow at the Hudson Institute, said that America's "cultural power," which he defined as the American "cultural empire," may be even more influential around the world than even its "political" power. What is "American cultural power"? It is American mainstream media, Hollywood and the entertainment industry, social media, and celebrity culture. These impact the opinions and prejudices of millions if not billions of peoples around the world

Hollywood hides behind freedom of speech when vilifying Arabs and Muslims, in the same vein as French President Emmanuel Macron as described above. What about the mainstream media, which touts journalistic integrity and intellectual honesty? I am a believer in the high standards in American journalism except when it comes to the "Middle East." For seven decades it has relinquished its responsibility to fairly and responsibly cover this region of the world and its peoples. The CBS weekly television news show, *60 Minutes*, is considered to be one of the most respected examples of probing investigative journalism in the US. It debuted in 1968, and at the time of writing this book in 2020, it has aired 2,325 episodes; with an average of three stories per show, it has investigated approximately 6,975 issues. I have been watching *60 Minutes* since I was a boy, and it is a show that is not shy about probing sensitive issues such as challenging US presidents and multinational corporations. In its over 50-year history and thousands of topics investigated, to the best of my review, it has not touched some of the crucial issues presented in this book: the impact of the evangelical Christian Zionist agenda on

US foreign policy in the "Middle East" and Hollywood's long-standing vilification of Arabs and Muslims. Another giant in journalistic standards is CNN, which airs a weekly show called *Reliable Sources* that focuses on the integrity and fairness of the reporting of the American news media. This show, which according to CNN "turns a critical lens on the media" debuted in 1992 and has aired over 1,000 episodes; to the best my knowledge, it has never assessed the fairness of the media coverage of the Arab–Israeli issue.

Let me give you a timely example of the power of the media in impacting public opinion and changing the path of nations. In the 1980s, Australian millionaire Rupert Murdoch created a media empire that now owns hundreds of news outlets around the world. The mainstream media claims that the model by which the Murdoch news empire operates, by deliberately conflating real news with opinion, is new. I posit that neither the election of Donald Trump as US president in 2016 nor the adoption of Brexit ("British" and "exit"— the withdrawal of the UK from the EU) in 2020 would have been possible without the Murdoch model's impact on public opinion. While the mainstream media criticizes Murdoch's Fox Networks for opinion-based news stories as not meeting journalistic standards, it is the exact model that the mainstream media has used for decades when covering the Arab–Israeli issue, Arabs, and Muslims.

## Trivializing Terrorism

Going back to the social experiment with the three groups I presented above, in which the aim was to stigmatize the Blue group as terrorists when the members of all three groups committed acts of terrorism equally: how do you make this label stick? The only way would be to call the acts of terrorism committed by the Red and White groups something less nefarious than terrorism, thereby trivializing the terrorism committed by those two groups as compared to that of the Blue group.

Terrorists planted a bomb in the basement of a church; in the ensuing explosion, four young girls—11-year-old Denise McNair and 14-year-old Addie Mae Collins, Carole Robertson, and Cynthia Wesley—were killed. This occurred on September 15, 1963, in the city of Birmingham, Alabama. The four girls who died that day were all African American. The terrorists who committed the bombing were White Christian extremists belonging to the KKK, for whom this was the third terrorist bombing they committed in Birmingham in 11 days. This was one of nearly 2,000 acts of terrorism committed by the KKK on American soil, not a single one of which was labeled as terrorism by the mainstream media nor the history books that generations of Americans grew up studying.

*Merriam-Webster's Dictionary* defines "terror" as "violence or the threat of violence used as a weapon of intimidation or coercion." In writing this book, I have attempted to mathematically quantify acts of terrorism committed by members of each of the three Abrahamic faiths, an example of which is provided at the end of Section 3, where I quantified acts of terrorism committed in the city of Jerusalem. There is no mathematical model that can objectively show that over the past 2,000 years, or even the past 100 years, more acts of terrorism have been committed by individuals of the Muslim faith among the three Abrahamic religions. The common misperception that exists around the world that Islam is the most violent religion is a result of deliberate actions of Hollywood and the mainstream media.

The renowned author and former priest, James Carroll, summarized it far better than I can when he said, "Islam is accused of violence as if Christianity is innocent."

By trivializing terrorism when committed by certain groups, we have weakened our collective stand against the scourge of terrorism in the US and around the world.

## The Third Revolution

The American Revolution (1775–1783) against a British king and the French Revolution (1789–1799) against a French king transformed human history. These two revolutions sparked one of history's largest civilizational, cultural, scientific, and economic advances. The British and the French kings were far less brutal toward their subjects as compared to the current kings and dictators in Arab countries.

The colonial powers, however, ensured that the Arab revolution during WWI failed. Based on fanatic religious beliefs, not only have they betrayed the Arabs who helped them during WWI, they Balkanized Arab lands and installed anchors in the ground, vassal kings and dictators who would assure that no pro-freedom movements ever succeed in the future.

I am sure you have noted that throughout this book, I have placed the term "Middle East" in quotations. This term did not come from any person or group who lives in the "Middle East." It is a colonial term to define a region that was created as an evangelical Christian Zionist experiment. The young generation of the "Middle East," as a first step, ought to remove this term. No people can achieve their potential when defined by their historical opponents. America sees Russia and China as its opponents and would never allow American cities or regions to be named by Russia or China. The British would never have allowed the Nazis to name cities in England. The French would never allow Algerians to name French cities with Arab or Muslim names.

The European Union (EU) is composed of 27 countries and 24 languages. On Arab land, there are 22 Arab countries, all of whom speak one language (Arabic), but there is no political and economic union like the EU. The Arab vassal kings and dictators are deeply opposed to any such union because it threatens their individual fiefdoms.

The US federal system would be ideal for the combined Arab countries as each state would still be able to keep its unique cultural characteristics. The combined population of the Arab countries is 422 million (based on 2018 data). That would put such a federation second in the world in land area after Russia and third in population after China and India. This federation would start out as fifth in the world in GDP after the US, China, Japan, and Germany. This would also bring to an end the internal conflicts in the region. Such a federation could enter into a collaborative relationship with its two neighbors, the historical civilizations of Iran and Turkey. The self-serving manufactured hatred by the Wahhabis in Saudi Arabia and the Mullahs in Iran between Sunnis and Shia would evaporate. Moreover, the sturdiness of the guardrails of genuine egalitarian societies are measured by how they treat their minorities. Such a new country (federation) would need to reach deep into the annals of its civilizational past in how it would treat its Christian and Jewish

minorities; it would have to replicate the high standards of humanitarian principles witnessed in the original caliphate of the seventh
century.

Based on deep-seated religious beliefs presented in this book,
Western powers will oppose any such freedom-seeking movement.
China and Russia, for their perceived strategic reasons, will likewise
oppose such a movement. Let me take you back to the 1770s in
America when people from all walks of life, collectively known as the
Sons of Liberty, came together to take a stand against the superpower
of that time, Great Britain. The end result was not just freedom, but
the creation of one of history's greatest civilizations. The inevitable
failure of the Arab Spring—a series of pro-freedom movements in
a number of Arab countries in the 2010s—was due to the fact that
these movements were spontaneous and did not lend themselves to
coordination across borders. The success of the American Revolution
against the British king was ultimately due to the coordinated efforts
of the Sons of Liberty and other grassroots groups in the 13 colonies.
Arab kings and dictators are admittedly brutal, but at the end of the
day they are only a few families standing in the way of the aspirations
of over 400 million people; they are nothing but paper tigers.

# Bibliography

## Chapter 1

Adamson, Peter. *Philosophy in the Islamic World: A History of Philosophy without Any Gaps*. Oxford: Oxford University Press, 2016.

Akyol, Mustafa. "Who's Afraid of Arabic Numerals?" *New York Times*, June 4, 2019. www.nytimes.com/2019/06/04/opinion/arabic-numerals.html.

al-Zahrāwī, Abū al-Qāsim Khalaf ibn ʿAbbās. *Albucasis on Surgery and Instruments*. Berkeley: University of California Press, 1973.

Alkhateeb, Firas. *Lost Islamic History: Reclaiming Muslim Civilisation from the Past*. London: Hurst and Company, 2014.

Aschoff, A., Paul Kremer, Bahram Hashemi, and Stefan Kunze. "The Scientific History of Hydrocephalus and Its Treatment." *Neurosurgical Review* 22, no. 2–3 (October 1999): 67–93. https://doi.org/10.1007/s101430050035.

Ayto, John. *The Glutton's Glossary: A Dictionary of Food and Drink Terms*. New York: Routledge, 1990.

Badeau, John S., and John R. Hayes. *The Genius of Arab Civilization: Source of Renaissance*. Cambridge, MA: MIT Press, 1983.

BBC. "Why Algorithms Are Called Algorithms." Produced by Dayglow Media and Pencil and Pepper. *BBC Ideas*, July 9, 2019. Video, 3:03. www.bbc.co.uk/ideas/videos/why-algorithms-are-called-algorithms/p07gdlwf.

Bennison, Amira K. *The Great Caliphs: The Golden Age of the ʿAbbasid Empire*. New Haven, CT: Yale University Press, 2009.

Boyer, Carl B., and Uta C. Merzbach. "The Arabic Hegemony." In *The History of Mathematics*. 2nd ed. New York: Wiley, 1991.

Brown, Daniel W. *A New Introduction to Islam*. Malden, MA: Blackwell, 2004.

Brown, Nancy M. *The Abacus and the Cross: The Story of the Pope Who Brought the Light of Science to the Dark Ages*. New York: Basic Books, 2010.

Clarence-Smith, William Gervase, and Steven Topik. *The Global Coffee Economy in Africa, Asia and Latin America, 1500–1989*. New York: Cambridge University Press, 2003.

Curiel, Jonathan. *Al' America: Travels through America's Arab and Islamic Roots*. New York: The New Press, 2008.

de Wulf, Maurice. *History of Medieval Philosophy*. Mineola, NY: Dover Publishing, 1952.

Esposito, John L. *The Oxford History of Islam*. Oxford: Oxford University Press, 2000.

Ganchy, Sally. *Islam and Science, Medicine, and Technology*. New York: Rosen Publishing, 2008.

Huff, Toby E. *The Rise of Early Modern Science: Islam, China, and the West*. Cambridge: Cambridge University Press, 1993.

Johnson, Steven. *Wonderland: How Play Made the Modern World*. New York: Random House, 2016.

Khan, Aisha. *Avicenna (Ibn Sina): Muslim Physician and Philosopher of the Eleventh Century*. New York: Rosen Publishing Group, 2006.

McFadden, Robert D. "Reagan Cites Islamic Scholar." *New York Times*, October 2, 1981. https://www.nytimes.com/1981/10/02/us/reagan-cites-islamic-scholar.html.

Morgan, Michael H. *Lost History: The Enduring Legacy of Muslim Scientists, Thinkers, and Artists*. Washington, DC: National Geographic, 2007.

Nicol, Robert. *A Treatise on Coffee: Its Properties and the Best Mode of Keeping and Preparing It*. London: Baldwin and Cradock, 1831.

Osler, William. *The Evolution of Modern Medicine*. Whitefish, MT: Kessinger Publishing, 2004.

Oweiss, Ibrahim M. "Ibn Khaldun: The Father of Economics." In *Arab Civilization*, edited by Ibrahim M. Oweiss and George N. Atiyeh. Albany: State University of New York Press, 1988. Accessed online at https://faculty.georgetown.edu/imo3/ibn.htm.

Pendergrast, Mark. *Uncommon Grounds: The History of Coffee and How It Transformed Our World*. New York: Basic Books, 2010.

Porter, Roy. *The Greatest Benefit to Mankind: A Medical History of Humanity*. New York: W. W. Norton and Company, 1997.

Rashed, Roshdi. *The Development of Arabic Mathematics*. Translated by Angela Armstrong. New York: Springer, 1994.

Robinson, Chase F. *Islamic Civilization in Thirty Lives: The First 1,000 Years*. London: Thames and Hudson, 2016.

Rubenstein, Richard E. *Aristotle's Children: How Christians, Muslims, and Jews Rediscovered Ancient Wisdom and Illuminated the Middle Ages*. Orlando, FL: Harcourt, 2004.

Smith, A. Mark. *Ptolemy's Theory of Visual Perception: An English Translation of the Optics with Introduction and Commentary*. Philadelphia: American Philosophical Society, 1996.

Truitt, E. R. *Medieval Robots: Mechanism, Magic, Nature, and Art.* Philadelphia: University of Pennsylvania Press, 2015.

Weinberg, Bennett Alan, and Bonnie K. Bealer. *The World of Caffeine: The Science and Culture of the World's Most Popular Drug.* New York: Routledge, 2001.

Zuraw, Lydia. "How Coffee Influenced the Course of History." *NPR*, April 24, 2013. www.npr.org/sections/thesalt/2013/04/24/178625554/how-coffee-influenced-the-course-of-history.

## Chapter 2

Adelson, Roger. *Mark Sykes: Portrait of an Amateur.* London: Jonathan Cape, 1975.

Ágoston, Gábor. *Guns for the Sultan: Military Power and the Weapons Industry in the Ottoman Empire.* Cambridge: Cambridge University Press, 2005.

Al-Enazy, Askar H. *The Creation of Saudi Arabia: Ibn Saud and British Imperial Policy, 1914–1927.* Abingdon, NY: Routledge, 2010.

Alföldi, L. M. "The Battle of Mohács." In *War and Society in East Central Europe.* Vol. 3, *From Hunyadi to Rákóczi: War and Society in Late Medieval and Early Modern Hungary,* edited by J. M. Bak and B. K. Király. New York: Brooklyn College Press, 1982.

Almond, Ian. *Two Faiths, One Banner: When Muslims Marched with Christians across Europe's Battlegrounds.* Cambridge, MA: Harvard University Press, 2009.

Anderson, Scott. *Lawrence in Arabia: War, Deceit, Imperial Folly and the Making of the Modern Middle East.* New York: Doubleday, 2013.

Andrew, Christopher M., and A. S. Kanya-Forstner. *The Climax of French Imperial Expansion: 1914–1924.* Stanford: Stanford University Press, 1981.

Antonius, George. *The Arab Awakening: The Story of the Arab National Movement.* New York: Capricorn Books, 1965.

Barker, Thomas M. *Double Eagle and Crescent: Vienna's Second Turkish Siege and in Historical Setting.* Albany: State University of New York Press, 1967.

Berdine, Michael D. *Redrawing the Middle East: Sir Mark Sykes, Imperialism and the Sykes-Picot Agreement.* London: I. B. Tauris and Co, 2018.

Berend, Nora. *At the Gate of Christendom: Jews, Muslims and Pagans in Medieval Hungary 1000–1300.* Cambridge: Cambridge University Press, 2001.

Brotton, Jerry. *The Sultan and the Queen: The Untold Story of Elizabeth and Islam.* New York: Penguin Books, 2017.

Bucsay, Mihály. *Der Protestantismus im Ungarn 1521–1978.* Vienna: Bohau, 1977.

Busch, Briton C. *Britain, India, and the Arabs: 1914–1921.* Berkeley: University of California, 1971.

David, Géza, and Pál Fodor. "Hungarian Studies in Ottoman History." *In The Ottomans and the Balkans: A Discussion of Historiography,* edited by Fikret Adanir and Suraiya Farooqhi. Leiden, Netherlands: Brill, 2002.

Davison, Derek. "Today in Middle Eastern History: The Battle of Aqaba (1917)." *Foreign Exchanges,* July 6, 2019. https://fx.substack.com/p/today-in-middle-eastern-history-the-332.

Dawn, C. Ernest. *From Ottomanism to Arabism: Essays on the Origins of Arab Nationalism.* Urbana: University of Illinois Press, 1973.

Denne, Luke, and Charlotte Gardiner. "Former U.S. Officials Criticize Trump's Decision to 'Abandon' Kurds." *NBC News,* November 17, 2019. https://www.nbcnews.com/news/world/former-u-s-officials-criticize-trump-s-decision-abandon-kurds-n1084156.

Fekete, Lajos. *Buda and Pest under Turkish Rule.* Budapest: Turkish Department, Lorand Eotvos University, 1976.

Finkel, Caroline. *The Administration of Warfare: The Ottoman Military Campaigns in Hungary, 1593–1606.* Vienna: VWGÖ, 1988.

Fodor, Pál. *In Quest of the Golden Apple: Imperial Ideology, Politics and Military Administration of the Ottoman Empire.* Istanbul: Isis Press, 2000.

Fromkin, David. *A Peace to End All Peace: The Fall of the Ottoman Empire and the Creation of the Modern Middle East.* New York: Holt Paperbacks, 1989.

Hourani, Albert. *The Emergence of the Modern Middle East.* Berkeley: University of California Press, 1981.

İnalcık, Halil. *Studies in Ottoman Social and Economic History.* London: Variorum, 1985.

Isaacson, Walter. "How Einstein Divded America's Jews." *The Atlantic,* December 2009. https://www.theatlantic.com/magazine/archive/2009/12/how-einstein-divided-americas-jews/307763.

Jacobson, Miriam. *Barbarous Antiquity: Reorienting the Past in the Poetry of Early Modern England.* Philadelphia: University of Pennsylvania Press, 2014.

Kedourie, Elie. *In the Anglo-Arab Labyrinth: The McMahon-Husayn Correspondence and Its Interpreters 1914–1939.* Cambridge: Cambridge University Press, 1976.

Kent, Marian. *Oil and Empire: British Policy and Mesopotamian Oil 1900–1920*. London: Macmillan Press for the London School of Economics, 1976.

Knolles, Richard. *The General Historie of the Turkes, from the First Beginning of That Nation to the Rising of the Othoman Familie*. London, 1602.

Lewis, Bernard. *The Jews of Islam*. Princeton, NJ: Princeton University Press, 1984.

Lloyd George, David. *Memoirs of the Peace Conference*. Vol. 2. New Haven, CT: Yale University Press, 1939.

Lloyd George, David. *War Memoirs of David Lloyd George*. Vol. 3, *1916–1917*. Boston: Little, Brown, 1934.

Lloyd George, David. *War Memoirs of David Lloyd George*. Vol. 6, *1918: Final Months of the War*. Boston: Little, Brown, 1938.

Lowe, C. J., and M. L. Dockrill. *The Mirage of Power*. Vol. 3, *The Documents, British Foreign Policy 902–1922*. London: Routledge and Kegan Paul, 1972.

Motlagh, Jason. "The Betrayal of the Kurds." *Rolling Stone*, December 18, 2019. https://www.rollingstone.com/politics/politics-features/trump-betrayal-of-the-kurds-927545.

Murphey, Rhoads. *Ottoman Warfare 1500–1700*. New Brunswick, NJ: Rutgers University Press, 1999.

Nevakivi, Jukka. *Britain, France and the Arab Middle East 1914–1920*. London: Athlone Press, 1969.

Peirce, Leslie. *The Imperial Harem Women and Sovereignty in the Ottoman Empire*. Oxford: Oxford University Press, 1993.

Riddell, George Allardice. *Lord Riddell's War Diary 1914–1918*. London: Ivor Nicholson and Watson, 1933.

Rogan, Eugene. *The Fall of the Ottomans: The Great War in the Middle East, 1914–1920*. New York: Basic Books, 2015.

Sachar, Howard M. *The Emergence of the Middle East: 1914–1924*. New York: Alfred A. Knopf, 1969.

Sanders, Ronald. *The High Walls of Jerusalem: A History of the Balfour Declaration and the Birth of the British Mandate for Palestine*. New York: Holt, Rinehart and Winston, 1983.

Shaw, Stanford J., and Ezel Kural Shaw. *History of the Ottoman Empire and Modern Turkey*. Vol. 2, *Reform, Revolution, and Republic: The Rise of Modern Turkey, 1808–1975*. Cambridge: Cambridge University Press, 1977.

Skilliter, Susan A. *William Harborne and the Trade with Turkey 1578–1582: A Documentary Study of the First Anglo-Ottoman Relations*. Oxford: Oxford University Press, 1977.

Stanwood, Frederick. *War, Revolution and British Imperialism in Central Asia.* London: Ithaca Press, 1983.

Sykes, Christopher S. *The Man Who Created the Middle East: A Story of Empire, Conflict and the Sykes-Picot Agreement.* London: William Collins, 2016.

Tahhan, Zena. "More Than a Century On: The Balfour Declaration Explained." *Al Jazeera*, November 2, 2018. https://www.aljazeera.com/features/2018/11/2/more-than-a-century-on-the-balfour-declaration-explained.

Trumpener, Ulrich. *Germany and the Ottoman Empire: 1914–1918.* Princeton, NJ: Princeton University Press, 1968.

Tuchman, Barbara W. *Bible and Sword: England and Palestine from the Bronze Age to Balfour.* New York: Funk and Wagnalls, 1956.

Weber, Frank G. *Eagles on the Crescent: Germany, Austria, and the Diplomacy of the Turkish Alliance 1914–1918.* Ithaca, NY: Cornell University Press, 1970.

Zeine, Zeine N. *The Emergence of Arab Nationalism: With a Background Study of Arab-Turkish Relations in the Near East.* Beirut: Khayats, 1966.

# Chapter 3

Al-Enazy, Askar H. *The Creation of Saudi Arabia: Ibn Saud and British Imperial Policy, 1914–1927.* London: Routledge, 2010.

Antonius, George. *The Arab Awakening: The Story of the Arab National Movement.* London: Hamish Hamilton, 1938.

Baker, P. Randall. *King Husain and the Kingdom of Hejaz.* Cambridge: Oleander Press, 1979.

Barnard, Anne, and Maria Abi-Habib. "Why Saad Hariri Had That Strange Sojourn in Saudi Arabia." *New York Times*, December 24, 2017. https://www.nytimes.com/2017/12/24/world/middleeast/saudi-arabia-saad-hariri-mohammed-bin-salman-lebanon.html.

Bell, Gertrude. *Letters of Gertrude Bell.* Edited by Florence Bell. 2 vols. London: Ernest Benn, 1973.

Ben Gurion, David. *My Talks with Arab Leaders.* New York: The Third Press, 1973.

Bennett, G. H. "Lloyd George, Curzon and the Control of British Foreign Policy 1919–22." *Australian Journal of Politics and History* 5, no. 4 (1999): 467–82.

Bullard, Sir Reader. *The Camels Must Go: An Autobiography.* London: Faber and Faber, 1961.

Busch, Briton Cooper. *Britain, India, and the Arabs: 1914–1921.* Berkeley: University of California Press, 1971.

Chait, Jonathan. "Nixon Disallowed Jewish Advisors from Discussing Israel Policy." *New Republic*, December 9, 2010. https://newrepublic. com/article/79829/nixon-disallowed-jewish-advisors-discussing-israel-policy.

Churchill, Winston S. *Winston S. Churchill.* Vol. 4, *1916–1922, The Stricken World*, edited by Martin Gilbert. Boston: Houghton Mifflin, 1975.

Churchill, Winston S. *Winston S. Churchill.* Vol. 4, *Part 2: July 1919– March 1921*, edited by Martin Gilbert. Boston: Houghton Mifflin, 1978.

Danahar, Paul. *The New Middle East: The World after the Arab Spring.* New York: Bloomsbury, 2013.

Danforth, Nick. "How the Middle East Was Invented." *Washington Post*, May 19, 2016. https://www.washingtonpost.com/news/worldviews/ wp/2016/05/19/the-modern-middle-east-is-actually-only-100-years-old.

De Onis, Juan. "Faisal's Killer Is Put to Death." *New York Times*, June 19, 1975. https://www.nytimes.com/1975/06/19/archives/faisals-killer-is-put-to-death-prince-is-beheaded-before-a-crowd-of.html.

Dickson's interesting diary of his visit between 20 January and 20 February 1920. In *Records of Saudi Arabia 1902–1960*, edited by E. Quick, P. Tuson, and A. Burdett, 253–254 and 253–289. Cambridge: Cambridge Archive Editions, 1992.

Evans, Harold. "His Finest Hour." *New York Times*, November 11, 2001. https://www.nytimes.com/2001/11/11/books/his-finest-hour.html.

Firestone, Reuven. *Journeys in Holy Lands: The Evolution of the Abraham-Ishmael Legends in Islamic Exegesis.* Albany: University of New York Press, 1990.

Gady, Franz-Stefan. "How Churchill Fought the Pashtuns in Pakistan." *The Diplomat*, October 24, 2015. https://thediplomat.com/2015/10/ how-churchill-fought-the-pashtuns-in-pakistan.

"General Repeats Remarks on Jews." *New York Times*, June 30, 1976. https://www.nytimes.com/1976/06/30/archives/general-repeats-remarks-on-jews-but-senate-panel-confirms-brown.html.

Golden, Tim, and Sebastian Rotella. "The Saudi Connection: Inside the 9/11 That Divided the F.B.I." *New York Times*, January 23, 2020. https://www.nytimes.com/2020/01/23/magazine/9-11-saudi-arabia-fbi.html.

Hitchens, Christopher. "Why the Suicide Killers Chose September 11." *Guardian*, October 3, 2001. https://www.theguardian.com/world/2001/oct/03/september11.usa2.

Howell, Georgina. *Gertrude Bell: Queen of the Desert, Shaper of Nations.* New York: Farrar, Straus and Giroux, 2006.

Khalidi, Rashid. *The Origins of Arab Nationalism.* New York: Columbia University Press, 1991.

Lacey, Robert. *The Kingdom.* New York: Harcourt Brace Jovanovich, 1982.

Lawrence, T. E. *The Letters of T. E. Lawrence.* Edited by David Garnett. London: Jonathan Cape, 1938.

Lawrence, T. E., and D. G. Hogarth, eds. *The Arab Bulletin 1916–1919.* Buckinghamshire, UK: Archive Editions, 1986.

Leatherdale, Clive. *Britain and Saudi Arabia 1925–1939: The Imperial Oasis.* London: Frank Cass, 1985.

Letter from Imam Sir 'Abdul 'Aziz ibn Sa'ud To His Excellency Sir Percy Cox. September 4, 1922. FO371/8936 E1363/46/92, pp. 1, 3, 4. In *Records of Saudi Arabia 1902–1960*, edited by E. Quick, P. Tuson, and A. Burdett. Cambridge: Cambridge Archive Editions, 1992.

Massoumi, Narzanin. "Why Is Europe Islamophobic." *New York Times*, March 6, 2020. https://www.nytimes.com/2020/03/06/opinion/europe-islamophobia-attacks.html.

Memorandum by Major H. R. P. Dichson, PA, Bahrain, to Cox, Civil Commissioner, Baghdad, on "Meeting with Ibn Saud at Hoffuf, Jan 20–Feb 20, 1920" 20 February 1920, LP/S/10, 2182, pts 11, 12, p. 5. In *Records of Saudi Arabia 1902–1960*, edited by E. Quick, P. Tuson, and A. Burdett, 282. Cambridge: Cambridge Archive Editions, 1992.

Mengin, Felix. *Histoire de l'Egypte sous le Gouvernement de Mohammed-Aly.* Bertrand, 1823.

Mousa, Suleiman. "Sharif Husayn and Developments Leading to the Arab Revolt." *New Arabian Studies* 1 (1993): 36–53.

Power, Carla. "Saudi Arabia Bulldozes over Its Heritage." *Time*, November 14, 2014. https://time.com/3584585/saudi-arabia-bulldozes-over-its-heritage.

Private conversation between Dickson with Ibn Saud, 10 February 1920, No, 2635, in LP/S/10, 2182, pts 11, 12, p. 1. FO371/5062 E6289/9/44, 11 June 1920. In *Records of Saudi Arabia 1902–1960*, edited by E. Quick, P. Tuson, and A. Burdett, 278. Cambridge: Cambridge Archive Editions, 1992.

Prott, Volker. *The Politics of Self-Determination: Remaking Territories and National Identities in Europe, 1917–1923.* Oxford: Oxford University Press, 2016.

Quick, E., P. Tuson, and A. Burdett, eds. *Records of Saudi Arabia 1902–1960.* Cambridge: Cambridge Archive Editions, 1992.

Quigley, John. *The Statehood of Palestine: International Law in the Middle East Conflict.* Cambridge: Cambridge University Press, 2010.

Rouillé, Guillaume. *Le Promptuarium iconum insigniorum.* Lyon, France, 1553.

Sardar, Ziauddin. "The Destruction of Mecca." *New York Times,* September 30, 2014. https://www.nytimes.com/2014/10/01/opinion/the-destruction-of-mecca.html.

Schneer, Jonathan. *The Balfour Declaration: The Origins of the Arab-Israeli Conflict.* New York: Random House, 2010.

Shamekh, Ahmed A. *Spatial Patterns of Bedouin Settlement in Al-Qasim Region, Saudi Arabia.* Ann Arbor, MI: University Microfilms International, 1975.

Shwadran, Benjamin. *Jordan: A State of Tension.* New York: Council for Middle Eastern Affairs Press, 1959.

Teitelbaum, Joshua. *The Rise and Fall of the Hashimite Kingdom of Arabia.* London: Hurst and Company, 2001.

Telegram from Colonial Office to FO on "King Hussein and Ibn Saud," No, 5163/23, 3 February 1923, FO371/8936 E1363/46/91. The CO telegram refers to previous FO371/8936 E/546/46/91 reporting content of dispatch No. 62 of 16 January 1923, from Baghdad "forwarding copies of correspondence between King Hussein and Ibn Saud on occasion of Nejd Pilgrimage" sent by Ibn Saud; see also telegram 15 September 1922, from High Commissioner of Iraq to Secretary of State for Colonies, No. 3860, LP/S/10, 7351/1920, pt. 1. In *Records of Saudi Arabia 1902–1960*, edited by E. Quick, P. Tuson, and A. Burdett. Cambridge: Cambridge Archive Editions, 1992.

Tharoor, Shashi. "In Winston Churchill, Hollywood Rewards a Mass Murderer." *Washington Post,* March 10, 2018. https://www.washingtonpost.com/news/global-opinions/wp/2018/03/10/in-winston-churchill-hollywood-rewards-a-mass-murderer.

Van Creveld, Martin. *The Sword and the Olive: A Critical History of the Israeli Defense Force.* New York: Public Affairs Publishers, 1998.

William, Kenneth. *Ibn Sa'ud: The Puritan King of Arabia.* London: Jonathan Cape, 1933.

Wilson, Jeremy. *Lawrence of Arabia: The Authorised Biography of T. E. Lawrence.* London: William Heinemann Ltd, 1989.

"US Ready to Invade Middle East in 1973." *Al Jazeera,* January 1, 2004. https://www.aljazeera.com/news/2004/1/1/us-ready-to-invade-middle-east-in-1973.

# Chapter 4

Bloom, Stephen G. "Lesson of a Lifetime." *Smithsonian Magazine,*
    September 2005. https://www.smithsonianmag.com/science-nature/
    lesson-of-a-lifetime-72754306.
Elliott, Jane. *A Collar in My Pocket: The Blue Eyes/Brown Eyes Exercise.*
    Self-published, Amazon Digital Services, 2016.
Kahneman, Daniel. *Thinking, Fast and Slow.* New York: Farrar, Straus
    and Giroux, 2011.
PBS. "Introduction." January 1, 2003. https://www.pbs.org/wgbh/
    frontline/article/introduction-2.
Semmerling, Tim Jon. *"Evil" Arabs in American Popular Film:
    Orientalist Fear.* Austin: University of Texas Press, 2006.
Shaheen, Jack G. *Reel Bad Arabs: How Hollywood Vilifies a People.*
    Northampton, MA: Olive Branch Press, 2009.

# Chapter 5

Kahneman, Daniel. *Thinking, Fast and Slow.* New York: Farrar, Straus
    and Giroux, 2011.
Leiby, Richard. "To the Players in Abscam, the Real-Life 'American
    Hustle,' the Bribes Now Seem Quaint." *Washington Post,* December
    26, 2013. https://www.washingtonpost.com/lifestyle/style/to-the-
    players-in-abscam-the-real-life-american-hustle-the-bribes-now-
    seem-quaint/2013/12/26/d67648c2-6c15-11e3-a523-fe73f0ff6b8d_
    story.html.
Morehouse, Ward, III. "'Abscam' Fallout: Atlantic City Casinos."
    *Christian Science Monitor,* February 6, 1980. https://www.csmonitor.
    com/1980/0206/020642.html.

# Chapter 6

Acocella, Joan. "How Martin Luther Changed the World." *New Yorker,*
    October 23, 2017. https://www.newyorker.com/magazine/2017/10/30/
    how-martin-luther-changed-the-world.
Applebaum, Anne. "History Will Judge the Complicit: Why Have
    Republican Leaders Abandoned Their Principles in Support of an
    Immoral and Dangerous President?" *The Atlantic,* July/August 2020.
    https://www.theatlantic.com/magazine/archive/2020/07/trumps-
    collaborators/612250.

aṭ-Ṭabarī, Muḥammad Ibn-Ğarīr. *The History of Al-Tabari*. Vol. 36, *The Revolt of the Zanj A.D. 869–879*. Translated by David Waines. Albany: State University of New York Press, 1992.

Benware, Paul N. *Understanding End Times Prophecy: A Comprehensive Approach*. Chicago: Moody, 2006.

Bump, Philip. "Half of Evangelicals Support Israel Because They Believe It Is Important for Fulfilling End-Times Prophecy." *Washington Post*, May 14, 2018. https://www.washingtonpost.com/news/politics/wp/2018/05/14/half-of-evangelicals-support-israel-because-they-believe-it-is-important-for-fulfilling-end-times-prophecy.

Burkett, Delbert. *An Introduction to the New Testament and the Origins of Christianity*. Cambridge: Cambridge University Press, 2002.

Carroll, James. *Constantine's Sword: The Church and the Jews, a History*. New York: Houghton Mifflin, 2001.

Coggan, Donald. *The English Bible*. Essex: Longmans, Green and Co. Ltd., 1968.

Donner, Fred McGraw. *The Early Islamic Conquests*. Princeton, NJ: Princeton University Press, 1981.

Drijvers, Jan Willem. *Helena Augusta: The Mother of Constantine the Great and the Legend of Her Finding the True Cross*. Leiden, Netherlands: E. J. Brill, 1992.

Dubnow, Simon. *History of the Jews*. Vol 2, *From the Roman Empire to the Early Medieval Period*. Frankfurt: Oulook Verlag, 1968.

Earl of Shaftesbury. "State and Prospects of the Jews." *Quarterly Review* 63 (January/March 1839): 166–92.

Ehrman, Bart D. *Peter, Paul and Mary Magdalene: The Followers of Jesus in History and Legend*. New York: Oxford University Press, 2006.

Esposito, John. *What Everyone Needs to Know about Islam*. New York: University Press, 2002.

Finkelstein, Israel, and Neil Asher Silberman. *The Bible Unearthed: Archaeology's New Vision of Ancient Israel and the Origin of Its Sacred Texts*. New York: Simon and Schuster, 2002.

Goldman, Sam. "It's Christian Politics, Not AIPAC Money, That Explains American Support for Israel." *Washington Post*, February 12, 2019. https://www.washingtonpost.com/news/monkey-cage/wp/2019/02/12/its-christian-politics-not-aipac-money-that-explains-american-support-for-israel.

Greatrex, Geoffrey, and Samuel N. C. Lieu. *The Roman Eastern Frontier and the Persian Wars: Part II, AD 363–630*. London: Routledge, 2002.

Groppe, Maureen. "Is Mike Pence Channeling Queen Esther? Or the Apostle John? A New Book Examines This and More." *USA Today*, June 20, 2019. https://www.usatoday.com/story/news/politics/2019/06/20/mike-pences-faith-book-portrays-vp-most-influential-evangelical/1499144001.

Grypeou, Emmanouela, Mark Swanson, and David Thomas. *The Encounters of Eastern Christianity with Early Islam.* Leiden, Netherlands: Brill, 2006.

Haldon, John. *Byzantium in the Seventh Century: The Transformation of a Culture.* Cambridge: Cambridge University Press, 1997.

Herzl, Theodore. *The Jewish State.* Anodos Books, 1917.

Hunter, Stephen. "'300': A Losing Battle in More Ways Than 1." *Washington Post*, March 9, 2007. https://www.washingtonpost.com/wp-dyn/content/article/2007/03/08/AR2007030802188.html?nav=hcmodule.

Kaegi, Walter Emil. *Byzantium and the Early Islamic Conquests.* Cambridge: Cambridge University Press, 1995.

Kaegi, Walter Emil. *Heraclius, Emperor of Byzantium.* Cambridge: Cambridge University Press, 2003.

Kennedy, Hugh. *The Great Arab Conquests: How the Spread of Islam Changed the World We Live In.* Philadelphia: Da Capo Press, 2007.

Kenyon, Sir Frederic George. *The Story of the Bible.* London: Murray, 1936.

Kohen, Elli. *History of the Byzantine Jews: A Microcosmos in the Thousand Year Empire.* Lanham, MD: University Press of America, 2007.

Le Strange, Guy. *Palestine under Moslems.* Beirut: Khayats, 1965.

Levi Della Vida, G., and M. Bonner. "Umar (I) b. al-Khaṭṭāb." In *Encyclopaedia of Islam*, edited by Peri J. Bearman, Thierry Bianquis, Clifford Edmund Bosworth, E. van Donzel, and W. P. Heinrichs. 2nd ed. Accessed November 4, 2020. https://referenceworks.brillonline.com/entries/encyclopaedia-of-islam-2/umar-i-b-al-khattab-SIM_7707.

Lindberg, Beth M. *A God-Filled Life: The Story of William Eugene Blackstone.* Chicago: American Messianic Fellowship, 1952.

Luther, Martin. "The Freedom of a Christian: Doctrine of Justification by Faith Alone." In *On Christian Liberty*, edited by Harold J. Grimm and translated by W. A. Lambert. Minneapolis: Fortress Press, 2003.

Luttwak, Edward N. *The Grand Strategy of the Byzantine Empire.* Cambridge, MA: Harvard University Press, 2009.

Maza, Cristina. "Trump Will Start the End of the World, Claim Evangelicals Who Support Him." *Newsweek*, January 12,

2018. https://www.newsweek.com/trump-will-bring-about-end-worldevangelicals-end-times-779643.

McCullough, David. *Truman.* New York: Simon and Schuster, 1992.

Mohtsham, Saeed M. "Vision and Visionary Leadership: An Islamic Perspective." *International Review of Research Papers* 3, no. 2 (June 2007): 248–77.

Mulrine, Anna. "Too Much Religion at Military Academies? West Point Cadet Revives Charge." *Christian Science Monitor,* December 7, 2012. https://www.csmonitor.com/USA/Military/2012/1207/Too-much-religion-at-military-academies-West-Point-cadet-revives-charge.

Murray, Iain. *The Puritan Hope: Revival and the Interpretation of Prophecy.* Edinburgh: Banner of Truth, 1971.

*National Geographic: The Holy Land,* January 1, 2014.

Nayeri, Dina. "Yearning for the End of the World." *Guardian,* August 25, 2017. https://www.theguardian.com/news/2017/aug/25/yearning-for-the-end-of-the-world.

Nicolle, David. *Yarmuk, AD 636: The Muslim Conquest of Syria.* London: Osprey Publishing, 1994.

Palmer, Andrew. *The Seventh Century in the West-Syrian Chronicles.* Liverpool: Liverpool University Press, 1993.

Powell, Mark Allan. *Jesus as a Figure in History: How Modern Historians View the Man from Galilee.* Louisville, KY: Westminster John Knox Press, 1998.

Rea, Steven. "Just 300, but CG on Their Side." *Philadelphia Daily News,* March 9, 2007. Accessed November 23, 2011. https://web.archive.org/web/20160304065951/http://articles.philly.com/2007-03-09/entertainment/25237355_1_persians-life-sized-iranians.

Rea, Steven. "Opening Haul by 300 Is a Stunner." *Philadelphia Inquirer,* March 13, 2007. https://www.inquirer.com/philly/entertainment/movies/20070313_Opening_haul_by_300_is_a_stunner.html.

Runciman, Steven. *A History of the Crusades.* Vol. 1, *The First Crusade and the Foundation of the Kingdom of Jerusalem.* Cambridge: Cambridge University Press, 1987.

Ṣallābī, ʻAlī Muḥammad Muḥammad. *The Biography of Umar ibn al-Khattab.* 2 vols. Riyadh, Saudi Arabia: Darussalam, 2010.

Sharif, Regina. *Non-Jewish Zionism: Its Roots in Western History.* London: Zed Books, 1983.

Sizer, Stephen. *Christian Zionism: Road-Map to Armageddon.* Downers Grove, IL: InterVarsity Press, 2004.

Smith, Allan. "Trump Signs Executive Order Targeting College Anti-Semitism, Israel Boycotts." *NBC News*, December 11, 2019. https://www.nbcnews.com/politics/donald-trump/trump-sign-executive-order-targeting-college-anti-semitism-israel-boycotts-n1099601.

Smith, Jean Edward. *Bush*. New York: Simon and Schuster, 2016.

Soloveichik, Meir. "Queen Esther, a Hero for Our Time." *New York Times,* March 8, 2020. https://www.nytimes.com/2020/03/08/opinion/queen-esther-purim.html.

Spellberg, Denise A. *Thomas Jefferson's Qur'an: Islam and the Founders*. New York: Alfred A. Knopf, 2013.

Stowasser, Barbara Freyer. *Women in the Qur'an, Traditions, and Interpretation*. New York: Oxford University Press, 1994.

Telford, William R. *The Theology of the Gospel of Mark*. Cambridge: Cambridge University Press, 1999.

Thompson, Craig R. *The Bible in English, 1525–1611*. New York: Cornell University Press, 1963.

Wagner, Donald E. *Anxious for Armageddon*. Scottdale, PA: Herald Press, 1995.

Wagner, Donald E. "Evangelicals and Israel: Theological Roots of a Political Alliance." *Christian Century*, November 4, 1998. https://www.christiancentury.org/article/2012-03/evangelicals-and-israel.

Wong, Edward. "The Rapture and the Real World: Mike Pompeo Blends Beliefs and Policy." *New York Times*, March 30, 2019. https://www.nytimes.com/2019/03/30/us/politics/pompeo-christian-policy.html.

Wright, Robin. "Pompeo and His Bible Define U.S. Policy in the Middle East." *New Yorker*, January 11, 2019. https://www.newyorker.com/news/our-columnists/pompeo-and-his-bible-define-us-policy-in-the-middle-east.

Zauzmer, Julie, and Sarah Pulliam Bailey. "This Is Not the End of the World, according to Christians Who Study the End of the World." *Washington Post*, March 17, 2020. https://www.washingtonpost.com/religion/2020/03/17/not-end-of-the-world-coronavirus-bible-prophecy.

# Chapter 7

Asbridge, Thomas. *The Crusades: The War for the Holy Land*. New York: Simon and Schuster, 2012.

Bauer, Conrad. *The Knights Templar*. Ireland: Maplewood Publishing, 2015.

Bellinger, Charles K. *The Genealogy of Violence: Reflections on Creation, Freedom, and Evil*. New York: Oxford University Press, 2001.

Brownworth, Lars. *In Distant Lands: A Short History of the Crusades.* London: Crux Publishing, 2017.

Brundage, James A. *The Crusades: A Documentary Survey.* Milwaukee, WI: Marquette University Press, 1962.

Carroll, James. "The Bush Crusade." *The Nation*, September 2, 2004. https://www.thenation.com/article/archive/bush-crusade.

Carroll, James. *Constantine's Sword: The Church and the Jews, A History.* New York: Houghton Mifflin, 2001.

Chazan, Robert. *God, Humanity and History: The Hebrew First Crusade Narratives.* Berkeley: University of California Press, 2000.

Davis, William Stearns. *"God Wills It!": A Tale of the First Crusade.* New York: MacMillan Company, 1924.

Edde, Anne-Marie. *Saladin.* Translated by Jane Marie Todd. Cambridge, MA: Harvard University Press, 2011.

Fisher, Ian. "Pope Apologizes for Uproar over His Remarks." *New York Times*, September 17, 2006. https://www.nytimes.com/2006/09/17/world/europe/17cnd-pope.html.

Gabriele, Matthew. "Against the Enemies of Christ: The Role of Count Emicho in the Anti-Jewish Violence of the First Crusade." In *Christian Attitudes toward the Jews in the Middle Ages: A Casebook*, edited by Michael Frassetto. New York: Routledge, 2007.

Gabrieli, Francesco. *Arab Historians of the Crusades.* Translated by E. J. Costello. Berkeley: University of California Press, 1984.

Giebfried, John. "The Crusader Rebranding of Jerusalem's Temple Mount." *Comitatus: A Journal of Medieval and Renaissance Studies* 44, no. 1 (2013): 77–94.

Girard, René. *Things Hidden since the Foundation of the World.* Translated by Stephen Bann (Books 2 and 3) and Michael Metteer (Book 1). Stanford: Stanford University Press, 1987.

Girard, René. *Violence and the Sacred.* Translated by Patrick Gregory. Baltimore: Johns Hopkins University Press, 1977.

Golb, Norman. *The Jews in Medieval Normandy: A Social and Intellectual History.* Cambridge, UK: Cambridge University Press, 1998.

Hillenbrand, Carole. *The Crusades: Islamic Perspectives.* Edinburgh: Edinburgh University Press, 1999.

Hilliam, David. *Richard the Lionheart and the Third Crusade.* New York: Rosen Publishing Group, 2004.

Hitti, Philip. *History of the Arabs.* Basingstoke, UK: Palgrave, 2002.

Holt, Peter Malcolm. *The Crusader States and Their Neighbours, 1098–1291.* Harlow, UK: Pearson Longman, 2004.

Hull, Michael D. "First Crusade: Siege of Jerusalem." *Military History*, June 1999. Accessed on HistoryNet.com. https://www.historynet.com/first-crusade-siege-of-jerusalem.htm.

Ibn Al-Qalānisī. *The Damascus Chronicle of the Crusades: Extracted and Translated from the Chronicle of Ibn Al-Qalanisi*. Translated by H. A. R. Gibb. Mineola, NY: Dover Publications, 2003.

Jacoby, Susan. "The First Victims of the First Crusade." *New York Times*, February 13, 2015. https://www.nytimes.com/2015/02/15/opinion/sunday/the-first-victims-of-the-first-crusade.html.

Jones, Dan. *The Templars*. London: Head of Zeus Ltd., 2017.

Krey, August C. *The First Crusade: The Accounts of Eye-Witnesses and Participants*. Princeton, NJ: Princeton University Press, 1921.

Maalouf, Amin. *The Crusaders through Arab Eyes*. London: The Folio Society, 1983.

MacAskill, Ewen. "George Bush: 'God Told Me to End the Tyranny in Iraq.'" *Guardian*, October 7, 2005. https://www.theguardian.com/world/2005/oct/07/iraq.usa.

Madden, Thomas F. *The Concise History of the Crusades*. Lanham, MD: Rowman and Littlefield, 2013.

Man, John. *Saladin: The Sultan Who Vanquished the Crusaders and Built an Islamic Empire*. Boston: Da Capo Press, 2016.

Mayer, Hans Eberhard. *The Crusades*. Oxford: Oxford University Press, 1965.

Montefiore, Simon Sebag. *Jerusalem: The Biography*. New York: Vintage Books, 2012.

Peters, Edward, ed. *The First Crusade*. Philadelphia: University of Pennsylvania Press, 1971.

Prawer, Joshua. *The Crusaders' Kingdom*. London: Phoenix Press, 1972.

Runciman, Steven. *The First Crusade*. Cambridge: Cambridge University Press, 1980.

Tyerman, Christopher. *The World of the Crusades*. New Haven, CT: Yale University Press, 2019.

Ulaby, Neda. "Scholars Say White Supremacists Chanting 'Deus Vult' Got History Wrong." *NPR*, September 4, 2017. https://www.npr.org/2017/09/04/548505783/scholars-say-white-supremacists-chanting-deus-vult-got-history-wrong.

Waldman, Peter, and Hugh Pope. "'Crusade' Reference Reinforces Fears War on Terrorism Is against Muslims." *Wall Street Journal*, September 21, 2001. https://www.wsj.com/articles/SB1001020294332922160.

Wasserman, James. *An Illustrated History of the Knights Templar*. Rochester, VT: Destiny Books, 2006.

# Chapter 8

Armstrong, Karen. *A History of God*. New York: Ballantine Books, 1993.

Armstrong, Karen. *Muhammad: A Biography of the Prophet*. San Francisco: Harper San Francisco, 1993.

Asbridge, Thomas. *The Crusades: The War for the Holy Land*. New York: Simon and Schuster, 2012.

Babinger, Franz. *Mehmed the Conqueror and His Time*. Princeton, NJ: Princeton University Press, 1992.

Barber, Malcolm. *The Crusader States*. New Haven, CT: Yale University Press, 2012.

Bauer, Conrad. *The Knights Templar*. Ireland: Maplewood Publishing, 2015.

Bellinger, Charles K. *The Genealogy of Violence: Reflections on Creation, Freedom, and Evil*. New York: Oxford University Press, 2001.

Blee, Kathleen M. *Women of the Klan: Racism and Gender in the 1920s*. Berkeley: University of California Press, 2008.

Brody, Richard. "The Worst Thing about 'Birth of a Nation' Is How Good It Is." *New Yorker*, February 1, 2013. https://www.newyorker.com/culture/richard-brody/the-worst-thing-about-birth-of-a-nation-is-how-good-it-is.

Brownworth, Lars. *In Distant Lands: A Short History of the Crusades*. London: Crux Publishing, 2017.

Brundage, James A. *The Crusades: A Documentary Survey*. Milwaukee, WI: Marquette University Press, 1962.

Choniates, Nicetas. *O City of Byzantium: Annals of Niketas Choniatēs*. Translated by Harry J. Magoulias. Detroit: Wayne State University Press, 1984.

Edbury, Peter W., and John G. Rowe. *William of Tyre: Historian of the Latin East*. Cambridge: Cambridge University Press, 1988.

Edde, Anne-Marie. *Saladin*. Translated by Jane Marie Todd. Cambridge, MA: Harvard University Press, 2011.

Evans, Richard J. *In Hitler's Shadow*. New York: Pantheon, 1989.

Evans, Richard J. *The Third Reich at War*. London: Allen Lane, 2008.

Flori, Jean. *Richard Coeur de Lion: le roi-chevalier*. Paris: Biographie Payot, 1999.

Flori, Jean. *Richard the Lionheart: Knight and King*. Translated by Jean Birrell. Edinburgh: Edinburgh University Press, 1999.

Forbis, Judith. *The Classic Arabian Horse*. New York: Liveright, 1976.

Girard, René. *Things Hidden since the Foundation of the World*. Translated by Stephen Bann (Books II and III) and Michael Metteer (Book I). Stanford: Stanford University Press, 1987.

Saleem I. Abdulrauf

Girard, René. *Violence and the Sacred.* Translated by Patrick Gregory. Baltimore: Johns Hopkins University Press, 1977.

Graetz, Heinrich Hirsch. *History of the Jews.* Philadelphia: Jewish Publication Society of America, 1891.

Gregory, Timothy. *A History of Byzantium.* Malden, MA: Wiley-Blackwell, 2010.

Guterl, Matthew Pratt. *The Color of Race in America, 1900–1940.* Cambridge, MA: Harvard University Press, 2009.

Halbertal, Moshe. *Maimonides: Life and Thought.* Princeton, NJ: Princeton University Press, 2013.

Hamilton, Bernard. *The Leper King and His Heirs: Baldwin IV and the Crusader Kingdom of Jerusalem.* Cambridge: Cambridge University Press, 2005.

Harris, Jonathan. *Constantinople: Capital of Byzantium.* London: Hambledon/Continuum, 2007.

Harris, Jonathan. *The End of Byzantium.* New Haven, CT: Yale University Press, 2010.

Hillenbrand, Carole. *The Crusades: Islamic Perspectives.* Edinburgh: Edinburgh University Press, 1999.

Hilliam, David. *Richard the Lionheart and the Third Crusade.* New York: Rosen Publishing Group, 2004.

Holt, Peter Malcolm. *The Crusader States and Their Neighbours, 1098–1291.* Harlow, UK: Pearson Longman, 2004.

Jones, Dan. *The Templars.* London: Head of Zeus Ltd., 2017.

Keen, Maurice Hugh. *Chivalry.* New Haven, CT: Yale University Press, 2005.

Kinney, Alison. "How the Klan Got Its Hood." *New Republic*, January 8, 2016. https://newrepublic.com/article/127242/klan-got-hood.

Knausgaard, Karl Ove. "The Inexplicable." *New Yorker*, May 18, 2015. https://www.newyorker.com/magazine/2015/05/25/the-inexplicable.

Lane-Poole, Stanley. *Saladin and the Fall of the Kingdom of Jerusalem.* London: G. P. Putnam's Sons, 1903.

Lay, Shawn, ed. *The Invisible Empire in the West: Toward a New Historical Appraisal of the Ku Klux Klan of the 1920s.* 2nd ed. Urbana: University of Illinois Press, 2004.

Le Goff, Jacques. *Saint Louis.* Translated by Gareth Evan Gollrad. Notre Dame, IN: University of Notre Dame Press, 2009.

Lower, Michael. *The Tunis Crusade of 1270: A Mediterranean History.* Oxford: Oxford University Press, 2018.

Lyons, M. C., and D. E. P Jackson. *Saladin: The Politics of the Holy War.* Cambridge: Cambridge University Press, 1982.

Madden, Thomas F. *The Concise History of the Crusades*. Lanham, MD: Rowman and Littlefield, 2013.

Man, John. *Saladin: The Sultan Who Vanquished the Crusaders and Built an Islamic Empire*. Boston: Da Capo Press, 2016.

Morgan, Michael H. *Lost History: The Enduring Legacy of Muslim Scientists, Thinkers, and Artists*. Washington, DC: National Geographic, 2007.

Nicol, Donald M. *Byzantium and Venice: A Study in Diplomatic and Cultural Relations*. Cambridge: Cambridge University Press, 1999.

Nicolle, David. *Saladin: The Background, Strategies, Tactics and Battlefield Experiences of the Greatest Commanders of History*. London: Osprey Publishing, 2011.

Nicolle, David. *The Second Crusade 1148: Disaster outside Damascus*. London: Osprey, 2009.

Nisar, Hasher. "What We Can Learn from Saladin." *Huffington Post*, December 9, 2015. https://www.huffingtonpost.com/hasher-nisar/saladin-lessons_b_8704244.html?ncid=engmodushpmg00000004.

Papayianni, Aphrodite. "Memory and Ideology: The Image of the Crusades in Byzantine Historiography, Eleventh to Thirteenth Century." In *The Crusader World*, edited by Adrian Boas. New York: Routledge, 2016.

Phillips, Jonathan. *The Life and Legend of the Sultan Saladin*. New Haven, CT: Yale University Press, 2019.

Phillips, Jonathan. "A Noble Enemy: How Saladin Became a Hero in the West." *Economist*, May 30, 2019. https://www.economist.com/books-and-arts/2019/05/30/how-saladin-became-a-hero-in-the-west.

Prawer, Joshua. *The Crusaders' Kingdom*. London: Phoenix Press, 1972.

Richard, Jean. *Saint Louis: Crusader King of France*. Edited and abridged by Simon Lloyd. Translated by Jean Birrell. Cambridge: Cambridge University Press, 1983.

Richard, King of England. *Chronicle of the Third Crusade: A Translation of the Itinerarium Peregrinorum Et Gesta Regis Ricardi*. Edited and translated by Helen J. Nicholson. Aldershot, UK: Ashgate, 1997.

Riley-Smith, Jonathan. *The Crusades: A Short History*. 2nd ed. New Haven, CT: Yale University Press, 2005.

Robert of Clari. *The Conquest of Constantinople*. Translated by Edgar Holmes McNeal. New York: Columbia University Press, 1936.

Rogers, William Warren, Robert Ward, Leah Atkins, and Wayne Flynt. *Alabama: The History of a Deep South State*. Tuscaloosa: University of Alabama Press, 1994.

Runciman, Steven. *A History of the Crusades.* Vol 2, *The Kingdom of Jerusalem and the Frankish East, 1100–1187.* 2nd ed. London: Penguin, 1990.

Seierstad, Asne. "The Anatomy of White Terror." *New York Times*, March 18, 2019. https://www.nytimes.com/2019/03/18/opinion/new-zealand-tarrant-white-supremacist-terror.html.

Shaheen, Jack G. *Reel Bad Arabs: How Hollywood Vilifies a People.* Northampton, MA: Olive Branch Press, 2009.

Sphrantzes, Geōrgios. *The Fall of the Byzantine Empire: A Chronicle by George Sphrantzes 1401–1477.* Translated by Marios Philippides. Amherst: University of Massachusetts Press, 1980.

Tyerman, Christopher. *God's War: A New History of the Crusades.* Cambridge, MA: Belknap Press of Harvard University Press, 2006.

Tyerman, Christopher. *The World of the Crusades.* New Haven, CT: Yale University Press, 2019.

Van Biema, David. "Saladin (c. 1138–1193)." *Time*, December 26, 1999. http://content.time.com/time/magazine/article/0,9171,36516,00.html.

Wasserman, James. *An Illustrated History of the Knights Templar.* Rochester, VT: Destiny Books, 2006.

Weir, Alison. *Eleanor of Aquitaine: By the Wrath of God, Queen of England.* New York: Vintage Books, 2008.

Wheatcroft, Andrew. *The Infidels: The Conflict between Christendom and Islam, 638–2002.* London: Viking Publishing, 2003.

William of Tyre. *A History of Deeds Done beyond the Sea.* Translated by E. A. Babcock and A. C. Krey. New York: Columbia University Press, 1943.

# Chapter 9

Abu Toameh, Khaled. "Palestinian Census: 4.7 Million in West Bank and Gaza Strip." *Times of Israel*, March 28, 2018. https://www.timesofisrael.com/palestinian-census-4-7-million-in-west-bank-and-gaza-strip.

Anderson, Scott. *Lawrence in Arabia: War, Deceit, Imperial Folly and the Making of the Modern Middle East.* New York: Doubleday, 2013.

Bell, J. Bowyer. *Terror out of Zion: The Fight for Israeli Independence.* Dublin: Academy Press, 1977.

Carter, Jimmy. *Palestine: Peace Not Apartheid.* New York: Simon and Schuster, 2006.

Ennes, James N., Jr. *Assault on the Liberty: The True Story of the Israeli Attack on an American Intelligence Ship.* New York: Random House, 1987.

Entous, Adam. "How Trump and Three Other U.S. Presidents Protected Israel's Worst-Kept Secret: Its Nuclear Arsenal." *New Yorker*, June 19, 2018. https://www.newyorker.com/news/news-desk/how-trump-and-three-other-us-presidents-protected-israels-worst-kept-secret-its-nuclear-arsenal.

Entous, Adam. "The Maps of Israeli Settlements That Shocked Barack Obama." *New Yorker*, July 9, 2018. https://www.newyorker.com/news/news-desk/the-map-of-israeli-settlements-that-shocked-barack-obama.

Goldman, Sam. "It's Christian Politics, Not AIPAC Money, That Explains American Support for Israel." *Washington Post*, February 12, 2019. https://www.washingtonpost.com/news/monkey-cage/wp/2019/02/12/its-christian-politics-not-aipac-money-that-explains-american-support-for-israel.

Guthridge, Ian. *The Rise and Decline of the Christian Empire*. Victoria, Australia: Medici School Publications, 1999.

Herzog, Chaim. *Heroes of Israel: Profiles of Jewish Courage*. Boston: Little, Brown and Company, 1989.

Hoffman, Bruce. *Anonymous Soldiers: The Struggle for Israel, 1917–1947*. New York: Knopf, 2015.

Lenczowski, George. *American Presidents and the Middle East*. Durham, NC: Duke University Press, 1990.

Levin, Bess. "Jared Kushner: Palestinians Have Never Done Anything Right in Their Sad, Pathetic Lives." *Vanity Fair*, January 29, 2020. https://www.vanityfair.com/news/2020/01/jared-kushner-peace-plan-palestinians.

Lewis, Bernard. *The Jews of Islam*. Princeton, NJ: Princeton University Press, 1984.

Maza, Cristina. "Benjamin Netanyahu Declares Israel Nation-State of Jews Alone, Not Arab Citizens, in Social Media Spat with Actress." *Newsweek*, March 11, 2019. https://www.newsweek.com/netanyahu-israel-nation-state-jews-1358133.

McCarthy, Justin. *The Population of Palestine: Population History and Statistics of the Late Ottoman Period and the Mandate*. New York: Columbia University Press, 1990.

McCullough, David. *Truman*. New York: Simon and Schuster, 1992.

McGowan, Daniel, and Marc H. Ellis, eds. *Remembering Deir Yassin: The Future of Israel and Palestine*. New York: Olive Branch Press, 1998.

McKinley, Jesse. "Play about Demonstrator's Death Is Delayed." *New York Times*, February 28, 2006. https://www.nytimes.com/2006/02/28/theater/newsandfeatures/play-about-demonstrators-death-is-delayed.html.

Morris, Benny. *1948: The First Arab-Israeli War*. New Haven, CT: Yale University Press, 2008.

Myre, Greg. "Israeli Army Bulldozer Kills American Protesting in Gaza." *New York Times*, March 17, 2003. https://www.nytimes.com/2003/03/17/world/israeli-army-bulldozer-kills-american-protesting-in-gaza.html.

Neuman, Johanna. "Truman's 1947 Complaints about Jews Set Off a Controversy." *Los Angeles Times*, July 17, 2003. https://www.latimes.com/archives/la-xpm-2003-jul-17-na-truman17-story.html.

Nirenberg, David. *Anti-Judaism: The Western Tradition*. New York: W.W. Norton and Company, 2013.

Pappé, Ilan. *The Ethnic Cleansing of Palestine*. Oxford: Oneworld Publications, 2006.

Pappé, Ilan. *The Idea of Israel: A History of Power and Knowledge*. New York: Verso, 2015.

Parker, Ned, and Stephen Farrell. "British Anger at Terror Celebration." *The Times*, July 20, 2006. Accessed via https://www.indybay.org/newsitems/2006/07/20/18290072.php.

"Population of Israel on the Eve of 2018: 8.8 Million." Israel Central Bureau of Statistics. December 31, 2017.

Rachel Corrie Foundation for Peace and Justice. "Rachel's Writing and Emails from Palestine." Accessed October 24, 2020. https://rachelcorriefoundation.org/rachel/emails.

Rodinson, Maxime. *Israel and the Arabs*. London: Penguin, 1968.

Sakran, Frank C. *Palestine Dilemma: Arab Rights versus Zionist Aspirations*. New York: Public Affairs Press, 1948.

Scott, James. *The Attack on the Liberty: The Untold Story of Israel's Deadly 1967 Assault on a U.S. Spy Ship*. New York: Simon and Schuster, 2009.

Segev, Tom. "The Spirit of the King David Hotel." *Haaretz*, July 23, 2006. https://www.haaretz.com/1.4858473.

Tamari, Salim. *The Great War and the Remaking of Palestine*. Oakland: University of California Press, 2017.

Vester, Bertha Spafford. *Our Jerusalem*. New York: Doubleday, 1950.

Wright, Clifford A. *Facts and Fables: The Arab-Israeli Conflict*. New York: Routledge, 2015.

Zakaria, Fareed. "Israeli Settlements; James Baker on U.S.-Russian Relations; Move U.S. Embassy to Jerusalem?" *CNN*. January 8, 2017. http://transcripts.cnn.com/TRANSCRIPTS/1701/08/fzgps.01.html.

Zauzmer, Julie, and Susan Svrluga. "Trump's Executive Order on Anti-Semitism Adds to the Fierce Campus Debate about Israel and

Palestinian Rights." *Washington Post*, December 11, 2019. https://www.washingtonpost.com/religion/2019/12/11/trumps-executive-order-anti-semitism-plunges-into-fierce-campus-conflicts-about-israel-palestine.

## Chapter 10

Allen, Beverly. *Rape Warfare: The Hidden Genocide in Bosnia-Herzegovina and Croatia*. Minneapolis: University of Minnesota Press, 1996.

Andreescu, Ștefan. "Military Actions of Vlad Țepeș in Southeastern Europe in 1476." In *Dracula: Essays on the Life and Times of Vlad the Țepeș*, edited by Kurt W. Treptow. New York: Columbia University Press, 1991.

Andreescu, Ștefan. *Vlad the Impaler: Dracula*. Bucharest: The Romanian Cultural Foundation Publishing House, 1999.

Babinger, Franz. *Mehmed the Conqueror and His Time*. Edited by William C. Hickman. Translated by Ralph Manheim. Princeton, NJ: Princeton University Press, 1978.

Baddeley, Gavin, and Paul A. Woods. *Vlad the Impaler: Son of the Devil, Hero of the People*. Hersham, UK: Ian Allan, 2010.

Bećirević, Edina. *Genocide on the Drina River*. New Haven, CT: Yale University Press, 2014.

Blinder, Alan, and Kevin Sack. "Dylann Roof Is Sentenced to Death in Charleston Church Massacre." *New York Times*, January 10, 2017. https://www.nytimes.com/2017/01/10/us/dylann-roof-trial-charleston.html.

Brooks, Dan. "What's the Panic over 'Joker' Really About?" *New York Times*, October 2, 2019. https://www.nytimes.com/2019/10/02/magazine/the-joker-movie.html.

Chalkokondyles, Laonikos. *The Histories*. Vol. 2, Books 6–10. Translated by Anthony Kaldellis. Cambridge, MA: Harvard University Press, 2014.

Crowe, David M. *War Crimes, Genocide, and Justice: A Global History*. New York: Palgrave Macmillan, 2013.

Dahlburg, John-Thor. "Bosnian Witness Says She Endured Series of Rapes." *Los Angeles Times*, March 30, 2000. https://www.latimes.com/archives/la-xpm-2000-mar-30-mn-14282-story.html.

Filkins, Dexter. "Blood and Soil in Narenda Modi's India." *New Yorker*, December 2, 2019. https://www.newyorker.com/magazine/2019/12/09/blood-and-soil-in-narendra-modis-india.

Fisher, Ian, and Sabrina Tavernise. "Pope Backs Turkey's Bid to Join European Union." *New York Times*, November 29, 2006. https://www.nytimes.com/2006/11/29/world/europe/29pope.html.

Florescu, Radu R. "A Genealogy of the Family of Vlad Țepeș." In *Dracula: Essays on the Life and Times of Vlad the Țepeș*, edited by Kurt W. Treptow. New York: Columbia University Press, 1991.

Florescu, Radu R., and Raymond T. McNally. *Dracula Prince of Many Faces: His Life and Times*. Boston: Back Bay Books and Little, Brown and Company, 1989.

Goodwin, Godfrey. *The Janissaries*. London: Saqi Books, 2001.

Goodwin, Jason. *Lords of the Horizons: A History of the Ottoman Empire*. New York: Picador, 1998.

Guerin, Orla. "Hagia Sophia: Turkey Turns Iconic Istanbul Museum into Mosque." *BBC News*. July 10, 2020. https://www.bbc.com/news/world-europe-53366307.

Jamaleddine, Ziad. "Hagia Sophia Past and Future." *Places*, August 2020. https://placesjournal.org/article/hagia-sophia-past-and-future.

Jefferson, John. *The Holy Wars of King Wladislas and Sultan Murad: The Ottoman-Christian Conflict from 1438–1444*. Leiden, Netherlands: Brill, 2012.

Kafadar, Cemal. *Between Two Worlds: The Construction of the Ottoman State*. Berkeley: University of California Press, 1995.

Kakissis, Joanna. "Hungary Has a Xenophobia Problem." *NPR*, April 27, 2018. https://www.npr.org/sections/parallels/2018/04/27/602375067/hungary-has-a-xenophobia-problem.

McNally, Raymond T. "Vlad Țepeș in Romanian Folklore." In *Dracula: Essays on the Life and Times of Vlad the Țepeș*, edited by Kurt W. Treptow. New York: Columbia University Press, 1991.

Nicolle, David, and Christa Hook. *The Janissaries*. London: Osprey Publishing, 1995.

Rohde, David. "Why Did Ratko Mladic Commit Genocide against Bosnia's Muslims?" *New Yorker*, November 27, 2017. https://www.newyorker.com/news/news-desk/why-did-ratko-mladic-commit-genocide-against-bosnias-muslims.

Serhan, Yasmeen. "Why Doesn't Steve Bannon Matter in Europe?" *The Atlantic*, October 12, 2019. https://www.theatlantic.com/international/archive/2019/10/why-doesnt-steve-bannon-matter-in-europe/599917.

Shaw, Stanford J. *History of the Ottoman Empire and Modern Turkey*. Vol. 1. Cambridge: Cambridge University Press, 1976.

Stoker, Bram. *Dracula*. Harmondsworth: Penguin, 2004.

Treptow, Kurt W. *Vlad III Dracula: The Life and Times of the Historical Dracula*. Las Vegas: The Center for Romanian Studies, 2020.

# Chapter 11

Ahmed, Muddassar. "Who Was Emir Abdel-Kader, the Hero of Humanity?" *Toledo Society Podcast*, May 20, 2020. https://toledosociety.com/1400-omg/e2-who-was-emir-abdelkader-the-hero-of-humanity.

Beverley, James A. *Islamic Faith in America*. New York: Facts on File, 2009.

Churchill, Charles Henry. *The Life of Abdel Kader: Ex-Sultan of the Arabs of Algeria*. Charleston, SC: Nabu Press, 2014.

Danziger, Raphael. *Abd al-Qadir and the Algerians: Resistance to the French and Internal Consolidation*. New York: Holmes and Meier, 1977.

Jennings, Ken. "The Odd Story of How Elkader, Iowa, Got Its Name." *Conde Nast*, September 15, 2014. https://www.cntraveler.com/stories/2014-09-15/the-odd-story-of-how-elkader-iowa-got-its-name.

Kiernan, Ben. *Blood and Soil: A World History of Genocide and Extermination from Sparta to Darfur*. New Haven, CT: Yale University Press, 2007.

Kiser, John W. *Commander of the Faithful: The Life and Times of Emir Abd el-Kader*. Rhinebeck: Monkfish, 2008.

MacSwan, Angus. "Libyan 'Lion of Desert' with Rebels in Spirit: Grandson." *Reuters*, March 25, 2011. https://www.reuters.com/article/us-libya-rebels-lion/libyan-lion-of-desert-with-rebels-in-spirit-grandson-idUSTRE72O46F20110325.

Marston, Elsa. *The Compassionate Warrior: Abd el-Kader of Algeria*. Bloomington, IN: Wisdom Tales, 2013.

# Chapter 12

Bailyn, Bernard. *The Ideological Origins of the American Revolution*. Cambridge, MA: Belknap Press, 1992.

Brands, H. W. *The Man Who Saved the Union: Ulysses Grant in War and Peace*. New York: Doubleday, 2012.

Calhoun, Charles W. *The Presidency of Ulysses S. Grant*. Lawrence: University Press of Kansas, 2017.

Chernow, Ron. *Grant*. New York: Penguin Press, 2017.

Columbus, Christopher. *The Four Voyages of Christopher Columbus: Being His Own Log-Book, Letters and Dispatches with Connecting Narrative Drawn from the Life of the Admiral by His Son Hernando Colon and Other Contemporary Historians*. Edited and translated by J. M. Cohen. London: Penguin Classics, 1969.

Curiel, Jonathan. *Al' America: Travels through America's Arab and Islamic Roots*. New York: The New Press, 2008.

Davidson, Miles H. *Columbus Then and Now: A Life Reexamined*. Norman: University of Oklahoma Press, 1997.

"Gen. Grant and the Jews." *New York Times*, January 18, 1863. https://www.nytimes.com/1863/01/18/archives/gen-grant-and-the-jews.html.

Grant, Ulysses S. *Personal Memoirs of U. S. Grant*. New York: C. L. Webster and Co, 1885.

Gugliotta, Guy. "New Estimate Raises Civil War Death Toll." *New York Times*, April 2, 2012. https://www.nytimes.com/2012/04/03/science/civil-war-toll-up-by-20-percent-in-new-estimate.html.

Haselby, Sam. "Muslims of Early America." *Aeon*, May 20, 2019. https://aeon.co/essays/muslims-lived-in-america-before-protestantism-even-existed.

Howland, Edward. *Grant as a Soldier and Statesman: Being a Succinct History of His Military and Civil Career*. Hartford, CT: J. B. Burr and Company, 1868.

Kahan, Paul. *The Presidency of Ulysses S. Grant: Preserving the Civil War's Legacy*. Yardley, PA: Westholme Publishing, 2018.

Lincoln, Abraham. "The Gettysburg Address." November 19, 1863.

Longacre, Edward G. *General Ulysses S. Grant: The Soldier and the Man*. Cambridge, MA: Da Capo Press, 2006.

Lopez, Barry. *The Rediscovery of North America*. Lexington: University Press of Kentucky, 1990.

McFeely, William S. *Grant: A Biography*. New York: W. W. Norton and Company, 1981.

Miller, Donald L. *Vicksburg: Grant's Campaign That Broke the Confederacy*. New York: Simon and Schuster, 2019.

Morison, Samuel Eliot. *Admiral of the Ocean Sea: A Life of Christopher Columbus*. Boston: Little, Brown and Company, 1942.

Morison, Samuel Eliot. *Christopher Columbus, Mariner*. Boston: Little, Brown and Company, 1955.

Nelson, William H. *The American Tory*. Oxford: Clarendon Press, 1961.

Phillips, William D., Jr, and Carla Rahn Phillips. *The Worlds of Christopher Columbus*. Cambridge: Cambridge University Press, 1992.

Simpson, Brooks D. *Ulysses S. Grant: Triumph over Adversity, 1822–1865*. Boston: Houghton Mifflin Company, 2014.

Smith, Jean Edward. *Grant*. New York: Simon and Schuster, 2001.

White, Ronald C. *American Ulysses: A Life of Ulysses S. Grant*. New York: Random House, 2016.

# Chapter 13

Adams, William Howard. *The Paris Years of Thomas Jefferson*. New Haven, CT: Yale University Press, 1997.

al-Hakem, Ibn Abd. *Dhikr fatḥ al-Andalus: Ibn Abd-el-Hakem's History of the Conquest of Spain*. Translated by John Harris Jones. Goettingen: Dietrich University Press, 1858.

al-Hibri, Azizah Y. "Islamic and American Constitutional Law: Borrowing Possibilities or a History of Borrowing?" *University of Pennsylvania Journal of Constitutional Law* 1, no. 3 (1999): 492–527.

Cartwright, Mark. "Timbuktu." *Ancient History Encyclopedia*. February 22, 2019. https://www.ancient.eu/Timbuktu.

Central Intelligence Agency. *The CIA World Factbook 2019–2020*. New York: Skyhorse Publishing, 2019.

Collins, Roger. *The Arab Conquest of Spain 710–797*. Oxford: Blackwell Publishing, 1989.

Collins, Roger. *Visigothic Spain 409–711*. Oxford: Blackwell Publishing, 2004.

Curiel, Jonathan. *Al' America: Travels through America's Arab and Islamic Roots*. New York: The New Press, 2008.

Curtin, Philip D. *The Atlantic Slave Trade: A Census*. Madison: University of Wisconsin Press, 1972.

De Villiers, Marq, and Sheila Hirtle. *Timbuktu: The Sahara's Fabled City of Gold*. New York: Walker and Company, 2007.

Dewey, Frank L. *Thomas Jefferson, Lawyer*. Charlottesville: University Press of Virginia, 1986.

Diouf, Sylviane A. *Servants of Allah: African Muslims Enslaved in the Americas*. New York: New York University Press, 1998.

Dumbauld, Edward. *Thomas Jefferson, American Tourist*. Norman: University of Oklahoma Press, 1946.

Farmer, Henry George. *Historical Facts for the Arabian Musical Influence*. London: Reeves, 1930.

Farmer, Henry George. *A History of Arabian Music to the XIIIth Century*. London: Luzac Oriental, 1994.

Gaustad, Edwin S. *Sworn on the Altar of God: A Religious Biography of Thomas Jefferson*. Grand Rapids, MI: William B. Eerdmans Publishing Company, 1996.

Gomez, Michael A. *Black Crescent: The Experience and Legacy of African Muslims in the Americas*. Cambridge: Cambridge University Press, 2005.

Hammer, Joshua. *The Bad-Ass Librarians of Timbuktu*. New York: Simon and Schuster, 2016.

Haselby, Sam. "Muslims of Early America." *Aeon*, May 20, 2019. https://
aeon.co/essays/muslims-lived-in-america-before-protestantism-even-
existed.

Hodgson, William B. *Notes on Northern Africa, the Sahara, and Soudan.*
New York: Wiley and Putnam, 1844.

Hopkins, J. F. P., and Nehemia Levtzion, eds. *Corpus of Early Arabic
Sources for West Africa History.* New York: Markus Weiner Press,
2000.

Ibn Idhari. *Histoire de l'Afrique du Nord et de l'Espagne intitulée Kitāb
al-Bayān al-Mughrib.* Arabic text ed. Translated by G. S. Colin and
E. Lévi-Provençal. Leiden, Netherlands: Brill, 1948.

Ibn Said, Omar. *A Muslim American Slave: The Life of Omar Ibn Said.*
Edited and translated by Ala Alryyes. Madison: University of
Wisconsin Press, 2011.

Izadi, Elahe. "Thomas Jefferson and the Long History of Defending
Muslims' Rights." *Washington Post*, June 26, 2018. https://www.
washingtonpost.com/news/retropolis/wp/2018/06/26/thomas-
jefferson-and-the-long-history-of-defending-muslim-rights.

Jefferson, Thomas. *Jefferson Abroad.* Edited by Douglas L. Wilson and
Lucia C. Stanton. New York: Modern Library, 1999.

Jefferson, Thomas. *Jefferson's Literary Commonplace Book.* Edited by
Douglas L. Wilson. Princeton, NJ: Princeton University Press, 1989.

Jefferson, Thomas. "Letter to John Page: February 21, 1770." In *The
Papers of Thomas Jefferson*, edited by Julian P. Boyd, Charles T.
Cullen, John Catanzariti, Barbara B. Oberg, and James P. McClure.
40 vols. Princeton, NJ: Princeton University Press, 1950.

Johnson, Sylvester A. *African American Religions, 1500–2000:
Colonialism, Democracy, and Freedom.* Cambridge: Cambridge
University Press, 2015.

Kimball, Marie Goebel. *Jefferson: The Scene in Europe.* New York:
Coward-McCann, 1950.

Kubik, Gerhard. *Africa and the Blues.* Jackson: University Press of
Mississippi, 1999.

Levtzion, Nehemia. *Ancient Ghana and Mali.* London: Methuen, 1973.

Macintyre, Ben. "'The Bad-Ass Librarians of Timbuktu,' by Joshua
Hammer." *New York Times*, April 28, 2016. https://www.nytimes.
com/2016/05/01/books/review/the-bad-ass-librarians-of-timbuktu-by-
joshua-hammer.html.

Malcolm X. *The Autobiography of Malcolm X: As Told to Alex Haley.*
New York: Ballantine Books, 1965.

Manning, Patrick. "The Slave Trade: The Formal Demography of a Global System." In *The Atlantic Slave Trade: Effects on Economies, Societies and Peoples in Africa, the Americas, and Europe*, edited by Joseph E. Inikori and Stanley L. Engerman, 117–44. Durham, NC: Duke University Press, 1992.

Manseau, Peter. "Why Thomas Jefferson Owned a Qur'an." *Smithsonian Magazine*, January 31, 2018. https://www.smithsonianmag.com/ smithsonian-institution/why-thomas-jefferson-owned-qur-1- 180967997/#:~:text=Historians%20have%20attributed%20the%20 third,a%20variety%20of%20religious%20perspectives.&tex- t=Jefferson%20bought%20this%20book%20while,of%20the%20 world's%20legal%20systems.

Mohamud, Naima. "Is Mansa Musa the Richest Man Who Ever Lived?" *BBC Africa*, March 10, 2019. https://www.bbc.com/news/world- africa-47379458#:~:text=With%20an%20estimated%20fortune%20 of,wrecked%20an%20entire%20country's%20economy.

Morgan, Michael Hamilton. *Lost History: The Enduring Legacy of Muslim Scientists, Thinkers, and Artists*. Washington, DC: National Geographic, 2007.

Nicolle, David. *The Great Islamic Conquests AD 632–750*. Oxford: Osprey Publishing, 2009.

Rice, Howard C., Jr. *Thomas Jefferson's Paris*. Princeton, NJ: Princeton University Press, 1976.

Ruane, Michael E. "When Few Enslaved People in the United States Could Write, One Man Wrote His Memoir in Arabic." *Washington Post*, January 20, 2019. https://www.washingtonpost.com/ history/2019/01/20/when-few-enslaved-people-could-write-one-man- wrote-his-memoirs-arabic.

Saad, Elias N. *Social History of Timbuktu: The Role of Muslim Scholars and Notables 1400–1900*. Cambridge: Cambridge University Press, 1983.

Shackelford, George Green. *Thomas Jefferson's Travels in Europe, 1784–1789*. Baltimore: Johns Hopkins University Press, 1995.

Spellberg, Denise A. *Thomas Jefferson's Qur'an: Islam and the Founders*. New York: Alfred A. Knopf, 2013.

Thompson, E. A. *The Goths in Spain*. Oxford: Clarendon Press, 1969.

Thompson, Mary V. "Mount Vernon." In *Encyclopedia of Muslim- American History*, edited by Edward E. Curtis, 392–93. Vol 2. New York: Facts on File, 2010.

Torrey, Charles Cutler. *Ibn Abd al-Hakam's Kitab Futuh Misr wa'l Maghrib wa'l Andalus*. New Haven, CT: Yale University Press, 1932.

# Chapter 14

Beglinger, Martin. "The Most Expensive Party Ever." *Alimentarium*, May 14, 2014. https://www.alimentarium.org/en/magazine/history/most-expensive-party-ever.

Buchan, James. *Days of God: The Revolution in Iran and Its Consequences*. New York: Simon and Schuster, 2013.

Burke, Jason. "Shah's Opulent Tented City Awaits Rebirth in Desert." *Guardian*, September 9, 2001. https://www.theguardian.com/world/2001/sep/09/iran.

Fisk, Robert. *The Great War for Civilisation: The Conquest of the Middle East*. New York: Vintage Books, 2005.

Ghattas, Kim. *Black Wave: Saudi Arabia, Iran, and the Forty-Year Rivalry That Unraveled Culture, Religion, and Collective Memory in the Middle East*. New York: Henry Holt and Company, 2020.

Halm, Heinz. *The Shi'ites: A Short History*. Translated by Allison Brown. Princeton, NJ: Markus Weiner Publishers, 2005.

Hyer, Marjorie. "Evangelical Christians Meet to Develop Strategy for 1980s." *Washington Post*, January 30, 1981. https://www.washingtonpost.com/archive/local/1981/01/30/evangelical-christians-meet-to-develop-strategy-for-1980s/3ee92602-35a7-413a-ae2a-bb786fb3b396.

Kinzer, Stephen. *All the Shah's Men: An American Coup and the Roots of Middle East Terror*. Hoboken, NJ: John Wiley and Sons, 2003.

Ruthven, Malise. *Fundamentalism: The Search for Meaning*. Oxford: Oxford University Press, 2004.

Tait, Robert. "Iran to Rebuild Spectacular Tent City at Persepolis." *Guardian*, September 22, 2005. https://www.theguardian.com/world/2005/sep/22/arts.iran#:~:text=Now%20Iran's%20Islamic%20rulers%20are,2%2C500%20years%20of%20the%20monarchy.

Van den Berg, Dirk, dir. *The Siege of Mecca*. Outremer Film and K2 Productions, 2018.

Wright, Robin. *In the Name of God: The Khomeini Decade*. New York: Simon and Schuster, 1989.

Wright, Robin. *The Last Great Revolution: Turmoil and Transformation in Iran*. New York: Vintage Books, 2000.

# Chapter 15

Agrawal, Ravi. "Why India's Muslims Are in Grave Danger." *Foreign Policy*, March 2, 2020. https://foreignpolicy.com/2020/03/02/india-muslims-delhi-riots-danger.

Asher, Catherine B., and Cynthia Talbot. *India before Europe*. Cambridge: Cambridge University Press, 2006.

Bapu, Prabhu. *Hindu Mahasabha in Colonial North India, 1915–1930: Construction Nation and History*. London: Routledge, 2013.

"Bollywood's Role in India's Heated Political Environment | The Quint's Films and Politics Roundtable." *The Quint*. January 1, 2020. YouTube video, 55:20. https://youtu.be/N8M4BgaTm38.

Bondurant, Joan V. *Conquest of Violence: The Gandhian Philosophy of Conflict*. Princeton, NJ: Princeton University Press, 1988.

Brown, Judith M. *Gandhi: Prisoner of Hope*. New Haven, CT: Yale University Press, 1991.

Chadha, Yogesh. *Gandhi: A Life*. New York: John Wiley, 1997.

Filkins, Dexter. "Blood and Soil in Narendra Modi's India." *New Yorker*, December 2, 2019. https://www.newyorker.com/magazine/2019/12/09/blood-and-soil-in-narendra-modis-india.

Frykenberg, Robert Eric. "Hindu Fundamentalism and the Structural Stability of India." In *Fundamentalisms and the State: Remaking Polities, Economies, and Militance*, edited by Martin E. Marty and R. Scott Appleby, 225–47. Chicago: University of Chicago Press, 1996.

Gandhi, Rajmohan. *Gandhi: The Man, His People, and the Empire*. Berkeley: University of California Press, 2006.

Gettleman, Jeffrey, Kai Schultz, Suhasini Raj, and Hari Kumar. "Under Modi, a Hindu Nationalist Surge Has Further Divided India." *New York Times*, April 11, 2019. https://www.nytimes.com/2019/04/11/world/asia/modi-india-elections.html.

Graham, Bruce Desmond. *Hindu Nationalism and Indian Politics: The Origins and Development of the Bharatiya Jana Sangh*. Cambridge: Cambridge University Press, 2008.

Hallissey, Robert C. *The Rajput Rebellion against Aurangzeb*. Columbia, MO: University of Missouri Press, 1977.

Pacey, Arnold. *Technology in World Civilization: A Thousand-Year History*. Cambridge, MA: The MIT Press, 1991.

Richards, John F. *The New Cambridge History of India*. Part 1, *The Mughals and Their Contemporaries: The Mughal Empire*. Cambridge: Cambridge University Press, 1995.

Robb, Peter. *A History of India*. London: Palgrave, 2002.

Schimmel, Annemarie. *The Empire of the Great Mughals: History, Art and Culture*. Edited by Burzine K. Waghmar. London: Reaktion Books, 2004.

Schultz, Kai, and Hari Kumar. "Narendra Modi's Estranged Wife Escapes Unhurt from Car Crash in India." *New York Times*, February 7, 2018.

Saleem I. *Abdulrauf*

https://www.nytimes.com/2018/02/07/world/asia/india-narendra-modi-wife.html.

Tripathi, Amish. "Let Ayodhya Ram Mandir Be a Reminder: Indian Ancestors Died for It, Up to Us to Rebuild." *The Print*, August 4, 2020. https://theprint.in/opinion/let-ayodhya-ram-mandir-be-a-reminder-indian-ancestors-died-for-it-up-to-us-to-rebuild/474213.

Varshney, Ashutosh. *Ethnic Conflict and Civic Life: Hindus and Muslims in India*. New Haven, CT: Yale University Press, 2002.

Yasir, Sameer. "Gandhi's Killer Evokes Admiration as Never Before." *New York Times*, February 4, 2020. https://www.nytimes.com/2020/02/04/world/asia/india-gandhi-nathuram-godse.html.

Zhou, Steven. "From India, Islamophobia Goes Global." *Foreign Policy*, July 1, 2020. https://foreignpolicy.com/2020/07/01/india-islamophobia-global-bjp-hindu-nationalism-canada.

## Conclusion

Alsultany, Evelyn. "How the New 'Aladdin' Stacks Up against a Century of Hollywood Stereotyping." *The Conversation*, May 26, 2019. https://theconversation.com/how-the-new-aladdin-stacks-up-against-a-century-of-hollywood-stereotyping-115608.

Basu, Nayanima. "Not Just Macron's Politics, It's France's Brand of Secularism That Always Clashed with Islam." *The Print*, October 31, 2020. https://theprint.in/opinion/newsmaker-of-the-week/macron-battle-liberalism-france-secularism-clash-islam/534316.

"Erik Prince and the Last Crusade." *Economist*, August 6, 2009. https://www.economist.com/democracy-in-america/2009/08/06/erik-prince-and-the-last-crusade.

Fox, Alex. "Nearly 2,000 Black Americans Were Lynched during Reconstruction." *Smithsonian Magazine*, June 18, 2020. https://www.smithsonianmag.com/smart-news/nearly-2000-black-americans-were-lynched-during-reconstruction-180975120.

Gilad, Elon. "Why Are Palestinians Called Palestinians?" *Haaretz*, October 29, 2015. https://www.haaretz.com/israel-news/.premium-why-are-palestinians-called-palestinians-1.5414906.

Gilad, Elon. "Why Is Israel Called Israel?" *Haaretz*, April 20, 2015. https://www.haaretz.com/.premium-why-is-israel-called-israel-1.5353207.

Goody, Jack. *Islam in Europe*. Cambridge, UK: Polity Press, 2008.

Helmore, Edward. "Donald Trump Jr Posts Crusader Symbol Image amid Middle East Turmoil." *Guardian*, January 7, 2020. https://www.

theguardian.com/us-news/2020/jan/07/donald-trump-jr-gun-crusader-symbol-iinstagram.

Mazzetti, Mark, and Emily B. Hager. "Secret Desert Force Set Up by Blackwater's Founder." *New York Times*, May 14, 2011. https://www.nytimes.com/2011/05/15/world/middleeast/15prince.html.

O'Reilly, Mick. "Is British Queen a Descendant of Prophet Mohammad?" *Gulf News*, April 9, 2018. https://gulfnews.com/world/europe/is-british-queen-a-descendant-of-prophet-mohammad-1.2202085#:~:text=Brooks%2DBaker%20said%20the%20British,IV%2C%20the%20UPI%20report%20concludes.

Singer, Peter W. "The Dark Truth about Blackwater." *Brookings*, October 2, 2007, https://www.brookings.edu/articles/the-dark-truth-about-blackwater.

Zakaria, Fareed. *Global Public Square*. "Nationwide Protests Continue in the Wake of George Floyd's Death; Anger in America Reverberates around the World; America's Policing Problem; The Coronavirus Race Gap." Aired June 7, 2020, on CNN. https://www.cnn.com/shows/fareed-zakaria-gps.

# Figure Credits

## Chapter 1

**1-1:** Ivan Vdovin / Alamy Stock Photo

**1-3:** Pictorial Press Ltd / Alamy Stock Photo

**1-4:** World History Archive / Alamy Stock Photo

**1-5:** Artmedia / Alamy Stock Photo

**1-6:** US National Library of Medicine and the Parke, Davis & Company (1958)

**1-7:** ugurhan / iStockphoto.com

**1-11:** Chronicle / Alamy Stock Photo

**1-13:** Malekas85 / iStockphoto.com

## Chapter 2

**2-7:** Q 59888, ©Imperial War Museum

**2-10:** Q 58863, ©Imperial War Museum

**2-12:** Courtesy of the Seven Pillars of Wisdom Trust (UK) and Double Day (US)

**2-14:** Q 12364, ©Imperial War Museum

**2-17:** World History Archive / Alamy Stock Photo

**2-18:** Royal Geographical Society (The National Archives—United Kingdom)

## Chapter 3

**3-2:** Xristoph, CC BY-SA 3.0

**3-3:** Félix Mengin: *History of Egypt during Mohammed Ali's Reign*, a book published in 1823.

**3-5:** Photographer Unknown

**3-7a:** Courtesy of the Center for the Study of the Built Environment (CSBE)

**3-7b:** Courtesy of the Center for the Study of the Built Environment (CSBE)

**3-9:** Photographer Unknown

**3-15:** Photo Dept., Library of Congress, Matson Collection

**3-16:** Richard Francis Burton, Second Edition of Burton's *Pilgrimage*

**3-17:** Engraving by Berthault (after L. N. de Lespinasse, *Vue de la Mecque* - Plate 45 from Ohsson, Tableau général de l'Empire Othoman, vol. 2, 1790. Paris: Imprimerie de Monsieur.

**3-22:** Photo by Uncredited/AP/Shutterstock (7402484a)

**3-23:** Photo by Uncredited/AP/Shutterstock (7402485a)

**3-26:** Abbie Rowe. White House Photographs. John F. Kennedy Presidential Library and Museum, Boston.

**3-28:** Archive PL / Alamy Stock Photo)

# Chapter 4

**4-1:** Courtesy of Jane Elliott

**4-3:** Album / Alamy Stock Photo

**4-4:** Archive World / Alamy Stock Photo

**4-5:** Masheter Movie Archive / Alamy Stock Photo

# Chapter 5

**5-2:** United States Holocaust Memorial Museum, courtesy of Gerard Gert

# Chapter 6

**6-1:** National Archaeological Museum of Athens

**6-2:** Moviestore Collection Ltd / Alamy Stock Photo

**6-5:** Photo by بلال الدويك, edited by AishaAbdel

**6-7:** CNG Coins

**6-9:** Courtesy: Paul Brandus / @WestWingReport

**6-10:** Hanan Isachar / Alamy Stock Photo

**6-11:** Alpha Historica / Alamy Stock Photo

**6-12:** © National Portrait Gallery, London

**6-14:** Republican National Convention 2020

**6-16:** Gage Skidmore

# Chapter 7

**7-1:** ©sorincolac /123RF.COM"

**7-2:** dpa picture alliance / Alamy Stock Photo

**7-4:** Signol, Emile (1804-92); 1847. Photographic rights The Bridgeman Art Library.

**7-6:** JAUBERT French Collection / Alamy Stock Photo

# Chapter 8

**8-2:** Peter Barritt / Alamy Stock Photo

**8-3:** The Print Collector / Alamy Stock Photo

**8-4:** CPA Media Pte Ltd / Alamy Stock Photo

**8-5:** Entertainment Pictures / Alamy Stock Photo

**8-7:** Jon Arnold Images Ltd / Alamy Stock Photo

**8-8:** From *Saladin* by John Man, copyright © 2016. Reprinted by permission of Da Capo Press, an imprint of Hachette Book Group, Inc.

**8-9:** Juniors Bildarchiv GmbH / Alamy Stock Photo

**8-12:** Victor Korchenko / Alamy Stock Photo

**8-13:** Morn, retouched by Tteske

**8-14:** National Military Museum of Egypt

**8-16:** David A. Barnes / Alamy Stock Photo

**8-17:** Bettmann / Contributor: Getty Images

**8-19:** *Rise of Empires: Ottoman.* Produced by Karga Seven Pictures and distributed by Netflix, Inc.

# Chapter 9

**9-5:** Dutch National Archives, The Hague, Fotocollectie Algemeen Nederlands Persbureau (ANEFO), 1945–1989 bekijk toegang 2.24.01.04 Bestanddeelnummer 902-2074

**9-6:** Eldan David

**9-8:** Frank Lowenstein, Special Envoy for Israeli–Palestinian Negotiations, US State Department

**9-9:** Frank Lowenstein, Special Envoy for Israeli–Palestinian Negotiations, US State Department

**9-10:** US Navy Photo # NH 97478

**9-11:** Photograph by Denny Sternstein

# Chapter 10

**10-4:** NoPunIn10Did

**10-5:** Stocktrek Images, Inc. / Alamy Stock Photo

**10-6:** ©porojnicu - Can Stock Photo Inc.

**10-8:** ENCYCLOPEDIA BRITANNICA/Almir Dzanovic

**10-9:** Gryf / Alamy Stock Photo

**10-10:** Jan Wlodarczyk / Alamy Stock Photo

**10-11:** Alex Segre / Alamy Stock Photo

**10-12:** Pictorial Press Ltd / Alamy Stock Photo

**10-13:** incamerastock / Alamy Stock Photo

# Chapter 11

**11-1:** Classic Image / Alamy Stock Photo

**11-2:** mosamem / Alamy Stock Photo

# Chapter 12

**12-2:** *General Ulysses S. Grant at his headquarters in Cold Harbor, Virginia.* [June 11 or 12, printed later], 1864. Photograph. https://www.loc.gov/item/2002736661/.

**12-3:** Photographer: Alexander Gardner

# Chapter 13

**13-1:** Image color restored and colorized by RubenVanKuik. Original photographer unknown.

**13-5:** Album / Alamy Stock Photo

**13-6:** PRISMA ARCHIVO / Alamy Stock Photo

**13-11:** Michaela McNichol, Library of Congress

**13-12:** Albert Knapp / Alamy Stock Photo

**13-13:** Library of Congress Rare Book and Special Collections Division Washington, D.C. 20540 USA

# Chapter 14

**14-3:** Historic Collection / Alamy Stock Photo

# Chapter 15

**15-5:** Manjik photography / Alamy Stock Photo

**15-7b:** from *Panipat.* Produced by Ashutosh Gowariker Productions and Vision World Films and distributed by Reliance Entertainment.

**15-7c:** from *Panipat.* Produced by Ashutosh Gowariker Productions and Vision World Films and distributed by Reliance Entertainment.

# Index

For the subject index, please visit www.threeinvaders.com.

## People

# Places

## A

Acre, 175–76, 177f, 183–84
Al-Diriyah, 54f, 56–59, 58f, 62, 62f, 77–78
Al-Jabal al-Akhdar, 260
Al-Uyayna, 56
Angola, 283–85
Antioch, 116, 157f, 158, 163, 173, 185. *See also*
    Outremer
Aqaba , 37, 37f, 79, 164–65
Aquitaine, 158, 169, 173–74, 179f
Ar-rur, 327
Argeş River, 239f
Arsuf, 177, 177f
Ascalon, 177f
Aydhab, 164–65
Ayn Jalut, 185
Ayyadieh, 175

## B

Balkan Peninsula, 242f, 243
Bangladesh, 323f
Banu Jadhimah, 116
Beersheba, 41, 197
Beit Nuba, 177f, 178
Benghazi, 261f, 262, 265
Benin, 284
Bosnia and Herzegovina, 241, 242f, 243, 243f,
    244, 346
Brindisi, 183
Burkina Faso, 284

## C

Cameroon, 284
Carpathian Mountains, 233, 239
Carthage, 186
Castile, 338
Cilicia, 157f. *See also* Outremer
Constantinople, 18, 22, 111, 116, 151f, 179–81,
    181f, 191–93, 237–38, 245
Cordoba, 9f, 11, 15, 146f, 338, 340
Cote d'Ivoire, 284
Curtea Veche, 251f

## D

Dabiq, 41–42
Damietta, 182, 184
Deir Yassin, 207, 209
Delhi, 321, 325, 327–28, 329f, 332

## E

Edessa, 157f, 158. *See also* Outremer

Edirne, 23, 237, viii
El-Arish, 42
Elkader, 264–65

## F

Fez, 10, 11f, vii

## G

Galicia, 338
Gambia, 284
Germany
    anti-Semitism in, 23–24, 42, 104, 139, 173
    crusaders in, 150–51, 151f, 183–84, 193
    evangelicals in, 286, 301
Ghana, 284, 286
Golgotha, 111
Gujrat, 324–25

## H

Hattin, 166–67, 175, 291
Hispaniola, 267

## I

India, 29, 33, 82, 206, 253–54, 321–28, 323f,
    329–30, 329f, 331–35, 331f, xi
Indian subcontinent, 82, 322, 323f, 327–30. *See*
    *also* Bangladesh; India; Kashmir;
    Pakistan
Iraq
    Al-Husayn massacre in, 311–12
    Churchill and, 80, 83
    Jews in, 196, 212–13
    media representation of, 4, 109
    US invasion in (2003), 131–32, 155, 343–45
Israel
    Bible and, 124, 134, 348–50
    establishment of, 44–45, 131, 198, 204,
        208–15, 213f
    media and, 222–27, 222f, 226f
    military of, 215–16
    Third Temple and, 137
    Umar's effect on, 118–19
    US politics and, 86, 133–34, 138–39, 215–
        20, 217f, 221f, 345
    war with Egypt and Syria and, 86
    Zionism and, 133, 136, 198, 200f, 208, 320

## J

Jordan, 21, 35, 39, 78–80, 80f, 115f, 164, 200f,
    210, 213, 216, 263, 265

Printed by Amazon Italia Logistica S.r.l.
Torrazza Piemonte (TO), Italy

17797024R00240